The Life of
DYLAN THOMAS

The Life of
DYLAN THOMAS

by Constantine FitzGibbon

with photographs

An Atlantic Monthly Press Book

LITTLE, BROWN AND COMPANY · BOSTON · TORONTO

for

CAITLIN

ATLANTIC–LITTLE, BROWN BOOKS
ARE PUBLISHED BY
LITTLE, BROWN AND COMPANY
IN ASSOCIATION WITH
THE ATLANTIC MONTHLY PRESS

PRINTED IN THE UNITED STATES OF AMERICA

Acknowledgements

A VERY GREAT many people have helped me with this biography, both by giving me information and by checking and on occasion correcting what I have written. Those whom I should most like to thank are Caitlin Thomas, John Davenport, Pamela Hansford Johnson, Trevor Hughes, Donald Taylor and, perhaps above all, Vernon Watkins. Their help and advice have been invaluable.

Others who have helped me, and whom I should like to thank, are Ralph Abercrombie, David Archer, E. F. Bozman, John Malcolm Brinnin, Arthur Calder-Marshall, Lord David Cecil, Sheila Cutforth, Dan Davin, Aneirin Talfan Davies, Nicolette Devas, Charles Fisher, Professor Idris Foster, Wyn Henderson, Rayner Heppenstall, David Higham, Estelle Holt, Eric Hughes, Richard Hughes, Alfred Janes, Glyn Jones, Merwyn Levy, Bill McAlpine, Dr. Charles McElvie, Yvonne Macnamara, the late Louis MacNeice, Professor Ralph Maud, Ivan Moffatt, Howard Moss, Professor Bill Read, George Reavey, Keidrych Rhys, Professor Ernest Stahl, Gordon Summersby, Randall Swingler, Margaret Taylor, Stuart Thomas, John Ormond Thomas, Wynford Vaughan Thomas, Kent Thompson, Ruthven Todd, A. E. Trick, Tom Warner, the late Oscar Williams, Ralph Wishart, Basil Wright. I fear that there may be others who have helped me, and whose names I have overlooked: if so may I, apologetically, express my thanks?

Most of Dylan Thomas's letters have by now found their way into American university libraries, in particular those of Harvard, New York State (Buffalo), and Texas. All these libraries, or rather their librarians, have been most helpful in allowing me to see his letters, some of which I quote. So, too, have been all but one of the private collectors of "Dylaniana." I should therefore like to express my gratitude to them as well.

Finally, I quote other writers, and for the courtesy of permission to reprint copyrighted material I should like to thank Kingsley Amis for a quotation from an essay in the *Spectator;* the BBC for broadcasts in which Dylan Thomas and others took part; Kay Boyle for an extract from *Portrait of Dylan Thomas* (copyright © 1955 the Nation Company); John Malcolm Brinnin, J. M. Dent and Sons Ltd. and Atlantic–Little, Brown and Co. for extracts from *Dylan Thomas in America* (copyright © 1955, John Malcolm Brinnin); George Barker and Phoenix House for an extract from *Coming to London;* Arthur Calder-Marshall and Rupert Hart-Davis Ltd. for a quotation from *Magic of My Youth;* Alan Hodge and *History Today* for the late Norman Cameron's "The Dirty Little Accuser"; Lawrence Durrell for a passage from an article in *Encounter;* Charles Fisher for an article on Dylan Thomas; Geoffrey Grigson for three extracts from his article "Recollections of Dylan Thomas" in the *London Magazine,* and for the answers by Dylan Thomas to a questionnaire from *New Verse,* copyright by Geoffrey Grigson; Lady Snow for an extract from her article "Portrait of Dylan"; Mervyn Levy for an extract from an article published in *John O' London's;* Jack Lindsay for an extract from a hitherto unpublished article; the *London Magazine* for an extract from an article by J. Maclaren Ross; New Directions for extracts from *Letters to Vernon Watkins* by Dylan Thomas, edited by Vernon Watkins, reprinted with the permission of New Directions, New York, copyright © 1957 by New Directions; editorial contributions copyright © 1957 by Vernon Watkins; New Directions for extracts from *Quite Early One Morning* by Dylan Thomas, copyright 1954 by New Directions, and for extracts from *Portrait of the Artist as a Young Dog* by Dylan Thomas, copyright 1940 by New Directions, reprinted by permission of the publishers; New Directions for extracts from *The Collected Poems of Dylan Thomas,* copyright 1950, 1952, 1953 by Dylan Thomas, copyright 1946 by New Directions, reprinted by permission of the publishers, New Directions, New York; Philip O'Connor and Faber and Faber Ltd. for an extract from *Memoirs of a Public Baby;* Jan Read for an extract from his introduction to the Dylan Thomas version of *The Beach at Falesa;* Mrs. Theodore Roethke for an extract from an article by Theodore Roethke; William Sansom and Phoenix House for an extract from *Com-*

ing to London; Lance Sieveking and Hulton Publications for a quotation from *The Eye of the Beholder;* Doubleday and Co. Inc. and Faber and Faber Ltd. for a quotation from *Conversations with Stravinsky* by Igor Stravinsky with Robert Craft (copyright © 1958, 1959, Igor Stravinsky); Caitlin Thomas, the Longacre Press and Atlantic–Little, Brown and Co. for extracts from *Leftover Life to Kill* by Caitlin Thomas (copyright © 1957 by Caitlin Thomas) and from *Not Quite Posthumous Letter to My Daughter* by Caitlin Thomas (copyright © 1963 by Caitlin Thomas); Vernon Watkins, Faber and Faber Ltd. and New Directions for two extracts from "Portrait of a Friend" from *Ballad of the Mari Lwyd.*

Note

SOME of Dylan Thomas's works appeared with different titles and in differing form in the United States and England. *The World I Breathe,* published in the United States in 1939, incorporated the English books *18 Poems* (1934), *Twenty-five Poems* (1936) and *The Map of Love* (1939). *Quite Early One Morning* was published in England in 1954 and in the same year in the United States with expanded contents. *A Prospect of the Sea,* published in England in 1955, was published in the United States with the addition of the novelette "Adventures in the Skin Trade" under the title *Adventures in the Skin Trade and Other Stories* in 1955. The title novelette of the American edition was not published in England until later.

Deaths and Entrances (1946) and *Quite Early One Morning* (1954) were published in England independently of any American edition.

Published in the United States independently of any English edition were *New Poems* (1943), *Selected Writings* (1947), *In Country Sleep* (1952) and *A Child's Christmas in Wales* (1955).

The Life of
DYLAN THOMAS

1

⚛ ⚛

DYLAN MARLAIS THOMAS was born on the 27th of October, 1914, in his parents' house, No. 5 Cwmdonkin Drive, which lies in that part of Swansea called the Uplands. He was the only son and younger child of D. J. Thomas and of his wife Florence Hannah, née Williams, their daughter Nancy being some eight and a half years older than the new baby.

His family on both sides came of rural stock, small or very small farmers from the Welsh-speaking part of South Wales, the counties of Western Carmarthen and Cardigan, north and west of English-speaking Swansea. In the last century those lovely counties had not yet been touched by the mining, the foundries and the general industrialization that had by 1914 utterly changed the character of so much of South Wales. Indeed even today they remain very largely unspoiled, as the travel brochures would say. It is not in general rich farming country, the land being hilly, even mountainous, suitable principally for the grazing of sheep and, in the valleys, of cattle. Life was lonely in those farmhouses among the hills one hundred years ago, lonely and inevitably introspective, their only books the Bible and volumes of sermons and the Welsh classics, their only entertainments the chapel on Sundays, the local Eisteddfod, market day in the little town, the recurring festivals of the seasons, and an occasional christening, wedding or funeral. Such was the world into which Dylan's grandparents grew up.

In most respects that life resembles the countryman's immemorial way of living in all Western Europe and in New England, too, in bygone centuries. There are, however, certain peculiarities which gave the Welsh countryman his unique qualities. Though not himself a true countryman, Dylan Thomas was steeped in memories, both personal and atavistic, of the life that lay behind his parents' lives, and some comprehension of those unique qualities is important if one would understand both the poet and his poems.

There is, in the first place, the matter of language. Both Dylan's parents had spoken Welsh in their own childhood homes, though Dylan himself had almost no knowledge of his native tongue. Indeed his father, whom everybody called "D.J.," seems to have deliberately rejected the Welsh language, a subject on which I shall have more to say later. Nevertheless Welsh was the natural mode of expression both of himself and of his wife. It is generally accepted that language not only expresses thought but also affects it. The Welsh did not, in large measure still do not, think exactly like the English. No "Celtic" nation does. This is a chicken-and-egg business, and it is impossible to say whether the Welshness of the Welsh or the Irishness of the Irish is due to the structure and nature of their languages or vice versa: the answer is probably both, the one reinforcing the other. And in almost isolated communities, such as those from which Dylan's or James Joyce's forebears came, men's vision of the world and their modes of expressing that vision accentuate one another generation by generation.

To give but one well-known example, Matthew Arnold, in his *Study of Celtic Literature*, has noted a passage from the Mabinogion, that great collection of Welsh tales: "And they saw a tall tree by the side of the river, one half of which was in flames from the root to the top, and the other half was green and in full leaf." No Englishman, as Arnold recognized, could naturally have written that, could have constructed such a pattern of imagery, or would indeed have wished to do so. Dylan, on the other hand, could and did write in this way.

This leads to a question which is not easy to answer. How long do these special qualities of imagery survive the loss of the language in which they are most naturally expressed? It would seem that this depends to a very large extent upon how far the cultural environment is preserved. And this in turn depends both on the toughness and virility of the culture and on the nature of the environment. It is an extremely complex problem, involving many factors such as education both at school and at home, stagnation or advance in the community's economic life, the degree of intermixture with those who naturally speak the new dominant language. Perhaps the most drastic examples, and the ones most easy to observe, are to be found in the United States since 1850. Imaginative, cultural distinctions do there appear to have a capacity to survive for one or two, exceptionally even for three, generations, particularly in highly cultured families, though the roots of that culture may have been snapped almost with immigration or sometimes even before. Thus Eugene O'Neill was at least as much an "Irish" playwright as he was an "American" one. (And one has only to think of second or even third generation Americans with a Russian-Jewish rabbinical background. A "rabbinical" view of the world and the style that goes with it will frequently have survived emigration, forgetfulness of the European language as well as of Hebrew, even a loss of religious faith a generation or two ago. On the other hand imigrants from families with a lesser culture, whether Jewish, Irish, Italian or anything else, very rapidly accepted and scarcely influenced the basic American cultural pattern.) In less dramatic circumstances, such as the decline of the language in a country that remains to some extent a cultural entity, the modes of thought and the original imagery may linger on, in translation as it were, for a very long time before they degenerate into mere provincialism.

With writers in particular this often, during the period of transition, produces a heightened awareness of the "new" language, even among writers who have never known the "old." Because the English words and syntax do not always and exactly fit the ideas and images to be expressed, the recently Anglicized "Celt" will examine his language with a very close attention. On the lowest level this becomes the "look you" and "I'll be after" of the music hall, and on the highest will produce the intensely self-conscious and beautiful prose of a Synge or a David Jones, the punning, stretching, verbal inventions of a Joyce or of Dylan Thomas himself. If this argument is accepted, the importance of the fact that, while Dylan's parents were bilingual and had been brought up as Welsh-speakers, he himself spoke only English, becomes apparent.

The second point to be made, one that is closely allied to the first, is social and cultural. Welsh rural society in the last century was essentially different from that of its two greater neighbors, England to the east and Ireland to the west. In England feudalism lingered on in those country districts — such as the Wessex of Thomas Hardy's youth — which in other respects were similar to Carmarthen. In Ireland, certainly after the Famine and probably before it, people of the class of Dylan's grandparents would most likely have regarded their social superiors as the representatives of an enemy occupying power. In Wales neither condition prevailed. There was, for all intents and purposes, no aristocracy in Wales. And this was not because Wales had been conquered by the English and its aristocracy wiped out but because the Welsh had in some measure conquered England and their old aristocracy, the Herberts, the Cecils, and above all the Tudors, had moved eastwards, into lusher pastures. Let me make my meaning plainer. The Welsh had of course been conquered by the Anglo-Normans in the late eleventh and again in the thirteenth centuries, just as Ireland had been partly conquered by Strongbow in the twelfth and again in the fourteenth. But medieval conquest was a very different matter from the later variety. It was in the sixteenth, seventeenth and early eighteenth centuries that Ireland was really conquered and planted. Wales was spared this terrible ordeal, though some might maintain that English conquest was only postponed to take an industrial and cultural form in the nineteenth and twentieth. Be that as it may, one hundred years ago most of the Welsh nobility had been long gone and had not been replaced, or in no great measure, by English aristocrats. Meanwhile the landlords who remained were severed from their tenants, indeed from the overwhelming majority of their rural compatriots, by reason of three great divides: they spoke English, not Welsh; they were High Church, not Nonconformist; and they were Tories, not Radicals. Since Tudor times they had intermarried with one another or with Englishwomen of their own class and had thus become increasingly Anglicized. So that by the nineteenth century they were no longer an organic part of their society. Rural Wales thus lacked the residue of feudalism, the class system, that the English knew and more or less accepted as the natural order, that the Irish knew and resented as an alien importation. There were landlords in Wales, but they were seldom squires. This produced a society which, if not classless, was at least not dominated by class. Again there is some resemblance here to the system that prevailed in New England.

And this in turn meant that the Welsh did not regard the man in the big house either as their leader or as their enemy, though they would perhaps incline more to the second opinion than the first. If so, their hostility would be economic rather than social or nationalistic, for the landlords in rural Wales, taken by and large, were landlords and nothing more. The Welsh looked elsewhere for men to admire, to emulate, to accept as their superiors.

They looked to their preachers and their poets. And here again I must stress this point, particularly for English readers. They respected their preachers and poets by reason of their sermons and their poems. In England, one hundred years ago as today, a writer or a clergyman was respected by the middle classes if he was in the first place a gentleman and secondly successful, that is to say a bishop or the author of best sellers: among the working class he was simply regarded as one of the bosses (there were a few exceptions, such as Dickens), cut off by reason of his education and his training from the mass of the people. In Wales this was not the case. The poets and preachers came, in general, from the shopkeeper or small-farmer class, the class in fact from which Dylan Thomas was sprung, but there was no reason other than the basic educational one why a man from the humblest background should not gain local or even national fame through his talents as orator or bard. The ministry, indeed, provided almost the only means by which a boy from a poor family could rise in the world: his local denomination, if impressed by his potential talents, would pay for his education, even sometimes to the extent of sending him to a Scottish university in the days when there was no university in Wales and when Oxford and Cambridge were closed to Nonconformists.

That such talents are likely to develop in an encouraging home atmosphere is self-evident. Here once again a parallel can be drawn with those Jewish families which have produced their people's spiritual leaders and, in bygone days, their cultural leaders too. The largely rural process that produced the Welsh preachers and bards was not dissimilar in nature, though quite other in practice, to the largely urban process which created the rabbis. In neither case did wealth or social position play a part. One result of this is that whereas the Welsh may be, and frequently are, as snobbish as anyone else, they do not base their snobbery on family background in the same way or to the same extent as do the English. They judge a man for what he is, for what he himself has made of his life. This means that while success is usually acceptable, moral condemnation is also always to hand. Hence the type of Welsh hypocrisy (though that is a very harsh word for what is a quite natural reaction if certain premises are instilled and accepted) that Caradoc Evans has written angrily about and that Dylan Thomas rebelled against, though more in his life than in his work. It also explains the curious, at times comical, attitude of certain Welshmen towards

[7]

him during his life, and even more so when he was famous and safely dead.

This leads to the third strand in his Welsh background, which is Welsh religiosity. Welsh Puritanism is by no means unique. It was at one time spread throughout the British Isles — Irish-Catholicism is ethically far closer in spirit to Welsh, Scottish or the more extreme forms of English Nonconformity than it is to the religion of France or Italy — and it provided an acceptable code of moral values for the working and lower middle class as those classes became increasingly alienated from the Established Church. In the essentially rural societies of which I am here writing, where the squire does not pass judgement or where his judgement is unacceptable for political, social or economic reasons, then the priest or the preacher will have to fulfil this function too. His becomes the last word, and it can be very harsh. It can of course also be gentle and sweet, but Puritanism has always been far more harsh when dealing with the weaknesses of the flesh, and particularly with sexual ones, than when castigating the sins of the spirit. One explanation of this may be that Puritanism was concerned with, and primarily practised by, men and women of limited education, little leisure, and thus with few means of self-expression. (Spiritual arrogance, cynicism or sloth are hardly likely to be their besetting sins.) For such people, as for almost everyone else, their manner of making love is their prime means of communication with others — indeed for them it may almost be the only means. Without pretending to any deep understanding of the forces involved, I would guess that one reason why the "Celt" and the Anglo-Saxon accepted Puritanism so easily is to be found in the basic human wish of men, and perhaps even of women, to be protected from the lawlessness of their own and others' passions. And in a simple society that passion is, in the first place, lust, while the second most prevalent of the deadly sins is gluttony in the form of drink.

For there were few means of communication in a society based upon those lonely Welsh farms and the little market towns that served them. There was almost no painting. There was music, but this was chiefly of a choral, interpretative, and not of a directly creative sort, and such music was closely connected with the chapels. There was no aristocracy to encourage talent, to bring in new ideas from the great and distant world, to display a way of life of which the deacons might disapprove but which they could not crush. There was not even a capital city of their own to which the young men might flee to find ideas and mistresses and friends.

Almost all that was left was poetry, poetry based, a little dangerously, upon the old Welsh pagan or semi-pagan myths and sagas. In this circumscribed world the word, in Welsh and later in English, was free within limits. A great deal of poetry was being written in Wales in the nineteenth century, by men of all conditions, for in those days it was no odder for a cobbler to be a bard than it is today for an industrial worker to become a trade union leader. And one of the bards of that age was William, or Gwilym, Thomas, who took a bardic name. It was customary for poets to adopt a name of their own choosing. The one he chose was Marles, or Marlais, from the clear, fast stream of that name which flows through Llandysul in Cardiganshire. He was a preacher too, and he was the uncle of Dylan Marlais Thomas's father.

Gwilym Marles was a remarkable man who handed down more than his bardic name to his great-nephew. In some ways he may be said to epitomize those particular aspects of nineteenth century "Welshness" which I have been attempting briefly to describe.

In 1905 the distinguished Welsh patriot, author and educationist Sir Owen M. Edwards published *The Poetry and Prose of Gwilym Marles*, to which he wrote an introduction, also in Welsh. Mr. Glyn Jones has kindly translated this for me, and it is from this introduction that I have taken the following facts.

He was born at Glan Rhyd y Gwiail, near the village of Llanybydder in Carmarthenshire, in the year 1834, but was brought up by one of his father's sisters at Gwernogle. Her husband was a deacon with the Independents, and their household was an intensely religious one. The Bible was the boy's constant study, both indoors and out. "Often," he later wrote, "did I pray in the sacred places and beneath the stately oaks about my home. I felt then and I feel now that I was enjoying a sweet and pure communion with the Great Spirit." At his school and at his college he met boys from more distinguished homes, where there were more books to read. But, says Sir Owen, Gwilym had been raised where Nature is at her most beautiful, and where God is also present.

At eighteen he went to the Presbyterian College in Carmarthen, better known as the Welsh Academy. Founded early in the eighteenth century, this establishment became a nursery of Arminian, Arian, and finally of Unitarian doctrine in West Wales. Indeed this area, from Llandysul to the Vale of Aeron, was known within living memory as Y

Smotyn Du, "the black spot," because of the numerous heretical worshippers who lived there, the "socins" as the orthodox nicknamed them. But Gwilym Marles was no Socinian. He went to Carmarthen an Independent and left it, with a scholarship to Glasgow University, a Unitarian. (The Unitarians have been described as the intellectual aristocrats of Nonconformity, and Gwilym Marles as the founder of modern Welsh Unitarianism. They are religious radicals who deny the divinity of Christ. Their enemies used to say of them that they believe in one God — at most.)

At Glasgow he won an honours degree, and in 1860 he was inducted as pastor of the Unitarian chapel of Llwyn Rhyd Owen and later of Bwlch y Fadfa. He also opened a school at Llandysul, where he was immensely popular. He had already published a volume of verse while still at the university, and he continued to write both in prose and in verse for the Welsh-language periodicals of the day. His language, we are told, was simple and rich; his emotions serious and gentle.

He also became deeply involved in local politics as a radical, a tribune of the people. This was a period of struggle in Wales between the landlords and the tenants, which took on a directly political form as a result of the increased franchise following on the Reform Bill of 1867. The preacher-bard was very active on behalf of the tenants. In 1876 his own landlord, motivated apparently by spite, evicted him from his chapel of Llwyn Rhyd Owen, where his wife and baby daughter lay buried in the churchyard. His congregation followed him to his new chapel. It was a *cause célèbre*, and for a while Gwilym Marles was the people's hero. He himself wrote at this time: "We have been mocked because we are poor people, without influence. So be it. Nevertheless we shall not measure greatness and honour by the standards of wealth, family, nor of worldly dignity."

It broke his heart, though. He had never been strong, and he had worked too hard. His health declined rapidly, and on December 11, 1879, he died at the age of forty-five.

Such was the great man of the Thomas family, "the towering dead with their nightingales and psalms" of Dylan's poem. His memory, if not his influence, must have played a great part in the life of his nephew, Dylan's father, so great that he gave his uncle's bardic name both to his son and to his daughter. The fact that it was the bardic and not the Christian name which he chose for his only son is also significant, as I hope to show in the next chapter. D. J. Thomas when a young man had himself wished to be a poet.

The character of David John Thomas is complex and baffling. He was born at Johnstown, Carmarthen, in 1876. His father was a minor employee of the Great Western Railway — his occupation on D.J.'s birth certficate is given as guard — but David had his Uncle Gwilym's literary and intellectual talents. He won a Queen's Scholarship to the University of Wales, Aberystwyth, where in 1899 he obtained a first class honours degree in English. Like many a poor young man who would be a writer, he chose teaching as his career. Whether he wrote in English or Welsh or both I do not know, for I have seen nothing that he wrote nor have I met anyone who has. I should guess, however, that he wrote in English, since he made no attempt whatsoever to teach his son Welsh. Indeed I have heard that he disliked his first language, even that he expressed a certain contempt for those who wrote and spoke in it. On the other hand he was proud of being Welsh. Dylan felt much the same, and with the same ambivalence. He was to write, in a film script, of a typical Welshman, with a hymn on his lips and a lie in his teeth; he was to write elsewhere, "Land of my fathers, and my fathers can keep it"; yet Dylan was also proud of being Welsh, and it was always to Wales that he returned, grumbling it is true but with the instinct of a homing pigeon. Mr. Robert Pocock has written: "I only once heard Dylan express an opinion on Welsh Nationalism. He used three words. Two of them were Welsh Nationalism." He would hardly have used that third word if he had been brought up with any particular respect for the Welsh language. On the other hand, D.J., who could and did discuss such very Welsh matters as styles of *penillion* singing, remarked more than once to Mr. Keidrych Rhys — the founder and editor of *Wales,* a magazine intended to serve as the mouthpiece for a Welsh literary renaissance — that he was "afraid Dylan isn't much of a Welshman." However, the fact that Dylan was brought up with the greatest possible love and respect for the English language does not mean that D.J. posed as an Englishman. The probable explanation is subtler than that.

There was a tragedy, perhaps more than one, in D. J. Thomas's life. In the first place he would have liked to be a poet and was not — a frustration which was to find its echo in Dylan's own last years. He got a job at Swansea Grammar School as soon as he left the university in 1899, and except for a brief interlude a couple of years later at a school in Pontypridd he remained at that school until his retirement in 1936. But he seems to have regarded the teaching of English to adolescent boys as a career not worthy of his talents. There is a rumour that when the University College of Swansea was founded in 1920, D. J. Thomas applied for the newly created chair of English and that he believed he had been shortlisted for the appointment. His lack of academic experience would make this appointment unlikely. In any event the chair was given to a man whom D.J. regarded, rightly I am told, as his inferior. He remained the provincial schoolmaster, nor did he attempt to write. Why did he acquiesce in this defeat of his ambitions?

There are hints of a darker tragedy, and one that is again very relevant to his son's life and death. At one point, it seems, D. J. Thomas decided that Dylan, then a boy or very young man, was drinking too much. According to what Dylan told Mr. Alfred Janes at the time, D.J. gave his son a talking-to, and what he said both shocked and surprised the young poet. The respectable, repected, reserved schoolmaster told his son that when young he too had drunk too much; that this had come close to ruining his life; but that by will-power alone he had conquered his self-destructive vice. Dylan may, of course, have invented this story, but I doubt it. It has the ring of truth. A story that I am sure Dylan did invent is that one evening, on his way home in the Uplands tram, he stumbled over a drunken man in the aisle and found it was his father. This story I am certain is a fabrication of Dylan's, and a typical one, but it may well have been based on the shock he received when his father told him about his past drunkenness. And there is a very faint confirmation in a tittle-tattle in Swansea that Mrs. Thomas, when first married, had to borrow from friends because D.J. was spending all his salary on drink. It is even specified that at this time of his life he was drinking whisky.

Dimly, then, one can perhaps glimpse the outlines of an obscure and distant tragedy. D. J. Thomas was enough of a critic to know that his poems failed to communicate that which he wished to express. He accepted another, and in his eyes inferior, career and sought refuge in the illusory compensations of drink to which so many poets, both good and bad, have resorted. And perhaps because of this, there came the second failure to achieve success even in his secondary ambition.

There were other heavy drinkers among Dylan Thomas's relations, as his stories show. The fact that there are alcoholics in a family does not, of course, condemn all its members to alcoholism, for if this were so it would be the fate of most of us. On the other hand it does indicate a tendency in that direction.

It should be remarked that at the time of this putative tragedy in Dylan's father's life the term alcoholism did not yet exist. It was not then recognized as a malady, akin to diabetes or gout, but was regarded as a failure of will, and nowhere more so than among Welsh chapel-goers. D. J. Thomas did not become a teetotaller, which in his day and in his society would have been a religious rather than a medical gesture. He adopted the far more difficult course of drinking less, and of limiting himself almost entirely to beer. The psychosomatic effort must have been very great indeed. All his life he drank, at times fairly heavily (and Dylan used to refer to him with wonderment as "the human beer-barrel"), but all the evidence goes to show that he never again got drunk. Such a man might well have both a terror and a hatred of drunkenness, but he would also understand. This, too, was to affect his son.

D. J. Thomas bore in his person the scars not only of his ancestry but also of the partial break-up of his society. He was the country boy come to town, even though the town was so remote a one, and one so close to the countryside, as Swansea. And in Swansea sixty years ago, more than in the country districts, not only was English the everyday language of almost everyone, but the Welsh Puritan ethos was already on the decline. D. J. Thomas was a highly educated man and he read the writings of his immediate seniors, men living in larger cities and more remote even than a Swansea free-thinker from the principles of Christianity. He had accepted the progressive, materialistic humanism which may seem dusty and dreary now but which was new and exciting at the turn of the century when Wells and Shaw were young. And for reasons that are undoubtedly both personal and historical, D. J. Thomas had decided that there was no God. The nephew of Gwilym Marles was an atheist.

Though this statement, too, may be an oversimplification. There was a particularly violent type of post-Nietzschean atheism abroad in the 1890s which toppled over backwards into what can only be described as God-hatred and for which Freud provides a fairly adequate explanation. Thus the Calvinist-reared Norman Douglas was perpetually engaged in a sort of private vendetta against the Christian God, or "the poisonous ghost" as he preferred to call Him. Edward Aveling, who lived with Karl Marx's daughter, wrote a book called *The Wickedness of God.* Similarly Dylan Thomas once described his father looking out of a window on a rainy day and exclaiming, angrily: "It's raining, blast Him!" Whether such an attitude can be correctly called atheism would appear doubtful, though both D. J. Thomas and Norman Douglas so described themselves. Perhaps an eccentrically extreme, and extremely eccentric, Manichean Nonconformism would be a better phrase.

His former colleagues and his old pupils are agreed on one point about D.J. He was an awesome figure, sarcastic, quick-tempered, even choleric, particularly during his last years at the school when his health was broken and he was frequently in pain. His colleagues were frightened of his tongue and he had only one close friend on the staff, a classics master whose scholarship, like D.J.'s, should have won greater recognition. His tongue, it is said, was even more vicious than that of the English master. D.J. would address the boys of his class, collectively and singly, as guttersnipes or worse. Nor was his violence purely verbal. If a boy earned his displeasure he would cuff him or kick him right across, sometimes out of, the room. The result was that they feared and respected rather than loved their English master. But what they did love was when he read aloud to his class, for he had a most melodious and beautiful voice and his knowledge and passion were such that he breathed life into the poems he read them.

He has been described to me as a vain man, well dressed, rather indolent. In physique he bore no resemblance to his son save that in middle age he too developed the beer-drinker's pot-belly, of which sickness deprived him in later life. D.J. was rather taller than Dylan, his features regular and inclining to the saturnine. Dylan closely resembled both his mother and his sister, as well, it is said, as his maternal grandfather. As for D.J.'s indolence, in 1929 he did not bother to claim the appointment of senior master, which was his due, because the position carried slight extra responsibilities without any increase in pay. The "honour" of the title presumably meant nothing to him. His knowledge of literature was great and was not confined to the classics. He liked the poetry of Edward Thomas, who was no relation, and he read modern novels. A former colleague, Mr. Morris Williams, has told me that at one time D.J. joined Boots' Library in order that he might read the latest fiction, particularly American fiction, Lewis, Dreiser, Hemingway. And as early as the middle 1920s he was reading and admiring D. H. Lawrence, which shows a pretty advanced and emancipated taste for the period.

He never invited guests to No. 5 Cwmdonkin Drive and if, on returning home, he found that his wife was entertaining ladies in the drawing-
room he would walk straight through to the "middle room," his study.
On the other hand he went out to the pub almost every evening. There,
in his special place, among his intellectual inferiors, he would relax and
feel at home. They called him "the Professor," they regarded him as a
wit, and his opinon was sought and valued on the matters of the day.
He suffered from poor health. So far as I have been able to discover he
never went abroad, only seldom to England, and was not in the army
during the First World War. His world was as narrow as the house in
which he lived, and as broad as the English literature he loved.

It is thus hardly surprising that Dylan's relationship with his father
should have been marked by reserve on the one side and by respect on
the other. But that there was great love, at least on Dylan's part and to
the end of D.J.'s life, bears witness to the fundamental decency and
kindness of his father's attitude towards him. In a letter to Pamela
Hansford Johnson, written when he was nineteen and anxious above all
to escape from his parents' home, Dylan yet said of his father: "a
broader-minded man I have never known." I only saw them together
once, in London in 1945, and I was struck then by how much Dylan
was on his best behaviour with his father, how anxious that his friends
too should make a good impression. And the pride that the old man
took in his famous son was quietly apparent. I believe that they were
always close to one another but that it was, by D.J.'s wish, a closeness
that found only limited expression. It was love rather than friendship.

Dylan's mother was a much simpler character and a far warmer one.
She too was sprung from the very heart of the chapel-going, farming
Welsh society of the nineteenth century, but hers was a humbler intellectual background than that of her husband. There is no Gwilym Marles
in the Williams family. Though she was actually born in Swansea, her
roots too lay in the countryside. Her father, George Williams, had left
the farm at Llangain, which is some twenty miles northwest of Swansea
near Llanstephan and just across the estuary from Laugharne, to become, like Dylan's other grandfather, an employee of the Great Western Railway. In 1867, when he bought the ninety-nine-year leasehold of
the new house in Delhi Street, which lies in the poorer part of Swansea,
his occupation was given as railway porter. Later he rose in the railway's
hierarchy to inspector, but he continued to live at No. 29 Delhi Street,

a dreary jerry-built cottage in a street where all the houses look alike.

His was a large family, and when he died in 1905 there were three sons and four daughters still alive. These, with their husbands and wives, are the uncles and aunts of Dylan's *A Child's Christmas in Wales,* sturdy, humble people. One son, Thomas, became a minister of the Gospel and had the Nicholston Hall Chapel at Gower, a few miles to the west of Swansea. Another, William, continued to farm in a very small way at the original home, Llangain. The third, John, lived at home and worked in the Swansea docks. Of the four daughters the eldest, Annie, married Jack Jones, who was a tenant farmer also near Llangain. She was Dylan Thomas's "aged, peasant aunt" and it was her "sour, humble hands" that he commemorated in one of his best and most famous poems, *After the Funeral:* their farm was Fern Hill, which was to play so important a part in his youth and in his poems. The second daughter, Elizabeth Ann, known as Aunt Polly, remained a spinster and is said to have been something of a musician. It may well have been she who sang like a big-bosomed thrush on that Christmas day in Wales long ago. Theodosia, "Aunt Dosie," married a preacher, the Reverend David Rees, who had the Chapel of Paraclete in what was then the village of Newton which has now been engulfed by the town of Swansea. Dylan saw a lot of Aunt Dosie, frequently staying with her when he was small, and it was almost certainly in Paraclete that he learned his Bible lore. The youngest child of the whole family was Florence Hannah, who married D. J. Thomas at the age of twenty-one, in 1903.

If it was from his Thomas forebears that Dylan inherited his literary talent and his brains, his mother's family played far the greater part in creating his early environment, both in town and country. Whether or not D. J. Thomas had any brothers or sisters — and there is some inconclusive evidence that he may have — he had severed all his family links at an early age and never, so far as I have been able to discover, had anything to do with any of his relations. None was present at his funeral. It is safe to say that the only members of the Thomas family known to Dylan were his father and his sister Nancy.

Florence, his mother, was from all accounts a sweet, gentle and rather childish woman, and she gave her son the measureless and uncritical love that comes more easily from a simple heart. He wrote, on his thirtieth birthday:

And I saw in the turning so clearly a child's
Forgotten mornings when he walked with his mother
Through the parables
Of sun light
And the legends of the green chapels.

She was a gay, garrulous woman, but her gaiety was tempered in D.J.'s household and her garrulity found its outlet in chatter with women of her own sort. She was a fundamentally happy woman, with the happiness that is squarely based on the love of God and the self-evident truth that it is better to be good, and kind, than the reverse. She is said to have had nothing in common with D.J. whatsoever. But it surely says much for D.J.'s character and for her own that that intellectual atheist did not impose his anti-Christian views upon her and that he allowed her to take little Dylan to chapel: while she, on the other hand, tolerated her husband's atheism and did not force her own beliefs upon her son. From this compromise came, I think, Dylan's totally unformulated love of God. From the early chapel-going, too, he derived much of his imagery. It was perhaps from his mother that he inherited the gaiety, sweetness and generosity that were such an essential part of his personality, just as it was from her that he inherited his looks.

Whether she ever read a book other than the Bible is doubtful, though she had a respect for books. As he reached late adolescence he was to find his mother's ignorance and her conventional views irritating. This crisis, if so it can be called, comes in most clever boys' youth. He outgrew it, and the home-smashing scene that opens *Adventures in the Skin Trade* is mere literary sublimation. Certainly he loved and looked after her in her old age. And the placid, simple love and pride she felt for him still shines, cosy as a fire in a cottage kitchen, in what she said about him after his death when she had become, and signed her letters, "Dylan's Mam." For she accepted even his death, as perhaps only a true Christian could.

The Swansea into which Dylan was born, and where he spent all his childhood and youth apart from visits to his relations' farms, was and is in many ways a unique town. All towns are unique, but what is peculiar about Swansea is that it marks the junction of many worlds, of many ways of life.

Swansea at the time of Dylan's birth had something over 100,000 inhabitants. It has almost doubled in size since then and most of the town centre, old Swansea, was destroyed by fire in the Second World

War and has been rebuilt: but in character, I am told, it has altered little. And one aspect of that character is that it is obviously and proudly middle-class. Such shabbiness as exists is tucked away in the eastern part of the town, down near the docks, which is where Delhi Street is located, out of sight and almost out of mind. What one sees, what one saw, in western Swansea, which is where Dylan spent his youth, are neither relics of the medieval past (even when Dylan was born the Old Castle dating from the twelfth century had entirely disappeared and only vestiges of the fourteenth century New Castle remained) nor the vast slums of a Cardiff. The *Encyclopaedia Britannica* of 1911 says: "All the main thoroughfares are spacious, and in two or three instances even imposing, but most of the residential part consists of monotonous stuccoed terraces. The climate is mild and relaxing, and the rainfall averages 40 in. annually." The stuccoed terraces, in one of which Dylan was born, are still there and the rain still falls upon them.

For Swansea is built like Rome on seven hills between which the River Tawe winds towards Swansea Bay. The town reaches around that handsome bay in a three-quarter arc and its setting has been compared, by Landor among others, to that of Naples. Such a comparison is valid, at least at night, when the great circle of lights above and about the dark water is a most lovely sight. By day bourgeois, busy Swansea has nothing in common with Naples whatsoever.

As a seaport its prosperity was originally based on the exportation of the mineral wealth of Wales, particularly coal from the more westerly mines of the great Welsh coalfield. Also copper was brought here by sea to be smelted at Hafod, immediately to the east of the town itself. It had, but has no longer, a fishing fleet. The smelting, too, ended early in this century when it was found cheaper to take the coal to the copper, and there is a great, blighted tract of land like an old battlefield where once that industry flourished: the smelting process released fumes that destroyed the vegetation, forever it seems.

And then, on the other side of the bay where the rise and fall of the tide is exceeded only by that of the Bay of Fundy in Canada, lies the Gower Peninsula, one of the most gorgeous stretches of cliff and heath, one of the most romantic and wild sceneries in the whole of Britain. From the top of the cliffs the waves seem to whisper as they break in the sandy coves or reverberate within the caves far below. Between the industrial Wales of the coal valleys and the vast steel and tin-plate works and the older Wales of the western counties, Swansea sits plumply in its stucco, as pleased and as prosperous as its mildly relaxed housewives window-shopping in their spacious commercial thorough-fares. When Dylan was born nearly two-thirds of Swansea's population spoke only English and a third both English and Welsh; only three per cent were monoglot Welsh-speakers.

The town in which Dylan spent his first twenty years, or more than half his life, was thus in three ways a frontier: geographically, in that it is a seaport and here was the junction between land and ocean; cultur-ally in that this was the meeting point of the Welsh and English lan-guages, and it is to this that Dylan was referring when he wrote of Swansea's "two-tongued sea"; socially, in that here lies the dividing line between ancient, agricultural Wales of "the good, bad boys from the lonely farms" and the Wales of the mining valleys with their own par-ticular and very vivid life. Such deep-seated conflict can be destructive and stultifying, especially if it leads to mutual hatreds. On the other hand it can also be highly stimulating to the questing mind. One of the functions, perhaps the most important and fruitful function, of the artist is to make a pattern out of chaos, to find an imaginative synthesis for the antitheses about him. And it was in the very nature of Swansea and of the Wales he knew that Dylan found one of his principal themes, for the divisions of the town passed, as it were, through his own body. He was a Welshman, but he was an English poet; no major English poet has ever been as Welsh as was Dylan. His instincts were those of a countryman, as is most of his imagery, yet he was in many ways a very urban character. He could not swim but he was only ever happy by the sea.

There are at least two ways in which his Swansea background was formative. Although in its fashion a frontier town, it bore no resem-blance to those places where the frontier is a place of hostility. The con-flicts were peaceable in that snug, rather smug town. And with its two theatres, its art gallery, its concerts and its university, it provided the bourgeois bases of knowledge without which culture, as we know it in the twentieth century, has a very hard struggle to exist at all. To this must be added, in Dylan's case, the fact that his father was a well-read man with quite a large library.

Finally Swansea is a long way from London. The talented young men were not, or not so quickly, sucked into the life of the English metropolis. In 1931 it was much easier to be quite unselfconsciously idiosyncratic in the Uplands than in Bloomsbury. In Wales a generation ago there was really no one for a writer to be formed, or misformed, by as he attempted to make his pattern of the world about him, unless perhaps it be Caradoc Evans. And it is quite astonishing what a wealth of talent Swansea produced in those years: Evan Walters, Ceri Richards and Alfred Janes in painting, Daniel Jones in music, Harry Secombe in the theatre, Wynford Vaughan Thomas in prose and radio, Vernon Watkins and Dylan, the youngest of them all, in poetry.

Furthermore the one quality that all these artists have in common is that they were and are extremely knowledgeable technically, they are pros, and none more so than Dylan in his "craft or sullen art."

For the very remoteness of Swansea from the cliques of London and the *idées reçues* of its artistic and literary worlds was a protection. In those worlds originality is rapidly copied into cliché, so that the original artist finds himself, within a year or two, encased in a chamber of mirrors where every glass holds a second-rate imitator. The temptation is then great for the artist to strive after a new vision, perhaps before he has perfected the old. In Swansea the young men had time to formulate their own artistic values, create their own techniques, and find their own modes of expression unpressurized by fashion.

In that pre-television age, when radio was not yet of any artistic or intellectual interest and even the mass-circulation national press still met with stiff competition from the local Welsh papers, the young men had to explore and exploit their own minds and their own talents if they did not wish simply to sink into the cosy, commercial world about them.

That Dylan with his ancestry and his character would have become a poet regardless of where he was born seems probable. But the fact that he was a Swansea boy was certainly of the greatest importance in moulding the mind and manner of the particular poet he became.

2

❧ ❧

Dylan Thomas was born in his parents' home as was customary in those days. It was not an easy birth, nor was an easy birth anticipated. Nancy, then eight, was not a healthy child and the Thomases' second baby had died within its mother's womb. Special care was therefore taken and a midwife who had attended Mrs. Thomas on previous occasions was brought over from the other side of Swansea and stayed in the house to await the birth.

Dylan was a small baby, weighing less than seven pounds. According to his mother he was a fairly healthy one, "but not what you would call robust." This would seem to be something of an understatement for he grew into a sickly child with weak lungs and also, perhaps, a liver complaint. He had exceptionally fragile bones, too, and throughout his life was repeatedly breaking what his widow, Caitlin, has called those "chicken bones of his." As a result of poor health he did not go to school at all until he was seven, and then only to a nearby dame's school for a few hours each day.

His health is a matter of the greatest importance if one would understand either his character or his poetry. Unfortunately there are very few facts available. Dylan himself talked with hyperbolic gusto about his ill health, past and present. For him a cold in the head was pleurisy, flu pneumonia, and every hangover incipient DTs. He told me, for instance, and as early as 1937, that he had had cirrhosis of the liver as a child; and, in his early days at least, his tuberculosis, the occasional spitting of blood, and the belief that he had only a very short time to live provided a favourite conversational theme. In this, however, as in other matters, there is little relying on what he himself said. Nor, unfortunately, have I succeeded in locating any doctors' records that might cast light on his childhood maladies. Any attempt, then, to establish his medical history must be largely speculative. Nevertheless it must be made.

Certainly he had lung hemorrhages, quite serious ones, as a child, and it was these that kept him in bed so much and prevented any proper schooling when he was a little boy. However, these seem to have been a thing of the past by the time he went to the Swansea Grammar School at the early age of ten, though there is some evidence that there may have been a recurrence when he was in his late teens. In any event he was left with a legacy of weakened, scarred lungs and a tendency to bronchitis. To this must be added asthma, aggravated from about the age of fifteen by chain-smoking. He had surely the worst smoker's cough there ever was, wheezings and hawkings and roarings on a truly Wagnerian scale that frequently went on till he vomited. The condition of his lungs at the time of his death is described in his autopsy, and I append the relevant passage as a footnote for those who may be interested technically.*

It was his bad lungs that caused him to be exempted from military service in the summer of 1940, not, as he sometimes said, a clever trick he had played on the examining doctors whereby he drank a bottle of Empire sherry just before his medical and "came out in spots." The hemorrhages left another and more important psychological legacy, but of this more later.

As for his liver, Nancy's husband has told me that she did have a liver complaint as a child, and she died of cancer of the liver at the age of forty-seven. It is possible that Dylan's father, himself a man of poor constitution, passed on bad livers to both his children. And Dylan's extraordinarily weak head, combined with the excessive violence of his hangovers even when young, would indicate that in his case, too, all was not well with the liver, that sly, intolerant organ. On the other hand

* *Lungs:* Lie in the posterior portion of pleural cavities which contain no fluid. Anteriorly, lungs slightly emphysematous; posterior somewhat atelectatic and also lumpy in consistency with many small punctuate haemorrhages in the pleura over the collapsed lumpy portions of the lung posteriorly. Bronchi deeply congested and also covered with patchy fibrino-purulent membrane. Lungs heavy for their size — left one, 750 grams — right one, 700 grams. On section, parenchyma dark red in colour; markedly diminished aeration with a patchy broncho-pneumonia very evident on the cut surface especially in the dependent portions. Lower lobes — pneumonic areas gray in color somewhat raised. All the lobes appear to be involved in this bronchopneumonic process. (Autopsy carried out by Dr. Milton Helpern, St. Vincent's Hospital, New York, November 10, 1953.)

he may merely have annexed his sister's early symptoms for his own hypochondriacal purposes. His autopsy describes his liver as having a "consistency somewhat firmer than normal: fairly evident fatty infiltration." This, I am told, proves nothing one way or the other: such a condition is to be expected in a man of thirty-nine who had drunk as much as he had.

What is quite clear is that his mother pampered and coddled him throughout his whole childhood to her, and his, heart's content — in part because such was her nature, but also in part because she regarded him as a semi-invalid, a role he accepted easily. At the age of seventeen, when having high tea at a friend's house, he did not know how to deal with a boiled egg: his mother had always taken the tops off for him. Nor does his rather remote father appear to have objected to this upbringing. Both his parents were of humble origin and such people, when physically able to do so, have often, perhaps usually, treated their children with an indulgence seldom shown by middle-class parents born in the last century, who used to be obsessed lest they "spoil" their children. In this sense Dylan was "spoiled" all right. Freedom from human controls and constraint was, to him, the natural order; such constraints as he was forced to accept were those exerted by his own body.

The name Dylan, which according to an early letter of his rhymes with "chillen" as in "all God's chillen got wings" but which Welsh purists prefer to pronounce "Dullan," is now a famous Welsh name. It was not so in 1914 when D. J. Thomas gave it to his infant son. Indeed twenty years later even so learned a Welsh scholar as Mr. Glyn Jones, when first writing to the unknown author of an admired poem, mistook his sex because the poem in question was called *The Woman Speaks*.

D. J. Thomas had found the name in the Mabinogion, in the Fourth Branch of the Mabinogi. There is it written of Math, son of Mathonwy, the magician king:

She was brought unto him. The maiden entered. "Maiden," asked he, "art thou a virgin?" "So far as I know, I am," said she. He took his magic wand and bent it. "Step over my wand," said he, "and if thou art a virgin I shall know." She stepped over the wand, and as she did so she dropped a fine he-child with golden-yellow hair. The boy gave a loud cry . . . And Math son of Mathonwy said: "I shall name this child, and the name I shall give him is Dylan." Thus was the golden-haired boy named, and straightaway he made for the sea. And when he reached the shore he became at once a part of the sea, he partook of its nature, and he swam as fast as the swiftest fish. And for that reason he was called Dylan Eil Ton, Sea Son of the Wave.

Now this choice of names, Dylan Marlais, was, we may be sure, D.J.'s and not his wife's, and it is surely an odd one. In the first place neither of these names is, strictly speaking, a Christian name at all, though this is perhaps not extraordinary in view of D.J.'s anti-Christian bias. Nor is the choice of Marlais unexpected, as I hope I have shown. But why Dylan? Why this obscure figure from a Welsh literature which D.J. regarded as so unimportant that he did not even bother to teach a few words of the language, his own first language be it remembered, to the boy on whom he bestowed the curious name?

Indeed he does not even appear to have explained to Dylan what it meant. In September of 1933 Dylan wrote to Pamela Hansford Johnson: "My unusual name — for some mad reason it comes from the Mabinogion and means 'the prince of darkness.' " Dylan was at that period of his life so preoccupied both with himself and with words that his curious error sounds like the echo of a dismissive reply on his father's part years before.

The choice of this highly "poetic" name was not, obviously, fortuitous. I have heard of fathers so unimaginative that they buy books of names before baptizing their children; there are Italians who simply number their sons, Primo, Secundo and so on until their wives stop bearing them; there are men so vain that they give their first-born all their own names, thus achieving a sort of spurious, semantic immortality; there are others who decide, perhaps as boys, that if ever they have a son they will call him Maximilian or Fortinbras because it sounds so much more romantic than their own boring Tom or Dick; and finally, in Wales where there are so few surnames, parents occasionally choose a deliberately unusual name in order that the child and future man can be easily distinguished from all the other Rhyses and Joneses and Williamses. Thus Mr. Richard Hughes, the novelist, told me that at one time he considered calling his son Mahomet because he would surely be the only Mahomet Hughes in the London telephone directory.

My guess would be that D.J. chose the name Dylan partly because it had pleased him in his poetic, Welsh-speaking youth, partly because it is, in its eccentricity, the very reverse of his own David John, than which nothing could be more banal in Wales. His own life had been, in a sense, a deliberate if only partial escape from the banality of his background typified in his name. Sixty years ago most Welshmen of his sort who wished to escape their background would jettison, as he had done, the Welsh language as a barrier to "progress" of any sort. He wished his son to escape yet further, but pride of blood remained and a Welsh name, particularly an unusual one, would be no hindrance. His wish was to be granted, but the cost was to be high, both to his son and to himself.*

Yet again, why the Son of the Wave? The Swansea schoolmaster had no connection with the sea, save for the fact that the town in which he taught sat next to it. Perhaps the explanation should be sought less in his circumstances or even in his geography than in the poetic tradition into which he had grown up. In 1914 Swansea "modern poetry" (and D.J. prided himself on being modern) was still pre-Georgian, was Flecker, Masefield, Bridges and perhaps a little Rupert Brooke, the fading cadences of an old Romanticism, echoing back through the exoticism of the 'nineties, of Thompson and Wilde, through Swinburne and Tennyson, to Coleridge and to Keats. Throughout that century, and indeed before it, the sea and its ships murmur and roll through English poetry, while Shelley's little boat lost in the storm off Lerici is the very quintessence of the Romantic tradition. T. S. Eliot had not yet quoted Wagner's despairing line, *Öd' und leer das Meer,* in the great poem that perhaps marks the real end of the Romantic agony. It would have been hard for a Welshman half a century ago to find a more poetic name with which to christen his son than Dylan. And there is evidence that from the day of Dylan's birth D. J. Thomas was determined that his son should be the poet he had failed to be himself.

No. 5 Cwmdonkin Drive is a narrow, semi-detached house, two storeys high, one room and a corridor wide, four rooms deep. It was built in 1914 and the plaster was still wet when Dylan was born there. It has a small yard at the back and a little porch in front, known as "the front." When Dylan was a very small boy — he was just four when the

---

* D.J. cannot fail to have been reminded of the name Dylan in the year of his son's birth. In July of 1914 an opera was staged at Covent Garden with the title *Dylan, Son of the Wave.* The music was by Joseph Holbrooke, the libretto by T. E. Ellis, which was the pseudonym of Lord Howard de Walden. This opera, of which D.J. must have heard from Dr. Vaughan Thomas the composer, whom he was seeing at the time, was part of an attempted "Welsh revival" on the lines of the recent Abbey Theatre "Celtic revival" in Dublin. Dr. Vaughan Thomas (he had not then added the Vaughan to his name) was, I am told, the first composer in modern times to set traditional Welsh poems to music, and would therefore have had every reason to be interested in the opera. His sons were near contemporaries of Dylan Thomas's and one of them, Wynford, was to be a lifelong friend.

war ended — and heard talk of men going to the front, it puzzled him that so many men should be in his parents' porch and yet invisible to him. (D.J., being forty when conscription was introduced in 1916, was theoretically liable to be called up, but only as a member of the oldest age group. Like most of his year he was not in fact conscripted.) The house is the epitome of modest neo-Georgian respectability and in the Thomases' time, I am told, the inside matched the exterior, flowered wall-paper, furniture mass-produced for the British professional class, reproductions of Greek statuary (in one of his letters Dylan says that he is writing beneath a plaster Echo), brightly coloured pictures of the Bay of Naples and such upon the walls. Only in one respect did it differ from thousands of such homes: the middle room on the ground floor, D.J.'s room, was dark with books.

It was a cosy home, snug and expected as the Sunday roast and two veg, with big windows to let in the summer's sun and the town's distant noises and the voices of the children playing in the park, comfortable, warm and yellow with gaslight in the wintertime when the gas meter ticked mysteriously in the cupboard beneath the stairs. And tucked away at the back was that most definitive of all status symbols, the walking talking proof that D.J. and Florence had risen above the class into which they had been born, a maid who "lived in."

Dylan Thomas described her as "Patricia" in his story "Patricia, Edith and Arnold," a pathetically cheerful girl, with the simple problems and easy dreams of her sort, impulsive, quick to scold and quick to cuddle, half-enamoured of the little boy's latent masculinity. She must have been his first experience of the world of people apart from his parents and "hockey-voiced" Nancy. Yet at the age of twenty-five he was to write about her with a curious mixture of affection and condescension. Though he was by then a complete egalitarian who had long since ceased to judge people by standards even remotely connected with class, she remained in his memory "the servant" with all the estrangement that that relationship implies and which he caught in one image, when the little boy in his story notices "the brown stains under her arms."

If the house in which he grew up was as standard to his parents' condition as is the thrush's nest to the thrush, the distant sea and the nearby park gave it that character of its own which lives on in his poems and in his stories of childhood. Cwmdonkin Drive is an extremely steep street, with a gradient of about one in six or seven, and is some two hundred yards long. And it points straight down to Swansea Bay, a mile or less away, to the sea that is always there, summer and winter, by day and even by night as the lights of the little ships cross its waters and The Mumbles Lighthouse spins.

To go to the sea was a journey for the little boy, but the park was almost part of his home. Opposite No. 5 was a playing field,

> . . . a capsized field where a school sat still
> And a black and white patch of girls grew playing.

It was capsized because it was horizontal, while the street was so steep as to seem nearly vertical. It was cap-sized because it was, for a field, as small as a schoolboy's cap. And the school that sat still were the deaf-and-dumb children, taken there from their special schoolhouse at the very top of Cwmdonkin Drive when the "big girls," girls as big and old and knowledgeable as Nancy, were not playing their hockey in their black-and-white gym tunics.

Beyond the field, which was really a part of it, lay Cwmdonkin Park. With the exception of Fern Hill it was the most important place in his childhood. It recurs again and again in his poems and in his prose, sometimes by name, sometimes thinly disguised as in the lines of *Lament*, one of his last poems in which he returns once again to his innocent childhood.

> I tiptoed sly in the gooseberry wood,
> The rude owl cried like a telltale tit,
> I skipped in a blush as the big girls rolled
> Ninepin down on the donkey's common.

Parks mean more to urban children than fields or gardens do to country boys. They are so rare, so peculiar, Hyde Park, Central Park, the Luxembourg, the Tiergarten, they offer such marvellous freedom from the tyranny of the streets that children in their harnesses tug towards them like dogs on their leashes. No city child can ever forget his own.

He wrote years later in his *Reminiscences of Childhood:*

And the park itself was a world within the world of the sea town. Quite near where I lived, so near that on summer evenings I could listen in my bed to the voices of older children playing ball on the sloping paper-littered bank, the park was full of terrors and treasures. Though it was only a little park, it held within its borders of old tall trees, notched with our names and shabby from our climbing, as many secret places, caverns and forests, prairies and deserts, as a country somewhere at the end of the sea.

And though we would explore it one day, armed and desperate, from end to end, from the robbers' den to the pirates' cabin, the highwayman's inn to the cattle ranch, or the hidden room in the undergrowth, where we held beetle races, and lit wood fires and roasted potatoes and talked about Africa and the makes of motor-cars, yet still the next day it remained as unexplored as the Poles — a country just born and always changing.

And the boy Dylan, playing in that park, he describes through the eyes of the park-keeper in *Return Journey:*

Oh, yes, yes, I knew him well. He used to climb the reservoir railings and pelt the old swans. Run like a billygoat over the grass you should keep off of. Cut branches from the trees. Carve words on the benches. Pull up moss in the rockery, go snip through the dahlias. Fight in the bandstand. Climb the elms and moon up the top like an owl. Light fires in the bushes. Play on the green bank. Oh yes, I knew him well. I think he was happy all the time. I've known him by the thousands.

The few trim and respectable acres of Cwmdonkin Park thus gave him his first and fascinated glimpse of the outer world. This was the place where Patricia and Edith went to meet their bigamous lover in the snow, where the hunchback ate his bread from a newspaper and each day, like Pygmalion, built his woman anew, where anything and everything happened. It is happening there for other children today. I was in Cwmdonkin Park, in November of 1963, when a simple monument, a carved stone, was unveiled in Dylan Thomas's memory. There were perhaps a score of grown-ups attending the little ceremony in the rain. But the boys whose park it is were there, a dozen or more, aged from four to ten. They stood together, unasked, interested, astonishingly silent and attentive while a couple of poems were read. And then it was over and they scuffled and whooped and hared away. And in the sentiment of the moment I wondered: if I were to count them, might there not be one too many, an Ali Baba among the wide-eyed boys "innocent as strawberries?"

He was sent from time to time to stay with his Aunt Dosie and the Reverend David Rees out at Newton, in the minister's house that is called The Manse. Mr. Rees regarded himself, quite correctly, as the leader of his little community. Being interested in music, botany and so on he arranged that his flock be also instructed in these matters. Outings took place to the Gower Peninsula and to sites of historic interest. He was loved and respected in Newton. Here we may be sure Dylan had his full measure of Sunday school, in the hall behind the Victorian chapel called Paraclete, a big room especially designed for that purpose which also housed a children's library containing secular as well as religious books. In the centre of what was then a steep village, where the roads meet, there stood in those days a pump and from it an open drain ran swiftly downhill. The Newton grocer has told me how as children he and Dylan would send their paper boats careering down this lovely boys' river. Here, as at home, Dylan had to find his friends outside, for there were no cousins.

But the real country holidays were at Fern Hill, near Llangain. It would be hard to find a more remote farm and when found it is a curious place, large for what is essentially a peasant's holding, yellow-washed, built around three sides of a tiny court, with the farmyard and the few farm buildings off to one side. It has pointed Gothic-revival windows and looks, from the outside at least, as though it was originally built about 1830 as a gentleman's residence but has gone badly to seed. On one side is the hill where the house-high hay grew forty years ago, on the other, before the ground drops steeply away to a little stream, it is just possible to detect what was once a small flower garden. There are tall trees about the house, which give to the farm a feeling of being enclosed, and there are the remnants of the orchard where Dylan was young and easy under the apple boughs.

Inside, though, there is nothing to suggest even the faintest echo of what had once been perhaps a modest grandeur. Dylan has described the inside of the Fern Hill he knew in "The Peaches," a dank, dark house where only the kitchen was bright with brass and firelight beneath the sides of bacon hanging from the rafters, while the front parlour with its stale fern and its stuffed fox mouldered away, dusty with disuse. "I climbed the stairs; each had a different voice. The house smelt of rotten wood and damp and animals. I thought I had been walking down long, damp passages all my life, and climbing stairs in the dark alone . . . The candle flame jumped in my bedroom where a lamp was burning very low, and the curtains waved. . . ." And as though all this were not enough the whole gloomy, oil-lit farmhouse was filled with the legend of the hangman.

[29]

The tales told about the hangman are few but gruesome. The ground-floor windows are barred and these bars are said to have been the hangman's handiwork. He had, it seems, married a rich wife and either Fern Hill was her house or he bought it with her money. She died, either in childbirth or when their only child, a daughter, was very young, leaving all her possessions to the girl. All went well for the hangman so long as she was a minor and even, indeed, when first she came into her inheritance. But then she met a "gentleman from Carmarthen" with whom she fell in love. They wished to marry. This did not suit the hangman at all, for with her would go his money, his comforts, perhaps his home. He forbade her to see the Carmarthen gentleman. She disobeyed. He therefore barred the windows and locked her in whenever he had occasion to go out, as for example to Carmarthen for a hanging. Even these precautions did not satisfy him, so determined was his daughter to escape. He built a windowless room, which now forms one side of Fern Hill's tiny court, and in this he proposed to incarcerate her. But in the nick of time, and just before her dungeon was ready, the young gentleman from Carmarthen arrived with a ladder and she escaped through an upper window. So great was the hangman's wrath and mortification on discovering that his daughter had fled that he hanged *himself*, in his kitchen or as some say in his hall. All this is supposed to have happened at the end of the last century.

What truth there is in this dark and country tale I cannot say. But it was certainly Brontë-ish enough to provide an imaginative boy with the ingredients with which to frighten himself in those dark corridors where his candle flickered in the draught. And of course he embellished it. The hangman had not only hanged himself at Fern Hill; he had despatched his innumerable victims not in Carmarthen gaol (where he seems to have been a sort of deputy or assistant hangman, officiating only when the real hangman was indisposed or on holiday) but in his own house. Their wretched ghosts could also be heard squeaking and gibbering when the floorboards creaked, could also be seen, out of the corner of the eye, grimacing at the hangman's pendulent ghost at the foot of the stairs. All his life Dylan enjoyed frightening himself, as he enjoyed every sensation and experience. He was ever ready to conjure up ghouls, warlocks and above all vampires. Vampires were his favourites. He slept with his windows closed, "To keep the vampires out, of course." And an unpublished poem of his, which so far as I know was never written down, I give as a footnote.* It was composed in conjunction with Wynford Vaughan Thomas in about 1941 and Vernon Watkins was perhaps also present on this occasion.

Fern Hill's hangman gave him an early chance to experiment in the macabre. He made use of these experiments in his earliest short stories, the ones that he published later in *The Map of Love*.

Whether or not it was from the hangman's daughter that James Jones, who was married to Dylan's Aunt Ann, rented Fern Hill, I do not know. Certainly Jones was a bad tenant farmer. Dylan has described how he drank his piglets, and how he left the little boy, fearful in the growing dark, outside the pub while he did so. He was a slovenly farmer and the landlord — the farm has changed hands since — saw no point in spending money on his ill-run property during a period of agricultural depression. It became increasingly shabby and tumbledown, gates off their hinges, paint peeling, ever more thistles in the hay. (Dylan, sometimes with a school-friend, would come out to help with the haymaking; as reward they were allowed to ride the old horse.)

The ramshackle outhouses had tumbling, rotten roofs, jagged holes in their sides, broken shutters, and peeling whitewash; rusty screws ripped out from the dangling, crooked boards; the lean cat . . . sat smugly between the splintered jaws of bottles, cleaning its face, on the tip of the rubbish pile that rose triangular and smelling sweet and strong to the level of the riddled cart-house roof. There was nowhere like that farm-yard in all the slapdash county, nowhere so poor and grand and dirty as that square of mud and rubbish and bad wood and falling stone, where a bucketful of old and bedraggled hens scratched and laid small eggs.

* At the corner of Pell Street a vampire appears
Singing "Garlic! Sweet garlic!" He's sung there for years.
See he taps at the window of Councillor Rees
And he sings as he taps a most sinister piece.

     Councillors, jugulars, suck-eyed with glee,
     Oh for the veins of a scrumptious J.P.
     Tremble you aldermen, town-clerks beware
     As I hoover the veins of your succulent mayor.

At the Guildhall's Bloodorium the Council's convened,
The motion: "Re Pell Street and Bloodsucking fiends,"
Proposer — Rev. Samuel, Labour, Landore,
When whoops! through the windows the vampires roar.

     Councillors, jugulars, suck-eyed with glee . . . etc.

The Joneses had a son, Idris, who was seventeen years older than Dylan but who provided a companion of sorts when he went alone to remote Fern Hill. Dylan has described him, in "The Peaches," preaching hellfire sermons to his little cousin and reading girlie magazines in the roofless earth closet. There is almost certainly a great deal of exaggeration in this portrait. I once met Idris when Dylan brought him to London just after the war — his first visit to the capital, I think. Dylan had described him, as he described everyone and everything, with such exuberant yet convincing fantasy that I expected at least a Welsh Heathcliff, perhaps a Carmarthenshire Billy Sunday, maybe a straight lunatic. He turned out to be a rather quiet, shy countryman. But of course this was London, and 1945, and Dylan a famous man. It may have been very different, at Fern Hill, twenty years before.

If Fern Hill is in some measure the inspiration of those dark, early stories in which the influence of Poe and the Brontës is as discernible as that of Caradoc Evans and T. F. Powys, from memories of that farm also spring the lovely country poems, and not only the one that bears its name. Dylan in later years looked back on his innocent childhood with longing and delight, and Fern Hill was at least as much a part of his lost Garden of Eden as was Cwmdonkin Park, indeed almost certainly more.

As he grew older he celebrated his own paradise lost with ever greater glory, but this did not begin until he had left Swansea in 1934, though it did start very soon after. Thus when his Aunt Ann died, early in 1933, he wrote a poem about her funeral, on February 10th to be precise. It begins, like the famous poem he wrote and published only five years later, with the line:

After the funeral, mule praises, brays. . . .

There the resemblance between the two poems ends. The first poem has no pity for "her scrubbed and sour humble hands"; she is no "sculptured Ann . . . seventy years of stone," but rather a silly, gossipy old woman whose funeral is a half-hypocrisy.

The mourners in their Sabbath black
Drop tears unheeded or choke back a sob,
Join in the hymns and mark with dry bright looks
The other heads bent, spying on black books.*

* MSS: Lockwood Memorial Library, Buffalo.

Fern Hill in fact only became *Fern Hill* and Auntie Ann was only transformed into *Ann Jones* when London and much else had polarized that summer country sunshine, had distilled the scent of the hay, and it is the *remembered* owls that are bearing the farm away.

Fern Hill also appears, quite frequently, in his prose reminiscences of childhood. In general these stories, particularly those collected in *Portrait of the Artist as a Young Dog*, are autobiographical but strongly flavoured with poetic licence. They are *Dichtung und Wahrheit* and should not be regarded as any more factual than Goethe's book of that title. For instance there is the splendid story of his Grandfather Thomas, on Carmarthen Bridge in his railwayman's waistcoat with the brass buttons, refusing to go home, since there is no purpose in being buried in Llanstephan "where a man cannot twitch his legs without putting them in the sea." Dylan may have heard such a story about his grandfather, though it would probably have been his Grandfather Williams, but he certainly never heard either of them driving his horses across the counterpane at night, for they were both dead before ever he was born.

The little boy who looks out from the first picture — which I found among his mother's possessions and which, I should guess, was taken when he was about four — is already and unmistakably Dylan, although the curly brown hair was still golden-yellow in those days. The weak chin, though, the loose mouth, and above all the questing, haunting, slightly hooded eyes, with their hint of timidity mingled with wonderment, were to change little in the years to come. Only his nose, his Shandyean nose as he used to call it, did not then exist, for it was broken a year or so after this photograph was taken. He was playing in the house of a little friend whose nursery was at the top of a winding stair. The friend had to find his mother, for the usual reason, and Dylan was mocking him, leaning over the banisters and calling : "I got a pain in my tummy, Mummy," when over he went, straight onto his nose, flattening it. It never regained its shape and remained the conk that Mervyn Levy's excellent drawings show, not the fine and aristocratic nose of Augustus John's famous and highly romanticized portrait. Still, broken or not, the nose worked, nor does it seem to have added to his respiratory troubles. Indeed he could even smoke through it, and sometimes did, to the surprise of strangers in public houses who expected to see cigarettes between people's lips.

His earliest education was a haphazard affair. According to his mother she used to read to him when he was ill in bed, but she could not really spare the time. He more or less taught himself to read, she said, from the innocent English comics of the day, *Puck, Rainbow* and *Tiger Tim*. Then, in stark contrast, there were the hours with his father. When D.J. came home from the Grammar School he would read to his little son, and what he read him was Shakespeare. Mrs. Thomas has said: "When he was very small I used to say to his daddy: 'Oh, Daddy, don't read Shakespeare to a child only four years of age.' And he used to say: 'He'll understand it. It'll be just the same as if I were reading ordinary things.' So he was brought up on Shakespeare."

D.J.'s pupils have never forgotten the passion, humour and conviction with which he read Shakespeare to his English classes. One of them has told me that if D.J. missed his real vocation it was not that of poet but of actor. The effect upon the little boy, in his sickbed or before sleep, was profound and lasting. The greatest poetry in the English language, perhaps in any language, flooded into an open, receptive and above all fresh mind, for the little boy knew nothing else. Until he went to the school run by Mrs. Hole, when he was seven, he seems to have had almost no lessons at all. He went there — it was a short walk from Cwmdonkin Drive — for four years.

"Never was there such a dame-school as ours," he wrote in his *Reminiscences of Childhood*,

so firm and kind and smelling of galoshes, with the sweet and fumbled music of the piano-lessons drifting down from upstairs to the lonely schoolroom where only the sometimes tearful wicked sat over undone sums or to repent a little crime, the pulling of a girl's hair during geography, the sly shin-kick under the table during prayers. Behind the school was a narrow lane where the oldest and boldest threw pebbles at windows, scuffled and boasted, lied about their relations—
    "My father's got a chauffeur."
    "What's he want a chauffeur for, he hasn't got a car."
    "My father's the richest man in Swansea."
    "My father's the richest man in Wales."
    "My father's the richest man in the world."
—and smoked the butt-ends of cigarettes, turned green, went home, and had little appetite for tea."

Smoking? The cigarette became almost his personal device, the first vice, maybe the worst. Dylan without a cigarette is Joyce without his spectacles. In a letter of 1933 he wrote: "I was first introduced to Tobacco (the Boy Scout's enemy) when a small boy in a preparatory school." And in *Return Journey* he described himself at that school:

In Mirador School he learned to read and count. Who made the worst raffia dollies? Who put water in Joyce's galoshes, every morning prompt as prompt? In the afternoons, when the children were good, they read aloud from Struwwelpeter. And when they were bad, they sat alone in the empty classroom, hearing, from above them, the distant, terrible, sad music of the late piano lesson.

According to Mervyn Levy, who attended the same school at the same time and the same age, they really learned nothing there at all. His sister, Mrs. Black, who was also there, has written me: "One of the teachers used to sit in a chair and we all sat around on the floor. She read us stories, and the whole time one of the children had to rub the back of her neck. We also had to kiss her goodbye every day when we went home." Mrs. Hole's establishment, which held a couple of dozen children, was less a school than a sort of dumping place for children whose mothers wanted them out of the way, boys aged between seven and eleven, girls till sixteen. Since fees (ten pounds per annum) were paid, it was socially above the state schools, but educationally their obvious inferior. Mrs. Hole, who was elderly, had a middle-aged son who was in a state of almost permanent inebriation, and his bloated, scarlet features and unpredictable behaviour fascinated the little boys and girls. Over the mantelpiece of the room in which he presided there was a large ring of puppy-dogs-tails, threaded into a circle, all — he told the children — bitten off with his own strong, sharp teeth. His choice of decorations and souvenirs was a further source of wonderment. So too was his death, which occurred while they were at the school and was a source of endless speculation among them. It is impossible to say what effect this realization of death at so early an age had upon Dylan, but it is unlikely that it had none.

There were other discoveries to be made about the human realities. Mervyn Levy has written:

We shared many little cameos of experience when we were boys. I will re-call just one. It occurred when we were around nine or ten years of age. My mother died when I was eight and after her death my father engaged a suc-cession of nurses to look after his three children. One of these was a particu-larly comely and buxom young girl whom Dylan and myself had long sus-pected of washing her breasts in the hand-basin. The glass panels of the bathroom door were masked with areas of variously coloured opaque paper, very thin, and imparting to the top half of the door the aspect of a crude, stained-glass window. One day, in the holidays, we carefully scraped away two minute peepholes, one on either side. . . . Around three p.m. we crept up the sleepy, dark, afternoon stairs, and with an eye each to our respective peepholes beheld, in ecstasy, like two tiny elders, our own Susannah.

Most little boys, if given the chance, would have done the same. But Mervyn Levy has told me that what made the escapade so vividly memorable to him was less this first conscious vision of a woman's breasts than Dylan's intensity and excitement and passionate curiosity.

There are other stories of childish naughtiness. Though in their nature usual and normal, there is again something unusual in their scale. For instance the gang outings to the Uplands Cinema, the great ambition to get in without paying, and once inside to make the maximum noise when bored — nothing odd about that. But smoking a *cigar* in the cinema while still in short pants aroused the wonderment of his contemporaries. So, too, did the brazen stealing of sweets from Fergy's sweet-shop across the way. And when he played "the colonel" in the Mirador School play he behaved so outrageously, winking, spitting orange pips at the audience, chasing the other actors off stage with his property cane, that the curtain had to be rung down. Was it then or later that he dressed up in Nancy's clothes and loitered about street corners, making eyes at the boys — to the fury of his sister whom he so closely resembled? And Mervyn Levy's sister, their junior by five years, has described how they would run her to the school, one holding each hand so that her little feet seldom touched the ground, shouting at the top of their voices: *"The dragoons are coming!"* Dylan — dragoon — even dared to collect money ostensibly for Dr. Barnardo's Homes, actually for himself and his friends. The world was beginning to reveal its weaknesses.

At a school like Mrs. Hole's, as at more distinguished establishments, most of what the children learn they get from one another. Dylan, when not ill at home, was an extremely sociable, gregarious child, a one for gangs and fights and adventures of all sorts, a very masculine little boy despite, or perhaps in part as compensation for, his small size and his delicate, almost feminine appearance. On one occasion he was brought home unconscious when a seesaw that he and another boy had constructed on a building site threw him down a dozen feet onto his head; on another, some bigger boys whom he had been annoying dumped him upside down in a barrel of lime, but he was none the worse for this either. As he wrote later: "All day long it was running, it was lovely . . . it was air and playing." All day long, when the days were not spent coughing in bed.

But something much more important had happened to the little boy while he was at Mrs. Hole's school. His mother has said: "The only way we could keep him in, when it was wet or anything, was to give him plenty of notepaper and pencils. He would go into his own little bedroom and write and write and write."

Mr. Colin Edwards, who tape-recorded an interview with Mrs. Thomas shortly before her death, asked her at what age he started to write. She replied, when he was about eight or nine. And what did he write?

"He started with poems. And, you know, he would ask his sister sometimes: 'What shall I write about now?' and you know what sisters are, not very patient with their brothers, and she'd say: 'Write about the kitchen sink.' He wrote a poem, a most interesting little poem, about the kitchen sink. And then another about an onion. That kind of thing."

Did he write prose at that age too?

"No, poems, always poems."

When trying to understand another man's life, perhaps even when thinking about one's own, it is difficult not to do this backwards, to look in the beginning for that which foreshadows the middle and the end. Though it is the very opposite of inevitable that the boy Dylan who sailed his ship in the hunchback's basin in Cwmdonkin Park should later have written *Vision and Prayer* and died in St. Vincent's Hospital, New York — no other of the thousands like him lived such a life — nevertheless it was that boy who became that man. Therefore a biographer will search for the semblance of a pattern, will try to find in the boy the man's embryo. Since Dylan himself affirmed this unity of character and experience more than most writers have done, more even perhaps than Proust, and since he regarded man's existence as a unity from the act of creation to the fact of death, I think I should suggest here very tentatively what in my view his earliest years portend.

The distance between his sister and himself was such that in practice he was an only child. His home life was thus a solitary one, and this solitude was made the greater by the loneliness of the sick-bed. Home meant his mother's care, his own thoughts, his father's reading of

Shakespeare, his first childish poems. Outside, on the other hand, it was all running, it was gangs, it was the others, it was competition, it was new experience. But always, at the end of the day, there was the cosy home, the indulgent mother, the warm gas-lit refuge; and the greatest refuge of all was sickness, when anything was allowed the little boy. Sickness, too, spurs the imagination as shapes dissolve and the mountain becomes magic, while coarse and exciting and dangerous reality awaits outdoors. Knowledge is then irrelevant, indeed is not wanted, while feeling becomes all, feeling that can be expressed through words even before it can be fully expressed through the body, feelings not only of love, but also of fear, even the ultimate fear which is that of death roaring through the chapels.

Such, I think, was the little boy who went to the Swansea Grammar School at the age of ten.

3

⊰ ⊱

THE Swansea Grammar School, which Dylan Thomas first went to in 1925, was founded by Hugh Gore, Bishop of Waterford, in 1682. It was partly destroyed by fire bombs in 1941, has since been rebuilt in another part of Swansea and renamed the Bishop Gore School. Now free, it was a fee-paying school, though it took many non-paying pupils and its fees were small, in 1925 some five pounds a term. The boys were in general the sons of small businessmen, the larger shopkeepers, professional men. The sons of the rich would occasionally, though by no means always, be sent away to the more fashionable boarding schools in England. The sons of the poor went to the free state schoools. (Swansea Grammar School was administered by the town council.) Thus in his school life Dylan Thomas found himself once again in an environment he knew well. He neither left his home physically nor socially. No particular scholastic level save basic literacy was required of the boys admitted to the school. Had such a requirement been made, one may venture to doubt whether Dylan Thomas could have attended the school at all, save perhaps as D. J. Thomas's son.

For the headmaster, Mr. Trevor Owen, had the greatest regard for D.J., by then the senior English master. One of Mr. Owen's first actions, when appointed head in 1901, had been to bring back D.J. from Pontypridd, and he can never have regretted this decision, for the standard of the English classes was very high indeed.

This Mr. Owen seems to have been an admirable man and his school a very good one. He was, by the standards of his age, a progressive headmaster; nor did he attempt to turn his school into a third-rate imitation of Eton or Winchester, as some other grammar schools were trying to become at this time. The boys were not regimented; there were no compulsory games; and religion was limited to a few brief prayers and a hymn at morning assembly. Every encouragement was given, and successfully, to those boys who wished to learn, and many won university scholarships. Those who did not so wish, however, were generally ignored rather than penalized. Indeed it might well be said that discipline outside the classrooms was almost non-existent, and even inside was not particularly strict. There is a story that Mr. Owen once found Dylan hiding in the shrubbery when he should have been in school and enquired, mildly, what the little boy was doing there.

"Playing truant, sir," he replied.

"Well, don't let your father catch you," the headmaster remarked, shook his head, and walked on.

And Mr. Morris Williams, a retired master from the school, has told me that the way Dylan managed to be sick in bed whenever examination time came round was a standing joke in the masters' common-room. He was always bottom of his class in every subject except English, in which he was always top. The study of English, the writing of poems and, soon, the editing of the school magazine were his only interests in the school. All others were rapidly abandoned. In a BBC broadcast, Mr. Williams recalled: "The boys came and educated themselves and asked the masters for what they wanted. Dylan did that with me. He wanted to hear a bit of Virgil, though I don't think he was a Latin scholar at all. He came for about two months, until it was time to edit the magazine, and then I didn't see him any more."

This, I imagine, is both the beginning and the end of Dylan's story that he could have gone to Oxford and been a great classical scholar had he so wished. Mr. Stuart Thomas, an exact contemporary and speaking in the same BBC programme, recalled Dylan's even briefer brush with mathematics:

I remember one occasion when he hadn't done any homework. He was hastily cribbing out something from the boy next door when he was spotted by the master, who said: "Thomas, you're cribbing." Whereupon Dylan said: "If that's what you think, I won't attend any more of your classes," and walked straight out of the room. As far as I remember he never did come back to Mr. Joseph Jones's mathematics lessons.

Years later, in a talk before a poetry reading, Dylan was to say of his own education:

I could talk about my education—which, critics say, I have not got. And they are right, too. (But I do wish I had learned some other languages, apart from English, Third Programme and saloon. Then, perhaps, I could understand what people mean when they say I have been influenced by Rimbaud.) You know the kind of mock self-deprecating writers who always boast that they were boobs at school; that their place in the form was always black-marked bottom. They wink and prod you in the wind and try to give you the impression that they were always rakes, rips, limbs and lads; that rule-of-thumb education was not for them. And see, they gloat, see what we are now: distinguished figures, three times the choice of the Masterpiece-of-the-Fortnight Club: Genius will out! Sedentary hacks, breathless and bloated from gobbling stale fried phrases and swilling them down with praise, they were probably the apple of the pedagogic eye, pubescent pedants and lick-spittles as well. Only — usually — a subtle, or a humourless, or an honest writer says he was extremely good at school. Neither particularly subtle nor honest, I must say I was awful. Whether this was because of stupidity or arrogance I am still not asking myself. But my proper education consisted of the liberty to read whatever I cared to. I read indiscriminately and all the time, with my eyes hanging out on stalks. I never could have dreamt there were such goings-on, such argie-bargies, such simoons and ice-blasts of words, such love and sense and terror and slashing of humbug, and humbug too, such and so many blinding bright lights breaking across the just-awakening wits and splashing all over the pages — as they can never do again after the first revelation in a million bits and pieces, all of which were words, words, words, and each of which seemed alive forever in its own delight and glory and right.

It was then, in my father's brown study, before homework — usually the first botched scribblings of gauche and gawky heart-choked poems about black bloomered nymphs and the impossible loves of the sardine-packed sky — that I began to know one kind of badness. I wrote endless imitations — though I never thought them to be imitations but, rather, colossally original, things unheard of, like eggs laid by tigers — I wrote imitations of whatever I happened, moon-and-print struck, to be goggling at and gorging at the time: Sir Thomas Browne, Robert W. Service, de Quincey, Henry Newbolt, Blake, Baroness Orczy, Marlowe, Chums, the Imagists, the Bible, the Magnet, Poe, Grimm, Keats, Lawrence, Austin Dobson and Dostoievski, Anon and Shakespeare. I tried my little trotter at every poetical form. How could I know the tricks of this trade, unless I tried to do them myself, for the poets wouldn't rise from the dead and show me how their poems were done by mirrors, and I couldn't trust the critical expositors of poetry then — or now. I learned that the bad tricks come easy; and the good ones, which help you to say what you wish to say in the most meaningful, moving way, I am, of course, still learning — though in earnest company I must call these tricks by other names. Nothing, in those days, was too much for me to try. If Paradise Lost had not already been written, I would have had a shot at it. Prodigious then my truculent presumption was! I bulldozed through print, tore through the babbling dead like a tank with a memory. On the very green fields of my youth I stomped pun-shod and neigh-nonnied in a nosebag of adjectives. I *had* to imitate and parody, consciously and unconsciously: I *had* to try to learn what made words tick, beat, blaze, because I wanted to write what I wanted to write before I knew how to write or what I wanted to. And as if I knew now.

There is apparent in these light-hearted remarks by a middle-aged man about his own youth one paradox that had come by then to assume considerable importance for him and that lingers on, even after his death, in some of the more controversial comments that have been written about his poems. It is probably true, as he said, that most good writers are more highly educated than, say, most bank presidents or barristers. And because Dylan was a very good writer certain academic critics, particularly in America, have endowed him with a profound knowledge of astronomy or theology, of Welsh metrics or even of biology, which he certainly did not possess. On the other hand, and in part because of his defective education and consequently somewhat restricted view of the world, certain English academics, particularly those who learned from Dr. Leavis himself how to pop poems into critical killing-bottles, have denied that he was an original and important poet at all, though he certainly was.

It would therefore be well, at this point, to try and see what was happening to him intellectually during his years at the Grammar School, between 1925 and 1931. John Davenport, who knew him well later in his life and who, being a man of the widest culture, is more capable than most of forming an objective judgement of Dylan's mind, has told me that in his opinion Dylan was very clever but intellectually almost incredibly lazy. This is true in a way, but it is not the whole truth. His best poems are not the product of a lazy mind, and even his minor writing, his light prose and his film scripts, show a mastery of arrangement and synthesis, and at times of analysis too, which should surely have enabled him to romp through his Latin and mathematics lessons. Nor is it enough to say that he was interested "only" in poetry. He was not. He enjoyed talking about almost any subject to almost any man or woman, provided the conversation was genuine and was not conducted at an academic level. He found the academic approach, particularly to poems, distasteful in the extreme, and never made the slightest attempt to conceal this. It was as though he sensed that they were after him. And this, I think, dates back to the Grammar School.

When he entered the Grammar School he suddenly found that from being the dragoon of Mirador he was now one of the youngest, smallest and weakest among four hundred boys. He was also one of the worst educated — but he had this one talent: he could write poems, and a poem of his appeared in the school magazine during his first term there. He was extremely sensitive and perhaps even more self-centred than most artists. He had always been the hub of his little world, the king of his Cwmdonkin castle, and on the rare occasions when his wishes or whims had not been gratified there had always been the refuge of the imaginary world or in extreme cases of sickness. Now, educationally ill-equipped, he found himself among boys who were his superiors not only in that respect but also in physique. To this must be added the fact that like so many undersized men he was determined to excel, to beat the record. (Was not one of his last recorded remarks: "I've had eighteen straight whiskies. I think that's the record"?) His ambition was enormous, but at this early age quite undirected even as to the sort of poetry he wished to write. If he could not be top of his class then very well, he would be bottom. Any place in between would have seemed to him unworthy of his stature. In another family or at another school this clever boy's flamboyant idleness would have been punished. He would have been compelled or at least encouraged to conform. But such compulsion, such encouragement, existed neither in his home nor at his school. Besides, he was so very good at English. And he was so lovable and small and odd that nobody had the heart to be hard on him. From the very earliest age he expected, and usually got, the treatment that was to be his throughout his life: there were always people to "look after" Dylan, to be delighted and astounded by him, to pick him up and dust him off, to accept him at his own idiosyncratic value. And if, as has so frequently been said, he never grew up, his friends too must bear some of the responsibility for this. He was so obviously vulnerable, and Dylan soon learned how this could be turned to his advantage.

There are two anecdotes from his early years at the Grammar School which show two aspects of his character as it was then developing.

He was a good runner, both short and long distances, and he won the hundred-yard and the one-mile races for the under-fifteens. But before then he had won the school cross-country race. This was, it is true, a handicap race and Dylan, being one of the smallest boys with an already legendary reputation for ill health, was given a good start. Still,

he won it. What is more he had pluckily forced his way through brambles and was scratched and bleeding when he reached the winning post.
The race, and his win, caused a quite disproportionate excitement in
the school and among his friends. It is still invariably referred to by
people who knew Dylan as a child and often by some who did not. His
picture appeared in the local paper. It was a public triumph, his first.
And Dylan, who lost everything, carried that newspaper photograph,
yellowing and dog-eared, in his wallet till the day he died.

The other anecdote is of a slightly later date. By March of 1929 Dylan had had many poems published in the school magazine and quite a
few elsewhere. The editor of the magazine was then E. F. McInerny,
who occasionally published poems of his own, anonymously. One of
these, published that March, began and ended as follows:

> There once was a poet
> (His name I don't know it)
> Who thought that whenever
> He wrote, whatsoever
> The theme, his endeavour
> Must be to be clever. . . .
> . . . I'll add, to be brief,
> That he soon came to grief.
> He discovered, one day,
> That the true poets say
> Just the simplest of things
> In a beautiful way.

Dylan decided that this was a barb directed at himself. (Mr. Mc-
Inerny has told Mr. K. E. Thompson, to whom I am indebted for this
story, that in fact it was not.) He went straight to the editor of the
school magazine and asked the older boy if he was the poem's author.
McInerny replied that he was. Dylan turned away and walked out of
the room without a word.

Such sensitivity to criticism was to remain with him until the end.
And his reaction to it was, as often as not, the violence that would
conceal pain, and was seldom as quietly pathetic as it had been in 1929.
Indeed in later years his well-known "outrageous" behaviour was often
a direct counter-attack upon people whom he *felt* were intellectually,
socially or physically contemptuous of him, even though they might
have said nothing to hurt him. It all surely dates back to the little boy

who believed himself inadequate to cope, in the normal way, with the new, big world of the Grammar School.

This is not meant to imply that Dylan was unhappy at the Grammar School. All the evidence points the other way, and not least what he himself wrote about his time there. But his almost total academic failure left a scar. Dr. Daniel Jones, his closest friend at this period of his life, has written: "This early stand against the academic was very valuable to Dylan; he would have needed twice the time to accomplish all he did accomplish if he had not discerned clearly and from the beginning the things that were of no use to him, or if he had not steadily ignored them."

This is probably true, but it is the truth of hindsight and of foresight. We know that Dylan died at thirty-nine. Dr. Jones and indeed all his early friends knew that he expected to die at a much younger age even than that. All his life the clocks ticked away his death for him as they did for his Lord Cutglass in *Under Milk Wood*. His father frequently said that Dylan would never see forty. When he was eighteen a "damned, diabetic doctor" told him that unless he drank and smoked less he would be dead in four years. So of course time was short, too short for study. A man who is to be hanged next week will not start to learn Chinese: and to some extent Dylan was all his life in the condemned cell, as his poems show. On the other hand, he did not die as soon as he had expected. And by the time he was thirty-five there is evidence that he was regretting his lack of education. It was one cause of insecurity, even of fear. He said to Randall Swingler, and to others: "One day they'll find me out," "they" being the clever, educated ones; he was afraid that he would be intellectually unable to cope with the opera he was to write with Stravinsky; he was afraid above all that he had exhausted his first lyric sources and that he was unequipped to move on. For by then the damage had been done, and it was done early. If you cannot be top of your class, the only place is at the bottom. If you have only four years to live, why not make it a record and do it in three? If you are a lyric poet, why not outplay Keats at all his games? (And at the end of his life he said to John Davenport: "I can't go on. I've already had twice as much of it as Keats had.") And if the outer world is too difficult, there is always, for a time, the inner one. Implosion has made much great poetry, though perhaps the critics, the finders-out, would say that it has not made the greatest. And again Dylan was aware of this, when he used to describe himself as "top of the second eleven."

In *Return Journey* he describes himself, through the eyes of a schoolmaster and in very blank verse, as the Grammar School boy he once had been:

Oh yes, I remember him well, the boy you are searching for:
he looked like most boys, no better, brighter or more respectful;
he cribbed, mitched, spilt ink, rattled his desk and
garbled his lessons with the worst of them;
he could smudge, hedge, smirk, wriggle, wince,
whimper, blarney, badger, blush, deceive, be
devious, stammer, improvise, assume
offended dignity or righteous indignation as though to the manner
    born;
sullenly and reluctantly he drilled, for some small
crime, under Sergeant Bird, so wittily nicknamed
Oiseau, on Wednesday half-holidays,
appeared regularly in detention classes,
hid in the cloakroom during algebra,
was, when a newcomer, thrown into the bushes of the
lower playground by bigger boys,
and threw newcomers into the bushes of the lower
playground when *he* was a bigger boy;
he scuffled at prayers,
he interpolated, smugly, the time-honoured wrong
irreverent words into the morning hymns,
he helped to damage the headmaster's rhubarb,
was thirty-third in trigonometry,
and, as might be expected, edited the school magazine.

Apart from the mysterious maladies which afflicted him when due to sit for examinations, his health was satisfactory during the Grammar School years: he could hardly have won those races had he then been tubercular. He continued, however, to break his bones. Shortly after entering the Grammar School he was in collision with a car while riding his bicycle. His mother told Paul Ferris:

He was only eleven years old, but they put him in the men's ward. He was always very thoughtful. "Look at that poor man there," he'd say to his father. "He fell down the hold of a ship. Bring him some cigarettes, Dad." When he came out his right arm was in plaster and the doctor told me to get him to practise writing left-handed. So the next day I put a table and a chair out in the garden, with a lot of paper and pencils. I said: "Go and write, there's a good boy," and out he went. A little later I was upstairs and I looked out through the window, and there he was, feet up on the table, not writing at all, puffing away at a cigarette. That's what came of being in that old ward for men.

Dylan has described his first meeting with Dan Jones in "The Fight," and Dr. Jones has confirmed the substance of this account. Describing Dylan as he then was, aged about twelve, Dr. Jones has written: "Dylan was slight, with curly hair, large, soft eyes and full lips; he looked almost effeminate, but he was very tough."

Like most of Dylan's qualities his "toughness" was, I think, largely cerebral and defensive. With one part of his mind he had no wish whatsoever to be the sickly boy his parents and his appearance told him he was. He would then pose as a tough school-boy, a tough journalist, a tough poet in the manner of his friends Roy Campbell or John Davenport. He was, as I shall show, a very good actor indeed, and his poses were frequently accepted as the reality. But they were often a deliberate, almost a desperate, act of cerebral will-power. When it came to the point he was not tough but plucky. If he fought, and he did fight, he lost — against other boys' and other men's fists, against the world's seductions (drink and women were to him so many challenges thrown down), and at last he lost, finally and forever, his fight against the need to adjust himself to what Traherne called the dirty devices of this world. His own devices were not enough.

One of those devices was a multiplicity of personality, a desire not so much to please as to fit in not only with the persona he had made for himself but with the idea that others had formed, or might form, of him. For centuries the conquered "Celt" has given, face to face, the answers that he thought the conqueror wished to hear; hence his reputation for lying. Dylan went further: he presented to others the man he believed they wished to see. This ability to present his very strong personality in so many different guises contains within itself both the most marvellous and enriching sympathy as well as a low and despicable cunning — and all the gradations that lie between. He could make the person with whom he was talking believe that that person, his life, his eccentricities, perhaps even his views (if they were not about poems) were of absorbing interest to Dylan. And so, briefly, they were. Intimacy (intellectual, boon-companion, even sexual) was established immediately by this technique of what has been called "instant Dylan." Technique, though, is the wrong word: only rarely, desperately and with ultimate self-contempt did Dylan use this ability of his for a material end. He was truly interested in all people who were neither pompous nor patronizing. In his own phrase, he liked talking to the cowboys and the horses, though he found himself increasingly in the company of the asses and the cows. But he would usually manage to find some interest even in them. And they would be enormously grateful, and they have remained grateful, and those who write have written as often as not that Dylan was their closest friend, and perhaps they were right; he probably, briefly, was.

Yet were they right? I knew him, as I thought, quite well during one period of his life and of mine. While preparing to write this book I have talked to a great many people, a number of them close friends of his, of mine, of us both, and have listened to their visions of him. Even allowing for subjective factors, the pictures painted, the memories retained, the stories told belong not to one man but to six or eight. And this was undoubtedly one of his deliberate devices — as was his habit of keeping his friends apart — a strategic element of his life-long campaign not to be caught, not to be trapped and tied down and labelled, not to be "found out" and thus to lose his freedom. For he valued his freedom almost, if not entirely, above all else.

This Protean aspect of the man was already present in some measure in the boy. He was not only the tough little fellow who smoked and fought and, very early, began to drink. At home, alone, he was very different:

I sat in my bedroom by the boiler and read through my exercise-books full of poems. There were Danger Don'ts on the backs. On my bedroom walls were pictures of Shakespeare, Walter de la Mare torn from my father's Christmas *Bookman*, Robert Browning, Stacy Aumonier, Rupert Brooke, a bearded man who I discovered was Whittier, Watts's "Hope," and a Sunday school certificate I was ashamed to want to pull down. A poem I had had printed in the "Wales Day by Day" column of the *Western Mail* was pasted on the mirror to make me blush, but the shame of the poem had died. Across the poem I had written, with a stolen quill and in flourishes: "Homer Nods." I was always waiting for the opportunity to bring someone into my bedroom — "Come into my den; excuse the untidiness; take a chair. No! not that one, it's broken!" — and force him to see the poem accidentally. But nobody ever came in except my mother.

The poems that he published in the school magazine fall into two easily recognized categories: many are comic, and he remained of course a first-class comic writer all his life. Others are serious but inevitably derivative. Thus in July of 1927 he published a poem, *Best of All:*

Rose-red banners across the dawn,
Brown sails at sea on a misty morn,
Racing shadows across the corn —
 These are the things I love.

First dim star in the twilight hour,
Drenchings sweet of the hawthorn flower,
Wallflowers kissed by a summer shower,
 And the clear sky above!

A wistful song as the shadows fall,
The whisper of trees and a soft bird-call
A glimmering moon — and over all
 The tang of a wind from the sea.

Just a year later the school magazine contained two of his poems, one comic and the other "serious." *Missing* is, I think, less obviously copied from Housman than is *Best of All* from Rupert Brooke. But first the comic one.

Life-Belt

I can't say when Columbus sailed
 To find the United States!
I don't know when the plague began!
 (I'll own I am not good at dates.)
If you say "Bosworth Field" to me
 The answer in my gullet sticks,
But when the Conquest's mentioned — ha!
 I'm on the spot with "Ten-Six-Six!"

"Can any boy," the Big Beak asks,
 "Tell me when Joan of Arc was burnt?"
Well, there you are, you know! That's just
 Another thing I haven't learnt.
"The First Crusade?" Oh, not for me!
 "Reform Bill?" It's a further fix.
"The Norman — ?" Only watch me now
 Raise the glad hand with "Ten-Six-Six."

I'm clear that Alfred burnt the cakes —
 "But when?" Alas, no figures come!
"Gunpowder Plot?" November fifth!

"What year?" Again I'm stricken dumb!
Washed out by the historic flood,
    Such chaps as I would sink like bricks,
Did not each wear around his waist
    A life-belt labelled, "Ten-Six-Six!"

Missing

Seek him, thou sun, in the dread wilderness,
For that he loved thee, seek thou him, and bless
His upturned face with one divine caress.

Lightly, thou wind, over his dear, dark head,
Where now the wings of dreamless sleep are spread,
Whisper a benediction for the dead.
Softly, thou rain — and for his mother's sake,
Shed thou thy tears on him; he will not wake,
No weeping through that deep repose can break.

These poems are quoted here for two reasons. The first is that they surely reveal an expertise in the composition of traditional verses that is not only astonishing in a boy of twelve or thirteen but which is also analogous to the ability to draw, in the classical manner, which has been the one common possession of all the great "experimental" painters of the last century and of this. The theory advanced by Mr. David Holbrook in his *Llareggub Revisited,* that Dylan Thomas wrote a sort of gibberish because he could not write anything better, was surely invalidated while the poet still stood on the threshold of his career.

The second point is that I cannot, in the school magazine, find any trace of the poems that were to come, though his notebooks show that he was beginning to write "Dylan Thomas poems" before he left the school. At an early age he was told by the editor that one line was too obscure, and amended it (without, as it happens, making it less obscure). This may have put him off publishing anything that can be called more than pastiches. People have looked. A German scholar, who researched lengthily in Swansea, did unearth one unsigned poem in the school magazine which gave him the transitional clue between Dylan-the-boy and Dylan-the-poet. I understand he had to scrap a whole thesis he was writing around this poem. Unfortunately it turned out to have been written by E. F. McInerny.

(Mr. McInerny has told me one curious anecdote about Dylan as a boy poet, of biographical rather than of literary interest. McInerny was then editing the magazine, and Dylan submitted a poem which Mc-Inerny recognized as being a poem by Thomas S. Jones, reproduced in Arthur Mee's *The Children's Encyclopaedia*. He felt it his duty to inform D.J., not in his capacity as Dylan's father but because he was the master ultimately responsible for the magazine. D.J. was extremely distressed at this apparent plagiarism on his son's part. However, Mc-Inerny has since wondered whether this may not have been a case of total, unconscious recall. Dylan at that age was writing so many poems that he certainly had no need to steal one.)

I believe that the early, derivative aspect of Dylan Thomas's poems can best be summed up in an article that he himself wrote when he was either fourteen or just fifteen, for it appeared in the school magazine only a few weeks after his fifteenth birthday. I quote it in full, not only because of the light it sheds on what he was reading and admiring at that formative age, but also because I think it is good proof of the high intellectual standard of the Swansea Grammar School. (A similar and equally knowledgeable article about contemporary music was published by Daniel Jones at the same time.)

MODERN POETRY

To attempt a comprehensive survey of Georgian poetry within a restricted space is to produce almost impassable difficulties. Poetry has never been so wide and varied as it is today, and the individualism of nearly every poet asserts itself to such an extent that no definite poetical schools can be discerned. It is obvious that in dealing generally with this subject, many poets must be either ignored or forgotten. Hardy, Bridges, William Watson, Newbolt, Binyon, Kipling, Noyes and many other important names cannot even be mentioned, none of them being typical of the modern artistic spirit, and none being strictly Georgian.

The most important element that characterises our poetical modernity is freedom — essential and unlimited — freedom of form, of structure, of imagery and of idea. It had its roots in the obscurity of Gerard Manley Hopkins' lyrics, where, though more often than not common metres were recognised, the language was violated and estranged by the effort of compressing the already unfamiliar imagery.

The first form of freedom was found in the poetry of Robert Bridges, who introduced free rhythms into the confines of orthodox metre. De la Mare enlarged upon this process of innovation within convention, and at the present time Sacheverell Sitwell presents a great deal of his strange confusion of thought and beauty in the heroic couplet.

The freedom of ideas can be found abundantly in any anthology. Assuming that no subject is an unpoetical subject, the neo-Romanticists (headed by T. S. Eliot, and, in the majority of his moments, by James Joyce) give us their succession of sordid details, their damp despondent atmosphere, and their attraction for the gutter, "the sawdust restaurants with oyster shells," "the yellow smoke of streets," and "cigarettes in corridors and cocktail smells in bars."

But this freedom does not confine itself to the writing of such crudities as would have disgusted our Victorians and Augustans. At the head of the twilight poets, W. B. Yeats introduces a fragile, unsubstantial world, covered with mysticism and mythological shadows. His entire poetic creation is brittle, and his cry,

> "I have spread my dreams under your feet,
> Tread softly because you tread on my dreams,"

is justified.

Neither is the variety of freedom composed only of vague shadows and bitter crudities. The simplicity of the early poets, Herrick and Lovelace, modernized in subject-matter and treatment, can be found in the best of our present hedgerow poets. W. H. Davies has written some of the most charming poems in the language, the simple beauty of which makes up for the lack of deep thought in most of his other work.

The freedom of imagery can best be exemplified by the small Imagist group, founded by John Gould Fletcher, the American. Richard Aldington, the best known Imagist of today, has adopted the original method of accentuating the image and making it first in importance in the poem, but has modified it and made it more intelligible. Fletcher loaded his work with colour and rich scintillation to such an extent that the real depth of one image was lost, owing to the blinding effect of the next. In such lines as:

> "Lacquered mandarin moments, palanquins swaying and balancing,
> And the vermillion pavilions, against the jade balustrades.
> Silver filaments, golden flakes settling downwards,
> Rippling, quivering flutters,
> The rain rustling with the sun,"

the glitter is mainly superficial, the rush of innumerable coloured words producing a kaleidoscopic effect that cannot stimulate or satisfy the imagination.

The position of the Sitwells in poetical art is indefinite, only because they are curiously regarded as obscurists, while a closer examination of their work cannot fail to impress the mind with images and thoughts of a new and astonishing clarity. They cannot be considered as a poetic whole. Admittedly the same philosophical principle governs both Edith's and Osbert's work, but it is only this basic quality which can make their poetry comparable. Building on the same foundations of dramatic lyricism and satire, their structures are entirely different. Edith achieves narrowness of poetical effect within wide psychological and natural fields. Her poems are essentially femiinine, with their shrewd grasp of detail, their sudden illuminations, and their intensity of emotion, and it is the more insignificant mannerisms of her femininity that make her poems difficult. Osbert, whose poetry is the least distinguished of the three, is a painter of more definite emotions, lacking the hard colour of Edith and the gradual beauty of Sacheverell. His satire is violent, but the violence carries with it a redeeming conviction. Sacheverell is the most difficult to become intimate with. His difficulty is genuine, the strangeness of the picture he sees and wishes to explain justifying the strangeness of the image he employs.

It is obvious that when a really revolutionary movement takes place in any art, there must be a justification for it, either material or intellectual. What changed the course of English poetry completely was the Great War, the brutality of which failed to warp man's outlook, and caused some of the bitterest and the loveliest poetry in the language to be written. Out of the darkness came the clear light of genius: Siegfried Sassoon, with his white-hot satire and beauty; Rupert Brooke, who sacrificed his ardour, his mental and physical sublimity for the country that was never allowed to realise him fully; Robert Nichols, whose wild impetuosity and deep reserve flamed and dwindled with the spirit of passion; Wilfred Owen, Robert Graves, Julian Grenfell, and the other heroes who built towers of beauty upon the ashes of their lives.

It is the more recent poetry of today that shows the clearest influence of the war. The incoherence caused by anguish and animal horror, and the shrill crudity which is inevitable in poetry produced by such a war, are discarded. Instead, we have a more contemplative confusion, a spiritual riot. No poet can find sure ground: he is hunting for it, with the whole earth perturbed and unsettled about him. Today is a transitional period. D. H. Lawrence, the body-worshipper who fears the soul; Edmund Blunden, who has immersed himself in the English countryside; Ezra Pound, the experimental mystic, are only laying the foundations of a new art. The poetry that will be ultimately built upon these foundations seems, as far as can be conjectured at present, to offer promise of a high and novel achievement.

This essay is surely a remarkable achievement when one recalls not only his age, but also the date at which he wrote it, 1929, for it shows at least an acquaintance, and often more than just that, with almost all the modern and indeed the most modern poets of the day. He was laying carefully and thoroughly the foundations for what was to be his own high and novel achievement. So far as writing went, though perhaps not much farther, he always knew what he was doing; as he liked to say in later years, he was a pro. And here we see him, the apprentice, mastering his profession. Soon enough he was to start writing his "own" poems, those that could not have been written by anyone else, which for some years remained hidden in those school exercise books marked

POMES. And by then he understood, as I think this essay already shows, what sort of poems he could and should write. With all this preparation and thought it is hardly surprising that he should have been hurt, when first he met T. S. Eliot in 1933, by his impression that the great man was treating him with polite condescension — in Dylan's phrase, as if he were a case of "pitboy to poet."

Meanwhile, and this is not fortuitous, he had made what was perhaps the most important friendship of his life. Dan Jones was and is a remarkable man, composer, writer, scholar, widely read in several literatures, with some knowledge of painting, and no hesitation in instructing his contemporaries as to how they should write, compose or paint. In a letter written during the summer of 1935 to Mr. A. E. Trick, Dylan was to say:

> We stayed with Dan Jones in Harrow for a few days. He reads all the time, and is cleverer than ever, but his mind is a mess for he doesn't know any direction. He isn't sure either of music or writing, though he does both competently and often brilliantly. I shouldn't be surprised to see him turn into a first-rate literary critic, producing a standard study or a comparison of European literatures. He has all that Jamison had with more wit, more sensibility, and, within his time limits, a far more comprehensive erudition.

It can thus be seen that he was Dylan's intellectual opposite, or rather his complement. He was, with the exception of D.J., the first highly cultured person whom Dylan really knew. And, what is more, they were contemporaries and could exchange ideas with the freedom and ease of equals. In Dan Jones's home, Warmley, Dylan found the most modern literature of the day, Joyce, Stein, Eliot, Pound, the Sitwells, as well as those rediscovered writers of the past who were then exerting a strong influence on young poets, Blake, Gerard Manley Hopkins, the minor Elizabethans. There, too, he picked up such superficial knowledge as he possessed of foreign poetry. He learned about the other arts as well. And all this again complemented the solid grounding in the English classics that he had received from his father and in his father's library. It would not be an exaggeration to say that his literary education was for all intents and purposes completed in Warmley and during his conversations with Dan Jones. By the time Dan Jones left Swansea for the university — in 1931 — Dylan's mould as a poet had been made. Although his style broadened and deepened, essentially it scarcely changed for fifteen years and reveals only small evidence of any new influences. For example, although of course he read the so-called " 'thirties" poets, there is no trace of them, scarcely even of W. H. Auden, to be found in his own poems written then or later. Indeed most of the poems he published before the war — and some that he published later — were already written, at least in embryonic form, before ever he left Swansea at the age of just twenty.

It must not, however, be imagined that his close friendship with Dan Jones was of a purely serious, literary nature. On the contrary, there was a great deal of play in it, and some of this play was also formative. There were one-a-side cricket matches; there were outings to the countryside and, not very much later, evenings in the pubs; there was the occasion when Dan Jones wrote an article about an imaginary composer, Dr. Zlepp, and Dylan persuaded D.J. that this phantom existed, and the article was published in the school magazine; there was the Warmley Broadcasting System. Two loudspeakers were linked to the radiogram, and the boys could broadcast from the upstairs to the downstairs rooms. Dr. Jones has written:

I still have some of the programmes: "The Rev. Percy will play three piano pieces, Buzzards at Dinner, Salute to Admiral Beattie, and Badgers Beneath my Vest"; "Rebecca Man will give a recital on the Rebmetpes"; "Locomotive Bowen, the one-eyed cowhand, will give a talk on the Rocking Horse and Varnishing Industry"; "Zoilredb Pogoho will read his poem Feffokorp." These broadcasters became real people to us, and we collaborated in a biography of the greatest of them, Percy. Here is a description of one of the trying experiences we inflicted on Percy's old mother: "Near the outskirts of Panama the crippled negress was bitten severely and time upon time, invariably upon the nape, by a white hat-shaped bird."

Above all there were the poems written in collaboration, and the word games. Again I cannot do better than quote Dr. Jones:

In poetry collaborations we always wrote alternate lines: I had the odd-numbered lines and Dylan the even-numbered, and we made it a rule that neither of us should suggest an alteration in the other's work. The poems, of which I still have about two hundred, are a different matter from the WBS fooling. It is still play, but it is what I would call serious play. The poetic style of Walter Bram, as we called ourselves, is bafflingly inconsistent: it is fragile, furious, laconic, massive, delicate, incantatory, cool, flinty, violent, Chinese, Greek, and shocking. One poem may begin "You will be surprised when I remain obdurate," and the next, "I lay under the currant bushes and told the beady berries about Jesus." Some of the poems are very, very beautiful; very. Especially those that tell of singularly gentle and godlike actions by the third person plural.

"They had come from the place high on the coral hills
Where the light from the white sea fills the soil with ascending
    grace.
And the sound of their power makes motion as steep as the sky,
And the fruits of the great ground lie like leaves from a vertical
    flower.
They had come from the place; they had come and had gone again
In the season of delicate rain, in a smooth ascension of grace."

We had word obsessions: everything at one time was "little" or "white";
and sometimes an adjective became irresistibly funny in almost any connection: "innumerable bananas," "wilful moccasin," "a certain Mrs. Prothero."
These word games and even the most facetious of our collaborations had a
serious experimental purpose, and there is no doubt that they played an important part in Dylan's early poetic development.

Thus did Dylan play with words for their own sake, with their colour
as he called it in a retrospective poem that contains its faint echo of
Rimbaud's *Voyelles*. (It would be surprising if he had not heard of
Rimbaud from Dan Jones, for Edgell Rickword's book about the
French poet had been published, even though Norman Cameron's fine
translations had not. At a very early age Dylan was referring to himself
as the Rimbaud of Cwmdonkin Drive, though he was probably thinking more of the boy-poet's dissolute and drunken myth than of his
poems.) Such play links the fascination a new word can have for a
small child with the absolute feeling for, and mastery of, language that
all poets must possess if they are to write well.

And there can be no doubt that in his early days, at least, the feel,
taste, colour, above all the sound of a word were infinitely more important to him than its sense. In this he resembled certain painters and
sculptors of the age for whom the paint, the stone, the wood were in
themselves more important than the idea or image that they were used
to express; indeed in large measure the material, rather than the artist's
cerebral processes, formulated through the hand, mind and sensibility
of the artist what he should express in that medium and how. Such was
Dylan's early use of words, and this accounts in large measure for the
obscurity of some of his early poems. In the beginning was the word,
and sometimes only the word was still there at the end too. He had
what he called his private dictionary, in which he compiled lists of
words that he particularly liked. As late as 1934 he was asking Pamela
Hansford Johnson, in a letter, if she did not think "drome" the most

beautiful word in the English language. This word's only meaning is that it was a common abbreviation for aerodrome. Dylan certainly did not regard an airport as a beautiful *thing*.

Two other facets of Dylan's creative life — less important obviously than his preoccupation with words — can be traced back to his Grammar School days. One is his passion for the cinema, the other his talent as an actor.

During the years between 1940 and his death, he wrote a great many film treatments and scripts. Indeed he probably put more words on paper in this professional capacity than in any other. Mr. Donald Taylor, who first employed Dylan as script-writer, has told me how surprised he was, from the very beginning, at Dylan's feeling for, and understanding of, films. Here again Dylan was, almost at once, a pro. But Mr. Taylor might have been less surprised had he read an article that Dylan had published in the school magazine at the age of fifteen. From internal evidence it would seem that Dylan had read Paul Rotha's recently published *The Film Till Now;* he had certainly assimilated its contents most thoroughly.

THE FILMS

The evolution of the motion-picture from the crude experimentalism of pre-war years to the polished artistry of today has taken place during a very short period. It was not until the beginning of the twentieth century that it was possible to present natural things in natural motion on a screen. Today, less than thirty years later, every shade of physical emotion, however slight or subtle, can be shown among natural and often naturally coloured surroundings.

The first picture that *could* be taken seriously was produced by D. W. Griffith in 1907. He brought a greater sense of balance and artistic understanding to the film than had hitherto been thought of, and introduced the now familiar tricks of the "close-up," the "fade-out" and the "cut back." He realised the importance of motion-pictures, not as freak exhibitions, but as works of art produced through an entirely new medium. The first film that *was* taken seriously was Adolph Zukar's "Queen Elizabeth," produced in 1912. Zukar had been for a long time contemplating the introduction of famous stage-stars to the screen, and he made his first attempt at this by casting Sara Bernhardt as Elizabeth. The film met with instant appreciation, but, with a few notable exceptions, stage-stars have not been successful on the screen, partly from the more exacting demands of silent presentation, and partly because good stage technique does not necessarily mean a good screen technique.

In 1914 D. W. Griffith produced "The Birth of a Nation." This was quite easily superior to every other pre-war film. It was devastating in its racial results, causing rioting and bloodshed, but it proved more than ever to him that motion-pictures were world-wide influences.

During the war, the few English studios that had been trying to compete with the many more American ones were entirely suspended. When English producers turned back to their trade in 1919 they found that America had got complete hold over the world, and dominated every market. It was not until two or three years ago that England woke up to the fact that English producers were bringing forth many fine films. Up to then the public had been so used to seeing thousands of American pictures and occasional and almost invariably bad English ones, that they did not get to know that there were some really intelligent producers at work in England. Now, the pictures produced in this country are quite as good and nearly as many as those produced in America.

The stories of the early films were simple and obvious, but as time went on and the public became more sophisticated, it was necessary to think of plots that did not always deal with the human triangle, or the hero, the heroine and the villain in a breathless intrigue with an inevitable ending. Consequently the hero became more humanised, and even the heroine had her faults, while the villain was not branded by a cloak and a series of sinister gestures, but was allowed more ordinary dress and movements. Then, as plots wore thinner and thinner, the classics were taken from their shelves, dusted, abridged, renovated by superior intellects, and finally were represented on the screen with more taste and understanding, until today many of the best films are those based upon, or woven round, famous novels and plays.

Film-acting requires distinct subtlety of action. Spoken words are, as often as possible, eliminated, and visual symbols used instead. That is, nearly the whole effect of a film depends upon the comprehensibility of features, facial expressions, and movements of the body. The early actors, dependent so much upon speech, found themselves at a loss to adapt themselves to the screen. Consequently their acting was exaggerated and absurd. They magnified every emotion and overstressed every facial expression. They indulged almost invariably in orgies of grief, hysteria and inarticulate anger. Henry B. Walthale, in 1914, showed that such exaggeration was unnecessary, by giving a new and delicate film performance in "The Birth of a Nation." He employed the slightest gestures and the most illuminating innuendoes. His acting was a landmark in the progress of the motion-picture. From his time has come a long line of actors and actresses who have made themselves universally admired for their brilliance and charm.

In the few points I have dealt with, I have made no mention of sound. The coming of the talkies has widened many fields and narrowed many others. There is no one way of treating the motion-picture with sound and without sound: they are far too differentiated. Sound-technique is in the same state now as silent technique was when D. W. Griffith evolved his own methods of pictorial representation, adding inestimably to its progress. Whether there will be a Griffith for sound-films is a matter that is best left to time.

Synchronized films up to 1930 have been distinctly disappointing. Crudity was expected, but both American and English producers have taken sound for granted, and have been over-confident of themselves. The older and established producers, especially, have merely added it to their screen-properties, without realising that it is something new which cannot be tackled by any old methods but which requires a special way of approach. Even film pioneers must start at the beginning of sound-film production, and learn what there is to be learnt.

This is obviously not a profound study of cinema techniques, but it does show that at fifteen he was aware that films, like poems, do have a technique and, furthermore, that in films too a new one must be learned. Despite the misspelt names and the grammar, curiously clumsy, the boy's interest in "the medium" is apparent. All his life Dylan was a passionate film fan. He would give himself up completely to whatever film he was seeing, would not only laugh aloud at the funny ones but would cry without shame when the actors demanded this of him. He had a fan's hero-worship for the stars, which persisted even when he was famous himself, and his pride and delight at being invited to Charles Chaplin's home was enormous and genuine. It was much the same when he met Danny Kaye, though on a lesser scale, for Kaye had not been a childhood hero. I think that he derived more sheer pleasure from being treated as an equal by Charlie Chaplin than he would have done had he been so treated by T. S. Eliot or W. B. Yeats. The world of poets was the world he knew: that other world was the infinitely more attractive world of dreams. . . .

Dylan himself had the makings of a good actor. He played the lead in school plays by Drinkwater and such, and though with his frail physique he was oddly cast as Cromwell and as the strike leader in *Strife*, he got good notices. His gestures, we are told, were somewhat weak, but his voice was already magnificently rich and powerful. (His father had already seen to it that both he and his sister, herself a keen amateur actress, have elocution lessons to eliminate any trace of Welshness. Hence his "cut-glass accent" as Dylan used to call it, which some of his Swansea contemporaries found odd and even affected.) Lord David Cecil has told me that when first he met Dylan, in about 1937 or 1938, it was with some of Augustus John's children and the Macnamara girls, and they all played charades. Lord David recognized at once, and with surprise, that Dylan's performance was quite different in quality from that of the others. Indeed when he was nineteen, and anxious somehow to escape from Swansea, he thought briefly of becoming a professional actor. And of course his performances on the wireless in England, both as reader and actor, and his public readings in America won him enormous popular acclaim. His poems would hardly have captured such a vast audience on both sides of the Atlantic if his voice had not done so first. Acting was his secondary career; the tragedy began when he was forced into making it his first.

Dylan's father wanted him to go to the university after the Grammar School, though it is hard to see why. Perhaps he hoped that Dylan would get a degree which would enable him, too, to fall back on teaching English should he fail to survive as a poet. But Dylan had every intention of surviving as a poet. Also he had no wish to go on studying, and in view of his miserable academic record, he was surely right. Besides, with his usual timidity and his skill at self-protection, he must have feared that he would make a fool of himself at a university, and be mocked. Cunningly he played on his father's hero-worship of Bernard Shaw: Shaw had had no higher education, and look what a fine, successful writer he had become! So why should Dylan go on studying? He only wished to be a poet, "as good as Keats," he told his mother at the time, "if not better." His parents seem, as usual, to have surrendered quite easily to this rather specious argument. And if he were not to go to the university there was really no point in his continuing at the Grammar School where, in his last year, he had really done nothing save act, edit and write most of the school magazine. Why not edit a proper magazine? Why not write poems all the time? In the summer of 1931, when he was sixteen and a half, he left Swansea Grammar School. His formal education was over.

4

D YLAN THOMAS left the Grammar School in July of 1931. He first
went to live in London in November of 1934. Until then his home
remained his parents' house at No. 5 Cwmdonkin Drive. These three
years were the most important period of his life as a poet.

It was in Swansea, living the somewhat anomalous life of an adolescent still at home but no longer at school, that he wrote all the poems in
his first volume, *18 Poems*, most of those in his second, *Twenty-five
Poems*, and, in embryonic form at least, a considerable number of his
later ones. Not only was this his most productive period, but it was also
the one in which his style became set, and it was to be scarcely modified
until about the middle of the war. Thereafter he wrote about twenty
poems in all, and these seem to me to mark a new departure. It is therefore no exaggeration to say that three-quarters of his work as a poet
dates in style, in concept and often in composition from this Swansea
period. Its importance is thus obvious.

Yet it is a difficult period about which to write biographically. The
basic facts of his life are known: that he worked as a journalist, first on
a paper and then free-lance; that he acted a great deal; that he began to
drink, and did not fall in love; and above all that during these years he
created not only his own poetry but also his own image of the poet,
upon which the Dylan Thomas legend is based. But to clothe these bare
bones with human flesh I have had to rely on the memories of others,
inevitably unreliable after thirty years and, as I have mentioned earlier,
often contradictory. Until the long series of letters to Pamela Hansford
Johnson begins, in September of 1933, there are very few written rec-

ords or letters. Nor did he himself write much about this period of his life. It did not interest him as his childhood had done, though in *Return Journey* he did describe himself as a young journalist.

He'd be about seventeen or eighteen and above medium height. Above medium height for Wales, I mean, he's five foot six and a half. Thick blubber lips; snub nose; curly mousebrown hair; one front tooth broken after playing a game called Cats and Dogs, in the Mermaid, Mumbles; speaks rather fancy; truculent; plausible; a bit of a shower-off; plus-fours and no breakfast, you know; used to have poems printed in the *Herald of Wales;* there was one about an open-air performance of *Electra* in Mrs. Bertie Perkins's garden in Sketty; lived up the Uplands; a bombastic adolescent provincial Bohemian with a thick-knotted artist's tie made out of his sister's scarf, she never knew where it had gone, and a cricket-shirt dyed bottlegreen; a gabbing, ambitious, mock-tough, pretentious young man; and mole-y, too.

The Swansea in which Dylan Thomas went to work in 1931 was not a happy place. What town was in that year of political crisis, of deepening depression and of massive unemployment? And South Wales was among the areas worst hit: the mining industry had never recovered from the terrible strikes of 1925 and 1926, and to this was now added the shut-down, partial or complete, of many steel mills and factories and the further closing of coal mines. There were small towns in the valleys where for all intents and purposes everyone was out of work; where the little shops gave credit until they too went bankrupt; where there was nothing for the young men to do save go away to England or stand in knots at street corners while hope became despair.

Since Swansea had a more diversified economy than, say, the Rhondda, its economic devastation was less total, but like any seaport it drew much of its sustenance from its hinterland. The Reverend Leon Atkin, a Christian socialist whom Dylan used to refer to as "my padre," has told me of the Swansea of this period, the Swansea he first knew where there were 28,000 unemployed. The young men, he said, were ashamed of their shabbiness and at night would avoid the well-lighted thoroughfares. Alfred Janes remembers walking down a Swansea street with Dylan during the depression. As they passed two youths, waiting, in a doorway, in the rain, they heard the one say to the other: "Nothing to do here. Let's join the fascists." There is perhaps an echo of this in Dylan's story of himself and the strange young men standing, waiting, with nothing to do, under the railway arch — the story that he called

"Just Like Little Dogs." There is another echo of the whole atmosphere in his early poem: *I see the boys of summer in their ruin.*

This was the time when young men with good degrees from Oxford or Cambridge were lucky to get jobs as shoe-salesmen; when shoe-salesmen whose shops had gone smash were lucky to get jobs as unskilled labourers; when unemployed labourers were lucky if the Means Test allowed them to draw a dole. Dylan was therefore lucky to be taken on, first as a reader's boy and then as a very junior reporter, by the *South Wales Daily Post,* now the *South Wales Evening Post,* when he was not quite seventeen.

He seems to have realized this and, in the beginning at least, to have taken his career as a journalist seriously. For a few weeks he even took shorthand lessons, about twelve in all, on the advice of his friend Charles Fisher, who also worked on the paper. Mr. Jeffreys, who tried and failed to teach him shorthand, has written: "I remember him as of medium height, a chubby, round red-faced boy. He used to come into my middle room and try to take an interest in what I was teaching him, but he seemed to be miles away — far off in a dream world of his own." And Miss Phoebe Powell, a telegraphist on the paper, remembers him as he then was: "nice, quiet boy. You couldn't get a word out of him. He was always well dressed — nice linen — and he had darkish curly hair. It was obvious his mother kept him beautifully turned out." His pay on the paper was of course very small, but since he lived at home it was all pocket money.

"For two years," he wrote to Pamela Hansford Johnson, "I was a newspaper reporter, making my daily call at the mortuaries, the houses of suicides — there's a lot of suicides in Wales — and Calvinistic 'capels.' Two years was enough." Indeed, it was considerably too much. His job on the *Post* lasted in fact for some fifteen months, during the first part of which he was employed reading proofs — and spent a considerable portion of his time writing doggerel on the back of the long green galley sheets. Mr. Eric Hughes, who worked on the same paper at the same time, has told me that when Dylan was promoted to reporting he was without doubt the worst newspaperman there ever was. Not only was he totally inaccurate, getting the names of the suicides wrong and bringing back false information from the mortuaries and the chapels, but he rapidly developed the habit of writing what he, rather than what his editor, wanted. Thus when ordered to report a choral rendition of *Hiawatha* he devoted two lines to the performance and the rest of his piece — which should of course have gratified the singers and their relations by listing all their names — to a sustained attack on the poetry of Longfellow.

As if this sort of thing were not enough he soon made a discovery which will eventually prove fatal to almost any cub journalist, namely that one hockey match, one bazaar opening, one auction, one local wedding is very like another and that it is possible to report them without having actually attended them, the time thus saved being devoted to billiards in the YMCA. Nor did he always take the rudimentary precaution of checking with someone who had attended. As was bound to happen sooner or later he filed, and the *Post* published, a report of a sporting event — a lacrosse match, I believe — which had in fact been cancelled. On another occasion he forgot to put in the routine telephone call to the fire station and the paper thus missed the news of a big fire at the hospital. Mr. R. M. Jones, who is still with the *Post*, has recalled: "In those days Dylan's chief beverage was coffee which he and his cronies would drink in the Kardomah while they put the world to rights after a morning's reporting in the police court. On arriving they would ask the girl at the cash desk where Malcolm Smith, the paper's manager and a regular client, was sitting. If he was upstairs they would go down: if he was down, then they went up."

By Christmas of 1932 it was agreed between the editor, Mr. J. D. Williams, and himself that it would be as well if his employment on the staff of the paper were terminated. At that time he wrote to his friend Trevor Hughes:

To answer a question of yours: I have left the *Post*. They offered me a five years contract in Swansea. I refused. The sixteen months or less I was on the staff were already showing signs of a reporter's decadence. Another two years I'd have been done for. Not that I was afraid of the Mermaid's grip. I still sedulously pluck the flowers of alcohol, and occasionally, but not as often as I wish, am pricked by the drunken thorn (an atrocious image!). No, what I feared was the slow but sure stamping out of individuality, the gradual contentment with life as it was, so much per week, so much for this, for that, and so much left over for drink and cigarettes. That be no loife for such as Oi!

I am attempting to earn a living now — attempting is the correct word — by free-lance journalism, and contribute, fairly regularly, humorous articles to the *Post*, less regularly literary articles to the *Herald*, now and then funny verses to the BOP (what a come-down was that, O men of Israel!), seasonable and snappy titbits for the Northcliffe Distributive Press . . . I still write poems, of course. It's an incurable disease. I write prose, too, and am thinking of tackling a short novel. Thinking, I said.

One may doubt whether the five years' contract had any existence outside of Dylan's imagination but the fact that he continued to contribute both to the *Post* and to its weekend stable companion, the *Herald of Wales,* shows that he and the paper parted on good terms. It was always very hard for anyone to remain cross with Dylan for long. To Pamela Hansford Johnson he wrote, late in 1933: "I, too, have a wicked secret. I used to write articles for the Northcliffe Press on 'Do Novelists make Good Husbands?' and 'Are Poets Mad?' etc. — very literary, very James Douglas, very bloody. I don't do that any more now: I ran the Northcliffe Press into a libel suit by calling Miss Nina Hamnett (who wrote the book called *Laughing Torso,* I don't know whether you remember it) insane. Apparently she wasn't, that was the trouble."

There were other troubles. For the *Post* he wrote a series of articles on the poets of Swansea. This was considered quite safe, and Dylan was given a free hand to say what he wished about the local bards, long dead and usually long forgotten until he dug up their literary remains for brief examination before final reinterment. Unfortunately, though, one local worthy was not dead. A Mr. Howard Harris arrived in an immensely bad temper at the *Post* offices. His anger was not lessened by the discovery that the critic who had so airily dismissed his life's work was himself not yet aged nineteen.

One of these articles is, I think, worth quoting here, less because of any intrinsic interest it may have than because it shows how Dylan, as a boy, was forming his own vision of what a poet is and how a poet lives and dies. The subject of the article was Llewelyn Prichard, an early nineteenth century writer of verse and prose. It begins:

No-one can deny that the most attractive figures in literature are always those around whom a world of lies and legends has been woven, those half mythical artists whose real characters become cloaked forever under a veil of the bizarre.

They become known not as creatures of flesh and blood, living day by day as prosaically as the rest of us, but as men stepping on clouds, snaring a world of beauty from the trees and sky, half wild, half human.

It is, on the whole, a popular and an entertaining fallacy.

But Llewelyn Prichard was a genuine figure of fancy. The gaunt, wide-eyed poet with the wax nose might have stepped from the pages of a romanticist's diary.

His life, strange and disordered, as poet, artist and strolling player, trembling on the verge of disease, one foot in the grave and the other in the workhouse, needs no glossing over. With Prichard eccentricity was no pose; it was bestowed upon him by contemporaries; it was ingrained in the man. . . .

And it ends:

Towards the end of his life Prichard's poverty became so great, and his physical reserves so low, that Samuel Chapman, his loyalest friend and greatest admirer, made a collection to keep him from the Union Workhouse. Chapman's efforts succeeded, but like many such actions were soon to seem futile. Prichard, coming home late one night to the cottage in Thomas Street, attempted to write in his own room. But he soon fell asleep. The candle fell on to the papers surrounding him. He was too drunk to know what to do, and died as strangely and as tragically as he had lived, "caught in a chaos of unrestrained words and passions, caught by the fire and the flames." . . . He failed to be great, but he failed with genius.

The article is headed: A FIGURE LOST IN LIES AND LEGENDS. The parallel is so obvious that it need not be drawn. What is of interest is that Dylan should have written in this way before ever a serious poem of his own had been published, that he should have been aware of the depressing fact that the public desires its poets to be not only "trembling on the verge of disease," consumption being, since Keats, regarded as the most suitable for lyric poets, but also eccentric and given to excess. He was enough of an actor to be aware, too, of the need to give the public what it wants.

There are no strolling players in this century or else who can doubt that Dylan too would have joined them — at least for a time? As it was, acting for him was more than a hobby and an amusement. It would be an exaggeration to say that he was a professional, though in the spring of 1934 he did think of applying for a job with the Coventry Repertory Company. On the other hand he was also more than a mere amateur who enjoyed dressing up.

I have mentioned his acting with the Grammar School Dramatic Society. Before he left the school he had also played minor parts with the YMCA Players. The entirely professional repertory company at the Grand Theatre also occasionally recruited extras; he and other amateur actors could thus earn a guinea or two. But it was at the Swansea Little Theatre that he did most of his acting. Miss Ethel Ross has made a detailed study of this aspect of his life, and I cannot do better than quote her article on the subject, published in the *Swan*:

✲   ✲   ✲

There was in Swansea, in the twenties, a rapidly growing enthusiasm for the theatre. From 1924 to 1928 the Amateur Dramatic Society staged plays like "Leah Kleschna," "The Laughing Lady" and "If Four Walls Told." There was a slight aura of sin hanging over the theatre in the eyes of many nonconformists, and these lively young people were often regarded as a little advanced. Nevertheless they succeeded very well with plays of a popular type.

From them broke away a group with a different idea — that of putting on plays which the local commercial theatre could not afford to stage: Chekhov, Ibsen, Shakespeare, for example. In 1929, therefore, the Stage Society was formed and it took over a little church school hall at Southend, Mumbles. Here plays by Capek, Barrie, Galsworthy, Malleson, Housman and Shaw followed in quick succession. Lectures, drama schools, playwriting contests and the presentation of original works helped to make a varied and interesting programme. Young people from school and college, guided by interested professional and business people, often family groups, worked to design sets and costumes, to play in the orchestra or to land a fat part.

Mr. J. D. Williams, editor of the *South Wales Daily Post*, was most liberal in his support and often over-generous in his reviews in the effort to consolidate this young and worthwhile movement. Dylan Thomas on leaving school had joined his staff and with his fellow-reporter, Eric Hughes, began to take an interest in acting with the company. Dylan's sister, Nancy, and her future husband, Haydn Taylor, were also members. In 1932 all four appeared in Noel Coward's *Hay Fever;* Eric Hughes as David Bliss; Dylan Thomas as Simon Bliss; Haydn Taylor as Richard Greatham; and Nancy Thomas as Jackie Coryton.

The *Post* said:

We are grateful to Noel Coward and the Little Theatre Players at The Mumbles for a bright evening with *Hay Fever*. Two hours of almost continual chuckling, with a crescendo at frequent intervals into hearty laughter, are gifts from the gods these days.

The critic from *The Mumbles Press* reported:

Simon, who is an artist with an explosive temper and untidy habits, asks a snakily beautiful creature to stay. Mr. E. C. Hughes was well cast as David Bliss. Equally well done was Simon's part by D. M. Thomas. Mr. Haydn Taylor was sufficiently convincing as Greatham. Miss Nancy Thomas, as the shy and maddeningly well-brought-up Jackie Coryton, executed one of the best efforts in characterisation it has been my privilege to see for a long time.

In April of the same year (1932) Thomas played Count Bellair in *The Beaux Stratagem* by Farquhar, remedying for all time the fault of being "innocent of gesture." It was even said that as the French prisoner at Lichfield speaking broken English he was excessively mobile.

He and Eric Hughes now had definite ideas of the parts they liked to play and by March 1933 after much effort, persuaded the Little Theatre Committee to put on *Peter and Paul* by H. F. Rubenstein.

Of this production Mr. J. D. Williams wrote in the *Post:*

Now the secret is out why the young lions of Swansea Little Theatre begged — even prayed season after season for the production of "Peter and Paul." No-one could understand their passion. One heard its praise at every general council. It became a kind of leading motif. The very fate of the Little Theatre, so it seemed by the pleadings of the young lions, was mixed up with and depended upon its presentation. The young lions were in love with the play because of the acting chances it gave them, gorgeous chances. Two men's lives stretched from youth into old age. The vigour of ravenhaired manhood: the accomplishment of grey-sprinkled middle age: the decline into snow-crowned old age. What fat parts! Yes! they were justified in their insistence, for whatever else "Peter and Paul" will do — it has already shown that the Little Theatre is an admirable school for acting and that it has trained players of real efficiency and intelligence.

Peter (Dylan Thomas), determined to write, has to buckle to and carry on his father's business, and in that atmosphere he forgets how to write and does a nobler thing: he rears a happy family. But Peter, in age reviewing his life, feels that he has missed its biggest meaning: the unwritten books haunt him.

Paul (Eric Hughes) who longed for the bourgeois comforts of a home is deflected on the path of the writer, and suffers long neglect and persecution and the breaking up of his home before the people acclaim his fame.

One will not detract a tiny bit from the merits of Eric Hughes and Dylan Thomas save to say that the latter might with advantage tone down a little of his acting in the first act.

A.D.B. in *The Mumbles Press* was not so critical:

Dylan Thomas and Eric Hughes came through with flying colours. The Little Theatre is fortunate indeed to possess two young men capable of sustaining with such convincing reality these characters from youth to old age. To do one thing or the other is comparatively easy to the task of appearing young, middle-aged or old in three short scenes. It needs not only great acting ability, but intense concentration to maintain the character of the moment.

Thomas's next big part was in Rodney Ackland's *Strange Orchestra*, produced in December 1933 by Eric Hughes. Again it was a role that now seems peculiarly relevant to his own life.

Mr. J. D. Williams, still pleased to review productions himself, wrote:

The Little Theatre Players, or perhaps mainly the younger spirits among them, gave us the racking disharmonies, individual and communal, concentrated in one household.

Near the end, when the play was deeply stirring, there are hints of approaching serenity for a few, achieved through suffering, but even so, it can hardly be complained that there are left any allurements in the "life" of these temperamental folk with their incessant introspection and selfishness, their swift "loves," their fun parties and clubs and their gin and sandwiches.

The lodgers include an amoral cad: a young novelist, Val, so absorbed in himself, in dramatising his friends for his novels that he cannot see the greatness of Esther's piteous realisation of life's cruelties. There was a pitiable inevitability about Mr. Dylan Thomas's Val.

The Mumbles Press did not approve at all. Neither in fact did many of the older members of the society who were suckled on Irving's *Bells* and *The Merry Widow:*

Rodney Ackland's "Strange Orchestra" comes perilously near to being a problem play, which experience shows is not the best material for amateur societies or the middle-class suburbanites which form their audiences.

Its people were all stamped with the fear and the "artificiality" of the post-war "artistic" London, and their emotions which were shown to be as real as those of the rest of us burst out into startling expression. This is not shallowness on the part of these neurotics — but the fact is that Chelsea and theatreland are a powerful forcing house which brings into public view those things which we normally think most decent to hide.

A month later in January 1934 Thomas was playing Witwoud in *The Way of the World,* giving a most impressive and clever representation in the view of the theatre critic. He had developed an elegance of movement and a mastery of gesture difficult to achieve in amateur productions of period plays.

His last big part was that of Julien, the Paris journalist, in Jean-Jacques Bernard's *Martine,* though he did not get as far as the first performance. It was customary for the young men of the theatre and the more daring girls, when not wanted on stage, to nip out to a mysterious hostelry known as Cheese's.

Naturally players were often called in vain and someone would be sent post-haste to fetch them from the bar. Some producers put up with it better than others but Doreen Goodridge, irritated to extremity, warned Thomas, who thought he had time for "a quick one," that if he left he needn't come back. He went. It was the dress rehearsal.

Gallantly Mr. Malcolm Graham read the part on the opening night and managed to memorize it later in the week. . . .

The clash caused much hurt on both sides. Dylan Thomas felt his freedom was being attacked and he never really enjoyed being unpopular. From this time he took much less interest in acting for the Little Theatre, though he did play a minor part in *Richard II* and in April 1934 acted in a revival of *Hay Fever* for charity. There was no comment this time on his acting in the local press. . . .

But to the Little Theatre he did most sincerely pay as great a tribute as he could. In 1933 *Electra* by Sophocles was produced by Mr. Thomas Taig in a Sketty garden. . . . Daniel Jones wrote the music for the sound effects and played it. He was then a student in the English department of Swansea University College.

Dylan Thomas came along one evening. I remember seeing him, slightly apart from the audience, leaning against a tree, a cigarette hanging from his lips. He looked extremely bored, so much so that one of his former masters was heard to remark, "If Thomas can't look a little more appreciative he'd better stay away."

I cannot recall that he made any comment to the cast, but a few days later the *Herald of Wales* published a thirty-two-line poem, containing the following stanza:

> A woman wails her dead among the trees
> Under the green roof grieves the living.
> The living sun laments the dying skies,
> Lamenting falls. Pity Electra's loving.

Shortly after Thomas left for London, and what acting I saw after that was at parties, impromptu. . . .

✿　　✿　　✿

I have quoted and paraphrased Miss Ross's article at such length not only for the information that it casts on Dylan's acting career — or rather his first acting career, for he was to have a second, public one, as well as a private one that went on, intermittently, throughout his life — but also for the incidental light that it casts on himself and his environment during these years. Dylan's type-casting is as relevant as is his article on Llewelyn Prichard. But equally relevant, surely, is the extraordinary attitude of the anonymous critic on *The Mumbles Press;* his fatuous comments on morality must, to the boy Dylan, have given every encouragement to react as violently as possible and as soon as ever he could. And *The Mumbles Press* presumably represented much that he heard from his mother's, though not his father's, friends. Finally there is the queer and muffled prose style of his own, friendly editor, another good reason for the rejection of journalism as a career.

It was during these years, 1931 to 1934, that he made those friendships which were to be the most durable of his life. Just as his childhood memories were of quite particular importance to him, so his Swansea friends held a special place in his affections, though this was of course more true of some friends — or rather of some groups of friends — than of others.

Once he had left the Grammar School he seems to have drifted away from most of his school-mates, with the exception of Dan Jones.

This is only to be expected, since his near contemporaries either re mained school-boys or went to the university or were launched on careers different from his own and thus acquired interests that were not his. His new friends were, very roughly, of three sorts: there were those that he met through his work on the paper; those he encountered at the Little Theatre; and those with whom he shared a common interest in literature and the arts. These three groups overlapped: Eric Hughes both worked on the *Post* and acted with him in the theatre; Charles Fisher was more than just a journalist and was thought by many at that time to show greater promise as a writer than did Dylan. And it was the third group, the friends who not only shared his background but also his interests, who were and remained closest to him.

One of the dangers that wait, like a sheer drop, for the biographer as he pursues his corniche course, is the assumption of excessive knowledgeability. An early biographer of Goethe is said to have written: "Goethe told Eckermann that of all his mistresses it was Lili whom he had loved the most. Here Goethe was wrong." I should prefer to avoid such judicial pronouncements about Dylan. Nevertheless I must give it

as my opinion that Dylan now found himself one of a group of talented
young men, and that this group remained with him in his memory,
ghostly as Fern Hill was even then becoming a ghost, all his life. Not, I
would add, that they became ghosts — they remained his friends, and
remain so to this day — but that the vision of the little group of friends
remained with him long after the group itself had dissolved and that
with some part of his being Dylan was forever trying to re-create it, in
other places and with other people. But friendship, like love, has its
springtime.

In *Return Journey* the Narrator is Dylan in search of his past:

NARRATOR

Near the *Evening Post* building and the fragment of the Castle I stopped a
man whose face I thought I recognised from a long time ago. I said: I wonder if you can tell me whether you used to know a chap called Young Thomas.
He worked on the *Post* and used to wear an overcoat sometimes with the
check lining inside out so that you could play giant draughts on him. He
wore a conscious woodbine, too, and a perched pork pie with a peacock
feather and he tried to slouch like a newshawk even when he was attending
a meeting of the Gorseinon Buffalos. . . .

PASSER-BY

Oh, *him!* He owes me half a crown. I haven't seen him since the old
Kardomah days. He wasn't a reporter then, he'd just left the grammar school.
Him and Charlie Fisher — Charlie's got whiskers now — and Tom Warner
and Fred Janes, drinking coffee-dashes and arguing the toss.

NARRATOR

What about?

PASSER-BY

Music and poetry and painting and politics. Einstein and Epstein, Stravinsky and Greta Garbo, death and religion and Picasso and girls. . . .

NARRATOR

And then?

PASSER-BY

Communism, symbolism, Bradman, Braque, the Watch Committee, free
love, free beer, murder, Michelangelo, ping-pong, ambition, Sibelius, and
girls. . . .

NARRATOR

Is that all?

How Dan Jones was going to compose the most prodigious symphony, Fred Janes paint the most miraculously meticulous picture, Charlie Fisher catch the poshest trout, Vernon Watkins and Young Thomas write the most boiling poems, how they would ring the bells of London and paint it like a tart . . .

NARRATOR
And after that?

PASSER-BY
Oh the hissing of the butt-ends in the drains of the coffee-dashes and the tinkle and the gibble-gabble of the morning young lounge lizards as they talked about Augustus John, Emil Jannings, Carnera, Dracula, Amy Johnson, trial marriage, pocket-money, the Welsh sea, the London stars, King Kong, anarchy, darts, T. S. Eliot, and girls. . . .

I remember a conversation I had with Dylan once on the subject of friends. We agreed that we liked people who were about the same age as ourselves, with about the same income and not too dissimilar social backgrounds, who drank more or less the same amount in the same sort of places, and who were interested in the things that interested us. I asked him if, on the whole, he found his Welsh friends more congenial than his English ones, as I myself tend, on the whole, to feel more at home with Irishmen or Americans. His answer, as I recall it, was a very firm negative, but he added: "It's different, of course, if I knew them in the old Swansea days." To have been Dylan's friend in Swansea was, so far as he was concerned, to be his friend for life. He might quarrel with them, he might be bored by them or unkind about them, nothing made any difference to the basic fact: they were his real friends.

And yet when one looks at them now, those friends of his youth, there is little that they have in common save those Swansea years and a vocation or at least respect for the arts. The little group in this distant Welsh town was unaware that it was a group. It was in a constant state of disintegration as the young men went away to study, or returned home to work and create. It had no norm, and it certainly did not revolve around Dylan, who was only one among half a dozen. But it existed nevertheless.

Dan Jones's family moved away to Harrow during this period and Warmley ceased to be a second home for Dylan, but Dan himself was reading English at Swansea University where he got a first class honours degree in 1934. We may be sure that he was passing on some of his newly acquired knowledge to Dylan, that he continued to be in some ways his guide to current trends in English literature, as he had been at the Grammar School. Just as Dan had first introduced him to the Imagists and then to the Symbolists, so it was probably now, and through his friend, that Dylan first made intimate acquaintance both with the English Metaphysical poets and with the idea of Rimbaud. Dan Jones's didactic and even dictatorial manner irritated Dylan at times as it irritated others. But when a friend complained about Dan's overbearing and snobbish behaviour on one occasion, Dylan replied to the effect that for him Dan could do no wrong.

Then there was Alfred Janes painting his exquisite semi-abstract still-lifes with meticulous care and extreme slowness. A lot of the time he was away, at the Royal College of Art in London. He did not write letters. (On the unique occasion when he did, some years later, Dylan wrote to Vernon Watkins: "So now I have decided to abandon the book I was going to write and devote myself to The Life and Letter of Alfred Janes.") But Dylan saw a lot of him when he was at home. Fred Janes was passing through a religious phase at this time, and they discussed religion. Indeed in January 1933 Dylan wrote to a friend: "One day I may turn Catholic, but not yet." Dylan also tried his hand at painting, and all his life he drew what he called his "literary pictures" with a pleasant, Thurberesque line and often with a caption. I remember one of a very angry-looking man driving a steam-roller and saying: "Ask me any question and you'll get a rude answer."

There was gentle Tom Warner, the musician, who did not live in Swansea but frequently visited his aunts there. He has told me how he and Dan and Dylan would improvise, a trio playing any instruments that were to hand, violin, cello, piano, comb-and-tissue-paper, a brass kettle for the percussion. Since Dylan's inevitable cigarette endangered Tom's violin, he was restricted to Dan's cello. He did not know how to play it, and could not read music, but nevertheless managed to make patterns of sound which were not displeasing and were sometimes of interest. It is untrue though, as has sometimes been suggested, that he had any real knowledge of music. I remember an occasion when he and I were listening to Beethoven's Eighth Symphony on my gramophone: he then remarked that he could understand every form of artistic creation save music: it was incomprehensible to him that any man could keep so much sound and so many patterns in his head at one time.

Mervyn Levy went away to London to study painting, but came home from time to time. There was also John Prichard, the very quiet and very good novelist. And at the very end of his Swansea years he met Vernon Watkins and Glyn Jones. His friendship with Vernon Watkins was perhaps, from the point of view of the poet, the most important of his life after Dan Jones's. His *Letters to Vernon Watkins,* which are almost exclusively about Dylan's own poems, show how very much he relied on the older poet's advice and ear. Indeed it would be no exaggeration to say that Vernon took over where Dan Jones left off. By the time Dylan met him it was a poet's opinions he wanted and valued, not a scholar's knowledge (though Vernon's knowledge of poetry, English, French, German and Italian, is immense). Essentially Vernon Watkins is an entirely dedicated poet with all the toughness of fibre that this necessitates. He is also a profoundly religious man. In manner, however, he is aethereal, otherworldly, and therefore did not ever really share Dylan's pub and public life. Indeed Dylan used to laugh affectionately at his gossamer-like personality and extreme sensibility. I recall one evening during the war when the three of us were walking along a Chelsea street in the blackout. Vernon tripped over something and fell to the ground. When we had helped him to his feet Dylan asked me, who held the torch, to see what he had stumbled on. He was delighted to find that it was a small, black feather. Glyn Jones, the other poet whom he met at this time, he saw less frequently, since Glyn lived in Cardiff.

There were new friends of a slightly older generation, too. Perhaps the first of these was Trevor Hughes, whom Dylan met just before he left the Grammar School, and in the following circumstances. Dylan wished to edit a magazine, and this announcement appeared on June 2, 1931, in the *South Wales Daily Post:*

A SWANSEA PUBLICATION

Some time ago it was announced in this column that Swansea might shortly expect a new literary publication, entitled *Prose and Verse.*

It was, as was then mentioned, to be published by subscription, and although the editor hopes to be able to reduce the price of subsequent issues, the price of the first copy is to be two shillings. It is necessary to sell at least two hundred copies at this price in order to cover the initial expenses.

The editor, who is to be found at 5 Cwmdonkin Drive, Uplands, wants contributions, and he says that "their only qualification must be originality of outlook and expression."

The magazine never came to anything under Dylan's editorship, though he continued to toy with the idea for some years, and was eventually of some assistance to Keidrych Rhys when in 1937 that Welsh poet began to publish *Wales*, which might be described as the successor, and a very good one too, to the still-born *Prose and Verse*. But among those who responded to Dylan's initial appeal was Trevor Hughes. He and Dylan became close friends and from him, too, Dylan learned a great deal, though his influence was a curious one.

Trevor Hughes's life was tragic. He had an invalid mother to look after. His brother, whom he loved deeply, had died of TB in his arms, vomiting blood. He himself was tubercular, though he did not know this at the time. This long domestic tragedy was reflected not only in his stories, which are frankly morbid in the style of E. A. Poe and his disciples, but also in his conversation which alternated between an almost hectic gaiety and the deepest depression. Dylan later drew a rather unfair picture of him in his story "Who Do You Wish Was with Us?" — unfair because it gives a false picture of their relationship. Trevor Hughes's preoccupation with disease and death was neither tiresome nor distasteful to Dylan at this period of his life. Indeed he found it fascinating and it reinforced his own tendency in that direction. The influence is evident in Dylan's own early stories and in some of the poems, too. It is even more evident in the persona of the sick poet that he was busily inventing for himself. His tubercular talk of coughing blood, collapsed lungs and so on must have derived from conversations with Trevor Hughes. Furthermore Hughes was, apart from Dan Jones, the first person to appreciate and understand Dylan's serious writing, though he did not advise Dylan as Dan was doing and Vernon was to do; rather was it the other way around and in their literary relationship Dylan appears to have been dominant, telling his older friend what and how to write. When Trevor Hughes went away to London, in 1932, Dylan missed him, as his letters show.

It was in the following year he met A. E. Trick, Bert to his friends. Dylan used to refer to him as "my communist grocer," but this is a characteristic exaggeration.

Bert Trick was sixteen years older than Dylan. He had been a skilled engineer and an official of the Amalgamated Engineering Union, an unpaid Branch Secretary. In 1921, when the first post-war slump hit the engineering and ship-building industry, he was thrown out of work. "For months I loafed around, playing football on Neath marshland, listening to classical records, and reading socialist literature." He also read much other literature as well, and began to write poems. Eventually he got a job as a clerk with the Inland Revenue Department and was posted to their Swansea office. In 1928 he wished to marry, but his salary was insufficient to support a wife and family. He therefore raised the money to buy a grocery shop at 69 Glanbrydan Avenue, over which he and his family lived. I have heard that his business did not prosper eventually owing to his excessive generosity and trustfulness; he gave too much credit to those of his customers who had been badly hit by the depression.

No longer a civil servant, he was free once again to engage in local politics, and he did so, in the Labour interest. He was a left-wing socialist and a Marxist, but never a member of the Communist Party. And here again we see, repeated in modern dress as it were, the Welsh bardic figure whom I attempted to describe in the first chapter of this book: a man of humble origins and small income but of considerable culture and high principles, a poet and a radical. Only here Marxism and political oratory play the part that Christianity and *hwyl* preaching would have played one hundred years before. Bert Trick, incidentally, though not a teetotaller was certainly not a drinking man.

It was Mr. Thomas Taig, who then lectured in English at the university and was, as we have seen, connected with the Little Theatre, who suggested to Dylan in 1933 that he show his poems to Bert Trick.

Bert Trick has described to me how Dylan arrived one evening, unheralded, at the flat above the grocery shop. He was very thin then, and looked even younger than his eighteen years, despite the cigarette between his lips and the "poetic" dark shirt and corduroy trousers and the "journalistic" pork-pie hat he then affected. He was shy, too, but as soon as he began to read his poems his shyness vanished, and so did Bert Trick's natural scepticism of the boy-poet. Making some excuse, he left the room to fetch his wife. He was anxious that she, too, should share the experience of hearing this extraordinary boy read his extraordinary poems for the first time in their flat, for Bert Trick recognized their power and virtuosity at once.

They became close friends, on the basis of their common interest in poetry or, to be perhaps more precise, in Dylan's poems. Dylan introduced his other friends to Bert Trick, and many of them used also to come to Glanbrydan Avenue for evenings of music and poetry and talk, though Dan Jones was not of their number; he and Bert Trick never got on. It was from Bert Trick that Dylan learned his rather rudimentary left-wing politics. In his long letters to Pamela Hansford Johnson written at this time Dylan frequently talked about music; it is a safe assumption that he was then quoting, more or less verbatim, what he had heard from Dan Jones and perhaps from Tom Warner. Similarly the following passage about politics, from a letter to her dated November 11, 1933, may be taken as an accurate reflection of what he was learning from Bert Trick at this time:

This is written on Armistice day, 1933, when the war is no more than a memory of privations and the cutting down of the young. There were women who had "lost" their sons, though where they had lost them and why they could not find them, we, who were children born out of blood into blood, could never tell. The state was a murderer, and every country in this rumour-ridden world, peopled by the unsuccessful suicides left over by the four mad years, is branded like Cain across the forehead. What was Christ in us was stuck with a bayonet to the sky, and what was Judas we fed and sheltered, rewarding, at the end, with thirty hanks of flesh. Civilization is a murderer. We, with the cross of a castrated Saviour cut on our brows, sink deeper and deeper with the days into the pit of the West. The head of Christ is to be inspected in the museum, dry as a mole's hand in its glass case. And all the dominions of heaven have their calculated limits; the stars move to man's arithmetic; and the sun, leering like a fool over the valleys of Europe, sinks as the drops in a test-tube dry and are gone.

This is a lament on the death of the West. Your bones and mine shall manure an empty island set in a waste sea. The stars shall shine over England, but the darkness of England, and the sarcophagus of a spoonfed nation, and the pitch in the slain souls of our children, will never be lit.

"And the earth was without form and void; and darkness was upon the face of the deep." The old buffers of this world still cling to chaos, believing it to be Order. The day will come when the old Dis-Order changeth, yielding to a new Order. Genius is being strangled every day by the legion of old Buffers, by the last long line of the Edwardians, clinging, for God and capital, to an outgrown and decaying system. Light is being turned to darkness by the capitalists and industrialists. There is only one thing you and I, who are of this generation, must look forward to, must work for and pray for, and, because, as we fondly hope, we are poets and voicers not only of our personal selves but of our social selves, we must pray for it all the more vehemently. It is the Revolution. There is no need for it to be a revolution of blood. We do not ask that. All that we ask for is that the present Dis-Order, this medieval machine which is grinding into powder the bones and guts of the postwar generation shall be broken in two, and that all that is in us of godliness and strength, of happiness and genius, shall be allowed to exult in the sun. We are said to be faithless, because our God is not a capitalist God, to be unpatriotic because we do not believe in the Tory Government.

We are said to be immoral because we know that marriage is a dead institution, that the old rigid monogamous lifelong union of male and female — the exceptions are the exceptions of beauty — is a corrupted thought.

The hope of Revolution, even though all of us will not admit it, is uppermost in all our minds. If there were not that revolutionary spark within us, that faith in a new faith, and that belief in our power to squash the chaos surrounding us like a belt of weeds, we would turn on the tap of war and drown ourselves in its gasses.

Everything is wrong that forbids the freedom of the individual. The governments are wrong, because they are the committees of prohibitors; the presses are wrong, because they feed us what they desire to feed us, and not what we desire to eat; the churches are wrong, because they standardize our gods, because they label our morals, because they laud the death of a vanished Christ, and fear the crying of the new Christ in the wilderness; the poets are wrong, because their vision is not a vision but a squint; they look at our world, and yet their eyes are staring back along the roads of the past centuries, never into the huge, electric promise of the future.

There is injustice, muddleheadedness, criminal ignorance, corrupted and inverted virtue, hypocrisy and stone blindness, in every sphere of life. If only for one moment the Western world could drop the veils that, ever since the Reformation, have clung around it like the films of a disease, and look, with lightened eyes, upon the cess it has created, on the greatness it has spilt and strangled, on the starvation it has fostered, on the perversions and ignorances it has taught, then it would die of shame. And we, who have not been long enough alive to be corrupted utterly, could build out of its manuring bones the base of an equal and sensible civilization.

I will not bore you with any more propaganda, though why it should bore you God knows, for it is near to you as it is to me. Later, in another letter, I will give you a more reasoned outline of Revolution, the hard facts of communism — which is above communism for it holds the individual above everything else — and hope that you, too, may don the scarlet tie. . . .

The factual letter was, of course, never written. The sustained piece of oratory that I have quoted above — that might have been written ten years earlier by any young German close to Stefan George, whether he be a Stauffenberg or a future Nazi — remains almost but not quite his only "political" pronouncement. But before continuing with this subject there is a red herring to be disposed of.

This matter of Dylan's politics has been much confused by a remark by Augustus John, who states in his memoirs that Dylan Thomas had at one time been a Communist. John's views of Dylan, both when painting him and when writing about him, were peculiar, flavoured with condescension, tinctured with jealousy, and swamped in incomprehension, and are even more to be distrusted in his writing than his painting.

Dylan, like many and perhaps most of his and my generation who were connected with the arts, held the radical, and in England left-wing, views which are expressed in the passage I have just quoted. But Bert Trick, who must surely have known, has assured me that Dylan was not a Communist during this Swansea period. If further proof of this is needed, it is provided by a rather incoherent letter that he wrote to the *Swansea and West Wales Guardian* on January 14, 1934. It is, so far as I know, the only letter he ever wrote to a newspaper, as it is his only public declaration of political belief. It shows, I think, less of Bert Trick's Marxist influence than does the letter, written two months before, to Pamela Hansford Johnson. Here it is:

TELLING THE TRUTH TO THE PUBLIC
EXPOSURE HUMBUG AND SMUG RESPECTABILITY

Sir — in this overpopulated breeding box of ours, this ugly contradiction of a town forever compromised between the stacks and the littered bays, the Philistines exercise an inevitable dictatorship and regard the first glimmerings of a social intelligence and the first signs of a godly abhorrence of the parochial diseases much as the black man must have first regarded the features of his lily-faced brother.

You have most worthily demonstrated the fact that a local newspaper need not exclusively confine itself to the printing of photographs of our more bovine notabilities; the detailed reports of crimes which, in a less criminal state of society, would be unnecessary; insipid gossipings on the topographical positions of vanished streets and the references in bad novels to our God-chosen town; the retelling of old jokes; running commentaries on the gradual break down of the parish pump; and the useless quibblings between Christ-denying Christians, irrational Rationalists, and the whitespatted representatives of a social system that has, for too many years, used its bowler hat for the one purpose of keeping its ears apart.

But the colour of a shirt counts little to the man who has no shirt on his back, and the musical heaven after death harped on by the gentleman with the harmonium is a poor substitute for the man whose heaven on earth — warmth, clothes, food, a woman, and maybe children — is denied him on all sides. You can do more than merely allow the amateur and professional politicians of the town to display their bad manners in public. It is within your power to force, up to the very limits of censorship, upon all your readers some little consciousness of the immoral restrictions placed upon them, of the humbug and smug respectability that works behind them all their handcuffed days, and to do this, not from any political bias, but from the undeniable conviction that the God is not the lukewarm soup and starch of the chapels, but the red hot grains of love and life distributed equally and impartially among us all, and that at our roots of being lies not the greed for property or money, but the desire, large as a universe, to express ourselves freely and to the utmost limits of our individual capabilities.

Fascism would sprout to life like a flower through a coffin's cracks, watered by the excreta of the dead, the droppings of the political dead, the spittle of the Anti-Christs who had crucified Him and His children since the kiss of a man who wanted thirty pieces of silver in order, perhaps, to bribe one of the councillors of Jerusalem with a sack of coal or a cask of wine, or, as a member of the Jerusalem Road Improvement Committee, to buy a row of houses that the committee had decided to knock down for extension purposes. It would still stink of the weeds of this decomposing system of society, and all the tails of all the black shirts in the world would not wipe away the mud and the black and blue bruises of the well kicked bottom of the British public.

That we know. The shirts are changed, but the masks remain, hiding the riddle faces of those to whom the beauty of the tangible world approximates to the individual leisure for observing it. To them there is no world that is not to be touched and felt and sensed by the ambiguous senses of the maltreated body. To them the individual is a factor towards a state, and still an intricate machine for work that sells its sweat and muscle or else starves and is broken down. To them the individual is not a world, a structure of bone, blood, nerves and flesh, all made miraculous by the miracle of the mind, but a creature that works for the profit of its fellow creatures so that it may drag out its days and eat what is provided it and be buried at its own expense.

Fascism would clear the working man's house of bugs and attempt to provide him with a little more of what he should never have been deprived of; the divine right to live, regardless of his own working capacity.

Fascism would do this and more, so that he might work the harder and be dragged deeper into a false state of security and a blasphemous content, with his position at the very bottom of an anti-religious world of class.

That we know. It is within your power to force the consciousness of that, and the hate of that, upon a thousand brains, and to show, through the medium of that consciousness, that the beautiful world has been made foul by the men who have worked against men, by the devil in man which has worked against the God in man.

Teach to hate, and then to believe in the antithesis of what is hated.

Yours etcetera

DYLAN THOMAS

Swansea

He was immediately, and publicly, given a firm rap over the knuckles by his Marxist political mentor for this effusion.

When he got to London he met a number of Communists, but he did not often like them or their ideas; and when they were poets he despised, and continued to despise, their poems. (Already, in March of 1934, he had written to Glyn Jones: "You are, I suppose, a Socialist. As a Socialist myself, though a very unconventional one, I like to read good propoganda [his spelling] but the most recent poems of Auden and Day Lewis seem to me to be neither good poetry nor propoganda.")

One Communist poet whom he did like as a man, and whom he met almost as soon as he arrived in London, was Randall Swingler. Randall Swingler was then very active, in the Communist interest, on the cultural front, acting as a sort of link between Party headquarters and Bohemia. Had Dylan ever been a Communist Randall Swingler would almost certainly have known of it, and he assures me that Dylan never was. Indeed he has gone further, and has told me that even if Dylan Thomas had wished to join the Party, the Party would never have accepted for long so wild and undisciplined a recruit. These are strong words when one thinks of some of the writers they were accepting at this period.

There is a story that he once went off to join the Young Communists, but found that he was too old. Dylan may well have said this, but that does not mean the story is true. That he wore a very red tie, talked bolshie, loathed an establishment which permitted mass unemployment at home and fascism abroad and did not honour any but the worst poets, was passionately on the side of the poor and the oppressed, and hated the rich and the smug, all this certainly *is* true. He was, in fact, a rebel against his society, as artists of originality usually are. Since his society was run by conservatives, he sympathized with their political enemies: had he lived in a communist society he would quite certainly have hated their order and values with at least an equal violence.

There was a fairly regular pattern to his life in Swansea at this time. On Sunday evenings he and his friends would go to Bert Trick's for music and readings aloud and talk, talk, talk. Mrs. Trick would give them the sandwiches and the sweet jellies and cakes of which Dylan was so fond. All his life he had a craving for sweets seldom to be found in a man who drinks and smokes as much as he did. This may have had a physiological cause, or it may have been just another example of his infantilism. It took odd forms at times. When he was staying with me in Chelsea at the end of the war his attitude towards the candy ration that I brought back from the army PX each week was that of a child to its filled stocking on Christmas morning. He would even hide bars of chocolate under his pillow, like an alcoholic with his hidden bottle. And in the morning he would travel halfway across London, by bus, to a certain public house that was next to a place that sold ice-cream. He would buy an ice-cream cone, take it into the pub, and put the ice-cream into a fizzy light ale. This faintly intoxicating and I should imagine quite disgusting ice-cream soda was at that time the only breakfast that he cared to eat.

On Wednesday evenings Dylan and his friends had the use of his father's "middle room," where his mother would bring them sandwiches and cocoa. When D.J. returned from the pub at closing time, the young men would go upstairs, to Dylan's room, to continue the talk, or to hear what he had been writing. At this time he wrote his stories, in his very small hand, on large white pieces of cardboard, either old boxes or the stiffeners that laundries used to tuck into shirts. These he would then pin to the wall, so that he could see the whole of a story in progress at once, without having to turn pages.

Saturday evening was a pub-crawl, to the Antelope, the Three Lamps, the Bush, above all the Mermaid, and sometimes to the rough sailors' pubs down by the docks. It was in one of these that an enormous tattooed seaman in a singlet said to the young, frail, almost effeminate-looking boy: "You wouldn't think I was a sod, would you now?"

To which Dylan replied: "No. And you wouldn't think I was either," and then proceeded to sing, very loudly and in a deep bass voice, "Were you there when they crucified my Lord?"

Other evenings were spent in Dan's house or in those of his other friends, or at the cinema. Once he had met Vernon Watkins, for instance, he would go out about once a week to Vernon's parents' house on the very top of the cliffs of the beautiful Gower Peninsula. He visited Bert Trick, too, in his bungalow out at Caswell Bay. And then there were the evenings rehearsing in The Mumbles, and sometimes he would have to attend dinners or concerts as part of his job on the paper. On February 14, 1932, he wrote to Trevor Hughes:

I am playing in Noel Coward's *Hay Fever* at the Little Theatre this season. Much of my time is taken up with rehearsals. Much is taken up with concerts, deaths, meetings, and dinners. It's odd, but between all these I manage to become drunk at least four nights a week. Muse or Mermaid? That's the transition I spoke about. M or M? I'd prefer M any day, so that clears the air a lot.

I should guess that his "drunk at least four nights a week" is a manly exaggeration as well as being part of his deliberate poet's persona. Quite apart from his busy social, theatrical and journalistic life, he was writing a very great deal at this time, as I shall show later in this chapter. That he got drunk occasionally is certainly true. He has described one such evening in his story "One Warm Saturday." But the very fact that this incident was so obviously memorable would indicate that it was not of almost nightly occurrence. In another story, "Old Garbo," he gives what I believe to be a much more accurate description of how and why he drank. "Mr. Farr" was another reporter on the *Post*.

The back room of "The Three Lamps" was full of elderly men. Mr. Farr had not arrived. I leant against the bar, between an alderman and a solicitor, drinking bitter, wishing that my father could see me now and glad, at the same time, that he was visiting Uncle A. in Aberavon. He could not fail to see that I was a boy no longer, nor fail to be angry at the angle of my fag and my hat and the threat of the clutched tankard. I liked the taste of beer, its live, white lather, its brass-bright depths, the sudden world through the wet-brown walls of the glass, the tilted rush to the lips and the slow swallowing down to the lapping belly, the salt on the tongue, the foam at the corners.
"Same again, miss."

There are many aspects to Dylan's drinking, and most of them are already apparent at this early age. In the first place drink was a sign of manhood, that is to say of freedom. Secondly, and particularly in Wales thirty years ago, drink was wicked. Temperance preachers stalked the Swansea sands and thundered in their pulpits. To drink was therefore an act of defiance directed against all the values that they represented. Thirdly, vice of all sorts was somehow connected with his rather old-fashioned idea of "the poet." Dylan at that age might well have preferred absinthe, Enoch Soames's *sorcière glauque,* but one cannot have everything. Beer was a substitute. Finally, he liked it. If his woodbine was his first badge, his tankard soon became his second.

His parents disapproved of course and, as the passage just quoted shows, though he relished in a way such disapproval, he did not enjoy it face to face. Fred Janes has told me how, when he and Dylan had had too much beer, they would often go to his sister's house — she lived just below Cwmdonkin Drive and thus on Dylan's way home — and have something to eat, to sober up. On one such occasion Dylan startled the company by eating a whole bowl of chrysanthemums which he washed down with the water in the vase. On at least one other occasion, being

frightened of coming home the worse for drink, he hid in the field opposite his parents' home until all the lights had gone out.

Even more than drink the traditional proof of manliness is women.
And here Dylan's biographer is on slippery ground. Dylan would, it
seems, boast about great goings-on down near the docks. On the other
hand Eric Hughes, fellow journalist and fellow actor who was at this
time in love with Dylan's sister, has told me that he has never, before or
since, known a boy of that age who was less interested in girls than was
Dylan. Not that even the keenest interest would have done him a great
deal of good with girls of his own background. In those days, as doubtless today, the respectable young ladies of Swansea went virgin to their
wedding service in the chapel. Certainly Dylan ogled them during the
Sunday evening promenade along the front, and he may even have
kissed one or two. But he had no steady girl friend in Swansea, let alone
anything that could be remotely described as a mistress. Indeed
throughout his life this fundamental lack of interest lingered on, perhaps an atrophied Puritanism. He never did have a mistress in the
French sense. Why should he? What would he have done with one? For
him there was his wife, Caitlin, and if she was not there, then there
were other women.

What about those others, before ever he left Swansea?

There was a barmaid to whom he was attracted; her eyes are said to
have been of different colours. In New York, shortly before his death,
he confided to a stranger that he had first slept with a woman when he
was fifteen; that he and a friend had shared her one night; and the
friend had since become a prominent servant of the law. The story may
or may not be true. But what seems to me more characteristic, and
certainly more authentic since it was written at the time, is his description of an evening with Dan Jones, in a letter to Trevor Hughes dated
1932.

Dan Jones is staying here for a few days, and last night and the night before we wasted our substances and distended our bellies with low company.
It's difficult to write, because the bending of the head hurts like fury. . . .

Last night, Dan and I, none too brightly, for the womb of the Mermaid
was empty and the radiogram blaring, discovered we had too little feeling.
We almost lost our tempers, proving how unfeeling we were. The petty emotions, hates, loves, and spites, we said grandly, were nothing to us. We were
artistic Ishmaels, and we scorned with a ha and ho the lusts that shut up
bushes, burning like cantharides, all over waterless places. Sex was an instrument to annoy women with, and the anachronistic loyalties, faithfulness,

holy-desires, gratitudes, mercies and charities were no more than words to cover over the evil intentions of our inferiors. (Because they are inferior, these blubbery-eyed old men, stiff-dickied, these shop-assistants with their ingrown virginities priced at 1/11¾, these friggin boys, these wailing mothers, and disappointed communists, and God help our Godheads if we can't play Christ, and Christ was always the white sheep among the black, the superior, the natty gent in the tramps' ward.) We started to remember old cruelties, the purposeful raising of desires in girls we knew and the purposeful unsatisfying of them, the tongue-cuts, the embarrassments, the ungrateful things we had done, the muck we'd uttered with our tongues in our cheeks. Our lowest feelings, when we sit drunk, maudlin, holding a whore's hand, are the highest feelings of the maggoty men around us. Artists don't have to die etc. They crucify themselves. All the old bullshit.

Why am I writing this? Is it to show the futility of effort? Are you playing Freud to me as I tell you that, like Havelock Ellis, I bore holes in the floor to piss through, or cut a pigeon's throat as I copulate? I don't know why or what, but last night we, who had no feelings, spoke passionately, waving our arms in the air, saying, Desire is nothing, as we stroked her buttocks, saying, Hunger is vanity, as we swilled and wallowed, damning the conventions as we took a bus home and lied when we got there.

This is hardly the letter of a boy who has any knowledge of women, and it is not hard to guess that the arousing of desires which are then left unsatisfied is a neat inversion of Dylan's relationships with the girls he knew. There is also the evidence of the poems and stories he was writing at this time. They show an intense preoccupation with sexuality, but it is all male sexuality, it is all his own body, and at least one poem is quite obviously onanistic. If he was not a virgin when he left for London, he was the next best thing. It was all theory, it was all cerebral. And in some ways it remained so, apart from his love for his wife. He once asked me, travelling on top of a bus, whether I thought about sex a great deal. I was twenty-five years old, and I replied that I did. He said:

"I think about it all the time."

A boy who had enjoyed any real sexual relations with a girl would hardly have written, as he wrote to Pamela Hansford Johnson in 1933:

. . . My experience of waking with a woman at my side has been necessarily limited.

The medieval laws of this corrupted hemisphere have dictated a more or less compulsory virginity during the period of life when virginity should be regarded as a crime against the dictates of the body. During the period of adolescence, when the blood and seed of the growing flesh need, for the first time and more than ever again, communion and contact with the blood and seed of another flesh, sexual relationships are looked upon as being unnecessary and unclean. The body must be kept intact for marriage, which is rarely possible before the age of twenty: the physical expression of sex must be caged up for six or more years until for the price of a ring, a licence, and a few simpering words, opportunity is presented with all the ceremony of a phallic religion. But so often the opportunity comes too late, the seed has soured, love has turned to lust, and lust to sadism; the mind has become covered and choked by the weeds of inhibition; and the union of two starved creatures suddenly allowed the latitude of their sexes, is doomed from the start. The woman carries her marriage licence about with her as a bitch might carry the testimony of her liberated heat.

Such things may not be pleasant to talk about, but they do exist, and they are evil.

Since he did not go to boarding school, he lacked the homosexual introduction to sex which has been the progression of most members of the English middle class and therefore of most English writers. Again to Pamela Hansford Johnson, late in 1933, he wrote:

Have you remarked upon the terrible young men of this generation, the willing-buttocked, celluloid-trousered degenerates who are gradually taking the place of the bright young things of even five years ago? Or is the degeneracy, the almost unbelievable effeminacy, the product of the Welsh slums alone? In an hotel last night a boy, wearing a light green hat, white shirt, red tie, light green trousers and tightly fitting fawn overcoat, went up to the bar and said "a whate and a smale Ardath, girlie." I heard him. He was the most perfect example I've ever seen, the sort of thing one hears of in coarse stories but rarely encounters in the flesh (God deliver me from the flesh; the outer trappings are enough). I see more and more of them every day. They always existed, but in recent months — it seems months to me — they are coming, unashamedly, out into the open. I saw one with a drunken nigger last night.

It is the only vice, I think, that revolts me and makes me misanthropic. I can — theoretically — tolerate even incest (Tell me, have you read Leonhard Frank's "Brother and Sister"; if not, get hold of it by some method and *do* read it; it's brilliant) and other domestic sins. But the sin of the boy with the nigger goes up like a rocketed scab to heaven.

Dylan did tell an American friend that he had once tried homosexuality "with an MP." If so, it was on the *une fois philosophe* principle, but I doubt it, and the introduction of the Member of Parliament gives the story an additional ring of Dylanesque fantasy. Furthermore I do not believe that he knew any MPs, at least not well enough for experimen-

[87]

tations of this sort. Finally the story was told to a man who is himself a homosexual; Dylan, with his usual social tact, was probably trying to make him feel at ease.

Indeed I would say that his dislike of homosexuals, though moderated as he grew older and met more of them, remained with him to the end. In his letters, when commenting on a famous contemporary literary figure who was at one time almost equally well-known for his sexual perversions, Dylan seldom fails to mention these proclivities, and usually in coarse terms.

On one occasion during the war Dylan and several other poets took part in a public poetry reading. At least one of the other poets was a well-known homosexual. In the audience was Queen Elizabeth, now the Queen Mother, and she expressed a desire to meet the men who had read to her. Caitlin, who was apparently unaware of what was going on, was taken by friends to a nearby pub, where Dylan was to join them. He was rather a long time arriving and Caitlin showed signs of fretfulness and worry. Somebody explained to her that he was talking to the Queen. Caitlin said, morosely, that she did not approve of Dylan spending so much time with all these old queens. "But it's the English Queen," the friend explained. "English queens," she grumbled, "Irish queens, American queens, it's all the same. They're bad for Dylan. They upset him."

She was quite right. They did upset that part of him which remained the Welsh Puritan. Earlier in this chapter I have attempted to describe the sort of men Dylan liked. If one were to make, with a mental identikit, a composite picture of the type of man Dylan disliked most, he would be a snobbish, homosexual poetaster, with pretensions in place of talent, who held right-wing views and a university job, and did not drink. He met quite a few who had one or more of these qualities on his travels through the American universities, and they did not make those grisly marathons any easier to take. I recall his laughter as he told me of a young Middle Western academic who had asked him if it was *really* necessary to be a homosexual before a man could hope to be a poet nowadays.

We know a great deal about what Dylan was writing during this Swansea period because his poetry notebooks have, with one exception, survived. There are four of these, starting in April 1930 and ending in April 1934. One, covering the period July 1932 to January 1933, is missing, but typescripts of some of the poems it contained were left with

Trevor Hughes, who has deposited them with the British Museum. Assuming that during these six months he wrote about the same number of poems as in the previous and subsequent half-year periods, we find that during these four years, between the ages of fifteen and a half and nineteen and a half, he wrote over two hundred and fifty poems which he considered successful enough to transcribe into his notebooks.

From those notebooks that have survived he published, in his lifetime, fifty-four poems, sometimes in their original form but more frequently in a revised form or even almost totally rewritten. It is again permissible to assume that some of the published poems, other than those in the British Museum typescripts, existed at least embryonically in the missing notebook. This means that of all the poems he chose to publish, over half were written, in at least their original form, before ever he left Swansea.

During this same period he wrote all the "poetical" short stories which together formed the unpublished volume called *The Burning Baby* (1938). Six of these later appeared in *The Map of Love* (1939) and were reprinted, with five more, in the posthumous volume *A Prospect of the Sea*, and again, with the addition of a further half dozen, in the American edition of *Adventures in the Skin Trade*. There are one or two other stories referred to in his letters: they may be these stories with other titles, or other stories that have got lost. We may therefore conclude that he wrote between twenty and twenty-five short stories in Swansea which are similar in style and content to the poems he was then writing. (These do not include any of the stories in the *Portrait of the Artist as a Young Dog*, all of which were written later, and which have nothing in common with his poems.) His output was, in fact, very considerable during those years.

Professor Ralph Maud, of New York University in Buffalo, where the notebooks have come to rest in the Lockwood Memorial Library, is at present preparing those notebooks for publication and will no doubt thus complete his scholarly and critical interpretation of the poet's early work which he has allowed us to sample in his *Entrances to Dylan Thomas's Poetry*. Since I am writing a biography and not a critical study, it is not my intention to duplicate his labours, nor do I possess the qualifications to do so.

All I would say is that during these four years the poet's style shows a progression towards an ever greater density of meaning as he twisted syntax, piled image upon image, and juxtaposed unexpected adjectival nouns in his determination to produce maximum effect and the greatest possible measure of poetic truth. This was to lead, a little later, to a considerable degree of obscurity, particularly in the sonnet sequence *Altarwise by Owl-light,* after which there came some relaxation of intensity.

While experimenting in the boldest way with the sound and meaning of words, his rhythms at this time were cautious, almost monotonous, the five-beat line or some minor variant thereof being his usual metre. And almost all these early poems are short. Nor does he seem to have been as preoccupied with rhyme as he was later to become when writing longer poems with a far more ambitious rhythmic structure. In the early days it was really all words; it was, as he put it, the colour of saying.

His principal themes are less easy to define, though enough critics have attempted to do so. The unpublished poems in the notebooks number among them attempts at almost every sort of lyric poetry; he has said, in the passage I quoted earlier, how he tried his poet's hand at everything he knew. Of the poems that he published from the notebooks, and of the short stories, some he subsequently found unsatisfactory and did not include in his books. And only one poem that he did include in early volumes was later excised from his *Collected Poems.* The others remained and remain central to his life's work.

One early theme, or set of themes, of which he quite quickly wearied was madness, witchcraft and diabolism in general; he soon recognized this type of morbidity as adolescent and essentially derivative. He disliked it when he encountered it, wearing new feathers, in the work of the Surrealists. And out it went. One of his earliest published poems, the first draft of which was written on August 24, 1933, has in its published form the following opening lines:

> That sanity be kept I sit at open windows,
> Regard the sky, make unobtrusive comment on the moon,
> Sit at open windows in my shirt,
> And let the traffic pass, the signals shine,
> The engines run, the brass bands keep in tune,
> For sanity must be preserved.
>
> Thinking of death, I sit and watch the park
> Where children play in all their innocence,
> And matrons on the littered grass,
> Absorb the daily sun.

This poem, in part perhaps because of the obvious influence of T. S. Eliot, he never reprinted.

On the other hand his preoccupation with death remained, and indeed grew stronger and more profound with the passing years. The subjective basis for this preoccupation — his belief that he had not long to live — was in some ways transcended by his own sort of pantheism, by the identification of himself and his mortal body with all nature:

> The force that through the green fuse drives the flower
> Drives my green age: that blasts the roots of trees
> Is my destroyer.

This famous poem was also first written in the summer of 1933, but the concept remains central throughout his work. Even earlier is *And death shall have no dominion*, in the original version of which occurs the line:

> Though lovers shall be lost love shall not.

Finally there is what might be loosely called a Freudian synthesis in his poems between the death-wish and the urge to procreate, expressed now through one set of images, now another, often through several sets simultaneously, physiological, biblical, even astronomical: death and life cease to be antitheses, but are the yin and the yan of one great, mysterious process that the poet shares through his own body with all nature. Such, in crude oversimplification, was Dylan Thomas's principal contribution to English poetry. And it is already present in many of his earliest poems.

5

THERE IS some uncertainty concerning the date of Dylan's first trip to London. George Reavey has told me that he first met him there in 1932, in a pub called The Plough, which is near the British Museum and which in those days was frequented by writers and other literary folk. He is sure of his date, since both before and after 1932 he was living in Paris. Furthermore he was impressed by the respect with which the Welsh boy of seventeen, who had then had nothing published in London, was treated by well-known poets and novelists. Trevor Hughes, too, believes that Dylan came to London in 1932 and stayed with him in his Bloomsbury lodgings. He recalls introducing him, for the first time, to the Fitzroy Tavern, in Charlotte Street, Soho, which was then beginning to take the place of the Plough as the writers' and painters' pub. He also took Dylan around the British Museum, where the boy was overawed by the treasures it contains. In an attempt to appear at ease Dylan expressed his admiration for what he took to be a large piece of abstract sculpture and was embarrassed to learn that it was in fact a meteorite.

I hesitate to contradict such vivid memories, but I am sure that they are both mistaken about the date. There is no further evidence whatsoever that Dylan visited London before August of 1933. Had he stayed with Trevor Hughes in 1932 it is curious that there should be no reference to this in his letters to Hughes written during that year. Nor is there any obvious reason why he should have gone to London during the time when he was working on the *Post*, even if he could have afforded to do so. True, Dylan did say that on the occasion of his first visit to London he was so frightened that he never left the precincts of

Paddington Station, always the London end of his lifeline back to Wales. Such a visit, if it ever took place, might have provided the raw material for his unfinished novel *Adventures in the Skin Trade;* it is equally likely that he told that fictional story as if it were the truth. In any event such a visit would not have been the occasion on which he met Reavey in the Plough or was taken to the Museum by Hughes. I am inclined to think that no such visit took place, and that he first came to London in 1933.

In the spring of that year his sister Nancy had married Haydn Taylor. They were living on a houseboat in the Thames Valley, and in July of 1933 Dylan wrote to Trevor Hughes:

I will be in London for a fortnight, from Bank Holiday on, staying on the Thames with Nancy, my sister, who married some months ago. Write and tell me where I can come to see you, or where I can meet you sometime. We might go to the ballet together. Or we might sit and talk. Or sit.

Bank Holiday in that year was August 7th. Either just before this visit, or immediately after his return to Swansea, he wrote to Geoffrey Grigson, who had earlier that year begun publication of *New Verse,* probably the most important poetry magazine, with the exception of *Poetry* (Chicago), to be published in the English language so far in this century. To him he wrote:

I am sending you some poems to be considered for publication in *New Verse.* . . . Out of a large number of poems I found it extremely difficult to choose six to send you. As a matter of fact, the enclosed poems were picked almost entirely at random. If you think the poems unsuitable for publication, and if, of course, you are sufficiently interested, I could let you see some more. I probably have far better ones in some of my innumerable exercise books.
A considerable period lies between the writing of some of the enclosed poems, as perhaps you will be able to see. Whether time has shown any improvement I find it hard to say, as I have developed, intellectually at least, in the smug darkness of a provincial town, and have only on rare occasions shown any of my work to any critics, generally uninterested or incompetent. If you could see your way clear to publish any of these poems, or find in them sufficient merit to the reading of some more, you would be doing me a very great favour. Grinding out poetry, whether good or bad, in such an atmosphere as surrounds me, is depressing and disheartening.

In fact this visit had for Dylan a far more important purpose than merely to visit his sister. (There he fell into the Thames after a long session in the local pub. He could not swim, but fortunately his brother-in-law managed to fish him out with a boat-hook.) It was a sort of reconnaissance into literary London.

He had then had only one poem and no prose published in London. The poem was *And death shall have no dominion,* in its original form, which he later revised drastically before including it in *Twenty-five Poems.* It had appeared the previous May in the *New English Weekly,* of which A. R. Orage was then editor. Politically rather eccentric — Orage advocated a sort of guild socialism and also Major Douglas's ideas on Social Credit — the *N.E.W.*'s literary side was very good. Ezra Pound kept a benevolent eye on it, and later George Orwell was its unofficial literary adviser. But unfortunately it could not afford to pay its contributors anything at all. Other outlets were essential.

During this August visit Dylan saw Orage who, Dylan claimed, opened the conversation by asking him if he were a virgin: whatever his reply it was apparently satisfactory, for the first of his stories appeared, a few months later, in the *New English Weekly.* He also saw Sir Richard Rees, who had recently taken over the editorship of the *Adelphi* from Middleton Murry. Rees accepted a poem, *No man believes, when a star falls shot* and published it in the next edition of his magazine, the first of Dylan's poems to be bought in London. It was probably with Orage and his friends that Reavey met Dylan in the Plough, for Rees lived in Chelsea, and Dylan went to see him there.

Trevor Hughes believes that it was at this time, too, that Dylan took some of his poems to T. S. Eliot, who then edited the *Criterion* and who, from Faber and Faber, was already publishing virtually all the good young English poets. The meeting, which may have taken place a few months later, was not a success. Not only did Eliot fail to find merit in Dylan's poems, but Dylan mistook his somewhat distant, though courteous, manner for condescension. He told Trevor Hughes that Eliot had treated him as if he were a case "of pitboy to poet," a curiosity in a raree-show. Anyone who ever met T. S. Eliot will know that this can only have been a gross misunderstanding on Dylan's part resulting from timidity and from that inferiority complex which I have described earlier. Eliot had himself no recollection of this first meeting. He wrote to me, shortly before his death:

I remember being shown a number of his poems before his work was taken on by Richard Church for Dents and I remember discussing the poems with Sir Herbert Read. I think he agreed with me but I will not swear to this, when I came to the conclusion that I wished all the poems were as good as the best. I regret having been so fussy because Dylan Thomas's work was always hit or miss. It was a peculiarity of his type of genius that he either wrote a great poem or something approaching nonsense and one ought to have accepted the inferior with the first-rate. I certainly regarded him always as a poet of considerable importance. I do not remember who or what brought him first to my attention. It may have been Herbert Read or someone else or he may have brought them to me himself.

I never knew Dylan Thomas well. I always liked him. . . .

Thus this first visit to London was neither an unqualified success nor a total failure. He had discovered which magazines and papers might publish his poems, and he had had at least a whiff of the literary atmosphere in the capital. Now back in Swansea he proceeded to post off his work, doubtless accompanied by the obligatory "stamped addressed envelope" the sight of which is the usual bad start to a young writer's day. (The story current in the 'thirties that Geoffrey Grigson used to steam off the stamps and sell them to the post office is, I am told, entirely untrue. Certainly he sent these first poems of Dylan's back at once.) But one editor besides Sir Richard Rees did not return his poems.

This was Victor Neuburg, who ran *Poets' Corner* in a newspaper called the *Sunday Referee*, of which Mr. Mark Goulden was editor and Mr. Hayter Preston literary editor. *That sanity be kept* was published there on September 3, 1933, and was described by Neuburg as "the best modernist poem I have yet received." On October 29th he printed *The force that through the green fuse*, which he called "cosmic in outlook . . . a large poem, greatly expressed." And before *Poets' Corner* was wound up, two years later, Dylan had had five more published there; by then he was famous in literary circles and could publish his poems almost where he wished. But it was *Poet's Corner* that gave him his start as a poet, and it was indubitably Victor Neuburg, with Mark Goulden's backing, who set him on the path that was to make him, within twenty years, the most widely read English poet of the age, indeed perhaps the most widely read since Byron. (Rupert Brooke and Rudyard Kipling may have sold more copies, but for reasons not directly connected with poetry.)

This was the age of newspaper stunts to promote circulation and thus increase advertising rates. Free insurance, competitions to win cars or paid holidays were baits that were then held out to the public by almost every popular paper. It was Mr. Goulden who realized, early in 1933, that one small section of the populace had not been appealed to, the amateur poets. And there are a great many of these in England where it sometimes seems that more people write poetry than read it. Furthermore the *Sunday Referee* already had a higher literary standing than any other English newspaper. It commissioned articles from the best writers of the age, a very unusual practice at that time when newspapers were written almost exclusively by journalists. Among those whom Mr. Goulden published were Robert Graves, Richard Aldington, the Sitwells, the Huxleys, Bertrand Russell, Constant Lambert, D. B. Wyndham Lewis, to name but a few. It was thus a suitable paper in which to appeal to poets and poetry-fanciers. He therefore arranged that there be a weekly poetry competition. The prizes were very small, half a guinea for the winner with curiously childish consolation prizes, such as a penknife or a revolving pencil, for the runners-up whose poems were also printed. (Later there was also a *Junior Poets' Corner*, for child poets; what their prizes were I cannot think.) The response was immediate and considerable. More than three thousand people submitted poems — mostly bad ones — and many people did so repeatedly.

To run *Poets' Corner*, and to write the critical and literary chit-chat that filled the two columns between poems, Mr. Hayter Preston imported his old friend Victor Neuburg, who was assisted by a woman named Runia Tharpe. Neuburg had a domicile in St. John's Wood, 64 Springfield Road, now demolished. He was paid an extremely small salary — two pounds a week, I believe, which is about what Dylan must have earned on the *South Wales Daily Post* — and indeed the whole enterprise was run on a shoe-string, as was only to be expected in view of the comparatively small numbers of readers it could be expected to attract. Thus the poets themselves helped lick the stamped, addressed envelopes. But at the back of Mark Goulden's mind and Victor Neuburg's there was always the hope that they might discover a new, major poet. And they did.

This Victor Neuburg, or "the Vickybird" as he was commonly called, was a weird and very kind fellow. Born in 1883, the son of moderately well-off German-Jewish immigrants, he fell, while at Cambridge in 1906, completely under the influence of Aleister Crowley, the self-styled magician who liked to be called the Great Beast or 666 when he was not employing the pseudonym of Lord Boleskine. This person engaged in deplorable practices with assorted young men and women, talked in a queer semi-cockney accent, celebrated the Black Mass, wrote execrable verse (Neuburg's was slightly better), and generally larked about in a manner intended to scandalize the British public. He had strange, piercing eyes and was said to possess hypnotic powers, particularly over the young. When young himself this may well have been true. By the time I met him, in about 1937, he was simply a gross old man in a kilt sponging drinks and babbling drivel about pentagrams and elementals. But then the appeal of such persons is perhaps limited to those who wish to be dominated, as did the masochistic and homosexual Victor Neuburg. Furthermore there are certain periods of history that provide a more suitable environment for "magicians" than do others. Like France before the Revolution, Europe just before and after the First World War was such a place. Aleister Crowley was of the generation of Rasputin, Gurdjieff, Axel Munthe, an epoch in which miracle-workers, faith-healers and charismatic political charlatans flourished abominably as Christianity declined but the need for faith remained. Some of those quacks did good; more did harm. Crowley was only interested in evil, and in his coarse, comic opera fashion he managed to damage and perhaps to kill a number of people. One of these was Victor Neuburg, who was completely in Crowley's power until Crowley went to America in 1914, and who remained terrified of him for the rest of his life. (I am indebted for the facts about Neuburg to Miss Jean Overton Fuller, who allowed me to read in typescript her book about Victor Neuburg, though I do not always accept the deductions that she draws from them.)

The story that Crowley once turned Neuburg into a camel and sold him to the Alexandria Zoo where he languished for several years is, Miss Fuller assures me, quite untrue. It may even have been invented by Dylan. Not only was Crowley quite incapable of this sort of magic, but according to Miss Fuller he was very bad at magic of any sort, being an esoteric ignoramus who could not work out simple astrological equations. Furthermore, though the now superb Dublin Zoo used to keep quite domestic animals, such as sheep, in cages, would the Egyptians have the wit to put a camel behind bars? The camel story can be discounted. But Mr. Arthur Calder-Marshall has written, in *Magic of My Youth*, that Neuburg believed Crowley to be directly responsible for another, very real and fatal tragedy.

What happened, briefly, is that Neuburg, in addition to his homosexual relations with Crowley, had a relationship with an actress who called herself Ione de Forest. She too was a neurotic. She married another man, an unconsummated marriage; Neuburg accompanied them on their honeymoon. A few months later, in August of 1912, she shot herself through the heart in her Chelsea studio after first bequeathing her clothes to Nina Hamnett.

Was Neuburg in love with Ione de Forest? Impossible to say. But, perhaps more important, did Crowley think he was? For according to Arthur Calder-Marshall, Neuburg blamed the tragedy on Crowley. Although Crowley's slogan, his *Heil Hitler!* as it were, was "Do what thou wilt shall be the whole of the law," to which his disciples had to reply: "Love is the law, love under will," in fact love was out. Sex yes, love no. Crowley, like other more spectacular and successful wizards, realized that if his disciples loved one another this could only be at the cost of their total devotion to himself. Orgies centered about his own unattractive person were what he prescribed for his followers. He would therefore have been most displeased if he had reason to believe that Neuburg, his slave, was emotionally involved elsewhere.

According to Arthur Calder-Marshall, Crowley dealt with the situation magically and brutally. He caused Neuburg to be possessed by an evil spirit, and then did not release him. The possessed Neuburg went to see his mistress, with whom he had a quarrel of exceptional violence. She threatened to kill herself. He, or rather the evil spirit speaking through him, told her to do so, and he then walked out. She did.

Two years later he broke with Crowley, but by then he was himself a broken man. His horrible past obsessed him, and he became increasingly eccentric, a recluse in Steyning where he ran a small private press for a while with Mr. Hayter Preston. He married a local girl. He grew odder and odder. It was at Steyning in the 'twenties that Arthur Calder-Marshall first met him.

He lived in what was then regarded as a tumbledown cottage but which today would probably fetch seven thousand pounds as a superb example of Tudor black and white. Swinging from a bracket set in the wall hung a sign announcing the Vine Press. The wall itself was almost hidden in summer by the leaves of an ancient and infertile vine, and in a window of the room below the vine stood a large, dusty hand-press . . .

Each morning he would emerge from Vine Cottage with a string bag and an obese white bitch and make for the High Street.

He carried an ash stick, and he was always dressed in a Norfolk jacket and knickerbockers, with stockings which rode in rucks around his spindly legs, and shoes so old that the leather was cracked.

He had thin venous hands and a head which, by nature disproportionately large for his body, was magnified by dark Medusa locks which rose from his scalp and tumbled curling down his forehead.

To judge from a painting of him in youth, he had been handsome beyond the ordinary. But he had later contracted an eczema which disfigured his nose, and a malady of the spirit which plagued his whole life. On the care of his teeth he was scrupulous. He brushed them after every meal, even taking his toothbrush with him if invited out to lunch. But in his person he had lost all vanity or self-respect. Smudges would remain on his face for hours, sometimes even days. He shaved customarily every third day, and it was hard to know which was the more distressing, his tramp-like half-beard or his face clean-shaven. For he never mastered the skill of shaving, and when he had done with hacking at his hairs, his face was as scarred and gashed, as if he had been dragged through a thicket of brambles.

To his clothes he paid as little attention as to his person. Though this was a time for plus-fours and beltless sports-coats, the people of Steyning would have accepted the knickerbockers and Norfolk jacket, if he or his wife had made some attempt to patch them up. But of the holes at his elbows and knees, the frayed ends of his sleeves, the Poet seemed oblivious, or, what was perhaps even worse, almost proud . . .

As he walked along the street with his stick over his arm and his string bag in his hand, he looked like a king in motley or Charlie Chaplin playing Haroun al Raschid. While the bitch alternately sniffed at the surfaces popular in canine society and made its own contributions to The Dog's World, that archetype of the wall newspaper, he would saunter along singing to himself, "The first time I met her she was all dressed in red" or *Johnny Hall*, that threnody of the unitesticular, which he had found so popular during his wartime service with the P.B.I.

To his friends . . . he could be a disconcerting companion. He had a loud and uncontagious laugh, as abrupt to begin and end as the cry of a parakeet. Walking with him in a public street, I used to try to avoid anything even remotely mirthmaking, because I was so embarrassed by his strident cackle. But his humour was so intricately wired that even the most circumspect conversation might set it off, clanging through the quaint old-fashioned market town, like those burglar alarms which in London are frequently to be heard outside foreign fur shops.

To friend, foe or complete stranger his manners were polite to the point of parody. See him, for example, in the Post Office, buying a penny stamp. At this moment the vicar's wife, a worthy woman with the sincere conviction that Vickybird is the anti-Christ, makes for the door. Vickybird leaps to anticipate her, and as he holds the door open for her to pass, he bows solemnly from the waist, with the palm of his hand placed on his stomach. "The top of this wondrous morning to you fayre ladye!" he exclaims.

At this moment the walking-stick falls off his arm and clatters to the floor. He bends down smartly to prevent it tripping her up. The door catches him from behind and his head strikes the vicar's wife in the pit of the stomach. He straightens up to apologise and knocks her shopping-bag to the ground. Carrots, butter, sausages and onions strew the floor and as Vickybird runs to collect those which have rolled the furthest, the dog sniffs at those he has retrieved.

A casual courtesy, but Puck with his deliberate malice could not create chaos quicker than Vickybird by a single act of unsolicited helpfulness. Little wonder then that those who disliked him believed his attentions were malevolent.

Such was the pixie whom Hayter Preston persuaded Mark Goulden to appoint as poetry editor of the *Sunday Referee* in the spring of 1933. Again in *Magic of My Youth* Arthur Calder-Marshall recalls, in Neuburg's own weird conversational style, how Neuburg told him of the new job:

"Many is the time, little Arthur," he said, "when I have said unto thee in the words of the Prophet, 'Cast thy bread upon the waters and it shall come unto thee with knobs on.' That is precisely what has happened. Many moons ago, in the days of my former prosperity, I lent a trifling sum to a colleague of mine in distress. I never thought to press him for repayment and perhaps for that reason he retained for me what is more important than gratitude, an affectionate regard. So it happens that when in the fullness of time my friend becomes editor of that pre-eminently intellectual organ, the *Sunday Referee*, and it is decided to send its rising circulation soaring still higher by means of a weekly Poetry Competition, who does he select for the key post of Poetry Editor, but yours truly?"

I confess that after the grandiloquent introduction I was expecting something rather more impressive, and I said the first thing which came into my mind. "Well, that will at least pay the rent."

"The emolument," said Vickybird, "if not princely, is more than adequate. But you see, surely, the true significance of this appointment. It gives me, after all these years of waiting, a Platform, a National Platform from which to spread the Word. It means that at last I can speak to Youth, in whom our great hope lies. It means . . ."

By this time Runia Tharpe appears to have dominated him as completely as Crowley once had done, though in this case for the good. (Jean Overton Fuller tells how, when she led him to a shoe shop to buy him a pair of boots, the salesman asked her, not him, if they pinched.) And now the two of them set about the creation of *Poets' Corner*. Most of the poets they published during the two and a half years of its existence have been forgotten, inevitably. But reading the list of contributors one comes, from time to time, upon a familiar or even a famous name: Pamela Hansford Johnson, David Gascoyne, Ruthven Todd, Theodore Roethke.

Vickybird's attempt to create a coterie was only a qualified success. The young people whom he published did indeed come to St. John's Wood, where he offered them tea or soft drinks in the overgrown garden and talked to them about what he called the Creative Life. Throughout 1934 Dylan, when in London, was often there. Jean Overton Fuller remembers him at these little gatherings, his conversation "perfectly drawing room," himself "a polite young man, friendly but not at all presuming." However an attempt to institutionalize these little meetings, to form a society with a subscription of five shillings a year, failed in the summer of 1935. Dylan was there, as was Pamela Hansford Johnson, the two stars of this little circle. Neuburg wished that his Creative Lifers call themselves "The Zooists," but Dylan realized, and said, that this would make them appear ridiculous. Furthermore, he and Pamela Hansford Johnson had brought along some bottles of beer, six among the eight young people, one of whom was a teetotaller. Before the emergence of their host and hostess from the back room in which they usually lingered, it was decided that the only way the beer could be fairly divided would be if Dylan drank two of the bottles, "because he was so fond of beer." Mrs. Tharpe, when at last they did emerge, was extremely angry. She maintained that the mere smell of beer made Victor Neuburg ill. It was clearly not a happy gathering. Dylan never came again. The Zooists soon broke up. Like Neuburg himself, this little literary coterie was too eccentric and too old-fashioned for the age of Hitler and the Dneprostroi dam. The groups of writers that were then forming in London to replace the moribund "Bloomsbury" of the 'twenties were of a very different stripe, and not necessarily a more attractive one.

When Mark Goulden resigned as editor, Neuburg was dismissed from the *Sunday Referee*, and he and Runia Tharpe attempted to continue *Poets' Corner* in a publication of their own called *Comment*. It was not a success, partly for the same reason that the Zooists had failed, partly because Neuburg devoted so much of its limited space to his own fusty ideas expressed in his own preposterous style. Dylan did, loyally, contribute to it, unpaid. Though he had always regarded the Vickybird as an essentially farcical figure with a deplorable taste in poetry, he remained grateful to him. According to Miron Grindea, the editor of

Adam, Dylan declared at the time of Neuburg's death in 1940: "Vicky encouraged me as no one else has done. He possessed, I believe, many kinds of genius, and not the least was the drawing to himself, by his wisdom, graveness, great humour and innocence, a feeling of trust and love that won't ever be forgotten."

This declaration sounds utterly unlike anything that Dylan would ever have said or written, but it is certainly true in essence. On June 19, 1940, he wrote to Jean Overton Fuller:

I hadn't heard anything from Vicky and Runia for years, until about a fortnight ago. Then Pamela Johnson wrote to tell me that Vicky had just died. I was very grieved to hear it; he was a sweet, wise man. Runia's address is 84 Boundary Road, N.W. 8. At least, I suppose she is still there: I wrote her a letter, but I haven't had a reply; probably she's too sad to write.

This disquisition about Neuburg has interrupted the chronology of this biography. When Dylan returned home, after his first visit to London in August 1933, he had neither met Neuburg nor been published in *Poets' Corner.*

Back in Swansea, Dylan felt frustrated and depressed, as the letter to Geoffrey Grigson quoted earlier in this chapter shows. (And when Grigson turned down his poems he became one of the two men Dylan hated most in all England, the other, according to a letter of the time, being Sir Edward Elgar). His friends were leaving or had left, Fred Janes to London to study painting, Dan Jones soon to Budapest on a music scholarship, and Tom Warner was a less frequent visitor. Nancy had gone, and 5 Cwmdonkin Drive was an unhappy house, for Dylan's father now had cancer of the tongue for which he was undergoing painful and protracted treatment with radium needles. There was no Fern Hill anymore, since his Aunt Annie had died earlier that year. There was Blaen-Cwm, also near Llanstephan, where his Uncle Bob and his Aunt Dosie lived in adjoining cottages, but this was not the same; the age of country heaven was, for the time being, over. Writing to Pamela Hansford Johnson in October 1933 from Blaen-Cwm, he described what it was like to be a boy of just nineteen who has tasted briefly the freedom and excitement of the city but has been forced back by frosty circumstance upon his own, dull roots:

I am staying, as you see, in a country cottage, eight miles from a town and a hundred miles from anyone to whom I can speak on any subjects but the prospect of rain and the quickest way to snare rabbits. It is raining as I write, a thin, purposeless rain hiding the miles of desolate fields and scattered farmhouses. I can smell the river, and hear the beastly little brook that goes gingle-gingle past this room. I am facing an uncomfortable fire, a row of china dogs, and a bureau bearing the photograph of myself aged seven — thick-lipped, Fauntleroy-haired, wide-eyed, and empty as the bureau itself. There are a few books on the floor beside me — an anthology of poetry from Johnson to Dryden, the prose of Donne, a Psychology of Insanity. There are a few books in the case behind me — a Bible, From Jest to Earnest, a History of Welsh Castles. Some hours ago a man came into the kitchen, opened the bag he was carrying, and dropped the riddled bodies of eight rabbits on to the floor. He said it was a good sport, showed me their torn bellies and opened heads, brought out the ferret from his pocket for me to see. The ferret might have been his own child, he fondled it so. His own eyes were as close-set as the eyes of the terrible thing he held in his hand. He called it "Billy fach."

Later, when I have finished this letter, I'll walk down the lane. It will be dark then; lamps will be lit in the farmhouses, and the farmers will be sitting at their fires, looking into the blazing wood and thinking of God knows what littlenesses, or thinking of nothing at all but their own animal warmth.

But even this, grey as it is and full of the noise of sanitating water, is better than the industrial small towns. I passed them in the bus coming down here, each town a festering sore on the body of a dead country, half a mile of main street with its Prudential, its Co-op, its Star, its cinema and pub. On the pavements I saw nothing but hideously pretty young girls with cheap berets on their heads and paint smudged over their cheeks; thin youths with caps and stained fingers holding their cigarettes; women, all breast and bottom, hugging their purses to them and staring in at the shop windows; little colliers, diseased in mind and body as only the Welsh can be, standing in groups outside the Welfare Hall. I passed the rows of colliers' houses, hundreds of them, each with a pot of ferns in the window, a hundred jerry-built huts built by a charitable corporation for the men of the town to breed and eat in.

All Wales is like this. I have a friend who writes long and entirely unprintable verses beginning, "What are you, Wales, but a tired old bitch?" and, "Wales my country, Wales my sow."

It's impossible for me to tell you how much I want to get out of it all, out of narrowness and dirtiness, out of the eternal ugliness of the Welsh people and all that belongs to them, out of the pettiness of a mother I don't care for and the giggling batch of relatives. What are you doing? I'm writing. You're always writing. What do you know? You're too young to write. (I admit that I very often look even younger than I am.) And I *will* get out. In some months I will be living in London. You shall call every day then and show me the poetry of cooking. I shall have to get out soon or there will be no need. I'm sick and this bloody country's killing me.

He then goes on to write a few thousand words about the poems she had sent him and went for his walk. He describes this in his next letter to her:

After my last letter to you, written from the despondency of a Welsh hill cottage, I ran out of cigarettes and walked three miles to the nearest village, Llanstephan, to buy some.

It was a fool of a night. The clouds were asses' ears. The moon was plough-ing up the Towy river as if he expected it to yield a crop of stars. And the stars themselves: — hundreds of bright-eyed urchins nudging each other over a celestial joke. It is a long road to Llanstephan, bounded by trees and farmers' boys pressed amorously upon the udders of their dairymaids. But the further I walked the more lonely it became. I found the madness of the night to be a false madness, and the vast horseplay of the sky to be a vaster symbol. It was as if the night were crying, crying out the terrible explanation of itself. On all sides of me, under my feet, above my head, the symbols moved, all waiting in vain to be translated. The trees that night were like prophet's fingers. What had been a fool in the sky was the wisest cloud of all — a huge, musical ghost thumping out one, coded tune. It was a sage of a night, and made me forgive even my own foolishness.

There was, of course, no cigarette machine in Llanstephan.

His correspondence with Pamela Hansford Johnson would seem, dur-ing this sad winter, to have been almost his sole intellectual outlet apart from more mundane conversations with Bert Trick. To the girl whom he had then not met he poured out his heart and soul, or at least such parts of them as he believed suitable for her inspection. It was she who had begun it all, writing him a fan letter when his first poem appeared in *Poets' Corner* on September 3rd. Neuburg had already published several of her poems, and Dylan was clearly delighted by this first letter of appreciation from the great world. That she was both a poet and a young woman — he hoped an attractive one, and was soon reassured when she sent him the photograph he had asked for — helped enor-mously. To begin with he was shy and, characteristically, did not know how to begin or end his letters to her. His first one simply starts:

> Blaen-Cwm,
> Llangain,
> nr. Carmarthen.

Beginning this letter in the way I do removes the necessity of using the formal "madam," the stiff "Miss Johnson" (rather ambiguous but entirely unmeant) and the impudent "Pamela" (also ambiguous, also unmeant). It removes a similar obstacle in your case.

But very soon he was adopting what he must have regarded as a masterful, masculine tone. It is typical that he should have done this through poetry, or rather through his sensitive, intelligent, kind but extremely firm criticism of the poems she sent him. He might not know how to start letters to young ladies, but poems were his world, and here he was the dominant male. Although she was then a much better known poet than he, and was soon to have a book of her poems published, this literary relationship was established almost at once and lasted as long as their friendship. It surely says much for her, both as a woman and as a writer, that she accepted it without hesitation.

She had recently escaped from a youthful love-affair which had collapsed because the man had shown insufficient comprehension of her emotional requirements that were finding expression in her poems. Her life in Battersea, an office worker by day and a poet by night, was not an exciting one. Nor did Victor Neuburg and the Creative Lifers satisfy her eager and curious mind, which is presumably one reason why she wrote to Dylan in the first place. There was thus, on her part as on his, every reason to welcome the huge correspondence that passed between London and Swansea before ever they met. It is sad that her side of it has been lost. We can only be grateful that she has preserved his and that it is now in the Lockwood Memorial Library of New York University in Buffalo. Seldom can there have been such literate pen-pals, and seldom had a poet on the very threshold of his career written as much about what he was and how he lived and what he hoped to do. In late 1933 he wrote to her:

Swansea.

Night and Day: a Provincial Rhythm.

At half past nine there is a slight stirring in the Thomas body, an eyelid quivers, a limb trembles. At a quarter to ten or thereabouts, breakfast, consisting of an apple, an orange, and a banana, is brought to the side of the bed and left there along with the Daily Telegraph. Some five minutes later the body raises itself, looks blindly around it, and, stretching out a weak arm, lifts the apple to its mouth. Waking is achieved between bites, and, over the now more or less clear scrutiny of the fruit, the webs of the past night's dreams are remembered and disentangled. Then, still weakly but with increasing certainty of touch, the banana is peeled and the newspaper opened. At the last bite I have taken complete possession of the Thomas body, and read the criminal court cases on page three with great concentration. The orange, incidentally, is never touched until I get downstairs, the process of peeling and pipping being too cold for such an hour of the morning. When the reports of rapes, frauds, and murders have been thoroughly digested, I light a cigarette, very slowly lay my head back on the pillow, and then, without any warning, leap suddenly out of bed, tear off my pyjamas, scramble into a vest and trousers, and run, as if the fiends of winter were at my heels, into the bathroom. There, holding the cigarette, I scrape the beard from my face and dab about with a futile sponge. And then downstairs where, after another cigarette, I seat myself in front of the fire and commence to read, to read anything that is near, poetry or prose, translations out of the Greek or the Film Pictorial, a new novel from Smith's, a new book of criticism, or an old favourite like Grimm or George Herbert, anything in the world so long as it is printed. I read on until twelve or thereabouts, when perhaps I have read a quarter of a novel, a couple of poems, a short story, an article on the keeping of bees in upper Silesia, and a review by somebody I have never heard of on a play I never want to see. Then down the hill into the Uplands — a lowland collection of crossroads and shops, for one (or perhaps two) pints of beer in the Uplands Hotel. Then home for lunch. After lunch, I retire again to the fire where perhaps I shall read all afternoon — and read a great deal of everything, or continue on a poem or a story I have left unfinished, or to start another or to start drafting another, or to add a note to a letter to you, or to type something already completed, or merely to write — to write anything, just to let the words and ideas, the half-remembered half-forgotten images, tumble on the sheets of paper. Or perhaps I go out, spend the afternoon in walking alone over the very desolate Gower cliffs, communing with the cold and the quietness. I call this taking my devils for an airing. This takes me to tea-time. After tea I read or write again, as haphazardly as before, until six o'clock. I then go to Mumbles (remember the woman of Mumbles Head) a rather nice village, despite its name, right on the edge of the sea. First I call at the Marine, then the Antelope, and then the Mermaid. If there is a rehearsal I leave there at eight o'clock and find my way to the Little Theatre, conveniently situated between the Mermaid and the Antelope. If there is no rehearsal, I continue to commune with these two legendary creatures, and, more often than not, to conduct metaphysical arguments with a Chestertonian toper (last night it was "Existence or Being") who apparently makes a good living out of designing scanty and dirty costumes for provincial revues. Then a three mile walk home to supper and perhaps more reading, to bed and certainly more writing. Thus drifts an average day. Not a very British day. Too much thinkin', too much talkin', too much alcohol.

The basic patterns of our lives are set at an early stage. This was to remain his: mooning about in the morning, writing in the afternoon, drinking and talking or writing at night. Later, though, he gave up writing at night; once he had left Swansea his evenings became more complicated and, besides, he soon realized that there is no purpose in a writer's trying to do any serious work if he has been drinking.

Early in November he was unwell, suffering from insomnia probably introduced by hypertension. On the 11th he wrote to Pamela Hansford Johnson:

In my untidy bedroom, surrounded with books and papers, full of the un-healthy smell of very bad tobacco, I sit and write. There is a beautiful winter sun outside, and by my side the oil-stove shines like a parhelion. On the wall immediately in front of me hangs my pastel drawing of the Two Brothers of Death; one is a syphilitic Christ, the other a greenbearded Moses. Both have skin the colour of figs, and walk, for want of a better place, on a horizontal ladder of moons. The hot water pipes are swearing at me, and, despite the nearness of the stove, my tiny hands are frozen.

Last night I slept for the first time this month; today I am writing a poem in praise of sleep and veronal that stained the ravelled sleeve. These twelve November nights have been twelve long centuries to me. Minute by minute through the eight hours of the dark I lay and looked up into the empty corners of this room. First I would seize upon some tiny thought, hug it close to me, turn it over and over in my brain, hoping, by such concentration, to find my senses dropping away into oblivion. But soon my lips would speak sentences aloud, and I listen to them.

"The man of substance never walks." Then my lips say, "He only wheels a truck," and, a thousand years later, I understand what I have spoken. Then I would repeat all the poetry I knew, but if I forgot a word I could never think of another to put in its place unless it was a mad word and had no meaning. Then I would hear my heart beat, and count its beats, and hear their regularity.

And now, thanks to the God who looked with benevolent eye upon the antics of Lot's daughters, I have slept. Now I can reply to your letter and do my dance around your poems.

What in fact was the matter with him? Here we are once again and reluctantly in the realms of medical speculation. Let me present such "facts" as exist, with the reminder that these derive in part from his own letters, and therefore from himself.

First of all, in a letter to Pamela Hansford Johnson which is lost he must have spoken of a doctor who had told him that he only had four years to live. That lost letter probably immediately preceded the one dated November 11, 1933, in which he wrote:

Four years, my sweet, 1340 days and nights. And thank you for the optimistic remarks. I don't believe it either, but then it would be very odd if I did. You should hear me cough, though — a most pleasing sound, exactly like a sea-lion peeved. No, I don't think consumption has very much effect on what I write.

In a later letter he speaks again of "that damned, diabetic doctor" who told him that he had only four years to live. Now 1340 days from November 11, 1933, is, allowing for leap-year, July 17, 1937. If this figure was not written down at random, therefore, the awful warning must have been given to him in July of 1933. But as we have already seen he was then writing cheerfully to Trevor Hughes about his forth-coming visit to his sister and to London. He saw a lot of Trevor Hughes in London that August. And Trevor Hughes has assured me that at no time when he was seeing Dylan did Dylan either show any symptoms of TB or talk about having had it. If Dylan really did have TB the fact that his close friend knew so much about it would surely have given him every inducement to talk about his malady. On the other hand if Dylan was only play-acting, then the one person with whom he would not wish to discuss his imaginary malady would be Trevor Hughes.

Furthermore, Mrs. Wyn Henderson remembers that in 1936 or 1937 he showed her some X-rays that had just been taken of his lungs, and she remembers his delight that these showed no trace of TB. Then, in 1946, when he was hospitalized with alcoholic gastritis and in a state of nervous hypertension, his lungs were again X-rayed, and the file on him in St. Stephen's Hospital shows that again the results were negative. Finally the fact that his lungs showed no trace of scars at the time of his death is further very strong evidence that he never had TB at all, even as a child; this, of course, does not mean that he did not have weak lungs. He did. Indeed he may have believed, and his parents too may have believed, that he had had TB as a little boy. The disease was, after all, much more common in those days than it is today; it was endemic in many urban areas. This was a time when X-ray facilities were not read-ily available, and antibiotics had yet to be discovered. Diagnosis and treatment — and hence the isolation of those affected — were more dif-ficult. Inevitably in such circumstances false diagnoses occurred. In Dylan's case, with his tendency to bronchitis and his habitual asthma, such a medical error is comprehensible. Even so, it is incredible that any doctor would have told Dylan in 1933 that this disease would kill him in four years. The course of TB is highly unpredictable; surely no doc-tor would have committed himself to so cruel and irresponsible a prophecy?

So what, if anything, was he told — and when? In January of 1934 he wrote to Trevor Hughes:

Now I understand a little, but only a little, of the circumstance that has played so hard with you, and if it has not swallowed me it is because of my self-centredness, my islandic egoism that allows few of the day's waves to touch me. Soon after I left you, my father went to the University College Hospital to be operated upon for cancer of the throat; today he went back to school, weak and uncured. And only a little while ago I learnt the truth of my own health. But the statement of Dad's disease and the warning of mine have left me horribly unmoved. I become a greater introvert day by day, though, day by day again, I am conscious of more external wonders in the world.

He had not then written to Trevor Hughes since the previous October, on the 10th to be precise. This had been a cheerful letter, full of his plans to revive the *Prose and Verse* idea with Bert Trick handling the administrative side while he did the editing. No mention here of sickness, let alone of death. Something then had happened between October and January, but for reasons of his own in writing to Pamela Hansford Johnson, Dylan had antedated this something to the previous July and had decided to "dignify" it with the poetic name of consumption. (This is assuming that the figure 1340 is not purely fortuitous: but it is far easier casually to let drop that one was condemned to an early death some time ago than to give an account of sentence being pronounced yesterday, an account that must be detailed to be convincing.)

Assuming, then, that he was sick early in November, the next question that arises is: what was wrong with him? He was certainly, as we have seen, healthy enough a few weeks before to walk six miles in the middle of the night in search of cigarettes. When he speaks of "that damned, diabetic doctor," he may be transposing the adjective. The doctor — if such a doctor existed, and the reference to valerian indicates that he had seen one and been given a prescription — may have told him that he, Dylan, had diabetes. His craving for sweets, to which I referred in the previous chapter, and his passion for beer provide some very vague evidence for such a hypothesis. And had he been diabetic this would not have been revealed in his autopsy; it would also have been sufficient reason for his rejection for military service in 1940. On the other hand the report from St. Stephen's Hospital in 1946 shows that a urine test was made. He was not diabetic then. Furthermore I find it hard to believe, had he been, that he would never have mentioned it to me nor, so far as I am aware, to anybody else.

It is possible, of course, that he regarded diabetes as somehow shameful, and certainly as less glamorous than consumption. But in that case, why mention it at all?

My guess — and the reader must accept or reject it on the evidence that has been given, for there is no other — is that Dylan was extremely worried and unhappy on his return from London, that he had been drinking and smoking too much, and that he had a minor nervous breakdown, to use a phrase current at the time, perhaps combined with an attack of gastritis, or bronchitis, or both. (Ten years later, talking about a friend who was alleged to have a "nervous breakdown," I asked Dylan what exactly that phrase meant. He replied: "Constantine, it is the way we feel always.") His mother called in a doctor, to whom Dylan explained, as he later explained to the doctor at St. Stephen's, that he drank in order to sleep. The doctor then prescribed valerian and, mistaking the symptom for the cause, told the boy that if he continued to drink and smoke at that rate he would be dead within four years. Perhaps the doctor added a little homily, hardly out of place in Swansea thirty years ago, about self-control; perhaps the doctor told the boy that he himself was diabetic and had therefore had to renounce sweets.

If this is the explanation, it leads only to a further question: why was Dylan so worried and unhappy in the autumn of 1933? Here it is possible to be slightly less speculative. In the first place there was his father's cancer. Dylan, as I hope I have shown, was always remarkably dependent on his father; his father's death was to be the event that probably upset him most in all his short life; and it is perhaps significant that he died less than a year after his father's death. In his letters he complains sometimes about his mother, never about his father. Now, in 1933, his father had cancer, and it is not hard to imagine how that dread word reverberated through Cwmdonkin Drive, nor the effect on Dylan of knowing that the crab was torturing his own father, probably to death. His claim, in the letter quoted to Trevor Hughes, that he felt nothing may have seemed to Dylan to be the truth; it would be a very natural defence mechanism on the part of one who was in fact feeling too much.

Secondly there was the frustration, in every sense and not the least sexual, of his own young life. There was a cruel Struwwelpeter myth then current that masturbation drives boys mad. Dylan must have heard this, would have had no reason to disbelieve it — particularly when one remembers the world of the fantastic in which, as a writer, he was then living — and he once years later told John Davenport that he had engaged in that practice all his life and to excess.

Thirdly, and perhaps most important of all, his own real work seemed to him then at best unappreciated, at worst a failure. Not only were all the brave new plans for *Prose and Verse* petering out admidst the apathy of the Swansea bourgeoisie (in January he told Trevor Hughes that it was once again dead) but his own poems were not being received as he had hoped they might be, after his London visit. Meanwhile Pamela Hansford Johnson, whom he quite rightly considered his inferior as a poet, was late in October awarded the *Sunday Referee's* big prize, which meant that her poems would be published in book form. Though Dylan wrote her a charming letter of congratulation, it is easy to sense the underlying jealousy.

Since September he had had one poem, and one poem only, *The force that through the green fuse drives the flower*, accepted for publication, and that by the *Sunday Referee*. His letters to Pamela Hansford Johnson show that he despised *Poets' Corner*, all the more when they chose her poems for the big prize rather than his own. His hopes had been pinned on Sir Richard Rees and the *Adelphi*, but now he received a rebuff from that quarter too and one which, to a boy as uncertain of his intellectual equipment as was Dylan, was particularly painful. This was almost certainly accompanied by the return of some of his poems. The pain it caused him is shown in two letters. To Pamela Hansford Johnson he wrote, on November 11th:

I received a rather disquieting note from Richard Rees of the Adelphi, who, last week, asked me to send him some recent poems. He compliments me upon the high standard and great originality exhibited, and said my technique was amazing (One Up for Formal Me), but accused me — not quite in so many words — of being in the grip of devils. "The poems have an unsubstantiality, a dream-like quality," he writes, "which non-plussed me." He then goes on to say that the poems, as a whole, reminded him of automatic or trance-writing.

Automatic writing is worthless as literature, however interesting it may be to the psychologist and pathologist. So, perhaps, after all I am nothing but a literary oddity, a little freak of nature whose madness runs into print rather than into ravings and illusions. It may be, too, an illusion that keeps me writing, the illusion of myself as some misunderstood poet of talent. The note has depressed me more than the usual adverse criticism. It shows not dislike, or mere incomprehension, but confession of bewilderment, and almost fear, at the method by which I write my poetry.

But he is wrong, I swear it. My facility, as he calls it, is in reality tremendously hard work. I write at the speed of two lines an hour. I have written hundreds of poems, and each one has taken me a great many painful, brain-racking and sweaty hours.

This must have hurt all the more, for it was roughly what his father, in other words, was saying to him. D.J. was proud that Dylan wrote poems, but saddened that these were poems which he could not understand. In his January letter to Trevor Hughes, Dylan was still upset by what Sir Richard Rees had written:

No, the great Eliot has not damned me, but he has been cautious. Rees, on the other hand, though printing two poems of mine and taking a peculiar interest in all I write, has made one very startling accusation: that much of what I write is not written consciously, that any talent I may have is clairvoyant, and my fecundity is accounted for by "automatic writing." Charles Williams of the Oxford University Press, and author, as you know, of several mystic books, has read many of my poems but confesses that he does not understand them. And so we go on, meeting nothing but courtesy and interest, and nothing but a rather bewildered refusal to print.

It was failure, it was the Grammar School exams all over again, and since sickness, real or more usually feigned, had provided the refuge then, so sickness was again to be the hiding place. But now it must be on a larger scale, as suited London editors rather than Swansea ushers. It had to fit his self-created character, which was that of the doomed, damned and dissolute poet. It had to be TB. Pamela Hansford Johnson has told me of his delight, in the following year, when he managed to cough up a minute speck of blood into his handkerchief. And Rayner Heppenstall in his *Four Absentees* has described setting off to a pub with him, on the morning of February 12, 1936.

As we went out into the cold Dylan began to cough and spit. He looked down at his spittle in the roadway and said: "Blood, boy! That's the stuff."

How much of this was conscious trickery and how much subconscious response to a hostile environment is irrelevant, since the two are inextricably intermixed. Furthermore, how much did he believe in his own TB? I suspect that he half persuaded himself that he had this sickness, and that his relief to find, from the X-rays that Wyn Henderson saw, that he had not was partly true pleasure at being pronounced healthy, partly relief that he could now drop a pose that had become wearisome. Besides, it had not worked. Competent actor though he was, nobody, so far as I can make out, who knew him at all well believed for long in his TB. He himself, being a man of the most extreme sensitivity, must have realized this quickly enough once he had come to live in London. He also found that the coughing poet was as out of date as cloaks and beards and broad-brimmed hats. And he soon discovered that a more effective defence mechanism and, when need be, a more powerful deterrent was provided by alcohol. All the same he never entirely scrapped the TB legend. He used it on occasion in America, and Mrs. Ivy Williams, the proprietress of Brown's Hotel in Laugharne, believes to this day that "he only had one lung."

He seems to have recovered quite rapidly from what I take to be his nervous breakdown in November. Within a month or two he was writing cheerfully to Pamela Hansford Johnson:

But enough of this. It sounds, and is not, an alcoholic remorse, the self-pity of gin, the result of constipation. Let me talk to you of rats, or rather of *a* rat with whom I have become acquainted. I was sitting in the porch of the Pwlldue Inn on a cold, sunny afternoon, eating an unnaturally large sandwich and sipping at a quart mug — both sandwich and mug were almost as large as me. In the midst of my meal I heard a loud stamping (that is the only honest word to describe it), and looking up, saw a rat standing immediately in front of me, his eyes fixed on mine. A rat? This was a rat with a capital R, a vast iron-grey animal as big as a big cat, with long, drooping white whiskers and a tail like an old frayed whip. Normally I am frightened to death by rats, even by mice, and certainly by moths, but this monstrosity of a creature did not alarm me at all. He couldn't move quickly anyway, he was much too fat. He merely stood there in front of me until I threw him a piece of cheese. He sniffed it, swallowed it, and stamped away. Again "stamped" is the only word: he went away like a fat old soldier from a canteen. Thinking of him when he had gone, I came to the conclusion that he must be the Father of all Rats, the First Rat, the Rat Progenitive, the Rat Divine.

He had sent her Robert Graves's poems for Christmas and when, in late February of 1934, he made what I take to be his second visit to London, he stayed with her and her mother at their house in Battersea. He had written to her:

I shall be coming up to stay with my sister during the next few weeks, but the sister is merely an excuse. There are only two reasons for my visit: one is to see you, and the other is to look for a job. I have suddenly decided that I must earn money. If not I shall very soon be on the streets. I am going to look for a job in a publisher's office, though God knows what I have to offer any publisher in return for a living wage.

I hope I won't cut my throat before this reaches you. If I do cut it, I shall start with a neat saw at the side and cut through and through till my head is hanging down my back.

He arrived at Battersea Rise, nervous and shy, on February 23, 1934, for a long weekend, straight from the train. As her diary shows, she was already half in love with him, or at least prepared to fall in love, and she therefore remembered his arrival vividly, twenty years later, when she wrote in the Dylan Thomas Memorial number of *Adam:*

He was nineteen, I was twenty-one. He arrived very late on a dull grey evening in spring, and he was nervous as I was. "It's nice to meet you after all those letters. Have you seen the Gauguins?" (He told me later that he had been preparing the remark about the Gauguins all the way from Swansea, and having made it, felt that his responsibility towards a cultural atmosphere was discharged.)

He was very small and light. Under a raincoat with bulging pockets, one of which contained a quarter bottle of brandy, another a crumpled mass of poems and stories, he wore a grey, polo-necked sweater, and a pair of very small trousers that still looked much too big on him. He had the body of a boy of fourteen. When he took off the pork-pie hat (which, he also told me later, was what he had decided poets wore), he revealed a large and remarkable head, not shaggy — for he was visiting — but heavy with hair the dull gold of threepenny bits springing in deep waves and curls from a precise middle parting. His brow was very broad, not very high: his eyes, the colour and opacity of caramels when he was solemn, the colour and transparency of sherry when he was lively, were large and fine, the lower rims rather heavily pigmented. His nose was a blob; his thick lips had a chapped appearance; a fleck of cigarette paper was stuck to the lower one. His chin was small, and the disparity between the breadth of the lower and upper parts of his face gave an impression at the same time comic and beautiful. He looked like a brilliant, audacious child, and at once my family loved and fussed over him as if he were one.

He stayed with us for a week or so on that occasion, for six weeks on the second, and for varying periods over a year or more. Gauguin wore off quickly. We walked over the Common on summer evenings to a little pub in Clapham Old Town, sometimes we took the bus to Chelsea — which seemed to us a cultural Mecca — and sat in the garden of the Six Bells, watching the little fountain drop on to its muddy stones, the men playing on the bowling green, which was still there in those days. I read his poems, and criticized them with a kind of bold reverence; he read mine and criticized them by ridicule which was hilariously funny and also perfectly just. Sometimes we wrote doggerel poems together, in alternate lines.

That first long weekend was, from her point of view, a success, as her diary shows. They went to the theatre, to see Sean O'Casey's *Within the Gates;* Victor Neuburg and Runia Tharpe came in one evening; but above all they talked, till one, till one-fifteen, on one occasion till almost three. By day he visited editors and publishers, and he also travelled to the country to see his sister. But in the matter of his search for a job, and for outlets for his work, the visit was not particularly successful. On Monday, March 5th, he returned home. Her diary entry for that day reads:

Thought I'd have lunch with Dylan but he couldn't manage it. Saw him after work — he'd sold 3 poems & 3 stories but had no job offers that suited him so after ½ an hour of supreme depression, I saw him off to Wales on the 5.55.

Three days later she received a letter from him telling her that he loved her, which took her by surprise.

Back in Swansea his life seemed, at first, to continue exactly as before. He was rehearsing at the Little Theatre for *Martine,* the play in which, in fact, he never appeared. He and Bert Trick were still tinkering with the idea of *Prose and Verse,* though now it was no longer to be a periodical but "an anthology of English poems and stories written by contemporary Welshmen." He wrote two or three poems that month, including *Where once the waters of your face* and *Our eunuch dreams,* and a short story which he sent to Pamela to type for him. And in the covering letter he complained that he had been feeling "too ill . . . to do anything but sit fatalistically by the fire, sip tobacco out of a most exotic Turkish pipe, and scribble small conceits on the backs of postcards." And round and round in his head went the problem of how he could escape from Swansea; since his literary talents had failed to find him a job in London, it was then that he contemplated becoming a professional actor with the Coventry Repertory Company.

Glyn Jones, the poet and novelist, wrote to him early in March from Cardiff having admired a poem called *The Woman Speaks,* which the *Adelphi* had just published. A correspondence began, which became a friendship. And in the middle of the month Dylan described his present condition as follows:

I am in my very early twenties. I was self-educated at the local Grammar School where I did no work at all and failed all examinations. I did not go to a university. I am not unemployed for the reason that I have never been employed. I have done nothing but write, though it is only recently that I have tried to have some things published. I have had two poems in the Adelphi, several in the Sunday Referee (a paper you should take), some stories & poems (there is one story in this week's issue of the New English Weekly, some poems in the Listener, (I have a very obscure one in this week's, too), many things in an atrocious rag called the "Herald of Wales," a poem in John O' London's, while the Adelphi, the New English Weekly & other papers including, I hope, the Criterion, are going to print some things in the fairly near future. And that's about all. Not a very formidable list. Oh, I forgot, a poem of mine was read over the wireless from London last year. I believe I am going to live in London soon, but as, so far at least, no-one has offered me suitable employment, living is rather an ambitious word. I will probably manage to exist, and possibly to starve. Until quite recently there had been no need for me to do anything but sit, read and write (I have written a great deal, by the way), and now it is essential that I go out into the bleak and inhospitable world with my erotic manuscripts thrown over my shoulder in a sack. If you know any kind people who want a clean young man with a fairly extensive knowledge of morbid literature, a ready pen, and no responsibilities, do let me know. Oh, would the days of literary Patronage were back again!

(This letter contains several obvious inaccuracies. He was nineteen and not in his early twenties; he had had a job; and he exaggerates the amount he has had published — for instance the poem then appearing in the *Listener* was his first to appear in that periodical, and very nearly his last. But then he was, after all, asking his unknown correspondent to find him a job.)

A more influential poet than Glyn Jones had also been reading Dylan's poems, and he too now wrote to him. This was Stephen Spender, who also spoke of him to Geoffrey Grigson and to T. S. Eliot with the result that Dylan once again sent poems to *New Verse* and to the *Criterion*. Spender did more: he said that he would try to get Dylan some reviewing to do, so that he might earn a little money, for Dylan had written to him: "The fact that I am unemployed helps . . . to add to my natural hatred of Wales."

Dylan was, in fact, beginning to be known. The circle that then knew his name might be a very small one indeed, but in the world of poetry it was the most important. And the publicity of a minor scandal helped.

The poem which the *Listener* published on March 14th was *Light breaks where no sun shines,* a poem about conception. The first two lines of the second verse are:

> A candle in the thighs
> Warms youth and seed and burns the seeds of age.

The *Listener* was and is the literary organ of the BBC, and the BBC at that time was directed by Sir John Reith, now Lord Reith, who approached his duties in the highest spirit of Scottish Calvinist morality. The purity, not to say the Puritanism, of the BBC's programmes at that time was a byword, and in certain emancipated circles a laughing-stock. And now letters began to arrive at the Corporation's enormous office complaining that the BBC had published an obscene poem.

They caused consternation among the BBC's many bureaucrats. A public apology was made. Furthermore it seems that a ukase was issued: Dylan Thomas was temporarily black-listed, and well over six months passed before another poem of his was published by the *Listener.*

(I must add that I have been unable to obtain any documentary confirmation of this, but I believe it to have been the case. And for the next ten years and more the BBC showed a marked reluctance to employ this broadcaster of genius for programmes audible in England. He did do a little work for the BBC before the war. On April 21, 1937, Wynford Vaughan Thomas arranged that he do a broadcast of modern poems from Swansea. John Pudney, the poet, found Dylan in a somewhat distraught state in a public house in London only an hour or so before he was due to broadcast from Swansea. Pudney most competently took Dylan to Broadcasting House, arranged that the cables be rearranged, and the broadcast, Dylan's first, went out on time. This expensive rearrangement annoyed the BBC — nor were they pleased to discover that Dylan had broadcasted poems by American poets which were still in copyright and for which the BBC had to pay fees they had not anticipated. Dylan's friends in Swansea were equally surprised, for they had been expecting to meet Dylan after the broadcast. Only Dylan's father was proud and delighted by the beauty of Dylan's reading. During the war he did broadcast for the Overseas Service, but it was only when friends of his back from the war, such as Roy Campbell and John Arlott, obtained jobs as BBC producers that his very great talents on the air began to be used at all regularly. Since his death the

BBC has claimed him as its favourite and most favoured protégé, but it was by no means always so.)

Nothing endears a writer to English high-brows more than a charge of obscenity. Since this charge, or the complementary one of blasphemy, has been levelled by the philistines at almost every writer of genius since Hardy's time and before, it is hardly surprising that many intellectuals have come to see a causal connection. The silly little fuss in the BBC did Dylan much good.

An event even more important for his future as a poet took place during this month of March. It was decided that he would be awarded the second major *Poets' Corner* prize, which meant the publication of a volume of his poems, the costs being covered in part by the *Sunday Referee*. When it is realized how extremely hard it is for a poet to find a publisher willing to risk an almost certain loss on a first volume of poems, the value of this prize becomes apparent. It must have been personally gratifying, too, for him to have caught up, as it were, with Pamela Hansford Johnson, the only other prize-winner to date. (One more such prize was later awarded, to Mr. A. L. Basham.) On March 25th, Palm Sunday, it was announced in the *Sunday Referee* that it had been given to Dylan.

But first Mark Goulden wished to see the young poet. Indeed he has told me that so great was the virtuosity revealed in these poems that he could not help doubting whether this very young Welsh boy had in fact written them, whether they were not perhaps really the work of another man. In order to be sure that he was not the victim of a hoax he arranged to pay Dylan's fare to London, and put him up for the night at the Strand Palace Hotel. This was probably Good Friday, and since the staff of a Sunday paper would be working on Saturday, it is most likely on that day that the confrontation took place. It was, Mr. Goulden has told me, almost an interrogation, with himself, his literary editor, Hayter Preston, and Victor Neuburg on one side of the table, Dylan on the other.

Dylan was extremely shy, as anyone in those circumstances might well be, but he quite quickly convinced Mr. Goulden that he was the author of the poems. When Goulden asked him how he wrote such remarkable poetry, he replied:

"It just flows."

The editor was satisfied, the award confirmed. Mr. Goulden believes that a cheque was handed over, though I suspect that this may be an error of memory. If there was a cheque, it was certainly a very small one. And then Dylan went off to spent Easter with Pamela and her mother.

It must have been a very happy Easter, too. Nothing is sweeter to a writer than recognition, and none so sweet as the first. He still had no job and no idea of how he would live when at last he should have succeeded in escaping from Swansea and his childhood. But at the age of nineteen such problems are relatively unimportant compared to the knowledge that a book of one's own poems is to be published within the year. It is not hard to guess how he felt in the big red bus that carried him through Chelsea towards Battersea, and his girl, and, he must surely have thought, fame.

6

※ ※

During the summer and autumn of 1934 Dylan was still living in Swansea, though he paid several visits to London. After winning the *Sunday Referee* prize he returned home on April 9th and set about preparing a volume of poems for publication. These poems came out of his old notebooks — though they were not old in those days — and he usually worked them over and partly or totally rewrote them, always in the direction of greater density and complexity. This meant putting aside a novel he had begun — "my novel about the Jarvis valley" — which was in fact a series of loosely connected stories, macabre and sombre, with a Welsh rural setting.

He was up again, with his typescript, on June 12th, and he stayed with Pamela Hansford Johnson and then with Trevor Hughes, who was now living out at Harrow, for a little over a fortnight in all. Back in Swansea throughout July, where he played some village cricket, he returned to London on August 10th and remained till September 15th. Then he took Pamela and her mother down to Swansea for a fortnight. He stayed on there for another month until, in early November, he and Fred Janes moved to London, to a room that Janes had rented off the Fulham Road, in that part of southwest London where Chelsea and Fulham and Kensington meet.

He was lonely in Swansea, when he got back there in April, and he missed Pamela. On April 15th he wrote to her:

I read over what I wrote this morning. All is silly, but why should I cross it out or throw it away. It's just a little more me for you to grapple with. Which sounds even more conceited than many of the other things I've put in my letters to you. I've often wondered — I thought of asking you, but am always so vastly happy with you that I don't like intruding morbid and egotistic subjects — whether you think me as conceited a little young man as I often think you must do. I'm not really; profoundly the other way. But I've noticed that when, for example, you — quite honestly and often misguidedly — run down your poetry, I never retaliate, as every true-blue poet should, by saying how very unsuccessful my own poetry is, too. I never say it, but not because I don't think it. I know it. And when you say, of a poem of mine, "That's bad," and I try to argue and show you how good it really is — that, too, must sound conceit. Darling, it isn't. I'd hate you to think that I was at all self-contented, self-centred, self-satisfied in regard to — well, only one little thing, the things I write. Because I'm not. And not half as brave, dogmatic and collected in the company of literary persons as I might have led you to believe.

It was almost certainly due to her wholesome influence that he was trying at this time to give up smoking, to drink only in moderation and generally to improve his health. On the 25th of April he wrote to her:

No, I haven't been doing anything I shouldn't. I have smoked only two cigarettes since I last saw you. You can't — yes you can — realize how terrible it has been to give them up. I've chain-smoked for nearly five years; which must have done me a lot of good. I am allowed a pipe — mild tobacco, not too much. That keeps me alive, though I hate it like hell. I take walks in the morning and pretend there's a sun in these disappointed skies. I even go without a coat (sometimes) in this cold weather, and tread bejumpered over the sheepy fields. . . . I like to be tidy-minded, but I so rarely am. Now the threads of half-remembered ideas, the fragments of half-remembered facts, blow about my head. I can write today only awkwardly and uneasily, nib akimbo. And I want to write so differently: in glowing, unaffected prose: with all the heat of my heart, or, if that is cold, with all the clear intellectual heat of the head. . . . And now I shall rise from the lovely fire, jam my hat hard and painfully on my head, and go out into the grey day. I am strong, strong as a circus horse. I am going to walk, alone and stern, over the miles of grey hills at the top of this my hill. I shall call at a public house and drink beer with Welshspeaking labourers. Then I shall walk back over the hills again, alone and stern, covering up a *devastating* melancholy and a tugging, tugging weakness with a look of fierce and even Outpost-of-the-Empire determination and a seven league stride. Strength! (And I'm damned if I want to go out at all. I want to play dischords on the piano, write silly letters or sillier verses, sit down under the piano and cry Jesus to the mice.)

In his letters to her at this time he wrote at very great length about the poems and stories she was sending him. Her volume of poems, *Symphony for Full Orchestra,* was published and he rejoiced with her at the good reviews it received, sympathized or was suitably angry when the critics were less kind. He wrote surprisingly little about his own work, though on May 2nd he reported on the progress of the book he was preparing:

Thank you for the abortive list of poems. I disagree heartily with you. "We see Rise the Secret Wind," "In Me Ten Paradoxes," "The Eye of Sleep" and "Thy Breath was Shed" are all very bad indeed. I have rewritten "The Eye of Sleep" almost entirely, and it is now a little better, though still shaky on its rhythms and very woolly as to its intentions (if any). But I know how hard it is to make any sort of comprehensive list for anyone else.

I am going to include some poems which have been printed, so "Boys of Summer," though altered and double the length, is to open the book. Other poems are:

"Light Breaks Where No Sun Shines," "Before I Knocked and Flesh Let Enter," "No Food Suffices" (revised), "When Once the Twilight Locks" (revised), "Our Eunuch Dreams," "A Process in the Weather," "The Force That Through the Green Fuse," "Where Once the Waters of Your Face," "That the Sum Sanity" (revised), "Not Forever shall the Lord of the Red Hail" (revised). And about six or seven others I am still in the process of pruning and cutting about. You say Vicky's obstinate. Well, you know I am, too. And nothing that I don't want goes in.

But it was difficult, as a letter written a week later shows:

The old, fertile days are gone, and now a poem is the hardest and most thankless act of creation. I have written a poem since my last letter, but it is so entirely obscure that I dare not let it out even unto the eyes of such a kind and commiserating world as yours. I am getting more obscure day by day. It gives me now a *physical* pain to write poetry. I feel all my muscles contract as I try to drag out, from the whirlpooling words around my everlasting ideas of the importance of death on the living, some connected words that will explain how the starry system of the dead is seen, ordered as in the grave's sky, along the orbit of a foot or a flower. But when the words do come, I pick them so thoroughly of their *live* associations that only the *death* in the words remains. And I could scream, with real, physical pain, when a line of mine is seen naked on paper and seen to be as meaningless as a Sanskrit limerick. I shall never be understood. I think I shall send no more poetry away, but write stories alone. All day yesterday I was working, as hard as a navvy, on six lines of a poem. I finished them, but had, in the labour of them, picked and cleaned them so much that nothing but their barbaric sounds remained. Or if I did write a line, "My dead upon the orbit of a rose," I saw that "dead" did not mean "dead," "orbit" not "orbit" and "rose" most certainly not "rose." Even "upon" was a syllable too many, lengthened for the inhibited reason of rhythm. My lines, *all* my lines, are of the tenth intensity. They are not the words that express what I want to express; they are the only words I can find that come near to expressing a half. And that's no good. I'm a freak user of words, not a poet. That's really the truth. No self-pity there. A freak *user* of words, not a poet. That's terribly true.

There are passages even in Dylan's earliest letters that are disingenuous or intended to surprise, but this one seems to me a true *cri du coeur*, and a very revealing one indeed. What he was trying to express in his poems was a view of the world for which the English language failed to provide the words, let alone the syntax. (Would the Welsh language, one wonders, have proved a more suitable medium? Vernon Watkins believes that the strict *cynghanedd* rules of Welsh verse would have cramped him.) Yet he was determined to achieve the near-impossible, and he forced himself as he forced the words. At the same time James Joyce was doing much the same with the work in progress that became *Finnegans Wake*. For both it was grinding, lonely work, with hopelessness never far away. And at the end of the day's work, a few lines written, what then? A few days after writing the passage above Dylan had, or said he had, a weird and unpleasant experience:

Last night, in the deserted smokeroom of a seaside pub, I found myself suddenly cornered by three repulsive looking young men with coloured shirts, who asked me, in a most polite and Turpin way, for my cigarettes. Since they all looked *exactly* like Wallace Beery in one of his less debonair moments, I gave them my cigarettes and enough money to buy three pints of beer. They then smiled — or rather showed me about ten (or less) broken teeth (between them) — and persisted in drinking their illgotten beer in front of me and making rude remarks about the length of my hair. Now, I don't mind communist ideas, or even the practice of them. But why *my* cigarettes, *my* beer, and *my* funny hair? It's little incidents like that that make one feel very weak and small in a country full of strong barbarians. Before they left me — probably to intimidate another lonely little person — they told me what was apparently a dirty story in Welsh. That was the last straw, and later the sun went out.

So the picture that emerges from the letters he was then writing to Pamela Hansford Johnson is of a young poet working extremely hard and trying to improve his health by not drinking or smoking too much. He was, of course, writing to a girl on whom he was most anxious to make a good impression and who was, as he knew, not at all impressed by his "poetical" *âme damnée* pose of which, indeed, he was himself beginning to weary. This picture is confirmed by Glyn Jones who was, and is, a most sober man with profound religious convictions and acute powers of observation. Here is his description of Dylan at that time, as published in the *Western Mail* in 1960:

In 1934, when I saw him for the first time, there was something angelic about him, angelic and endearing. He was very slim and rather small — above medium height for Wales, he himself said — five-feet six-and-a-half.

The proportions of his head were not unlike those of Swinburne, i.e. all the development was in the brow and the chin was meagre. He had fair, wavy hair parted in the middle and large, wide-open brown eyes, the irises not quite touching the lower lids.

He was pale, almost girlish in appearance, but he gave the impression of some inner toughness, so that one could not think of him as delicate, much less fragile.

He was wearing that intellectual get-up made familiar, but not invented, by Mr. Colin Wilson, namely a black polo-neck sweater and shabby grey trousers.

In "Portrait of the Artist as a Young Dog" Dylan describes, with his customary self-deflation, the room in his parents' house where his early writing was done — the bedroom with the hot-water tank in the corner and pictures of the poets around the walls torn from his father's "Bookman."

But Dylan was 19 when I met him, and that first afternoon together we spent in the room referred to in "Especially when the October wind," the suburban parlour described as the "tower of words" with "behind the pot of ferns the wagging clock" and "the rows of star-gestured children in the park" close by.

His conversation I found to be self-disparaging, iconoclastic, quick-witted, delightful. But even more than by his conversation I was struck by his extreme awareness, his sensitiveness and response to every subtle change of mood and direction in our talk.

I had never met anyone with comparable gifts who possessed comparable charm, and I soon felt strongly that warm sympathetic flow of which several of Dylan's friends have written.

We talked mostly about poetry and prose — about short stories, that is — which seemed to interest Dylan very much indeed. And after that conversational probing in which new acquaintances have to indulge we found, I believe to the satisfaction of both of us, that our families had their origin in the Llanstephan area of Carmarthenshire.

Although I knew only of Dylan's poetry then, he showed me some of his stories, and he seemed anxious to know what I thought of them. I brought away with me after that first visit the typescript copies of, among others, "The Mouse and the Woman," "The Visitors," and "The Enemies," the stories in fact which were later to appear in *The Map of Love*.

I was enchanted with these pieces at the time; they seemed new, vital, strange, the reverse side of the obverse poetry.

He had drawings to show me, too — they were all destroyed, I learnt recently, in the home of Mr. Geoffrey Grigson during the "blitz" — fantastic, highly-coloured pastels which might have served as illustrations for the more esoteric passages of his prose. Poems, stories and pictures all obviously came out of one and the same world.

The two young friends went off to Laugharne for the weekend of Whitsun, which that year fell on May 20th. There was a ferry in those days across the estuary that separates Llanstephan from Laugharne, and Dylan must frequently have visited the town in which he was to spend so much of his short life and with which his name has become so closely linked. This letter that follows, which Pamela Hansford Johnson described in her diary as "a darkling letter from a dreary Dylan," is his own description of that town as he saw it on the occasion of this visit.

I am spending Whitsun in the strangest town in Wales. Laugharne, with a population of four hundred, has a townhall, a castle, and a portreeve. The people speak with a broad English accent, although on all sides they are surrounded by hundreds of miles of Welsh country. The neutral sea lies at the foot of the town, and Richard Hughes writes his cosmopolitan stories in the castle.

I am staying with Glyn Gower Jones. . . . He is a nice, handsome young man with no vices. He neither smokes, drinks, nor whores. He looks very nastily at me down his aristocratic nose if I have more than one guinness at lunch, and is very suspicious when I go out by myself. I believe he thinks I sit on Mr. Hughes's castle walls with a bottle of rye whisky, or revel in the sweet confusion of a broad-flanked fisherwoman. . . . I seem always to be complaining that I cannot fit the mood of my letters into the mood of the weathered world that surrounds me. Today I complain again for a hell-mouthed mist is blowing over the Laugharne ferry, and the clouds lie over the chiming sky — what a conceit — like the dustsheets over a piano. Let me, o oracle in the lead of the pencil, drop this customary clowning, and sprinkle some sweetheart words over the paper (paper torn slyly from an exercise book of the landlady's small daughter). Wishes, always wishes. Never a fulfilment of action, flesh. The consummation of dreams is a poor substitute for the breathlessness at the end of the proper windy gallop, bedriding, musical flight into the Welsh heavens after a little, discordant brooding over the national dungtip.

My novel of the Jarvis valley is slower than ever. I have already scrapped two chapters of it. It is as ambitious as the Divine Comedy, with a chorus of deadly sins, anagramatized as old gentlemen, with the incarnated figures of Love and Death, an Ulyssean page of thought from the minds of the two anagramatical spinsters, Miss P. and Miss R. Sion-Rees, an Immaculate Conception, a baldheaded girl, a celestial tramp, a mock Christ, and the Holy Ghost.

I am a Symbol Simon. My book will be full of footlights and Stylites, and puns as bad as that, kiss me Hardy? Dewy love me? Tranter a body ask? I'll Laugharne this bloody place for being wet. I'll pun so frequently and so ferociously that the rain will spring backwards on an ambiguous impulse, and the sun leap out to light the cracks of this sow world. But I won't tell you my puns, for they run over reason, and I want you to think of me today not as a bewildered little boy writing an idiot letter on the muddy edge of a ferry, watching the birds and wondering which among them is the "sinister necked" wild duck and which the terrible cormorant, but as a strong-shouldered fellow polluting the air with the smell of his eightpenny tobacco and his Harris tweeds, striding, golf-footed, over the hills and singing as loudly as Beachcomber in a world rid of Prodnose. There he goes, that imaginary figure, over the blowing mountains where the goats all look like Ramsay MacDonald, down the crags and the rat-hiding holes in the sides of the hill, on to the mud flats that go on for miles in the direction of the sea. There he stops for a loud and jocular pint, tickles the serving wench where serving wenches are always tickled, laughs with the landlord at the boatman's wit ("The wind be a rare one, he be. He blows up the petticoats of they visiting ladies for the likes of me. And a rare thirst he give you. Pray fill the flowing bowl, landlord, with another many magnums of your delectable liquor. Aye, aye, sor." And so on), and hurries on, still singing, into the mouth of the coming darkness. Or he hies him manfully to the Hikers' Hostel, removes his pimples with a bread knife, and sprinkles a little iodine over the one and forty bats that ring the changes in the Hikers' belfries.

But the eye of truth, tired of romancing, turned back with a material squint on myself, and marks the torture in my too-bony hand. . . .

I am tortured by every doubt and misgiving that an hereditarily twisted imagination, an hereditary thirst and a commercial quenching, a craving for a body not my own, a chequered education and too much egocentric poetry, and a wild, wet day in a tided town, are capable of conjuring up out of their helly deeps. . . .

I wish I could describe what I am looking on. But no words could tell you what a hopeless, fallen angel of a day it is. In the very far distance, near the line of the sky, three women and a man are gathering cockles. The oyster-catchers are protesting in hundreds around them. Quite near me, too, a crowd of silent women are scraping the damp, grey sand with the torn-off handles of jugs, and cleaning the cockles in the little drab pools of water that stare up out of the weeds and long for the sun. But you see that I am making it a literary day again. I can never do justice to the miles and miles and miles of mud and grey sand, to the un-nerving silence of the fisher-women, and the mean-souled cries of the gulls and the herons, to the shapes of the fisherwomen's breasts that droop, big as barrels, over the stained tops of their overalls as they bend over the sand, to the cows in the fields that lie north of the sea, and to the near breaking of the heart as the sun comes out for a minute from its cloud and lights up the ragged sails of a fisherman's boat. These things look ordinary enough on paper. One sees them as shapeless, literary things, and the sea is a sea of words, and the little fishing boat lies still on a tenth rate canvas. I can't give actuality to these things. Yet they are as alive as I. Each muscle in the cocklers' legs is as big as a hill, and each crude footstep in the wretchedly tinted sand is deep as hell. These women are sweating the oil of life out of the pores of their stupid bodies, and sweating away what brains they had so that their children might eat, be married and ravished, conceive in their wombs that are stamped with the herring, and, themselves, bring up another race of thick-hipped fools to sweat their strengths away on these unutterably deadly sands.

But now a piece of the sun comes out again. I am happy, or, at least, free from the morning's tortures. Glyn has gone fishing, and in another half hour the "Three Mariners" will have undone their waistcoats. I shall drink beer with the portreeve, and no crimping pussyfoot will say me nay. . . .

Oh hell to the wind as it blows these pages about. I have no Rimbaud for a book or a paper rest, but only a neat, brown rock. . . . It's getting cold, too cold to write. I haven't got a vest on, and the wind is blowing around the Bristol Channel. I agree with Buddha that the essence of life is evil. Apart from not being born at all, it is best to die young. I agree with Schopenhauer (he, in his philosophic dust, would turn with pleasure at my agreement) that life has no pattern and no purpose, but that a twisted vein of evil, like the poison in a drinker's glass, coils up from the pit to the top of the hemlocked world. Or at least I might do. But some things there are that are better than others. The tiny, scarlet ants that crawl from the holes in the rock on to my busy hand. The shapes of the rocks, carved in chaos by a tiddly sea. The three broken masts, like three nails in the breast of a wooden Messiah, that stick up in the far distance from a stranded ship. The voice of a snotty-nosed child sitting in a pool and putting shellfish in her drawers. The hundreds and hundreds of rabbits I saw last night as I lay incorrigibly romantic in a field of buttercups and wrote of death. The jawbone of a sheep that I wish would fit into my pocket. The tiny lives that go slowly and languidly on in the cold pools near my hand. The brown worms in beer. All these, like Rupert Brooke, I love because they remind me of you. Yes, even the red ants, the dead jawbone and the hapless chemical. Even the rabbits, buttercups, and nailing masts. Soon I see you. Write by the end of this week. Darling, I love you. xx

Was it overwork, boredom, frustration of every sort, loneliness, or a combination of these and perhaps of other, darker, forces that had led him into this frame of mind? His reaction in the days that followed was characteristic of him, and by no means unknown in others when in such a frame of mind. His next letter to Pamela Hansford Johnson is not written in his usual small, neat hand with the letters sloping backwards — the hand that so closely resembled Emily Brontë's that when Lawrence Durrell, noticing the resemblance, sent him a photograph of a manuscript poem of hers, Dylan at first glance thought it was a manuscript of his, returned by a magazine. No, the next letter is a most untidy scrawl, the lines wandering up and down, the product of a hand as shaky as the heart was distraught. It is dated only Cwmdonkin Drive, Sunday morning, bed. I take it to have been written and posted on May 27th, and there is corroboration for this in her diary entry for May 28th, which reads: "Appallingly distressing letter from Dylan. I cried lustily nearly all day and had to write telling him it must finish. So an end to that affair."

This is the letter he had written to her:

Question One. I can't come up.
Two. I'm sleeping no better.
Three. No, I've done everything that's wrong.
Four. I daren't see the doctor.
Five. Yes, I love you.

I'm in a dreadful mess now. I can hardly hold the pencil or hold the paper. This has been coming for weeks. And the last four days have completed it. I'm absolutely at the point of breaking now. You remember how I was when I said goodbye to you for the first time. In the Kardomah when I loved you so much and was too shy to tell you. Well imagine me one hundred times worse than that with my nerves oh darling absolutely at the point of breaking into little bits. I can't think and I don't know what I'm doing. When I speak I don't know if I'm shouting or whispering and that's a terrible sign. It's *all* nerves and more. But I've never imagined anything as bad.

And it's all my own fault too. As well as I can I'll tell you the honest honest truth. I never want to lie to you. You'll be terribly angry with me I know and you'll never write to me again perhaps. But darling you want me to tell you the truth, don't you. I left Laugharne on Wednesday morning and went down to a bungalow in Gower. I drank a lot in Laugharne and was feeling a bit grim even then. I stayed in Gower with ———, who was a friend of mine in the waster days of the reporter's office. On Wednesday evening ——— his fiancée came down. And she was tall and thin and dark and a loose red mouth and later we all went out and got drunk. She tried to make love to me all the way home. I told her to shut up because she was drunk. When we got back she still tried to make love to me, wildly like an idiot in front of ———. She went to bed and ——— and I drank some more and then very modernly he decided to go and sleep with her. But as soon as he got into bed with her she screamed and ran into mine. I slept with her that night and for the next three nights. We were terribly drunk day and night. Now I can see all sorts of things. I think I've got them.

Oh darling it hurts me to tell you this but I've got to tell you because I always want to tell you the truth about me. And I never want to share. It's you and me or nobody, you and me and nobody. But I have been a bloody

[128]

fool and I'm going to bed for a week. I'm just on the borders of DTs darling and I've wasted some of my tremendous love for you on a lank redmouthed girl with a reputation like a hell. I don't love her a bit. I love you Pamela always and always. But she's a pain on the nerves. For Christ knows why she loves me. Yesterday morning she gave her ring back to ————. I've got to put a hundred miles between her and me. I must leave Wales forever and never see her. I see bits of you in her all the time and tack on to those bits. I've got to be drunk to tack on to them. I love you Pamela and must have you. As soon as all this is over I'm coming straight up. If you'll let me. No, but better or worse I'll come up next week if you'll have me. Don't be too cross or too angry. What the hell am I to do? And what the hell are you going to say to me? Darling I love you and think of you all the time. Write by return. And don't break my heart by telling me I mustn't come up to London to you because I'm such a bloody fool.

xxxx Darling. Darling oh.

I have quoted this correspondence at such length, and this tragic letter in full save for omitting the names of the man and his fiancée, because they seem to me to be intensely revealing to anyone who would understand the life and the death of Dylan Thomas.

Its first and most immediate effect was upon his relations with Pamela Hansford Johnson. Although she soon and generously forgave him, she was henceforth more cautious and, understandably enough, far more reluctant to commit herself and her love to a young man who could write to her in this fashion. It is, of course, possible that he was anxious to bring their relationship to a climax of one sort or another; that he unconsciously wished to be free of her or that he thought to force her into bed with him by showing her that if she would not come, there were others who would. But neither interpretation seems to me to be consistent either with Dylan's character or with the tone of the letters. I believe he said exactly what he meant, and that what he meant was a cry for help. But help from what?

Perhaps truly to appreciate the significance of this "Sunday, bed" letter one must look much further ahead. There is a parallel between the frame of mind which it reveals and the description of Dylan as he was during his last days in New York. In 1953, according to John Malcolm Brinnin in his *Dylan Thomas in America*, he had or thought he had DTs and he said more than once that he had seen the Gates of Hell. This letter, though, shows that he had seen them long before, at least as early as that May of 1934, on the Gower Peninsula; and these gates were guarded, like those of any good chapel-goer's hell, by a drinker's glass filled with poison and by a red-lipped woman. Were his pain not so evident, and the final outcome so lethal, it would be almost comic in its banality, this "cigarettes and whiskey and wild, wild women, they'll drive you crazy they'll drive you insane" concept of sin. And I think there can be no question of "poetical" posing in his "Sunday, bed" letter. He does not here see himself as "the Rimbaud of Cwmdonkin Drive" — or if that is what he must be, then he wishes to be saved from his fate. It is a desperate cry for help and sympathy to the woman who loves him and who therefore, like his mother in years past, will surely, somehow, come to his succour. But Pamela has assured me that "darling" was definitely not amused. Few young women would be, in the circumstances. After all, she was not even his mistress. That she forgave him, though with reservations, within a very few days is proof not only of her affection for him but also of her young self-assurance.

Augustus John, who first met him a year or so later, has written: "The truth is that Dylan was at the core a typical Welsh Puritan and Non-conformist gone wrong." This facile judgement contains its element of truth. Just as his father's "atheism" was in fact a sort of God-hatred, so the son's defiance of conventional morality implied, in its intensity, an acceptance of that morality in its crudest manifestations. Dylan expressed more than once his astonishment, even his admiration, that Augustus John could commit his multiple adulteries and what-not without a twinge of conscience, could be drunk at night and remorseless in the morning. Dylan might be a-moral about money and possessions, but not about sex and drink. He suffered, as this letter shows, paroxysms of guilt, and was to do so all his life. Caitlin Thomas, who should know if anyone does, wrote in *Leftover Life to Kill:* "Though Dylan imagined himself to be completely emancipated from his family background, there was a very strong puritanical streak in him, that his friends never suspected; but of which I got the disapproving benefit."

His friends formed the impression that his attitude towards sex at this time was purely cerebral and practically negative. Trevor Hughes has told me two anecdotes. The one took place in a Swansea pub. It was empty save for Dylan and himself and two girls obviously ready to be picked up. Dylan was quite uninterested. Later, in London, they found themselves in the Fitzroy Tavern — this was, I imagine, June or August of 1934 — and a chorus girl picked them up. Her conversation verged on the obscene, and she made it quite plain that she would like one of them, preferably Dylan, to take her to bed. Dylan's response was to fall silent and doodle, moodily. On both occasions, of course, he was sober. On the other hand one must not exaggerate the extent of his "Puritanism." Though he might write with the greatest horror about the red-lipped woman of Gower to Pamela Hansford Johnson, whom he must have felt he had betrayed, ten days later he could be as boastful as any adolescent about this same incident to Trevor Hughes: "Here I am getting older and no wiser, and have lately become entangled with an erotic girl with whom I indulge in unrepeatable displays of carnality."

Later it was to be a different tale. The first two years in London, the years before Caitlin, were "sardined with women," but all the same the basic Puritan disapproval of sex without love, perhaps even of sex without marriage, remained. Rayner Heppenstall remembers a remark of February 1936:

Dylan was uncertain where he was going to stay the night. There was my floor. There were possible beds elsewhere. There was one in a Bloomsbury square. A telephone call was made from a kiosk, and Dylan decided on a bed.

As we rolled along the Euston Road, he suddenly raised miserable eyes and said:

"Oh God, I'm so tired of sleeping with women I don't even like."

Sex minus love might equal sin, but Dylan was not the sort of spiritual masochist who enjoys the sensation of guilt. I would venture to guess that he seldom, if ever, went to bed with any woman other than Caitlin his wife except when he had been drinking — and I would even go further and suggest that this was probably true even before he met her. And when he did go to bed with girls it was companionship that he wanted at least as much as the satisfaction of lust. But of course there were many, many occasions when he had been drinking, and the incident with the red-lipped woman of Gower is the prototype of many more to come.

Why did he drink so much? I have touched earlier on possible hereditary and physiological reasons. There was also his insomnia, to which he found an answer in alcohol. But none of these provides an adequate explanation for why he became, as he boasted in America, "the drunkest man in the world." Was he an alcoholic? I have never been quite sure that I understand the meaning of that fashionable word. (Dylan himself once defined an alcoholic as "a man you don't like who drinks as much as you do.") If my understanding is correct, an alcoholic is a man who has a compulsive craving for drink which he will go to any lengths to satisfy, but who derives no pleasure from the bottle which he both hates and fears. This was certainly not true of Dylan, who all his life could and did go for weeks on end drinking only a few glasses of weak beer, which he enjoyed. If alcoholism is a psychosomatic illness, then I think one can fairly say that Dylan was not an alcoholic. I believe that true alcoholics are, in any case, as rare as true nymphomaniacs. These words get bandied about, but Dylan drank as a woman may be promiscuous, and for many of the same reasons.

Poets, indeed artists generally, are not a particularly abstemious lot. One reason for this deplorable state of affairs is the acute mental pressure that goes with the act of creation. Since an artist's basic raw material is his own personality, his own thoughts, emotions and state of mind, he cannot as easily shut away his work as, say, a lawyer can lock up his briefs for the night or a scientist can close the door of his laboratory behind him. (I am aware that some scientists are, in this respect, in precisely the same circumstances as poets.) Furthermore a good artist's sensibilities, his mental and emotional antennae, must be developed to an almost monstrous degree. (And this is hardly necessary even among the most subtle scientists, whose work is almost purely intellectual.) A "thick-skinned" poet is a bad poet. And though the converse is not necessarily true, never was there a poet with a thinner skin than Dylan's. For all of us, and regardless of skin-thicknesses, the human condition requires an occasional sedative, which is presumably why the Greeks worshipped Bacchus. There are many such escapes available, from religion to opium. But in our irreligious society the most easily available is alcohol which is also, for most people, comparatively harmless.

Having a few drinks to relax is not, of course, the same as getting drunk, though the difference is one of degree rather than of quality. Once, after the war, Dylan was complaining to John Arlott, as he often did to others, about how ill he felt all the time. Arlott asked him bluntly why he got drunk so often. To this question Dylan gave a curious reply. He said: "Because it's different every time." This can be interpreted in at least two ways. He may have meant that each time the circumstances were different; that he never intended to get drunk, but that these constantly differing circumstances led him into drunkenness, willy-nilly. Such a feeble and disingenuous excuse might be expected of some men, but hardly from Dylan and certainly not when talking to so close a friend as John Arlott. (At the beginning of one term at the Swansea Grammar School, his form-master had asked Dylan if he intended to try harder in class. After some thought Dylan replied, very slowly: "No!" That was always far more his style than the making of silly excuses.) A far more likely interpretation is that he found in drink a constantly shifting and apparently new experience and vision of the world. As Coleridge found new shapes and colours and word-combinations in laudanum, as Yeats used mystical practices to dissolve the tedious world of reality, as St. John of the Cross drew his inspiration from the dark night of the soul, as innumerable artists have been fascinated by their dreams, so Dylan found, or thought to find, new perceptions in a vision of the world distorted by alcohol. Many poets have done the same; one has only to think of Beddoes, whom Dylan admired from his earliest youth, and of Rimbaud, whose legend fascinated him. If he was making an excuse, then this was it.

Another man also once asked Dylan why he drank so much, and to him he replied, briefly: "Because they expect it of me." This was undoubtedly true of his later years, and particularly in America. It stems, of course, from that poetic persona he had created for himself in early youth. But he drank little at home, and Caitlin has explained why, in one sentence: "His home was to Dylan a private sanctum, where for once he was not compelled, by himself admittedly, to put on an act, to be amusing, to perpetuate the myth of the *Enfant Terrible:* one of the most damaging myths and a curse to grow out of." Away from home, in London when he was not living there and far more so in America, Dylan-the-actor played the part he had created for Dylan-the-poet, and as the years rolled on one of the most celebrated manifestations of that character was drunkenness. Part of Dylan-the-actor's charm and success lay in his ability to give his audience what they wanted. When they wanted him witty, he was. When they wanted him outrageous, he was that too. Increasingly they wanted him drunk.

There are other aspects to his drinking. In his early days, before the legend had been created, nobody cared much whether Dylan drank or not. In the Soho pubs of the middle 'thirties there were a great many young people who drank as much as Dylan and quite a few who drank considerably more. Dylan felt at home in those pubs and with those people. If he there acted a part it was that of the consumptive poet, not that of the hell-raising boozer or lecher, for in these fields there was altogether too much competition. However, when he found himself in what he regarded naively, and perhaps even correctly, as more "distinguished" company, he would seek defence in drink. He was, as I hope I have shown, an almost excessively timid man. He was frightened of the famous, and the more he might admire their achievements as artists, the greater his fear of their contempt. "One of these days they'll find me out," he had remarked to Randall Swingler. In his writing, as he frequently said, obscurity was a defence — "Bewilder 'em!" — and in personal contacts alcohol provided a protective shield of almost unbreakable glass. Even if "they" saw through Dylan drunk, they would not have fingered his soul. Furthermore, drink gave him the Dutch courage to face the sort of social occasions that frightened him most. Geoffrey Grigson, in his unkind way, has described such an evening.

So far as I know the first of the genius-parties at which Dylan defended himself, or tried to save his face, by being drunk, was given for him by Cyril Connolly in the King's Road in Chelsea, a reluctant, beery Dylan having been despatched, late, by Norman Cameron from a bar in the Fulham Road: he told the celebrities, whose dinner he had spoiled, dirty chestnuts they had all heard in their childhood.*

Finally there was another and altogether happier aspect of Dylan's drinking, and this was his love of company. This was the drinking that his real friends saw and shared. There can be few occupations that are lonelier than a writer's. When he is working he is entirely alone with his piece of paper and whatever his mind may produce. He lacks even the physical stimulus of the painter or sculptor, the possibility of immediate expression that is most composers'. When his day's work is done he may, if he is lucky, have a wife or a friend to whom he can show it. Caitlin has described with bitter regret how Dylan would sometimes follow her about, anxious to read her a poem just completed, while she bustled about with housework and children and sometimes could not find the

---

* This would seem to be a good example of the mythmaking, usually unconscious, that has pursued Dylan's memory. Those present at Cyril Connolly's dinner party in question included the late Robert Byron, the late Desmond McCarthy and his wife, Anthony and Lady Violet Powell and Evelyn Waugh. Mr. and Mrs. Geoffrey Grigson were not present, and his account of the evening derives from what Dylan himself told Mr. Grigson on the following day. Both Mr. Waugh and Mr. Powell assure me that this account is incorrect. The evening was a gay and relaxed one. It was not Dylan's habit to tell dirty jokes, nor did he do so on this occasion. One may assume that it was part of his *enfant terrible* pose to give this quite misleading account to Mr. Grigson on the following day.

time to listen. Trevor Hughes has told me how Dylan would meet him by appointment in the street, during that summer of 1934, and would immediately produce a poem from his pocket. With the greatest intensity he would watch his friend's face while the poem was read. And if all was well, then Dylan was happy and they would walk on to the Fitzroy; and in the very noisiness and crowd of the bar with its honky-tonk piano, they found a protection to exchange ideas they might have been too shy to utter in a silent room. But even so, even if a writer has a wife, a girl, a friend who is prepared to put up with the tedium of reading, or listening to, his day's work, most writers have doubts that nag. The real judgement can only come when the piece of paper has become a page of print and that must be weeks or months later. With the case of a poet as consciously and deliberately original as was Dylan, the verdict was not given for years, indeed has not really been given yet. His was, in its most important aspect, an intensely lonely life.

He therefore wished, when not working (and he worked in the utmost physical solitude, so that few of even his closest friends ever saw him at it), to be with people, with friends. The Kardomah in Swansea, which Charles Fisher has described to me as "our Dôme and our Rotonde in one," set the pattern. He even tried to repeat it when first in London, and Fred Janes has told me how they used to go to the Lyon's Corner House and talk over coffee. But such places, in London even more than in the provinces, are a poor substitute for Paris cafés. In the 'fifties coffee bars did something to fill this need, though I hear that they too no longer provide a suitable meeting place. In the 1930s, certainly, young people who were interested in painting or writing or, to a lesser extent, music met one another in half a dozen pubs, mostly in Soho or Chelsea, where they drank beer. The pub, for Dylan, was the place where one went when one stopped working, always. And the drink was beer. That was how our generation behaved.

Dylan soon recovered from his red-lipped remorse, and apparently from his fear of DTs too. Pamela was expecting him in London on June 5th, but he was a week late, perhaps because he was getting his health back or perhaps because he was not at all sure of the reception he could expect in Battersea. On the 6th, though, she "wrote to the darling old fishface forgiving him," and on the next day he wrote to Trevor Hughes, who was also a bachelor: "I am looking forward to the day when Mr. and Mrs. Hughes in their two-backed beast face the double-faced world. That way, perhaps, lies your salvation and mine, though I doubt whether I, personally, could remain sober and faithful for more than a week on end."

This oblique and unpromising reference to matrimony was not purely theoretical. Almost as soon as he got to London in the following week he proposed to Pamela. Her diary entry for June 14th reads: "Met darling Dylan after work and we had a coffee. Met his friend Trevor Hughes and had a drink in Denman Street and at the Fitzroy. D. and I got home about 8.15. Had lovely evening — D. pressing me to marry him but I won't — yet." Nevertheless, as her diary shows, it was a very happy week for them both: "evening too happy for words," "a lovely, lovely evening sitting in the garden of the Six Bells, arguing, laughing," "Dylan and I over to the Six Bells again sitting in the garden. Very, very lovely evening." In her eyes they were, almost, a conventionally engaged couple.

But she had not committed herself, for she was worried. She was very young and he was even younger, though this she did not then know, for he had added a couple of years to his nineteen in order to appear older than she. Sweet, enchanting and amusing as he was, his pose as a wild boy confused and at times distressed her. She has told me that on one occasion when they had spent the evening over a couple of glasses of beer in the garden at the back of the Six Bells, Dylan met someone he knew on the way out and pretended to be drunk. Even a girl of her acute intelligence and possessing, as her novels show, a perspicacity for psychology far above the average, could hardly be expected to understand the extremely complex motivation behind such behaviour. She was, quite simply, worried about Dylan and drink. And on June 22nd she confided to her diary that she and Trevor Hughes "came to a very definite understanding re forming a watch committee over Dylan."

There were to be many such watch committees in the years to come, almost always the creation of a woman who was, or thought she was, in love with Dylan. And there was no more certain way of arousing his alarm and, ultimately, his hostility. He always wanted women to look after him when he was ill, or in trouble, but not to prevent him from making himself ill or getting into trouble. Such had been the childhood pattern. And since drink was to him, among other things, a means of self-defence he could only interpret the good ladies' efforts to stop his drinking as a dangerous attack upon his freedom; and he valued his freedom above all things, for without freedom there would be no poems. Caitlin never made this mistake, which was why she was, and remained, the only woman he ever really loved. Once Pamela set about "reforming" him, their relationship was doomed. Yet who can blame her? For her, marriage to an unreformed Dylan, to Caitlin's Dylan, would have been an impossibility. She loved him, and she tried, and throughout that summer of 1934 she thought that perhaps she might succeed. But her doubts increased.

During this summer and autumn his reputation as a poet grew as more and more of his poems were published in *New Verse*, the *Criterion*, the *Adelphi* and elsewhere. He was selling his short stories, too. Charles Williams, the author who wrote theological thrillers and who, for the Oxford University Press, had rather reluctantly declined to publish a book of his poems earlier that year, now recommended that he put his affairs in the hands of Curtis Brown, the literary agency. They were there less interested in his poems than in his prose, and they arranged with a publisher that he be commissioned to write his novel "all about my Jarvis valley." From Swansea in July he wrote to Glyn Jones: "I've done a few thousand words already: about 100,000 are needed. Work for the winter." In fact very little more of this novel was ever written. What he was writing in July was probably intended as part of it, but it ended up as a short story called "The Vest," which I published in my short-lived magazine, *Yellowjacket*, five years later. Unfortunately Curtis Brown's records for this period no longer exist, and I have not succeeded in discovering which publisher commissioned the novel. According to Dylan's letters he received no advance; payment was to be on delivery.

Other people were helpful as well. Sir Richard Rees gave him some reviewing to do for the *Adelphi* and Geoffrey Grigson, who in addition to running *New Verse* was also literary editor of the *Morning Post*, saw to it that he was able to earn a few guineas there too. Grigson later took a dislike to Dylan, both as a man and a poet, but in those early days he was a good friend to him. In 1957 he published in the *London Magazine* his memories of their first meeting, which must have been in April of 1934.

The rumour which was to increase to the legend of the purest genius had scarcely begun, at this moment . . . when, in a tea-room, an awkward *Mr.* Thomas faced an awkward, also an unconvinced, *Mr.* Myself across a corner table. The tea-room was in a courtyard between the dull quiet of the Temple and the dull mumble of Fleet Street.

[137]

Young *Mr.* Thomas was up from Cwmdonkin Drive, Swansea, in big London, where poets existed. He was uncertain of his part. He might, sitting there in the corner below the grey panes, have been acting a new Rimbaud. In features, still unpoached at this time, he looked rather like the Rimbaud portrayed in a group by Fantin Latour. But he had not heard of Rimbaud, in Swansea;* he wore a different poetic uniform, imitated, I rather think, from a frontispiece of Rossetti when young. Curls thatched his head, a Bohemian poetry tie flowed down and out below his soft collar. He talked poetry, his biographers might be surprised to learn. Young but not quite so young *Mr.* Myself suspiciously regarded this tie, and suspiciously heard a proffer of names he had not expected. Rossetti was one of them, Francis Thompson was another, James Thomson (B.V.) was a third. Stephen Spender, though, was a fourth.

Names, as I saw, were proffered: were held out, withdrawn, held out again, much as one might offer bits of food to a beast of uncertain nature and temper with whom one found oneself unexpectedly but ineluctably roomed or cabined or boxed.

Our presence with each other was Stephen Spender's direct doing. Odd poems above the name Dylan Thomas had appeared in the *Sunday Referee.* . . . I think Stephen Spender must have been one of the first unloony persons to remark on these poems and to enquire about their author, so fixing a label to him as "someone to be watched." I recall Stephen assuring me that at any rate I ought to ask Dylan Thomas for contributions to *New Verse.* He may have given me Dylan's address. Letters had gone to Wales, letters and poems in pale blue ink in that slow, leftward-sloping, pre-adolescent, unpersuasive hand from which Dylan never freed himself, had returned from 5 Cwmdonkin Drive and perhaps another Swansea address; and now we *mistered* each other and investigated each other and *mistered* each other again, in the grey tea-room.

Dylan had not yet succeeded enough, or sloughed off enough of lowest-middle-class Swansea, to resemble the painting of him by John. He was not so cocky. He needed assurance, with which he was never generously and liberally supplied. But London quickly intimidated him less, and was entered by him more frequently. Art adulating zanies in Parton Street, near Red Lion Square, eyed him first like schoolboy butterfly-collectors eyeing a Camberwell Beauty on the wing. They were persons of a kind needing shots of the notion of art as others need shots of insulin. If Mr. John Malcolm Brinnin's America is fantastically full of such people, whom Dylan Thomas learnt rapidly to use and kept on using till they lapped around his death in a New York Hospital, the London supply of them is never to be despised.

But by the time he came up in August, Grigson noticed a great change in Dylan's style and manner:

* This is incorrect. He knew about Rimbaud in Swansea.

Rossetti and the waterfall tie had vanished. Dylan Thomas found that London preferred to aesthetic debauch, or its uniform, the Toughish Boy, the Boy with a Load o' Bear, in and out, so boringly, of the pubs. The part was more congenial and more genuine, with a scope for virtuosity. It was defensive already — defence, release, escape.

Much has been written about the political nature of the literature produced in the 1930s, though recently the pendulum has swung the other way and it is now fashionable to allege that political influences were in fact negligible. The truth lies, as usual, somewhere between the two. Certainly, when midnight chimed in the new decade, the writers of England did not obediently replace their Proust and their Yeats and their Lawrence in the shelves and reach for *Das Kapital,* and Lenin's *Imperialism.* Most of the serious writers at work in the 'thirties were in fact untouched by Communism, and almost none had fascist sympathies. There were of course Communist writers at work then, as there are now, and these could be roughly, perhaps even rudely, divided into categories: the serious Communists who knew their Marxism-Leninism and produced stodgy and forgotten works of socialist realism (there were exceptions to this, to mention only Jack Lindsay, Edgell Rickword and Randall Swingler) and the frivolous salon-Communists, who knew little about their professed creed but often, and perhaps for that reason, wrote extremely well. One thinks particularly of the Oxford group of poets, Auden, Spender, Day Lewis, and their novelist friends, Isherwood and Upward and Calder-Marshall, all of whom had views which at one time or another were identical or very close to those of the Party, in it but never really of it. But behind this, and indeed responsible for these essentially bourgeois writers' profession of Communism, was a widespread feeling in intellectual circles that the economic crisis marked the end of capitalism and that Communism provided the only effective opposition to fascism and war. And if there was one place where the "pink decade" was just what the legend says, it was David Archer's bookshop in Parton Street.

Parton Street, which ran off Red Lion Square in the Borough of Holborn, exists no longer. It was a short crescent of three-storey Georgian houses run to seed, and next to the bookshop were the offices of Lawrence and Wishart, who published Communist literature. Across the way was Meg's Café, where Archer and his friends spent almost as much time as they did in the bookshop.

David Archer, a willowy young man in those days with a high-pitched giggle and a fondness for extravagant gesture, had started his bookshop shortly after coming down from Cambridge in 1932. A general's son, he was almost a classic case, a period piece, of reaction against the values his parents and his school, Wellington College, had attempted to instil into him. His political views were of the extreme left, and he regarded his bookshop as a social rather than a commercial venture. His purpose was to help young poets, and in the early years at least it was primarily a poetry bookshop, though well stocked with Communist literature too. In 1934 control passed to his partner, Ralph Abercrombie, who was much more serious-minded politically, and for this reason among others politics gradually ousted poetry, though never completely. It achieved considerable notoriety in the yellow press in 1934 when Esmond Romilly, who was news because he was Winston Churchill's nephew, ran away from Wellington and sought and found refuge in an unfurnished room above the bookshop from which he proceeded to issue a magazine, called *Out of Bounds*, the purpose of which was to undermine those bastions of reaction, the English public schools. Philip Toynbee, the son of a famous father, also fled there from Rugby, and the place was soon besieged by journalists and filled with adolescents who had run away from school for political reasons. It had, from the beginning, been decorated with those large coloured posters depicting happy, sturdy Russian peasants gathering in the corn or riding gleefully on tractors. And beneath them were to be found the young poets and the school-boy Communists, talking endlessly, borrowing the books they could not afford to buy — David Archer was extremely generous — as they engaged upon the eternal tasks of youth, the reformation of society and the creation of a new literature. It was, as I recall it, a cheerful, noisy place.

Archer not only sold books of poems, he also occasionally printed them. The first was a volume of Surrealist poems by David Gascoyne, who was then sixteen years old. The second was the first volume of George Barker's to be published, in 1933, when he was twenty. George Barker, in his *Coming to London*, has described the bookshop as it then was.

It was Michael Roberts who told me to look around the corner at a bookshop from which the *20th Century Magazine* was intermittently issued. But before doing so I took the reckless precaution of sending the editor one of my poems: I received in reply a note of invitation to call from a Mr. David Archer who was, I gathered from his notepaper, the proprietor of the bookshop itself. I called one clear and sunny morning, at about eleven o'clock, and entered a showroom in which bright books on Marxism and bright books of verse were unneatly displayed everywhere. Up a ladder in a corner was the tall and elegant figure of a character who might have stepped equally well out of Wodehouse or Proust — or, more probably, both — this figure, crucified against the upper wall, turned to me with a look of despair and relief as I entered. "Be an angel," it said, "hand me that hammer." This was Archer, whose posture of crucifixion up a ladder has never forsaken him, and whose insight into contemporary verse helped to form the poetic opinion of a generation. He invited me to take coffee. We went across the street into a café full of overcoated poets and truant schoolboys. There was an atmosphere of industrious conspiracy and illegal enthusiasms. Mr. David Archer was looking for a young poet to publish. Mr. Grigson, like a feline mandarin in shadows, was preparing his first or second issue of blood, entitled *New Verse*. A dark young horse was pointed out to me as the bright hope of the new poetry; he had a sad ingratiating face and bore his responsibility with deliberation. This was Mr. Charles Madge, most gracious of poets. Somewhere else an elongated Blue Boy of 15 was preparing to live down his recently published first novel. I can never remember whether David Gascoyne really spoke only in French at this time, or whether he merely happened to give this impression. . . .

Colonel Lawrence sidling into Archer's Bookshop, toying with a cold cup of tea and then disappearing in front of our eyes like a Middle Eastern fakir. John Cornford, filthy and consumed with a ferocity of nervous energy, ashamed and delighted when it was disclosed that he had written the two beautiful poems published in *The Listener* under a Welsh pseudonym. A rubicund young sheep farmer from the hinterland of Australia who really did know the words and the tune that the fishy girls sang and how Achilles hid himself among women: I mean Albert Lancaster Lloyd, singer, scholar, whaler. And a small, thin Dylan Thomas with a dirty wool scarf wound around himself like an old love affair, looking liker to a runaway schoolboy than Esmond Romilly, who really was one. The 20 year old matinee idol perpetually fiddling with a self conscious pipe, the critic and snake charmer Desmond Hawkins, explaining how he could never finish his novel because when he reached the last page the first one revolted him.

I do not know how many juvenile revolutionaries were temporarily harboured on the top floor of this bookshop, but they came and went like a rotation of furious tiger moths, always at night. Mothers arrived, weeping, in taxicabs. Did all the conspirators die, I wonder, in Spain?

There were the scalds and there were the heroes, almost none of them at the legal majority, milling frenziedly around the abstracted proprietor or impresario, David Archer, who could, with a single word, bring all these restless temperaments into an even more hysterical chaos of convulsive irresolution. If women and drink have saved many poets from madness and death, here, in Parton Street, politics and poetry saved many of us from women and drink.

It was inevitable that Dylan should be attracted to that atmosphere. Furthermore he derived a great deal of help from David Archer. The *Sunday Referee* was having difficulty in getting a commercial publisher to bring out *18 Poems*. The delay irked Dylan, and in August of 1934 he asked David Archer if he would consider publishing the book. When Archer agreed Victor Neuburg and Runia Tharpe went to see him. Having had his own press at Steyning, Neuburg was fully competent to discuss the technicalities with Archer and they soon came to an agreement, which Mark Goulden then underwrote. Archer agreed to print five hundred sets of sheets, of which two hundred and fifty were to be bound at once and sold at three shillings and sixpence. The printing costs were to be shared, the *Sunday Referee* providing thirty pounds, the Parton Bookshop twenty pounds. And the book appeared on December 18, 1934.

Miss Rosalind Wade in her *Parton Street Poets* remembers Dylan Thomas in the bookshop.

Young though he was, he seemed old: a strange grubby figure, dressed in a skimpy, green sweater, with tousled hair and bitten nails, he had early rebelled against the comfort of his home and might well have been labelled the forerunner of the Angry Young Men. He saw the perilous and ugly condition of his native Wales in the 'thirties through a mature child's eyes, gripped in the same depression as certain districts of George Barker's riverside London, and similarly it was the first thing to inspire him, although he interpreted it with far more humour and gusto. . . . Some of his admirers likened him to Chatterton. Others expected him to commit suicide quite soon; his enemies described him as a boor. In a white-painted, tasteful drawing-room he felt compelled to shock and swear: if the poems themselves had not proved otherwise, he could be said to have had little use for the graces of life.

And both John Pudney and Ruthven Todd remember him, at this time, in the café and bookshop, talking endlessly and obsessively about Beddoes.

Throughout the whole of August and the first half of September Dylan was staying with Pamela and her mother in Battersea. Her diary echoes the love and affection she felt for him, but there are some ominous entries. On several occasions he came in very late and the worse for drink; the next day she would be angry with him. And one can assume that living in the same house he found the platonic nature of their love affair an increasing strain. Nevertheless she continued to regard herself as his girl, if not his fiancée. He took her down to meet his sister and she noted in her diary that she *thought* she had made a good impression. And then, on September 15th, Pamela, her mother and Dylan all went down to Swansea for two weeks, to meet his mother. His father they already knew and liked. He stayed with his parents, Pamela and her mother at the Mermaid.

The visit, had it been successful, might perhaps have resulted in marriage, but it was not. In the first place the weather was appalling, and though they did their best to appreciate the beauties of the Gower Peninsula they were usually confined to the cinema, hotel lounges and No. 5 Cwmdonkin Drive. Then Mrs. Johnson found Mrs. Thomas, ". . . who gabbled all day till we nearly went frantic," increasingly tedious and irritating. Dylan does not appear to have introduced them to any of his Swansea friends (his usual tendency to keep his friends apart; perhaps he was afraid of more watch committees being formed). They discovered, too, that Dylan was only nineteen. And towards the end of the visit Pamela had a nervous collapse, so that a doctor had to be called in. Four days later the two women returned, sadly, to London. There had been no rupture with Dylan, no quarrel, but Pamela now realized that there could be no question of her marrying Dylan for a long, long time, if ever.

He had no financial prospects of any sort. Indeed from that point of view his position had, if anything, deteriorated, for D.J.'s failing health had compelled him to resign from the Grammar School and his salary had consequently been reduced to a pension. He was planning to sell his house in Cwmdonkin Drive and buy a smaller and cheaper one in the suburbs, though he did not in fact do this for another two years. But it was now imperative that Dylan go away, to London if he wished, and become self-supporting. The problem of a lodging was solved. He and Fred Janes would share a studio in Redcliffe Street, where they were joined by Mervyn Levy and, after they had moved to another address, by William Scott the painter. But what he was going to use for money was a more intractable question. As he himself later wrote: it was understood that young Mr. Thomas would soon be moving to London where he hoped, vaguely, to live on women. . . . But Pamela and her mother, fond of him as they were, had decided that he was not going to live on them. . . .

It was, indeed, high time he left. He was developing a hatred of smug, snug Swansea and of Wales in general which he was making less

[143]

and less attempt to conceal. Already in August he had caused a scandal when invited to address the John O' London Literary Society, at a meeting held above a Swansea ironmonger's shop. There were road works in progress outside, and he and Bert Trick had fallen into an exceedingly muddy trench, so that they arrived wet and filthy. He described what then happened in a letter to Pamela.

A definite success. There were thirty-five people in the audience, that's all, and thirty of them were women. But what women! All of a dim, uncertain age, most of them virgins, and all with some smattering of Freud and Lawrence. The Chairman, a big-bellied bore, introduced me as a Young Revolutionary (I was becomingly clad in red) who was tackling A Difficult and Courageous Task. I then gave them the works. At the beginning there was a frozen and horrified silence, but eventually I induced a few titters, and, at last, real, undeniable interest. A glassy look came into the eyes of the spinsters. I put in several wisecracks, and ended with "Let copulation thrive." Then the ladies, in one solid mass, bombarded me with questions. In the Communist Erewhon I had dealt with, would there be no perversions? What we consider as perversions, I replied (excuse the novelette form of this report) are, for the most part, healthy and natural bypaths of sexual life. How could a woman defend her honour in such a state? Tin drawers, I replied with Ready Humour. Do you believe in preventatives? The day, I replied, that legalized birthcontrol and clinical abortion come into practice, will go down as a French Letter day in the annals of history. And so on for two hours, until middle aged ladies, who, before that night, would have blushed or been horrified at the mention of pyjamas, were talking gaily about whirling sprays, Lesbianism, sanitary towels, latrines, fornication and other everyday and normal things. Trick made a nice little speech about the inevitability of Revolution, a gentleman defended repression with a very blood-shot eye, Janes made a joke about gallstones, and the meeting closed. God knows what we've done to these ardent and earnest ladies, but I hope it hurts. The more I see of Wales the more I think it's a land completely peopled by perverts. I don't exclude myself, who obtain a high and soulful pleasure from telling women, old enough to be my mother, why they dream of two-headed warthogs in a field of semen. (I heard, later, that a committee meeting has been held, and that care must be taken in future as to who is invited to lecture.) Those bloody women woke up in the cold light of morning and regretted those few hours of — if nothing else — verbal freedom.

And in the same letter he described, briefly, a visit that he and Glyn Jones had paid to Caradoc Evans in Aberystwyth the previous weekend:

He's a great fellow. We made a tour of the pubs in the evening, drinking to the eternal damnation of the Almighty and the soon-to-be-hoped-for destruction of the Tin Bethels. The university students love Caradoc, and pelt him with stones whenever he goes out.

It was obviously high time that Dylan left Wales, before they began pelting him.

This autumn of 1934 was a climacteric in his life. His first book of poems was about to be published, and he himself had at last to leave the cosy, ugly, boring, lovely gas-lit home of his childhood. (He was back soon enough, but with a difference. Henceforth he was a visitor.) October was the month of packing up, though the packing was more mental and poetical than physical. And there are, from precisely this period, two documents that show what the poet thought he was taking to London with him.

The first is not in his own words, though it is easy enough to detect his voice behind them. *Poets' Corner* gave prizes not only for poems but also for criticism. On November 25, 1934 — that is to say four weeks before *18 Poems* was published — the critical prize was awarded to Bert Trick for the following brief remarks about the poems of Dylan Thomas.

Modern poetry is roughly divided into two schools: that which works towards words, and that which works from words. The latter is abstract and purely intellectual in its appeal. Mr. Thomas is its best exponent. . . . Each line is so impregnated with images, allusion, and antithesis, that it becomes a poem within the poem. Words are treated like vials, new meaning being poured into them.

And in the previous month *New Verse* had published answers to a questionnaire addressed to its contributors. Dylan's reply is well-known and has often been republished, but is worth quoting again here. For this, together with a pullover, a few shirts, a red tie, some poems and some stories, is what Dylan took to London with him when he and Fred Janes set off on Sunday, November 11, 1934.

1. Do you intend your poetry to be useful to yourself or others?

To both. Poetry is the rhythmic, inevitably narrative, movement from an overclothed blindness to a naked vision that depends in its intensity on the strength of the labour put into the creation of the poetry. My poetry is, or should be, useful to me for one reason: it is the record of my individual struggle from darkness towards some measure of light, and what of the individual struggle is still to come benefits by the sight and knowledge of the faults and fewer merits in that concrete record. My poetry is, or should be, useful to others for its individual recording of that same struggle with which they are necessarily acquainted.

2. Do you think there can now be a use for narrative poetry?

Yes. Narrative is essential. Much of the flat, abstract poetry of the present has no narrative movement, no movement at all, and is consequently dead. There must be a progressive line, or theme, of movement in every poem. The more subjective a poem, the clearer the narrative line. Narrative, in its widest sense, satisfies what Eliot, talking of "meaning," calls "one habit of the reader." Let the narrative take that one logical habit of the reader along with its movement, and the essence of the poem will do its work on him.

3. Do you wait for a spontaneous impulse before writing a poem; if so, is this impulse verbal or visual?

No. The writing of a poem is, to me, the physical and mental task of constructing a formally watertight compartment of words, preferably with a main moving column (i.e. narrative) to hold a little of the real causes and forces of the creative brain and body. The causes and forces are always there, and always need a concrete expression. To me, the poetical "impulse" or "inspiration" is only the sudden, and generally physical, coming of energy to the constructional, craftsman ability. The laziest workman receives the fewest impulses. And vice versa.

4. Have you been influenced by Freud and how do you regard him?

Yes. Whatever is hidden should be made naked. To be stripped of darkness is to be clean, to strip of darkness is to make clean. Poetry, recording the stripping of the individual darkness, must, inevitably, cast light upon what has been hidden for too long, and, by so doing, make clean the naked exposure. Freud cast light on a little of the darkness he had exposed. Benefiting by the sight of the light and the knowledge of the hidden nakedness, poetry must drag further into the clean nakedness of light more even of the hidden causes than Freud could realise.

5. Do you take your stand with any political or politico-economic party or creed?

I take my stand with any revolutionary body that asserts it to be the right of all men to share, equally and impartially, every production of man from man and from the sources of production at man's disposal, for only through such an essentially revolutionary body can there be the possibility of a communal art.

6. As a poet what distinguishes you, do you think, from an ordinary man?

Only the use of the medium of poetry to express the causes and forces which are the same in all men.

Many critics have extracted a great deal of meaning from these answers. While they do contain some interesting thoughts, they seem to me to represent Dylan at his worst, as he always was in grappling with abstract concepts. And therefore to conclude this chapter I would quote, by way of contrast, from a letter he wrote to Charles Fisher, his close friend, shortly after he had come to London. The letter is undated, but as it comes from 5 Redcliffe Street, it must have been written very early in 1935.

You asked me to tell you about my theory of poetry. Really I haven't got one. I like things that are difficult to write and difficult to understand; I like "redeeming the contraries" with secretive images; I like contradicting my images, saying two things at once in one word, four in two and one in six. But what I like isn't a theory even if I do stabilize by dogma my own personal affections. Poetry, heavy in tare though nimble, should be as orgastic and organic as copulation, dividing and unifying, personal but not private, propagating the individual in the mass and the mass in the individual. I think it should work from words, from the substance of words and the rhythm of substantial words set together, not towards words. Poetry is a medium, not a stigmata on paper. Man should be two-tooled, and a poet's middle leg is his pencil. If his phallic pencil turns into a pneumatic drill, breaking up the tar and the concrete of language worn thin by the tricycle tyres of nature poets and the heavy six wheeler of the academic sirs, so much the better; and it's work that counts, madam, genius so often being an infinite capacity for aching pains.

That seems to me to sum up his views on his own poetry at the time when *18 Poems* was published.

7

⊱ ⊰

SOHO. It is not a borough of London and therefore has no fixed boundaries or borders. Yet it certainly does not extend to Shaftesbury Avenue in the south, where theatre-land begins, nor beyond the Tottenham Court Road in the east, where Bloomsbury lies, the more sedate world of the British Museum, London University and publishers' offices. To the north it probably ends somewhere between Fitzroy Square and Warren Street, and to the west before Poland Street and Portland Street, where the mantlemen and the semi-criminal second-hand car-dealers sell one another cheap clothes and unreliable automobiles. It is thus bisected by busy, noisy Oxford Street, which has nothing to do with Soho. But no two people would agree where Soho stops, for Soho is and was not so much a geographical concept as an atmosphere and a frame of mind.

Both have changed radically in the thirty years since Dylan Thomas arrived in London. It was then, as it is now, the "Latin Quarter" of London in that a great many foreigners lived there, though in those days they were mostly Frenchmen and Italians, whereas now Maltese and Cypriots appear to predominate. Before the war, too, it was a considerably less vicious place than it is today. Though it always had its criminal element — one pub near Rathbone Place was known as the Burglars' Rest because Nina Hamnett once found a jemmy on the bar-billiards table — it was not then the headquarters of the London underworld. Nor did it pullulate with prostitutes. There were a few about, but most of the girls had their beats and their beds further west, where the money was. And though there were sleazy Soho nightclubs, and a great many afternoon drinking clubs, strip clubs had not been invented.

Nor do I recall either dope peddlars or dirty-book shops in those distant days. Pep pills still lay in the future, though benzedrine began to be taken in the late 'thirties. Opium, cocaine and the like were too expensive for most of the people in Soho, where the French and Italian restaurants that are now so expensive were usually very cheap and often very good. It was an altogether more innocent and attractive place then than it is now, and the presence of the foreigners gave to its public life, its street-and-pub life, a greater measure of colour and vivacity than was to be found in the rest of western London.

Of Soho proper there were two halves, separated by Oxford Street. To the south lay Soho Square, Greek Street, Frith Street and Dean Street. Here were most of the restaurants and also the little foreign shops that served them, Italian grocers, French patissiers, German delicatessens, assorted bakers, a shop that sold rope-soled shoes and chefs' high hats, another where customers could buy freshly made pasta, two or three foreign newsagents, countless wine-merchants. Here, too, were the foreign pubs, the "Swiss" and above all the "French" where Victor Berlemont, with huge and curving mustachios that recalled Napoleon's Old Guard, presided behind an exotic glass contraption that could drip water into four Pernods simultaneously.

On the other side of Oxford Street lay what later became known as Fitzrovia. Its main thoroughfare was Charlotte Street, another street of restaurants and food shops, running from Fitzroy Square in the north to Percy Street and Rathbone Place in the south. Here, in Charlotte Street, was the Fitzroy Tavern, then run by an enormous Russian named Kleinfeld, a man whose coarse appearance and gross manners concealed a very kind heart: his principal activity, apart from serving drinks and bouncing drunks, was the collection of money to take East End children on seaside outings. He was also, very occasionally, good for a little credit or even, it was said, a small loan. It was this pub rather than Fitzroy Square, handsome, eighteenth century and down at heel, that gave the quarter its name. Rents were low and it was here that the young, and therefore almost always poor, modern painters lived. The expensive Chelsea studios by now belonged to Royal Academicians or to amateurs of art who liked the life but not the work.

Opposite Kleinfeld's was Bertorelli's Italian restaurant, where a dish of spaghetti with grated cheese and butter was almost the cheapest meal to be had, though there was a creamery in Rathbone Place and also Buhler's Café where the food was even cheaper. Indeed Mrs. Buhler, whose son Bob was then just beginning to paint, would often see to it that his penniless friends and their girls did not go to bed hungry.

Where Charlotte Street meets Percy Street and Rathbone Place there is a tiny and nameless square. Here stands another pub, the Marquis of Granby. As I recall the neighbourhood in the 'thirties the Marquis, to the cognoscenti of such matters, was very slightly rougher in atmosphere than the others. This may have been because of a quirk in the licensing laws: a borough boundary ran along the middle of Charlotte Street and of Rathbone Place. While the Fitzroy and the Wheatsheaf were in Holborn, the Marquis was in Marylebone where the pubs closed half an hour later. There was, as a result, a trek across the street, a small mass-movement, as the other pubs closed their doors. I remember quiet, early games of shove-ha'penny or bar billiards in the Marquis, but the stronger memory is of a jostling, deafening bar filled to bursting point late at night with determined drinkers from three or more other pubs, set on having one, two or three last ones. The proprietor of the Marquis was a colourless figure compared to Kleinfeld. He was, I think, a retired boxer with a broken nose. He gave no credit and seemed to prefer the company of bookmakers and such above that of artists and writers. I once had my wallet stolen in there, by a tart: the trash it contained cannot have done her much good.

The Wheatsheaf in Rathbone Place was very different in atmosphere both from the Marquis and from Kleinfeld's. It is said to have been George Orwell who first led the migration there from the noisy, garish Fitzroy already, in 1934, becoming too famous and a magnet for tourists. The Wheatsheaf was smaller, quieter, a long, narrow bar panelled in dark wood and, being a Scotch House which sold delicious Scotch ale, suitably decorated with the tartans of the clans. The landlord was a calm, quiet man and there were two extremely pretty and quick barmaids. Betty and Sadie were quick, but they were not fast. It was a recurrent topic of conversation between some of the young men, mostly writers, who had followed Orwell to the Wheatsheaf, whether it might be possible to establish contact with Betty or Sadie without a bar counter in between. So far as I know none ever did, though there was a story that a young man who later made a considerable name as a playwright had followed one of them upstairs and had rapidly come down again with one very red cheek.

It must not be imagined that the customers in these bars were exclusively, or even predominantly, intellectuals and artists, as they were in some Parisian cafés or Greenwich Village saloons. London pubs, in those days, were even more working class than they are today. The poets and painters of the 'twenties had discovered the joys of country inns but they did not then frequent London pubs. There were a very few exceptions, such as the Plough near the Museum, the Six Bells in Chelsea and the journalists' Fleet Street pubs, but members of the middle class did not usually go to pubs, and certainly not in the evening except for quick drinks or to buy a bottle, unless they were "slumming" or were themselves *déclassé* by alcohol or sexual perversion. (There was one pub in Mayfair that was frequented entirely by homosexuals and footmen; the police closed it, and somebody even pulled it down.) Even in the early 'thirties writers and painters did not often go by choice to the pubs; they entertained at home or in restaurants.

It was the economic depression that changed this. There was suddenly much less money about. A young man who was studying art or writing poems would be expected by his parents to survive on a much smaller income in 1932 than, say, in 1893. The characters of *Trilby*, "Bohemians" in their own view, were bourgeois millionaires in ours, with their chambers and their feasts and always, in the background, their parents' money. What the young men of the 'thirties could afford was a bed-sitter and beer and sometimes Bertorelli's. Those who could run to more expensive eating and drinking — which meant almost everyone who had had even a minor success — usually ate and drank elsewhere. Usually, but not always.

For there must be added the "political" factor. The poor young who wanted to write or paint were, as I have said in an earlier chapter, almost all of left-wing views. They believed that their and the world's future lay with the workers, and though they came almost entirely, like Dylan, from the middle class, "bourgeois" was the dirtiest French word in their English dictionary. To go to the pubs, to mix with the workers, was therefore not only economically attractive but also politically virtuous.

It did not work out that way. The club-and-class traditions of the English prevented any but the most superficial mingling. The Wheatsheaf's old regulars might at best tolerate, at worst resent, this influx of young men and women into their local. They went on going there because it was their pub, but there was very little mixing — perhaps a game of darts now and then, perhaps a beer offered and accepted, very little real contact. The young men and women who were interested in the arts formed a group or groups of their own which tended to grow larger as more such people, some of them neither young nor poor, went to these few pubs in search of company. And George Orwell, who desperately longed for real contact with the working class and who had therefore left the over-bourgeoisified Fitzroy for the simpler Wheatsheaf, soon found that there too he was hearing nothing at his end of the bar but Oxford voices talking to one another, and he departed for the deeper disillusions, the profounder disappointments of a workers' war in Spain. For many of us who remained the Second World War with its enforced contacts was to prove equally revealing.

Thus the Soho pubs remained, in the 'thirties, essentially what they were before and what they have become again, the clubs of the working class, and the presence in them of these middle-class young people was not always appreciated. Miss Kay Boyle, the well-known American short story writer, accustomed to the more rationalized minuets of Parisian intellectual life, described in the *Nation* of January 29, 1955, an evening with Dylan Thomas in Kleinfeld's. I am sure her memory has played her false; that she has extrapolated a remark made perhaps too loudly into this leaping upon the bar (which I find incredible, and the declamation of prose more so); but nonetheless I believe it casts some light on the Soho atmosphere of the mid-1930s.

It must be twenty years ago that I was in London one bleak winter night, going towards closing time through the icy fog into the warmth — comparative that is — and the uproar of a public house. Its name was the Fitzroy Pub, my husband told me, and it was a place, he said, where those who struggled with the arts, and struggled with poverty as well, came in the evenings to talk and drink. Even now I can see those fierce-eyed old women, not artists or writers but scrubwomen by day, who huddled and cackled inside the door, those toothless witches, with wool scarves bound like windingcloths around their heads, who sat on the chairs along the wall, or slipped from them, rattling with alcoholic laughter, and slept, like ancient mummies, on the floor. And I remember one other figure in the smoke of the place, a young man in a blue-green suit and an open-neck shirt, with a lightish shock of hair on his head, a stocky young man, with eyes that burned so eloquently that once you had looked at him you could not turn away.

At this moment I feel him standing here before me as he stood that night, his mouth wide open in something intended to be singing but was not, and I feel still the quality of tenderness that was behind the savage impact of his gaze. I have never forgotten the salute, or embrace, or whatever it was, that was in his eyes. He gave it to every human being he turned to, and he sang out so lustily in celebration that he was told by the men and women around that he was disturbing the so-called peace of the Fitzroy Pub.

He would climb up on the bar and tell the press of people from there what the hills and the sky were like where he came from, and how far away he was from the place he wanted to be. But nobody wanted to hear a word of it; in fact some of them wanted to knock him down, and others wanted to smash his face in once they had succeeded in dragging him down from his height. Feeling was running so high against him that my husband and I started through the people to where he was being shouldered from pillar to post.

I thought he was an Irishman, and I wanted to save him from British violence because of that as much as I wanted to save an individual from mob brutality. But my husband had recognized the accent as he sang, and he said, "He's Welsh." I thought of him then as a coal miner's son, connected by blood and birth with D. H. Lawrence, a young miner, I thought, come to the city and attacked for his gusto and his simplicity. So we pushed the men and women aside, and my husband shouted the worst of them down, and I can still see the Welshman's face, so young, so ruddy, and his eyes on us in that blind and tender salute as we got him clear of their hands. He said he had come out without a coat; so we got his muffler around his neck, and we took him out past the witches asleep in the filth and rot of their ragged shrouds. We went other places from there, the three of us, and we talked about different countries, and about high mountains, and the sea, and sometime toward the end of the night he said, "What's your name?" I told him mine, and I asked him his. By that time it did not seem strange that I'd known his poetry for a year, and could say lines of it to him, or that he'd read a story or two I'd written and remembered the endings of them, although where he'd read them he couldn't say. His name was Dylan Thomas, and I never saw him again after that, but I've always remembered how we fought for him, with something like dedication to someone who was more than a young man out of his country in that alien place where he was.

So did the Fitzroy appear on one evening, to one American writer, for whom the atmosphere was alien in the extreme, and whose memory I am sure has played her false. To Philip O'Connor, on the other hand, Soho was home in the 'thirties. He did not go there to see the funny people; he was one of them. He was as poor as Dylan, and at least as odd, and in his autobiography, *Memoirs of a Public Baby*, he described Fitzrovia as he then saw it, from the inside.

Fitzrovia was a national social garbage centre. But its inhabitants had the sweetness as well as the gameness of humanity gone off. They lived a life of pretence among themselves, and the successful ones pretended also to become outsiders, leaving the district to slander it; I have done this too, but in my case, my leaving had been mainly geographical. In London there were two chief bohemias, the rich and the poor. The rich, or relatively rich, lay around Hampstead and the Bloomsbury the other side of Tottenham Court Road. They were cultured, naturally, and held in scorn by the poor; contacts were infrequent, though they did occur. The poor were recruited from the lower-middle-class, coming of a suburban agony and couched in the clichés of the latter part of the French nineteenth century, with some Wilde. They sometimes settled, cohabited, bred in Fitzrovia, then attaining a slightly higher, if less hopeful status of settled bohemians, acquired the little grace of such, and began to refuse beds to the poorest recruits. In those days, before the war, many painted there. The district almost, never quite, became "interesting enough for a residence in it to serve as a *cachet* to the more substantial world of art-patrons and fans." But it never quite achieved its purpose. The uprooted in England, such a small minority, are more uprooted than anywhere else, due to the profundity of English conventions, which can support such a mass of unconventionality merely as a social headdress. The atmosphere was unique; we were like the magic paper flowers that starrily unfold rather chemical loveliness in water. We were babies who prattled ourselves into worlds of great achievements. We looked at and felt about each other amazingly deeply. We were all superbly, and socially surreptitiously pregnant; but never delivered except of disaster; and we watched, sportingly, out for each other's blood. So-and-so's misfired liaison was our only source of security, as was so-and-so's awful picture at the Tate, and the charlatan R.'s memoirs. The charms of the district were those of minimal effort, of peddling in sensations wafted in by the busy proper people surrounding our encampment. A feature before the war was the contact between Fitzrovia and Oxford and Cambridge; it was a minor convention for the misfits at the universities to spread their wings, sometimes on the way down, for a while to stay with us; we clustered around them, of course, like wasps round a jampot, and drove them quickly away with our needs as well as our stings. Somewhat, we overdid our parts for their entertainment; but there was always a shop-window element in bohemianism. We felt we might be spotted either as characters or as artists (the distinction was usefully confused) by the powers. But all that is in the past. A diminishing bohemian spirit met half-way an increasingly bohemianised conventionality, notably under the Labour government, whose composition was in part bohemian-inclined. Moreover, after the war, the council classed the district as industrial and it died of the incursion of tailoring sweat-shops; agents probably discouraged such poor rent-payers as artists were wont to be.

Over this fluctuating, frenzied and (despite Mr. O'Connor) fundamentally friendly society or crowd — the pubs mysteriously combined the qualities of a railway station buffet at rush hour with those of a literary and artistic society — there presided, like tatterdemalion hostesses, three or four ladies of uncertain age: the Countess (was she really a countess? She may well have been), Sylvia Gough, who had a grandly mysterious past, but above all Nina Hamnett and Betty May.

Nina was queen of the Fitzroy. To enter Kleinfeld's and not to buy Nina a drink — if one had the price of two — was in those days and in that world a solecism that amounted to a social stigma. The payment was an anecdote or two from an apparently (but alas only apparently, for repetition quite soon set in) inexhaustible fund concerning the artistic and literary great. A tall, bony, angular woman with a voice like a stage duchess and a laugh like a man, Nina had been a painter of very considerable talent. She had known everyone, both in London and Paris, in the years of the École de Paris, years that were already becoming mythical and, to the young men in London, fascinating not only because they were past but also because they were French. (Paris in those days was still believed to be the artistic and literary capital of the world, a belief which few in London questioned.) A childhood friend of Augustus John's — they both came from Tenby in Wales, but her background was odder than his solidly rich one: her father, who used to appear from time to time, was both an aged London taxi-driver and a retired colonel — she had married a Polish painter named Zawadowski with whom she had lived in Paris before the war. Then she had lived with Gaudier-Brzeska, that excellent sculptor who died too young. She called her memoirs (which Dylan had reviewed, libellously, in the *Western Mail* in 1933) *Laughing Torso*: that torso of her, by Gaudier, is in the Tate Gallery. She had been a very close friend of Modigliani's. She had done the drawings for Sir Osbert Sitwell's *The People's Album of London Statues*. Her stories about Gertrude Stein, André Gide, Hemingway, Picasso, indeed almost anyone her listener might care to mention, were amusing, usually involved drink, and may even have been true. Improper conversation, however, aroused her instant disapproval. To tell Nina a joke that was even slightly off-colour resulted in an immediate rap over the knuckles. Nor were her personal reminiscences amorous. Aleister Crowley, it is true, claimed to have been to bed with her, and was very rude about the experience, but he was almost certainly lying. There was something oddly Victorian and *grande dame* about Nina. She was also extremely kind and could be maternal: once when she decided I was not getting enough to eat she led me forcibly to the creamery in Rathbone Place, sat over me while I ate, and then paid for my meal.

Betty May, her old friend and old enemy, was usually to be found in the Wheatsheaf in those days. The two women were very different. Betty May had a face like a Pekingese, and though she must have been at least forty her body was still rounded and attractive. She too had written her memoirs, or at least a book had appeared over her name with the title of *Tiger Woman*. She had adopted the tiger, that Edwardian sex symbol, as her personal heraldic beast, and always wore its skin as coat or hat or both. She could and did scratch and fight like one, too. Her background was obscure. Had she, in fact, been brought up in a Paris brothel? Certainly she had known as many famous men in that city as Nina, indeed often the same men, but she had been a model, not an artist, and her entrée into artists' society had been made through the bedroom. Nor did she attempt to conceal this fact, or her continuing fondness for young men whom she instructed most competently in the art of love. Arthur Calder-Marshall in his *Magic of My Youth* has described his first glimpse of her, a year or two before Dylan moved to London.

As we left the Museum gardens there burst from a hotel almost opposite a woman followed by five men. "Taxi!" she shouted imperiously, "taxi!", first at a private car and then at a cab with the flag down.

She was conspicuously dressed in a coat of tigerskin with a cap to match. With breeches, top-boots and a whip I could have fancied her putting a troupe of large cats through their routine, so masterful was her manner. Yet as she stood at the head of her echelon of retainers, there was nothing unwomanly about her. Domination was not the denial of her sex but its prerogative.

Her coat was not done up, and though it was not possible to see exactly what she was wearing beneath it, a medley of bright colours was revealed so startling in contrast, that it seemed impossible that they could harmonise; and yet, with a flair for colour like a Romany, she had so arranged them that they were brilliantly effective. Her beauty, too, was like a gipsy's, her unpainted face achieving beauty by the clear curve of the jaw, the arching nostrils, the high, broad cheekbones and the sharp, catlike eyes.

She was not young by my standards, at least thirty-five; yet age was not a thing which entered my mind. Even into the summoning of a taxi she put an energy that made the men behind her look like dummies.

Dylan soon met her, and within a week or two of arriving in London had tasted the gin-and-lime of her breath. In a long letter to Bert Trick, probably written in late November of 1934 and from which I shall be quoting more fully later in this chapter, he wrote:

To continue this egoistic survey: I've met a number of new notabilities including Henry Moore, the sculptor, Edwin and Willa Muir, Wyndham Lewis, and certainly not least Betty May. Betty May is, as you probably know, an artist's model, who posed, though that is perhaps not the most correct word, for John, Epstein, and the rest of the racketeers. She wrote a book, too, describing herself as "the tiger woman of Paris." At least she didn't write the book, she sponsored it; it was really written by —— ——— for the sum of £40. I am going to write an article for her, under her name, for *The News of the World*. My payment will not be monetary, but, and although she is now not as young as she was, that will not matter.

And in this context the name of Crowley comes up once again. In the early 1920s Betty May had married an Oxford undergraduate named Raoul Loveday who was a follower of Crowley's. She had neither interest in nor understanding of magic, but her young husband insisted that they go to Crowley's establishment at Cefalu in Sicily, where Loveday died. She always maintained that Crowley had killed him by exposure after having failed to smash their marriage by compelling him to take part in orgies. Indeed she wrote as much in her *Tiger Woman,* and Crowley sued for libel. He lost his case. (Nina Hamnett was subpoenaed as a witness, and when a Scottish newspaper published a picture of one lady with the other's name beneath it, it is said that both collected damages.) Crowley's disgusting practices became an important ingredient in Betty May's conversation, for she regarded him as a very real danger to her young men. She must certainly have warned Dylan against the Great Beast. And Dylan, with his infantile or peasant's fear of the supernatural — of vampires and hobgoblins and things that go bump in the night — was duly scared. Some years later, in 1941 or 1942, he was sitting with my former wife Theodora in the "Swiss," doodling as he frequently did when in a bad mood. The cause of his bad mood that evening was the presence, at the far end of the pub, of Crowley. When Crowley walked across and placed in front of Dylan a duplicate of his doodle, Dylan was extremely frightened. He insisted that Theodora and he leave the pub immediately, without waiting for the man they were supposed to meet. She has told me that he remained in a state of the highest agitation all evening.

There is much more to Soho than these few pubs I have mentioned, though they certainly gave it its focus. Opposite the Marquis, in Percy Street, was the Eiffel Tower Hotel, owned and run by an aged citizen of the former Austro-Hungarian Empire named Stulik, who was said to have been at one time chef to the Emperor Franz-Joseph, to whom he bore a certain physical resemblance. The food was good but expensive, and we in the pubs looked upon it as the height of luxury, a place to which we went only by invitation, Augustus John being the usual host. The few bedrooms, I am told, were dark and cluttered with huge articles of central European furniture, but no questions were asked as to who was in whose room. Stulik's friends could run up enormous bills; Augustus once asked for his bill after a dinner party, Stulik produced his accumulated account, and Augustus took out three hundred pounds from his pocket with which to pay it. One result of this was that Stulik himself was sometimes penniless. On one occasion when John Davenport ordered an omelette there, Stulik asked if he might have the money to buy the eggs with which to make it. On another occasion, when Augustus grumbled at the size of his dinner bill, Stulik explained calmly in his guttural and almost incomprehensible English that it included the cost of Dylan's dinner, bed and breakfast for the night before. The Eiffel bore, in fact, a certain resemblance to Lottie Crump's hotel in Evelyn Waugh's *Vile Bodies*: the Cavendish was not the only one in London at that time.

The English licensing laws have always required a certain ingenuity on the part of those who do not wish to work in the afternoon or to go home at an unreasonably early hour. In those days the problem of afternoon drinking was solved, at least in Soho, by a multitude of clubs. These clubs consisted usually of a single room, with a bar in it and a lavatory at the back. The price of membership was low or even non-existent, and drinks cost only a penny or two more than what the pubs charged. Such was the Jubilee, upstairs and next to the Eiffel Tower. It was run by Izzy, whose features were so grotesquely Jewish that he might have posed for the anti-Semitic cartoons in the Nazi papers of the day. For many years, perhaps throughout the entire decade, Nina Hamnett was engaged in painting murals on Izzy's four walls, during the hours when the pubs were closed, in exchange for an occasional drink.

Another such was Wally's, a basement on the opposite side of Percy Street. Here Betty May was easily persuaded to sing her only song, "*The Raggle-taggle Gipsies*," while doing a little dance that necessitated the removal of her skirt, which she then waved rather as if it were a toreador's cloak. There was Welsh Peggy's. There were many, many more.

Charles Duff, the philosophic anarchist and author of *A Handbook on Hanging* among many other books, first met Dylan in just such a club, in November of 1934. In the revised but at present unpublished second edition of his autobiography, *No Angel's Wing*, he writes:

I knew Dylan Thomas from about a week after the day he arrived in London. I first met him in a very dull and fusty little drinking club in Soho — The Klomp Club — which attracted me chiefly because it was small and quiet, and a few friends of mine always went there in the afternoons. I had not heard of him before that. All my life I have relied on first impressions of people, and, on the whole, I have seldom modified them very greatly afterwards. It did not take me long to realize that here was a very pleasant drinking companion, a young man who was tender-hearted, sensitive, quick in the uptake, and one of the best pub-storytellers I had met. I was drinking fairly heavily at the time, using alcohol as a shock-absorber as people now use the far less effective pharmaceutical drugs. A very fine physician had told me that I had had some shocks and that alcohol *plus* good food would put me right in a month or so, adding: "Just go on a good binge and forget your troubles." This was my first day of the regime that was to cure me. How glad I was to meet an amusing companion at that moment! So we drank and drank . . . and then had a good meal. I met Dylan nearly every day after that, and looking back on nearly three weeks with Dylan, I can honestly say that he had as much to do with my recovery from what was then called "a nervous breakdown" as the alcohol or the food: perhaps more, for we amused each other rambunctiously every day, which to me was a magnificent catharsis. So much so that I do not remember a word of what we talked about. "There is no malice in Dylan," I told myself. When I heard of his death in America, my first thought was: poor Dylan, I never found a scrap of malice in him.

After the pubs closed in the evening the place to go, unless someone were giving a party, was the Café Royal in Regent Street. In those days it was not at all as it is now. A balcony, with tables for dinner or supper, circled an enormous room which was itself divided into two by a low barrier. In one half were more tables laid for dinner, while in the other the tables were bare and marble-topped. At these it was possible to buy a cheap ham sandwich, after which it was legally permissible to order a lager or any other drink. (Lager was the cheapest.) The Café Royal, more than other places in London, provided that Parisian café atmosphere which London missed and wanted. The rich and successful went there, as well as the poor and ambitious. If one moved in the world of the arts, even in its more obscure by-ways, one could be almost sure of finding friends or acquaintances in the Café Royal after the pubs closed and the theatres emptied. John Betjeman, in a poem describing it as it then was, with its vague memories of earlier generations, of Wilde and Beardsley and Beerbohm, has called it "London's fairyland." It was, indeed, an enchanting place.

The management, because of the licensing laws, had obviously to be very careful. Noticeable drunks were rapidly evicted, and if the offence were repeated, were barred altogether, at least for a time. (Dylan was barred for a while in 1935. I am told he had scraped his tongue with a cardboard menu and presented the result to a well-known writer of whimsy who had somehow offended him, and who screamed.) A young woman who arrived alone was not allowed to enter the big room unless she could point out the man she was meeting. And there was a character known as Rattlesnakes who was a most respectable businessman by day and who lunched regularly at the Café Royal, where he was then treated with the utmost civility. At night, however, after a few drinks he suffered from the optical illusions from which he derived his nickname. It was said that every night he tried to force his way back into the Café Royal and every night was ejected with total rudeness and contempt — "You bugger off out of here, Snakes!" — by the very same waiters who had served him with such deference at midday and who would do so again tomorrow.

And then, when at last the Café Royal closed and the uneaten ham sandwiches were removed, if still no party had been organized, there were the nightclubs. First and foremost was the Gargoyle in Dean Street, with its famous Matisse glass murals. This, though, was for the rich, not the real rich who went to the Embassy or the Four Hundred, but the Bohemian rich who ate at the Eiffel Tower and did not *have* to sit on the red plush benches around the marble-topped tables in the Café Royal. However David Tennant, who owned the Gargoyle and had a flat there, was extremely generous to his friends, and from quite early days Dylan went there a great deal, usually as his guest. For others there were much simpler nightclubs, or "bottle-parties" as they were then called. Even these were expensive, though, even so simple a place as the Negro "Joe's" in Bateman Street. If that was impossible financially, then there was coffee and more talk at an all-night Lyons'. There was even, in extreme circumstances, bed.

Now it must not be imagined that the same group of people led this same life day after day, let alone year after year. Fitzrovia was not really a society, and it was certainly not a club, though sometimes, meeting others who were there, it seems so in retrospect. But almost every day there were some people behaving in the fashion I have described. And it was to them that Dylan gravitated when he was in London. They were by no means all drunks and layabouts, just as they were by no means all dedicated artists. But one could say that Soho was a place of refuge for people — mostly young people, which is what gave it a curiously fresh charm — who had, more often temporarily than permanently, chosen to escape from an English middle-class society that was then far more rigid than it is today. And it was this of course that appealed to Dylan, who had rebelled against bourgeois conventions in Wales and who found the English equivalent even less to his taste. Also, being at that time a rather naive Swansea boy, he found Soho life exciting, even wicked. He wore himself out living that life, and after a few weeks in London, a few weeks of what he later called "the capital punishment," he would retire, exhausted, to Wales, to his parents now, to his wife later.

Dylan's home life in London, if such it can be called, was at this time certainly Bohemian in the George du Maurier sense. Theoretically he shared a series of rooms with Fred Janes, Mervyn Levy and William Scott, near the Royal College of Art, a poet among painters. It is hard to make out exactly who was where when, nor does it matter. Dylan, who sometimes slept at home, was supposed to share with the small rent, but never had the money, and on at least one occasion Fred Janes held him upside down and shook a shilling or two from his pockets. Trevor Hughes writes me:

And what a shambles of a room it was. Dylan pointed to a half loaf of bread and a saucer of butter almost hidden beneath a jumble sale conglomeration of books, painting materials, an ancient typewriter and heaven knows what else, on the table. There was no sign of crockery, but just one small butter-covered and badly discoloured knife with which he invited me to help myself to bread and butter. I assured him that I was not hungry — I was starving — and he was hugely amused by the look of horror which I could not conceal. He told me that they always lived like that and that the knife had been washed that very week.

In the letter to Bert Trick of November 1934 from which I have already quoted, he describes the atmosphere in the studio:

I live with Fred Janes just off the Fulham Road on the borders of Chelsea, Fulham, South Kensington and Brompton, in a large room with a bathroom and a sort of inferior wash-up adjoining. . . . Another Swansea boy — Hark, Hark, the Parish Pump — lives in the room above us. He is Mervyn Levy, a small and cunning Jew who does small and cunning drawings, and at present does not work in the Royal College Kensington. . . . I'm not at the moment working very hard. I find it difficult to concentrate in a room as muddled and messy as ours is nearly all the time. For yards around me I can see nothing but poems, poems, poems, butter, eggs, mashed potatoes, mashed among my stories and Janes' canvases. One day we shall have to wash up, and then perhaps I can really begin to work.

And a week or two later he was writing in much the same vein to Glyn Jones:

I am, as I think I told you when, during the famous Caradoc expedition, we last met, staying with a painter called Janes. We possess one large room in a quiet street in South Kensington — in South Kensington, that is, officially, but we are near Chelsea, Fulham and Brompton. Everything is in rather a mess, but, if you don't mind that, and I don't somehow think you do, then I do really wish you would sleep with us. Janes spends most of his time indoors and cooks his own meals, but I have most of my scanty meals in cafés — scanty not for the reason of utter penury, although I have had and do have and am having at the moment a particularly lean period, but for the sake of the demon alcohol who has become a little too close and heavy a friend for some time now. Pile in with us, will you? We shall also have the greatest pleasure in providing quite nice breakfasts free of all charge. Does that induce you? Yes, of course it does. So when are you definitely coming up? I'm not, I don't think so at the moment at least, going home for Christmas. My book of poems is coming out then, and I hope to make just sufficient money to keep me happy for the few most important days of the holiday.

Fred Janes recalls Dylan, in bed, fully dressed with overcoat and even hat on, waiting for his breakfast. Dylan himself would cook nothing, would not even slice his own bread. And Mervyn Levy, in a BBC broadcast, gives an echo of his early morning conversation at this time.

On those rare occasions when Dylan was at home for breakfast he liked nothing better than beer, cake and perhaps an apple. To my knowledge, in those days he never varied these basic breakfast components, except sometimes to omit either the cake or the apple or both, but never the beer. Anyway we didn't always have cake and apples, but we were never without beer when Dylan was in residence, simply because he was prudent enough to bring home a flagon or two of ale at night, thoughtfully sparing a half-bottle or so for breakfast the following morning. . . .
He never actually possessed a room of his own. . . . He was far too erratic and unpredictable in tenancy of any accommodation to qualify for a particular apartment, but he did have a mattress, and whenever he wanted to spend a night or a week — or a month, even, for that matter — this was laid on the floor of whichever of our three rooms it was most convenient at the time for him to share. Sometimes, when one or other of the permanent occupants was away, Dylan would sleep in the deserted bed, and my break-

fast recollections cover those occasions when he had the temporary use of such a splendid and luxurious facility. He liked sitting up in bed with his back against the wall, grinning through the broken brown bars of his teeth, drinking his beer from a teacup and nibbling at his cake or apple. The drinking and nibbling were interspersed with drags at a cigarette, a lot of coughing and, of course, a ceaseless flow of brilliantly comic and entertaining chatter. He didn't wear official night attire — nothing like pyjamas that is, usually having scratched his way into bed the night before in some combination of his day clothing. . . .

I would often visit him around nine in the morning, carrying my own breakfast of sausage, eggs, toast and a mug of tea. I would shake Dylan awake, hand him a cigarette and a light, and wait for the first low rumble of coughing to build up to a shattering, purple-faced crescendo. Then, relaxed and settling himself cosily against the wall, Dylan would establish his first human contact of the day with a beaming, good-natured: "Morning, Mervy!" . . . He always got the most out of his coughing-fits, by the way, which he really enjoyed in a curious, perverse way. He liked to spread around the entirely romantic idea that he was dying of T.B. The breakfast cigarette was a great help here. . . .

He was a tremendous actor. Now his third method of opening the breakfast chatter was to run straight in on a note of pure fantasy. "The magpies have been chewing my feet all night," or: "I was up at four. Those bloody dwarfs crushing up the mice again!" And on rare occasions he would set the cup of beer gently on the floor, stub the last fragment of cigarette, and speak in his dark-brown voice something of his poetry:

> "The force that through the green fuse drives the flower
> Drives my green age; that blasts the roots of trees
> Is my destroyer.
> And I am dumb to tell the crooked rose
> My youth is bent by the same wintry fever."

But most of all I enjoyed the breakfast-time fantasy weaving.

"Supposing the world and everything in it, Mervy, the men, women, animals, trees — and all the inanimate things — supposing it was all covered and dripping with thick films of oil. We'd be living in an oilyverse, wouldn't we?"

I clearly remember this particular fantasy which Dylan began one morning and, one of us having made a start, it would be up to each of us to elaborate and develop the basic idea. This particular fantasy went something like this, if I remember:

"We'd be slipping all over the place, wouldn't we?" I said, "all the time, slipping like mad."

"Of course," Dylan chuckled, "that would be one of the most natural conditions of existence in such a world. Everyone and everything would be hurtling about all over the place. It'd be horribly difficult to remain upright at all."

"And the cars and bicycles and trains would be slipping on the roads and railway lines," I replied.

"And the Pope would be his oiliness," Dylan continued, "and we'd have the Oilmas instead of Christmas."

"And we'd tell people to oil off," I suggested.

"And when the skies were pouring oil, we'd say: 'It's oiling cats and dogs.' "

And so the fantasy would continue to grow until we'd worry it into a stalemate, or one of us had to push off into the world — I to the Royal College, Dylan into those mysterious reaches of London beyond our ken and knowing, where the seedy and the élite lay in wait for him.

Another such elaborate fantasy that Mervyn Levy remembers involved mice, of which Dylan was as frightened as some Victorian spinster. If an engine of so-and-so many horsepower could pull the Royal Scot from Edinburgh to London at 100 mph, how much mousepower would be needed to do this, or rather how many mice? And how would you make these thousands, these tens or hundreds of thousands, of mice all gallop at 100 mph in the same direction at the same time? Cats on either flank of the column? Dwarfs with whips? And if mice, why not worms, how much wormpower would be needed . . . ?

And then there was the "British woman" campaign. I recall this from the war, but Ruthven Todd assures me that it started before the war, at the time of the government's *Buy British!* propaganda. Dylan's variant was: Wear a British Woman this Winter. The British man was supposed to wear his small British woman next to his skin, to keep him warm, she standing on the top of his feet, her arms about his waist, her head reaching to his chest, so that he could pass her a dry sherry between the buttons of his shirt. The elaboration was immense.

It is difficult, probably impossible, to reproduce verbal humour or wit on the printed page; the media are as different as sculpture and photography. And when a man is as much an actor as was Dylan, the voice, the manner, the circumstances and above all the reactions of others are as important as the content of what is said. I hope, though, that these anecdotes do, palely, reflect one quality of his humour, the piling of joke upon joke — as in his poems he piled image upon image. He built elaborate edifices of fantasy, cloud-castle wedding-cakes of words, tier upon tier, enormous confections of wit. To hear Dylan at his fanciful best, when he had had just enough to drink and not too much, was as good as the circus and not unlike some of the acts: can the trapezist catch even that swinging rope, can the horseback human pyramid grow still higher on yet another dappled grey? We hold our breath, and almost always they can, and almost always he did.

It must not be thought that he went in for monologue, like an Oscar Wilde or some others one might mention. His conversation, even at its most imaginative and elaborate, remained a communication between himself and his friends. His rich, appreciative chuckle when a friend made an amusing remark or told a good story is lost forever, as all conversation must and should be. And the reader who never knew him can only accept the word of those who did that he was delightful, exceptional company. His broadcast talks, prepared with sweat and groans and Alka-Seltzer, give to posterity only a part of his wit and charm. They are candied fruit: his conversation was the peach plucked fresh from the tree.

*   *   *

He did not in fact remain in London over Christmas, but returned exhausted to Swansea, bringing with him fifty copies of *18 Poems*, most of which he deposited with his friend Tom Warner, whom he used as a sort of book-bank, asking him from time to time to send a copy to a new friend. (The book, published on December 18th, was reviewed only in the *Morning Post*, of which Goeffrey Grigson was literary editor, the *Times Literary Supplement*, and in the Swansea papers; the edition of two hundred and fifty was sold out about a year later.) He had thus been in London for only six weeks, and this was to be the pattern for the next three years: too much talk, too much to drink, too many girls, exhaustion, and the escape home. He was up again in late January or early February of 1936, and he wrote to Bert Trick on February 12th:

London is good; Porth is better; and the nostalgia for open and grassy space is, as they say in sentimental diaries, or even dairies, strong upon me. I go my way and the rest of London go theirs. All London is out of step except me.

My book is selling well. A few complimentary reviews have appeared. And Edwin Muir is to write another in *The Listener* in about a week's or a fortnight's time. My chest complaint is bad and my nose runs. Janes has got a rash. There are mice in my room. Work is sporadic. Two and two is still, to my disordered Muse, five or even six. And algebra is the study of curves. I'm working on a story to be called "The Lemon" . . . and I have just finished two poems. . . .

Some people have invited me to spend part of the summer with them in the hills of Derbyshire, and I think of accepting. Conditions have more to

[165]

do with writing than I realized. It may seem affected but I really do need hills around me before I can do my best with either stories or poems. The world here is so flat and unpunctuated, like a bad poem by ——, I am moving from be-artized (in two senses) Chelsea soon anyway. And will let you know my change of address. There are all sorts of plans in my head: Derbyshire, Ireland, East End tenement, Richard Hughes in Laugharne (he's invited me), and even a short tramping existence around England, and I don't know what's going to happen yet.

The plan to share an East End tenement with Rayner Heppenstall came to nothing, and no more did the tramp around England, while the reference to Richard Hughes is premature. Dylan had not then met that distinguished novelist, but Hughes had expressed admiration for his poems to the gossip-writer of the *Swansea Evening Post*, the first really "established" author to do so. What did in fact now happen was an almost immediate return to Swansea, and early in March he was writing to Glyn Jones from Cwmdonkin Drive:

As you see, the trials of life have proved too much for me, the courts have found me guilty, and, rather hollow eyed and with little real work to my credit, I've returned home for a few weeks' holiday. I'm leaving, I believe, in the first week of April, but for the country then, and not for London — Surrey, Cheshire, Derbyshire, I don't know which. It's very lonely here in Swansea, and the few old friends I have spend their days in work and their evenings in indulging in habits which I've had quite enough of — at least temporarily. As it is, I'm working on some short stories. . . .

It must have been on this return journey that Dylan met Vernon Watkins, who was to become a very close friend and in every sense one of Dylan's most loyal helpers. Vernon has described the birth of that friendship in the introduction to his *Dylan Thomas: Letters to Vernon Watkins*.

We met a few months after his first book, *Eighteen Poems*, had been published. I remember turning over the pages of the book in the bookshop where it was prominently displayed, with a curiosity which was mingled with a determination not to buy it. Then I ran into his uncle whom I had known when I was a child, and he gave me his address. Soon after this I called at the house at the top of Cwmdonkin Drive, high above Swansea, and his mother told me that he was expected back from London in a few days. We arranged that as soon as he arrived he should come out to see me. In a few weeks, on the day after his return, he arrived.

He was slight, shorter than I had expected, shy, rather flushed and eager in manner, deep-voiced, restless, humorous, with large, wondering, yet acutely intelligent eyes, gold curls, snub nose, and the face of a cherub. I quickly realized when we went for a walk on the cliffs that this cherub took nothing for granted. In thought and words he was anarchic, challenging, with the certainty of that instinct which knows its own freshly discovered truth. . . .

My first impression of rooted obstinacy, which was really a rooted inno- cence, was reinforced whenever we met. We met often, either at his house or mine. At our first meeting at my house I had read poems of my own; on the first evening I spent with him at Cwmdonkin Drive he began to read his. He unfolded a large file, marked in black letters POMES. The first poem he read to me was "Ears in the Turrets Hear," and he followed this with others which he intended to print in his second book. . . .

Besides poetry, Dylan read me stories. One of the first he read was "The Orchards," printed in the *Faber Book of Modern Stories* and afterwards collected with other early stories in his third book, *The Map of Love.* It was in this story that the trick name Llareggub first appeared. Dylan alone could have devised so Welsh an invention, but it was also an example of the word- play he had learnt from Joyce, his most admired prose writer, whose "Dub- liners" made him deprecate his own short stories. "Llareggub" became, much later, the provisional title of "Under Milk Wood," and was printed as such in the first version, half of which was published in *Botteghe Obscure* in 1952. . . .

Another story Dylan read me at this time was "The Lemon," which *Life and Letters* afterwards printed. In this he explored almost scientifically the link or skin between the interior and exterior worlds, for the two were still mysteriously separated in his imagination, and in both his poetry and his prose he was very much more conscious of the first than of the second. But the best story of this period was one which he read me while it was still in the course of composition. It was to be called "A View of the Sea," and was to be dedicated to his friend Tom Warner who had written a piece of music with that title. Tom Warner was one of several friends who used to meet Dylan regularly at the Kardomah in Swansea every Wednesday during my lunch hour; Alfred Janes, the painter, another very close friend, was invariably there, and one or two storywriters and journalists came almost as often. Dy- lan was always ready to accept suggestions when he read aloud. He would return to them afterwards, testing them many times on his tongue. In this particular story one or two small alterations were made, and one of these made it necessary to change the title, which became "A Prospect of the Sea."

When Vernon Watkins writes of Dylan's imaginative separation, and also relationship, between the interior and the exterior world he might also be explaining the origin of one of the most persistent Dylan Thomas myths or legends. Even as early as the period of which Vernon Watkins is here writing one evidence of the paradox had already as- sumed geographical form. Cyril Connolly has expressed this paradox perfectly, in a phrase that Dylan adopted as his own and used frequently: that the ideal place to be was a womb with a view. Swansea and the villages of his childhood were Dylan's womb, unsatisfactory, cramped and boring as this might often be; London and later New York provided the view, even though what was there to be observed was frequently frigid, frightening adults or other grown-up public babies with their bottles and their screaming fits. He moved from the one to the other, and only in the very last years did he come to see that his was a hopeless quest for a place that cannot exist.

One of his earliest and closest friends in London was Norman Cameron, that excellent and unjustly neglected poet. William Sansom, in his *Coming to London,* has described Cameron as he then was. Sansom, then a very young man, was working in the advertising agency of J. Walter Thompson.

At the advertising office, my room was changed. I was put in an office for two with a strange tall man with an uncombed mop of hair and a long woollen tie. He came in with a kind of breezy, serious gusto, carrying a lot of dangerous-looking thin books, private stuff, poetry. After an affable greeting or two, he turned to write copy about a liver-medicine on the bright yellow paper provided for such purposes. I returned to dealing with a nail-polish remover, literally only, but meanwhile stole a glance or two at the stranger's visionary pale eyes and his suit, which seemed to be made of hair. I had seen nobody like this ever before: or if I had, had averted my smooth little eyes.

At midday this man suddenly turned and said: "How about some gudfud?" As a new boy I was prepared to agree to anything. But within a couple of hours I had understood exactly what Norman Cameron meant by his soon-to-be-well-known invitation to good food, had met my first poet and been astounded that he laughed and drank, ate and enjoyed life like other people. It was the first of many such lunches. . . .

During the next months Norman wrote medicinal copy in the morning and translated Rimbaud in the afternoon. . . . When the office closed, we would often walk along to a wineshop where goodish cheap hock was served on heavy wood tables, and there I met a number of Norman's friends — an astounded cherub called Thomas, a clerkly-looking fellow called Gascoyne, egg-domed Len Lye like an ascetic coster in his raffish cap, and many others whose names I cannot immediately remember but who, with hock and words, signed and resigned this new lease to my life. What impressed most was that, unlike certain other writers *manqués* back in the office, they did not discuss literary theory or whine about their souls and sensitivities — they made up things there and then, grabbed down extraordinary stories and myths from the air, wrote down doggerel and verse. "I am the short world's shroud, he said" — said Mr. Thomas, I remember — "I share my bed with Finchley Road and foetus." Not much, you may think. But it was preposterous and euphonious — and if you add the movement of faces and laughter and the hock, the evening smoke and the evening loll-together, and at least the freshness of such a statement — the impact may be guessed at. For until those times I had still thought of a poet as a cartoonist's poet, a sort of gangling sissy dancing among lambs in spring.

This was the sort of evening in London that Dylan liked best, among poets, among his peers. With them more than with anyone else, apart from his childhood friends, he could be his natural self. In such society he did not stand out particularly, save by his talents and his wit. These real companions were not likely to be impressed or shocked, though they might be irritated and at times angered by his feckless, childish ways. Norman Cameron was nine years older than Dylan and comparatively rich since he had a regular, well-paying job. He often put Dylan up in Chiswick, but on one occasion at least he turned him out. He wrote an excellent poem about this, which expresses, to my mind perfectly, how so many of Dylan's true friends felt about him. And it is important to remember that this poem was written long before Dylan's death. (Dylan, indeed, outlived Cameron, though only by a few months.)

THE DIRTY LITTLE ACCUSER

Who invited him in? What was he doing here,
That insolent little ruffian, that crapulous lout?
When he quitted a sofa, he left behind him a smear.
My wife says he even tried to paw her about.

What was worse, if, as so often happened, we caught him out
Stealing or pinching the maid's backside, he would leer,
With a cigarette on his lip and a shiny snout,
With a hint: "You and I are all in the same galère."

Yesterday we ejected him, nearly by force,
To go on the parish, perhaps, or die of starvation;
As to that, we agreed, we felt no kind of remorse.

Yet there's this check on our righteous jubilation:
Now that the little accuser is gone, of course,
We shall never be able to answer his accusation.

It was through Norman Cameron that Dylan met Mr. A. J. P. Taylor, the historian, and his wife Margaret, who was to play an important part in Dylan's life in years to come. Mr. Taylor was then a lecturer at Manchester University, and they had a small cottage on top of a steep hill near a place called Disley, in Derbyshire, where they often went in the vacation. They invited Dylan to visit them there, in the spring of 1935, and he arrived in April and stayed for some weeks. Mrs. Taylor remembers his excitement on arriving: he had, he said, seen the Queen of Sheba in the train. He was, as usual, worn out after a few weeks in the city and, again as usual, his behaviour changed as soon as he was away from it. He read Rabelais up there, and wrote a bad patriotic poem about Wales. He also got up a ladder to help paint the cottage, and for this he was paid in beer, which was rationed by his host and hostess. He seldom went to the pub, because he had no money, until he discovered a small colony of very left-wing Jews halfway down the hill, presided over by a Mr. Bloom, whose Joycean name delighted Dylan. He became very friendly with the "Wingers" as he called them, and they would occasionally invite him out for the evening. Dylan, incidentally, always had a marked fondness for Jews. Both their quick wit and their "underdog" qualities appealed to him, as they have to so many "Celts."

Back in London briefly, he was soon down in Swansea again. There he borrowed a small sum of money from Fred Janes "to get his hair cut" and set off for Ireland with Geoffrey Grigson, probably in July. Grigson has described his memories of that summer in the same article from which I have already quoted.

There was a valley above the Atlantic entered by no road, not even a well-defined path, over a ridge of rock, peat and heather. In this valley of Glen Lough between Ardara and Killybegs, I knew a solitary farmer and his wife. A year or two before, the place had been discovered by the American artist Rockwell Kent, who liked its wilderness and loneliness between mountains, or mountains and lakes, and the sea. He had concreted a donkey-shed into a sleeping-room and studio and had abandoned it. It was in that shed, on the edge of a small stream from the lakes, that Dylan and I lived for a while, building turf fires to dry ourselves out and keeping a quart bottle of potheen — illegal, colourless whiskey — hidden in a potato patch outside, below a lushness of chickweed. If indeed he had been in danger of T.B., I daresay he ought not to have been in the dampness and softness of Ireland; but here he was drinking less potheen, at any rate, than he had drunk of beer and spirits in London, and less porter than milk and buttermilk.

The Swansea Changeling, who might at any time go back to his own people, waded through mixed flames of loosetrife and corn marigold which floored the valley. From the cliffs he watched gannets drop and fleck the Atlantic; or climbing steeply to the lakes at the back of the farm and the converted stables, we shouted up to the surrounding, ringing mountains *We are the Dead*, for the multiple echo to reply in sequence *We are the Dead, the Dead, the Dead, the Dead*. We shouted to these mountains above the lakes one evening till we frightened ourselves, stumbling down afterwards through heather and fern and sog to the comfort of the cottage, where Dylan stretched stained white feet, Swansea feet, to the warm turf, alongside the brown, huge feet of the farmer Dan Ward. At times we sneaked down the enormous cliffs to a cold soul-tightening ocean, and sang the *Ram of Derbyshire* to black seals. There was no sand, no gravel, below these cliffs, only white pebbles shaped like eggs or heads by Brancusi. We drew faces on them with black crayon, we named them, set them against rock, and cracked them, with fling after fling of other huge white pebbles, into literary nothingness — since the faces were of authors — and literary oblivion. Several faces were those of people who were to find Dylan, to Dylan's dangerous surprise, a vessel of holiness.

I do not know how much, if at all, Dylan was moved by this peculiar valley in which man was camping as he camps so small in the cruel wilderness of Hercules Seghers. It is again, though, my feeling that he received only what was given him by childhood's environment of place, person, and literature.

> "Stroke and a stress that stars and storm deliver,
> That guilt is hushed by, hearts are flushed by and melt —"

He, in a way, knew that energizing, quietening, flushing and melting influence, that preamble to a deeper poetry; but, in Hopkins's added words, what did Dylan *fable*, what central reality did he then miss, what reality *riding time like a river?*

After about a fortnight I had to go home, Dylan staying in the glen for several more weeks, looked after by Dan Ward and Rose Ward, who felt his magnetism — to their cost, because he left suddenly one day, walking over the mountain towards Wales or London without paying them (though he had ample money) a penny of the agreed sum for all his food and lodging.*

Once Grigson had gone Dylan was alone, really alone for days on end, and for the only time in his life. He worked hard, and he grew up, even physically. He had been staying with Trevor Hughes shortly before he went to Ireland, and he stayed with him again immediately after his return. Hughes has told me that not only did Dylan seem much older, but those weeks of milk and buttermilk had caused him to grow out of his clothes; the sleeves of his jacket no longer reached his wrists, nor his

---

*Mr. Grigson has assured me that it is exactly true that he left Dylan with "ample money." Yet on August 3rd he was writing to John Lehmann, who had agreed to publish a poem of his in an anthology, that he was penniless. Mr. Lehmann has told me that he sent Dylan "a very small sum" which enabled him to return to Wales. But that Dylan did not pay the farmer would seem probable.

trousers his ankles. At the age of twenty he was ceasing, at last, to be a boy. His face, too, was changing from that of a cherub to the face which his friends knew in later life.

His work shows no such drastic change, though the poems that he wrote or rewrote during this summer and autumn are of an even greater density than those he had published in *18 Poems*. It was probably in Ireland that he began preparing a second volume for publication, which appeared the following year as *Twenty-five Poems*, published by Dent's. These were, again, mostly poems from the notebooks, usually revised to an extent that amounts to rewriting, though at least one, *The hand that signed the paper*, was published exactly as first written on August 17, 1933. It is the simplest poem in the book. Others existed, embryonically at least, even earlier (*Today this insect* was written in its original form as early as 1930) but were now altered almost out of recognition. For the exact chronology of *Twenty-five Poems* the reader is referred to Professor Ralph Maud's scholarly *Entrances to Dylan Thomas's Poetry*. It is enough to say here that only six entirely new poems, that is to say poems written in the year and a half between the publication of *18 Poems* and the despatch of the second volume to the printers, are to be found in that volume. These six, however, include the "sonnet sequence" in ten parts, *Altarwise by Owl-light*, which in length foreshadows the more spacious poems to come while in intensity, indeed at times incomprehensibility, it marks perhaps the culmination of his early work. This sequence was certainly being written in Donegal, where many of the revisions were also made. He was also writing prose there, as is shown in a long letter to Bert Trick, from which the following passages are taken.

I'm ten miles from the nearest human being, with the exception of the deaf farmer who gives me food. And in spite of the sea and the lakes and my papers and my books and my cigarettes (though they're darned hard to get and I've few of them left) and my increasing obsession with the things under the skin, I'm lonely as Christ sometimes and can't even speak to my father on an aetherian wavelength.

I came here — "here" is a cottage studio, once owned by an American artist, perched in a field on a hill facing a bit of the wild Atlantic — with Geoffrey G. but he's gone back to town. And here is a wild unlettered and un-French-lettered country, too far from Ardara, a village you can't be too far from. Here are gannets and seals and puffins flying and puffing and playing a quarter of a mile outside my window where there are great rocks petrified like the old Fates and Destinies of Ireland, and smooth white pebbles under and around them like the souls of the Irish dead. There's a hill with a huge echo. You shout and the dead Irish answer from behind the hill. I've forced them into confessing that they are sad, grey, lost, forgotten, dead and damned forever. There are St. Brigid shapes crossed in the rafters to keep away what and who should be kept away. They're superstitious here or mad, whimsy or barmy, and the blood sports are blood sports, but I can break a trout's back now as skilfully as Geoffrey (who gave me the killing rod) but with more conscience.

My days these days are planned out carefully, or at least conveniently, to the clock I haven't got (if time is the tick of a clock, I'm living in a funny dimension, in an hourless house): I rise at 9, I breakfast and clean up till 10, I read or write from 10 till 1, I lunch at 1, then I walk over the cliffs to the sea, stay or walk about there till half past 3 or 4, then tea. After tea I write until the early dusk, then I climb over the hills to the high lakes and fish there until dark. Back, supper, bed. I have a little illegal poteen whiskey with my supper. I smoke black shag in a bad pipe. One day a week I shall walk to Glendormatie where there is a shop and a porter bar. It rains and it rains. All the damned seagulls are fallen angels. Frogs and storms and squids and clegs and muttonbirds and midges and killing beetles. Dead sheep in the bracken. But this is by no means a despondent letter. Words are coming nicely. And the rain can't get in through the roof. I have a blazing turf fire and the only sound is the sea on the million stones. I have a beard too, a curly ginger growth, nearly regular, sweetly disorderly. I'll keep it for good I think, or long enough anyway for the Tricks and the Thomases and my Mumbles Mermaid (bless her hair and her tail) to admire and finger it. I have my homesicknesses, but they vanish all right like all the thought of permanency and the Uplands and the Park go up in wet smoke. In my sicker moments I think of my writing by my gas fire opposite the tall Greek nudes, or walking past your shop to the tram stop, and rattling along to a beery and fleshly Oystermouth, or walking to your house in the Sunday rain and sitting by the fire until we've set the whole world straight, and the whole Welsh world is dark. But I wouldn't be at home if I were at home. Everywhere I find myself seems to be nothing but a resting place between places that become resting places between resting places themselves. This is an essential state of being, an abstraction as concrete as a horse-fly, that's always worrying the back of your neck, plaguing and bothering before it draws blood. I'm at home and the blood's spilt, but only until the pricked vein heals up again and my water and sugar turn red again, and the body and brain, all the centres of movement, must shift or die. It may be a primary loneliness that makes me out-of-home. It may be this or that, and this and that is enough for today. Poor Dylan. Poor him. Poor me.

I wish I could provide you with notes on the financial, political, economic, industrial and agricultural conditions of this lazy and vocal land, but my powers of natural observation, never very clear, would give me less Marx every day. I find I can't see a landscape, scenery is just scenery to me, botany is botany or Bottomley Horatio, oblique; little he wotted when he made the trees and flowers how one of his Welsh chosen would pass them by, not even knowing that they were there. My own eye, I know, squints inwards. When, and if, I look at the exterior world I see nothing or me; I should like very much to say that I see *everything* through the inner eye, but all I see is darkness, naked and not very nice. What can be done about it? The birds of the air peck my mustache. Idly I shoo them aside engrossed in thoughts concerning the spiritual anatomy of the worms of Donegal. This is a poor, dirty land, and the pigs rut and scrabble in the parlors. There are few political feelings in the West, though most people seem to favour a mild republicanism. My deaf farmer believes in fairies, and burns a red lamp under a religious magazine reproduction of somebody's hideous head of Christ; even his calendars are Christian. I always expect to find a cross in the soup, or find a chicken crucified by skewers to a fatty plate. . . .

It's morning again with the wind sweeping up from the sea, and a straight mist above the hills. I've had breakfast, built a tiny stone bridge over the stream by my front door, fallen twice into the muddy gutters by the side of the stream, and banged my thumb with a hammer. In half an hour or so I'm going to work on my new story "Daniel Dom." Did I tell you about it when I saw you last? It's based on the "Pilgrim's Progress," but tells of the adventures of Anti-Christian in his travels from the City of Zion to the City of Destruction. I've been commissioned to write it but I won't be given any money until the first half a dozen parts or chapters are completed. The agents are rather frightened of blasphemy and obscenity (and well they might be) and want to see how clean the half dozen chapters are before they advance me anything. The poor fish don't realize that I shall cut out the objectionable bits when I send them a synopsis and first chapters, and then put them immediately back. . . .

I don't know how long I shall be here; it all depends on how the silence and the loneliness attack me. I had thought of staying here until September, but the hot months are long months. And though I can't say I like my fellows very much and though my social conscience is becoming more flea-bitten every day, I can't indefinitely regard my own face in the mirror every day as the only face in the world, my beard as the only beard, my undisciplined thoughts as the only thoughts that matter under the sun, or the lack of light, and as the thoughts that revalue the egg-shaped earth. I will want more than an echo, sad, grey, lost, forgotten, and damned forever, to answer me in August, and more than the contaminated sheep to roger on the high cliffs. But if I can, I'll stay here until September, come home for a few weeks, and then return to London when the season commences.

Whether or not *Daniel Dom* is the same book as "my novel all about the Jarvis Valley" I do not know: probably not, since he says that it is the fore-runner of his "Anti-Pilgrim's Progress" novel. On the other hand the crying to the dead beyond the mountain surely finds another echo in one of his finest poems, the poem about the dead women written fifteen years later, *In the White Giant's Thigh.*

In this strangely peaceful letter to Bert Trick he also remarks, philosophically enough: "Pamela has spurned me as a small but gifted Welshman of unsocial tendencies and definitely immoral habits." He had seen a certain amount of her that summer, while in London, and they had paid a last visit to the Vickybird together, but they were drifting further and further apart, and in the following year she married another man.

❁   ❁   ❁

Mr. Richard Church was at this time working for Dent's, a most respectable and solid firm of publishers perhaps best known for their publication of the classics in the *Everyman's Library* at prices available to all. He was editing a poetry series for Dent's, and the young poets he was publishing included Norman Cameron and Clifford Dyment. With the exception of Faber and Faber's imprint, which carried with it Mr. T. S. Eliot's imprimatur, this was the best house for a rising poet. It was Lascelles Abercrombie, himself a distinguished Georgian poet in those days and whose son was David Archer's partner and successor in Parton Street, who drew Mr. Church's attention to *18 Poems* a few months after its publication. Writing in the *Adelphi*, in 1954, Mr. Church says:

> His name was new to me, and I looked at his book, together with a bundle of unpublished poems, with some degree of bewilderment, and that unmistakable sensation at the centre of the stomach, which A. E. Housman recognized as the most reliable reaction to authentic poetry.

He goes on to say that disregarding his bewilderment (an action that troubled his conscience), and indulging the promptings of his diaphragm, he decided to publish a collection of Dylan's poems. This, however, is a slight exaggeration; the final decision concerning publication was to be made after the poems had been submitted. Such was the beginning of Dylan's relations with Dent's. Despite periods of stress and strain it was to continue for the rest of his life. There can be no doubt, after reading the correspondence that passed between him and Dent's, that that firm, and particularly its editorial head, Mr. E. F. Bozman, were very good to Dylan, repeatedly helping him financially in the years when he was not making them much money. They were not

[175]

only kind, they were also far-sighted, for in the end he made Dent's a very great deal of money indeed.

It was this volume of poems that he was preparing in Ireland. Back in Swansea, and with Vernon Watkins's help and advice, he completed the book. His relationship with Vernon Watkins was henceforth to be close and special. He had a great admiration for Vernon's own poems and perhaps even more, or more selfishly, for his friend's technical knowledge. Their ways of life were very different, for Vernon worked in a bank, and though he was not a teetotaller, like Glyn Jones, he was also a profoundly religious man. He had enjoyed a more English education than Dylan, having been to Repton and then to Cambridge. His culture was wide and international, and he knew Yeats, Eliot and other internationally famous poets, even though he was only a few years older than Dylan. He was and is a quiet and gentle man, though a witty one too. He is of the stuff of which friends are made, rather than "boon-companions," and he provided the Welsh counterpoint to Dylan's roaring London friendships, but did so with an ease and flavour that some of Dylan's Welsh friends, such as Dan Jones, lacked. Dylan both respected and liked him greatly. And the fact that Vernon's very good mind was concentrated, like a searchlight, on the writing of poems, his own, Dylan's and those of others, was a true bond, as Dylan's published letters to him show.

The collection of poems for the new volume was sent off to Richard Church on October 4, 1935, and Church acknowledged receipt two weeks later. Dylan then turned his attention once more to the writing of his novel, but there came a delayed action from Dent's. What Richard Church has called his bewilderment when reading *18 Poems* gradually gained the upper hand over the reactions of his diaphragm, which is hardly surprising since he had now to take on the responsibility of publishing poems he could not understand and which were, in any case, often considerably more difficult than those in the first volume. On November 26th he wrote a letter to Dylan which almost, but not quite, amounts to a rejection of the poems. He said:

I have read your poems over and over again, and I have a lot to say about them. To begin with, I will be candid about my aim in the tendency of our series of modern poetry. I want to create a public which at present does not exist. Accordingly I have to some extent to woo that public with work that is not too frightening. Secondly, I believe that poetry should be simple as well as sensuous and beautiful; that is, it should be fully distilled from the obscurations of emotion and thought. It should be the expression of the poet's personality after the conflict and not during the conflict. This may be demanding a maturity of view which is impossible in a young poet, but on the other hand it is urging him towards a clarification of technique which ultimately must be to the advantage of his work.

With these axioms, I look upon surrealism in poetry with abhorrence. To me it is an experiment in art which has led its practitioners up a blind alley, and has divorced them from the public upon which they should feed. Dissociated symbolism is a private eccentricity, and there is no reason why a reader should tease his wits or his imagination to elucidate a meaning where possibly there may be none. Surrealism is to me an anti-social activity, and therefore destructive. I am distressed to see its pernicious effect in your work, because I believe you to be outstanding amongst your generation as a poet with an original personality and the fine fire of spiritual passion. There are not many such today. I am therefore content to wait a little longer to see whether you cannot produce some work with the same simplicity as such poems as "Ears in the turret," "I have longed," and "The hand that signed."

The new group on which you are working I cannot stand for, because I do not believe that it is really you speaking. It is only you caught up in the delirium of intellectual fashion of the moment.

You may resent this candid criticism, but I value your work too highly to be anything but honest about it, and I beg you to think over what I have said and to be patient until we can meet at a later date and discuss the whole question of your work and its future in more detail. I hope meanwhile that your health will improve, and that you will be able to finish the novel with a minimum of exhaustion.

It would be hard to imagine a letter more calculated to annoy Dylan than this: the clichés in the first paragraph were precisely those against which he had set his face; the accusation of "automatic" writing which he had had to face before was now once again presented to this most conscious and self-conscious of poets under the more up-to-date guise of Surrealism, concerning which Mr. Church was obviously not very well informed; the poems he liked, though this he could not know, were Dylan's earliest, while he rejected Dylan's more mature work, an attitude that many writers have encountered and all have found annoying; and, finally, the patronizing reference to Dylan's youth would have hurt or even infuriated him.

His reply was immediate and strong, but courteous. It is worth quoting in full. The letter is dated December 9, 1935.

Thank you for your letter, and for the candid criticism of my poems. I do appreciate the trouble you have taken to make your attitude towards these poems quite clear, and am glad that you value my work highly enough to condemn it when you find it — though wrongly, I believe — to be influenced by such a "pernicious" experiment as surrealism. Far from resenting your criticism, I welcome it very much indeed, although, to be equally candid, I think you have misinterpreted the poems and have been misled as to their purpose. I am not, never have been, never will be, or could be for that matter, a surrealist, and for a number of reasons: I have very little idea what surrealism is; until quite recently I had never heard of it; I have never, to my knowledge, read even a paragraph of surrealist literature; my acquaintance with French is still limited to "the pen of my aunt"; I have not read any French poetry, either in the original or in translation, since I attempted to translate Victor Hugo in a provincial Grammar School examination, and failed. All of which exposes my lamentable ignorance of contemporary poetry, but, surely, does disprove your accusations. As for being "caught up in the delirium of intellectual fashion of the moment," I must confess that I read regrettably little modern poetry, and what "fashionable" poetry I do come across appears to be more or less communist propaganda. I am not a communist.

I hope you won't object, but I took the liberty, soon after receiving your letter, of writing to a very sound friend of mine and asking him what surrealism was, explaining, at the same time, that a critic whose work we both knew and admired had said that my own poems were surrealist. In his reply he told me what he thought the principal ideas of surrealism were, and said that surrealist writing need not have any "meaning at all." (He quoted some dreadful definition about "the satanic juxtaposition of irrelevant objects etc.") I think I do know what some of the main faults of my writing are: Immature violence, rhythmic monotony, frequent muddleheadedness, and a very much overweighted imagery that leads too often to incoherence. But every line *is* meant to be understood; the reader *is* meant to understand every poem by thinking and feeling about it, not by sucking it in through his pores, or whatever he is meant to do with surrealist writing. Neither is the new group on which I'm working influenced, in any way, by an experiment with which I am totally unfamiliar. You have, and no doubt rightly, found many things to object to in these new poems; all I wish to do is to assure you that those faults are due neither to a delirious following of intellectual fashion nor to the imitation of what, to my ignorance, appears a purposely "unreasonable" experiment inimical to poetry.

In conclusion, I have quite a number of poems as simple as the three you liked, but poems, to my mind, not half as good as the ones you cannot stand for. Do you wish me to send those on to you, or would you rather we wait until we can discuss everything when I come to town in the early new year?

Again, I trust you will not find this letter pretentious or impudent. I have thought a great deal about what you said in your letter, and my only excuse for the possible pretentiousness of my reply is that I really do want you to realize that you have — my obscurity is to blame — misinterpreted the purpose of my obviously immature poetry, and attributed to it experimental absurdities I hardly knew existed.

What is of interest in this letter is not only Dylan's spirited defence of his own poems, and particularly of the "sonnet sequence" which is "the new group on which I am working." It is also a revealing example of the mixture of honesty and dishonesty in Dylan's self-defence. Fundamentally, everything in this letter is true, everything, that is, that applies to his own poems. And yet it contains several quite pointless lies. (Caitlin wrote, after his death, that he could not help telling pointless lies; he would, she said, pretend that he had been to one cinema when in fact he had been to another.) So here, it is true that he could not read French, but quite untrue that he had read no modern French poetry in translation. Was not his close friend, Norman Cameron, even at that time translating Rimbaud, to whom Dylan refers more than once in other letters? It is perhaps true that he had read no French Surrealism, but he had certainly read the poems of David Gascoyne, the leading English Surrealist poet of the time whom he also knew personally. Again it is a half-truth; other letters show that he disliked Gascoyne's poems very much indeed, but he had certainly read them and almost certainly discussed Surrealist theory with him and others. To say, too, that he had read regrettably little modern poetry was a downright lie; he had read it all. And as for the quite gratuitous remark that he was not a Communist, this was certainly true, but it is equally certain that he did not talk this way in the Parton Street Bookshop. What we have here, in fact, is Dylan using, cashing in on, his lack of education for his own purposes. But he must have hated writing that letter.

Nevertheless it worked, as did the interview with Church early in January in London. He agreed to do some more work on the poems, and on March 17, 1936, he submitted them once again. In his covering letter to Richard Church he insisted that even the most difficult ones, which Church still mistrusted, be published. And he ended this letter with dignity:

If, after this final reading — and believe me I'm not being snooty at all — you come to the conclusion you could not honestly print them in your series, am I at liberty to try to have them published elsewhere? I hope, of course, most sincerely, that you will be able to publish them: if not, the day *may* come when none of my poems will be indecently obscure or fashionably difficult.

With some evident reluctance, Dent's accepted them, sonnet sequence and all. On April 28th Richard Church wrote:

Still I cannot understand the meaning of the poems, but in this matter I have decided to put myself aside and let you and the public face each other. I am accordingly taking steps to have the book set up in type. . . .

And in this same letter he suggests: "Why do you not give your attention to a tale of the world where your early years were spent?" Such, perhaps, was the genesis of the *Portrait of the Artist as a Young Dog*. Dylan's reply was to offer the short stories he had already written, of which more later. Meanwhile in May Church was writing to him for more poems, in order to bring the book up to sixty-four pages. After much badgering Dylan produced these in late June. There then ensued some correspondence as to what the book should be called, but finally and once again Dylan's views prevailed, and *Twenty-five Poems* was published on September 10, 1936, but before then much had happened to him.

He remained in Swansea throughout the winter of 1935-1936, until late March. To Vernon Watkins, whom he was seeing two or three times a week now, he described his work on *Twenty-five Poems* as "very like plumbing: getting things in the right position so that they function properly." He was also writing prose. On February 6th, in a letter to his friend Rayner Heppenstall, he said: "Now I'm better, no cold, no rheumatism, 3/2d, and a short story — called most beautifully 'The Phosphorescent Nephew' — finished, typed and accepted by a half-doped American editor." (I can find no trace of this story, nor of any American prose publication at this time; perhaps it was a fantasy.) His poems were now being accepted by English and American magazines almost as quickly as he finished or revised them, though few of these magazines paid more than a pittance, if that. And throughout the winter he was reviewing batches of thrillers almost every week, for Geoffrey Grigson, in the *Morning Post*, as well as an occasional more serious book in the *Adelphi* and elsewhere. He was, in fact, hard at work.

He did, however, make brief visits to London which followed the usual pattern. Sometimes he dossed down with the painters, but now he more often stayed with Norman Cameron.

Edith Sitwell, who had begun by mocking him in a parody that aroused his fury, had by this time become an admirer. Her praise — particularly her glowing review of *Twenty-five Poems* later that year in the *Sunday Times* and her subsequent defence of those poems in the correspondence columns of that paper — did more to establish his reputation outside the narrowest world of avant-garde poets than any other single factor. Meanwhile she was anxious to meet him, and in February of 1936 she invited him to a party in London. It was she who had given him his first real public acclaim when she wrote about his poem *A Grief Ago*, in the *London Mercury* a week or two before. Characteristically Dylan wrote to Robert Herring, then editor of *Life and Letters,* to enquire: "Can you tell me all about Miss S.? She isn't very frightening, is she? I saw a photograph of her once, in medieval costume." He went to the party where, as he wrote next day, there were "more dukes than drinks," and he made an immediate and immensely good impression on his hostess. There is a story that he got drunk on this occasion. This is untrue, though he apparently did get drunk *after* the party, which must have been a great strain for him. Wynford Vaughan Thomas asked Dame Edith how Dylan had behaved on this occasion, their first meeting, and she replied, over the air in a BBC broadcast: "Beautifully. I've never seen him behave anything but beautifully with me. He always behaved with me like a son with his mother."

She became his loyal friend and remained so to the end. She was also, in some ways, his patroness, always ready to defend both the man and the poet in print, and at times able to help him a little financially, though she has told me that he only rarely asked her for money, when the situation was truly desperate, and that she was never in a position to give him more than very small sums.

As for him, his feelings for her were those of affection and gratitude, an emotion of which he was quite capable. Although he had no overwhelming admiration for her poems, he would frequently include them in his later broadcasts of verse. His attitude towards her was tinged with humour, but it was a gentle, friendly humour, and once they had become friends he never again wrote unkindly about her in his letters. There is an anecdote that in a way shows the affectionate regard in which he held her.

Towards the end of Dylan's life, when Goronwy Rees was connected with the University of Wales in Aberystwyth, he asked Dylan if he would be interested in an honorary degree from that university. Dylan said at once that he would be delighted. Mr. Rees has told me that he was rather surprised at this, as he had imagined that Dylan might despise all such honours, and he asked Dylan, whom he had known for twenty years, why he wanted it. Dylan replied: "Because then, when I meet her coming towards me down the Tottenham Court Road like a galleon in full sail, and I say: 'Good morning, Dr. Edith,' she can reply: 'Good morning, Dr. Dylan.'"

It must have been during one of these early spring visits, too, that Dylan first met Augustus John. They too were to remain friends for the rest of his life, though this relationship was of a far more turbulent nature. The meeting took place in the Fitzroy, and according to John's rather unreliable autobiography, *Chiaroscuro*, it was Nina Hamnett who introduced them in a pub so full and noisy that even Augustus's deafness was not sufficient defence against the blast. Of their friendship I shall have more to say in the next chapter. It was one of Dylan's few friendships with a man who had neither comprehension for nor interest in his verse. But of all this, more later.

Meanwhile, back in Swansea, the poems were finished in mid-March, and the womb was becoming intolerably cramped once again. It was time he was off, and off he went, to London first of all. It was in London, in April of 1936, that he met Caitlin Macnamara.

8

CAITLIN MACNAMARA, whose name rhymes with catkin, though some pronounced it Kathleen, was born on December 8, 1913. Dylan was always under the impression that she was born in 1914 and was thus a few weeks younger than himself. This harmless, traditional and indeed endearing bit of feminine mendacity was given "official" status by their marriage certificate and, I am told, by her passport. Her father, Francis Macnamara, was an Irishman from Ennistymon, in the wild and barren western part of the County Clare; her mother, Yvonne, was half Irish and half French.

In their part of the County Clare the Macnamaras were grand people, proud of their lineage and contemptuous of their own poverty. The picture of the "big house" in nineteenth century Ireland gradually decaying as the country sank beneath the twin scourges of English misrule and agricultural depression is too well known to need repetition here. It was from such a house that Francis Macnamara came, and it was reflected in his character. His close friend, Arland Ussher, has written me: "Though the reverse of a snob, there was a grandeur and panache — and impatience of all constraint — about everything he did, which was extremely attractive . . . I think it would not be surprising if he gave Caitlin a superiority-complex, because he gave that to everyone who was associated with him. Personally I would always forgive such fellows for the delusive-but-pleasant 'top of the world' feeling which they inspire." He had a first class brain and was widely and deeply read. He moved as an equal among the best Irish writers of his day, that is to say the best that his country has produced, and it was long expected that he himself would produce a work of philosophy of a high order. That he never did so was due perhaps to a sort of aristocratic fastidiousness, perhaps to a specifically Irish passion for conversation — than which nothing is more destructive to a writer.

He was a believer in short cuts, and Mrs. Macnamara has told me that once, in his capacity as mathematician and philosopher, he invented a system for making money. Needless to say it did not work. Again to quote from Arland Ussher's letter to me:

Irresponsible he was, but he was certainly very unlike Dylan, whom he never met — though I know he sent Dylan and Caitlin money at a time when he could ill afford it. He was extremely generous (though he probably disapproved of education!), and also rather strict in money-matters — I think he never left an unpaid bill. Though he died from drink (cirrhosis — among other things) this was a late phase, when cares and worries were settling thick on him; when I first knew him, we used to meet chiefly in tea-shops. He was a very civilized person, and used to boast that he liked China Tea (of which he always made a great ceremony) as much as stronger beverages. . . . Francis had little time for modern writing, and to speak of Dylan's poetry to him was to put him into a paroxysm of rage. (It was easy to do that in any case). On the other hand — to be "cussed" — he praised highly the *Portrait of the Artist as a Young Dog*. "The best short stories in the English language," he used to say. All his judgements were extreme.

His first wife, Yvonne, had a background similar to his own and is also well and widely read in two languages. They had two daughters and a son before Caitlin was born, in London. There they moved in artistic and literary circles, and one of their closer friends was Augustus John who, in those pre-war years, promised to become a great painter. That he failed fully to keep this promise was due above all to his extravagant tastes, which required extravagant commissions, and in the inter-war years these could only come from the painting of fashionable portraits.

Shortly after Caitlin's birth her mother and father separated, and later divorced. Mrs. Macnamara took the children to live near Ringwood, in Hampshire, at no great distance from Fordingbridge where Augustus John and his large, chaotic family were installed. It was here on the edge of the New Forest, in a pleasantly shabby and book-lined cottage that had once been an inn, that Caitlin spent most of her childhood, though she also visited her father in Ireland.

Francis Macnamara could only afford to send his former wife three hundred pounds a year for herself and the children, so there was not

Dylan as a little boy.
This photograph was his mother's.

The Rimbaud of Cwmdonkin Drive.
This photograph was sent by Dylan to Pamela Hansford Johnson in 1933.

Dylan and Caitlin,
shortly after their marriage.

Dylan and Caitlin
View, Laugharne, 1938.

In their Chelsea studio, 1944.

This day winding down now
At God speeded summer's end
In the torrent salmon sun,
In my seashaken house
On a breakneck of rocks
Tangled with chirrup and fruit,
Froth, flute, fin and quill
At a wood's dancing hoof,
By scummed, starfish sands
With their fishwife cross
Gulls, pipers, cockles, and sails,
Out here, birdsible, mean
Tackled with clouds, who kneel
To the sunset nets,
Geese nearly in heaven, boys
Stabbing, and herons, and shells
That speak seven seas,
Eternal waters away
From the cities of nine
Days' night whose towers will catch
In the religious wind
Like stalks of tall, dry straw,
At poor peace I sing
To you, strangers, (though song
Is a burning and crested act,
The fire of birds in
The world's turning wood,
For my sawn, splay sounds),
Out of these seathumbed leaves
That will fly and fall
Like leaves of trees and as soon
Crumble and undie
Into the dogdayed night.
Seaward the salmon, sucked sun slips,
And the dumb swans drub blue
My dabbed bay's dusk, as I hack
This rumpus of shapes
For you to know
How I, a spinning man,
Glory also this star, bird
Roared, sea born, man torn, blood blest.
Hark: I trumpet the place,
From fish to jumping hill! Look:
I build my bellowing ark
To the best of my love
As the flood begins,
Out of the fountainhead
Of fear, rage red, manalive,
Molten and mountainous to stream
Over the wound asleep
Sheep white hollow farms

The finished manuscript
of *Prologue*,
completed in 1952.

To Wales in my arms.
Hoo, there, in castle keep,
You king singsong owls, who moonbeam
The flickering runs and dive
The dingle furred deer dead!
Huloo, on plumbed bryns,
O my ruffled ring dove
In the hooting, nearly dark
With Welsh and reverent rook
Coo rooing the woods' praise,
Who moans but blue notes from her nest
Down to the curlew herd!
Ho, hullaballoing clan
Agape, with woe
In your beaks, on the gabbing capes!
Heigh, on horseback hill, jack
Whisking hare! Who
Hears, there, this fox light, my flood ship's
Clangour as I hew and smite
(A clash of anvils for my
(Hubbub and fiddle, this tune
On a tongued puffball)
But animals thick as thieves
On God's rough tumbling grounds
(Hail to His beasthood!).
Beasts who sleep strong and thin,
Hist, in hogback woods! The haystacked
Hollow farms in a throng
Of waters cluck and cling,
And barnroofs cockcrow war!
O kingdom of neighbours, finned
Felled and quilled, flash to my patch
Work ark and the moonshine
Drinking Noah of the bay,
With pelt, and scale, and fleece:
Only the drowned deep bells
Of sheep and churches noise
Poor peace as the sun sets
And dark shoals every ringing field.
We shall ride out alone, and then,
Under the stars of Wales,
Cry, Multitudes of arks! Across
The water lawned lands,
Manned with their loves they'll move,
Animal islands, haunch to haunch,
Huloo, my prowed dove with a flute!
Ahoy, old, sea legged fox,
Tom tit and Dai mouse!
My ark sings in the sun
At God speeded summer's end
And the flood flowers now.

Photo by John Deakin, courtesy of Vo

"Time has ticked a heaven round the stars."
Dylan in the graveyard at Laugharne, 1952.

One of the many worksheets of the unfinished *Elegy* on which Dylan was working during the last two years of his life.

Dylan in his shed at the Boat House, summer 1953. Note his broken arm. The photograph on the wall is of W. H. Auden.

Photo by Rollie McKenna

enough money for the girls to be sent away to school. They were educated at home by a series of mademoiselles, for Mrs. Macnamara was determined that her daughters should learn French if nothing else. Later, when Francis Macnamara's father died, there was a little more money and Caitlin, then in her teens, was sent for a few terms to an academy for young ladies in nearby Bournemouth. In the circumstances it is hardly surprising that she was not much of a scholar. Though she was and is a clever woman, Dylan never needed to fear those "academic" attitudes nor that educational superiority which grated so upon him.

She liked books and read a great deal, but with almost incredible slowness. Her sister has told me that it then took Caitlin a year to read a novel. In her *Not Quite Posthumous Letter to My Daughter* Caitlin has spoken of her "cold, reserved family relations" — she is referring to Hampshire, not Ireland — and of her childhood home as a place where "no remotely dramatic incident" ever occurred. She inherited this reserve from her mother, and in company would often be silent for hours, though I do not believe that she was at all shy. These silences of hers were not, or not usually, hostile in intent but derived, I think, from a difficulty in formulating her thoughts into words. She herself was conscious of this in her relations with Dylan and has written, in *Leftover Life to Kill:*

Dylan was always about three jumps ahead of me, and had already put the argument backwards, inside out, and upside down, by the time I had eventually got it standing up straight. And this . . . used to make me hopping cross; presumably because I was out of my depth. And he insisted, though I never agreed, that women have *no* sense of fun: verbal fun I think he meant; and were a spewing mass of generalizations and . . . clichés . . . only fit for the bed and the kitchen.

From her father she inherited the flaming Macnamara temper. Caitlin in a rage was an awe-inspiring sight. She once lost her temper with me, over some quite trivial matter — I had innocently used a phrase which she regarded as offensive to herself as a lady — and then the words flowed all right. When the words dried up, though fortunately on this occasion they did not, she would use her fists, teeth, nails, bottles, anything that was to hand. When she was a very young girl she and her father, with whom she had a most violent love-hate relationship, quite often came to blows. Later, with Dylan, such fights, particularly late at night and usually in drink, were almost part of the marital routine. Mostly they meant nothing; they were Caitlin's way of expressing herself, of overcoming her communications barrier, even of showing her love. She has written:

But these fights, which were an essential part of our everyday life, and became fiercer and more deadly at each onslaught, so that you would have sworn no two people reviled each other more; and could never, under any fabulous change of circumstances, come together again: were almost worthwhile because, when the reconciliation did take place, according to how long we could stick it out, it was so doubly, trebly, quadruply sweet, and we could never have ventured to conceive of such a thing happening again.

Apart from her parents the most formative influence on the growing girl was the John family, with whom the Macnamara children were more or less brought up. There were a dozen or so John children, about half of them the sons and daughters of Augustus's two wives, the rest an illegitimate miscellany. Nicolette Devas, Caitlin's elder sister, has told me that the atmosphere at Fordingbridge was one of unabashed sexuality, the old patriarch being the least abashed of all. Nicolette has said that the choice for the Macnamara girls was either to dive into, or keep right out of, this eroticism. She kept out; Caitlin dived in, and her first passion, which was not returned, was for one of the John boys fifteen years her senior. Almost her second, which was returned, was for Augustus himself, though he sometimes became confused and thought she was his daughter as well.

She was quite unpredictable as a girl, and hardly more so as a woman. Lord David Cecil recalls a picnic he went on with her and the John children, when she was eighteen, near Poole. When it was time to go, Caitlin had vanished. At last he and Vivienne John found her, on board a cargo ship that was about to set sail, seated on the knee of a rather surprised Dutch sailor.

She was by then a very pretty girl indeed, with corn-coloured hair, blue eyes and a high, Irish complexion. She was small, smaller than Dylan to the delight of them both, but with a figure so perfectly proportioned that she never gave the impression of being a little woman. She dressed beautifully and eccentrically. At a time when most women wore tight-fitting, almost mannish clothes of careful colour, Caitlin chose bright and brilliant dresses, or more usually blouses and skirts, loosely flowing, gipsy-like. During the war, when women's clothes became tediously standardized, Caitlin found that the only shop where she could buy what she wanted was a theatrical costumier's.

She and Vivienne John ran away from home together, to London, to go on the stage. Caitlin there took dancing lessons, but she was by then too old for ballet, so she learned free-style dancing, in the manner of Isadora Duncan. She got a job as a chorus girl at the London Palladium, but was sacked quite quickly for unpunctuality and, oddly enough, untidiness. She then wished to go to Paris as a Folies Bergères girl, but this her mother refused to sanction. She now fell under the influence of a woman who taught her rhythmic dancing, and this woman did take her to Paris, but she found no work there, she had no money, and she was forced to come home.

Caitlin's dancing was and remained very important to her. Although, as her books show, she is a good writer, she hardly dared to write while Dylan was alive. Or rather she wrote secretly, hiding what she had written when he came home, for he could not bear the idea of another writer in his home. And though she danced secretly too, here the secrecy was of her own choosing, for Dylan was proud of having a dancer for a wife. She also danced publicly, at parties late at night; but this was a form of exhibitionism which sometimes embarrassed her audience and displeased Dylan, for her private dancing was in some ways less a means of self-expression than an auto-erotic act. She has described this in *Leftover Life to Kill:*

I am not, to my unlimited sorrow, a spontaneous person; not since my halcyon Isadora Duncan days, when I chose to fancy myself as flowing with melody, movement, and everything but the kitchen sink, including Grecian draperies, and Mercurian sandals, no half measures for me. It did not occur to me that all that flows is not, of necessity, gold; was it not *me* who was flowing? As a matter of fact it was not; being me, I was tying myself in knots, and refusing to respond to the music, though I could hear, quite distinctly, what it was saying to me; and one hitch of the brain too late, would spring into action. Whenever I did come, triumphantly one with the music: I am not using the expression "come" loosely, I mean in the loving sense; no loving come ever gave such prolonged ecstasy. And I did, comparatively often when I was alone; but as soon as I spotted the "glance" of an audience, I was finished: the brain on the alert, all suspicion again, put the pincers on, and the capricious flow stopped abruptly.

She derived almost equal pleasure from swimming, no matter how cold the water might be. Such physical exercise was, for her, a means of escape from the tensions of her being. Violence alternating with lethargy might define Caitlin's rhythm, though she has described her own nature and character far more fully and with much greater subtlety in her own books.

She and Dylan met shortly after her Paris escapade, in April of 1936. He had come up to London in late March, to see Dent's about his forthcoming volume of poems and, as he wrote to Vernon Watkins, to have "Nights Out with those I always have Nights Out with: Porteous, Cameron, Blakeston, Grigson, and old Bill Empson and all . . . Also I had lunch with Pope Eliot, as I said I would have; he *was* charming, a great man, I think, utterly unaffected. . . ." Then, after a week or so of what he described, in the same letter, as "Life No. 13: promiscuity, booze, coloured shirts, too much talk, too little work," he went down to Cornwall, to stay with Wyn Henderson in her cottage at Polgigga, near Penzance.

This was Norman Cameron's idea. In that small and intense world Wyn occupied a special position, being neither a Bohemian nor stuffily respectable. She knew a great deal about writing and painting (she had had her own press, and was to run Peggy Guggenheim's ultra-modern art gallery) and her comprehension of what, for lack of a better word, is called the artistic temperament was total. She herself, though, was and is a calm and sensible Freudian for whom such words as guilt and sin scarcely exist except as metaphor. She was then in her late thirties, the mother of two boys. A disastrous marriage had not embittered her, but had reinforced her tolerance and equanimity. It would be wrong to say that she was maternal. Rather was she that admirable sort of woman to whom one turns easily and willingly for sympathy and help, all the more so because these are given with such good grace, such apparent pleasure in the giving, and without criticism or any overt attempt at reformation. Dylan was extremely fond of her, as was Norman Cameron, who used her cottage in Cornwall as a sort of country retreat to which he sent his friends of either sex when he felt that they needed fresh air and her calm good sense. Watching Dylan's Life No. 13 in London during his winter visits, Cameron decided that, come the spring, Polgigga was the place for him. Early in March Wyn wrote to Dylan in Swansea, and he accepted her invitation with delight. In early April she, Oswell Blakeston (another poet) and Dylan would drive down to Cornwall. Rayner Heppenstall and the wife he had just married would be in a cottage nearby, and there were other friends in the neighbourhood as well, for this part of Cornwall was then by way of being an artists' colony.

It was during this London period, before his visit to Cornwall, that Dylan met Caitlin. It was Augustus John who introduced them in the Wheatsheaf. Dylan used to say that they were in bed together within ten minutes of their first meeting — a characteristic exaggeration. Caitlin, however, has informed me that they did have an immediate and most passionate affair. Augustus had gone, and she and Dylan spent several days and nights at the Eiffel Tower Hotel at Augustus's unknowing expense. Seldom were they ever so rich again. But, as she writes me, "deaf and obtuse as Augustus might be" they began to fear that he would find out. They parted, he to go to Cornwall, she to return to Hampshire where Augustus was painting her portrait. But it had happened. He had fallen in love with her at first sight, and was to remain so until the day he died seventeen and a half years later.

This did not mean that he was faithful to her from then on. He was having an affair with a woman who lived nearby in Cornwall, and when he came back to London there were several other girls and one such escapade ended, as I shall show, in disaster. Years later he was to say, in New York: "It doesn't matter who I go to bed with, because they're all really Caitlin." Certainly he would rather make love to her than to any other woman, but when she was not there it did not occur to him that he must be faithful, or if it did he dismissed the idea. Not to have indulged his desires to the full would have been, in his eyes, to be untrue to himself as he saw himself, and a denial of that personal freedom to which he set so fantastically high a value — let the subsequent sensations of guilt be rack, thumbscrew and wheel combined. Meanwhile she, to the best of my knowledge, and of those whose opinions I accept, was always a loyal wife to him, though she did flirt with other men. Her principal object then was to arouse Dylan's jealousy. In this she was always, and instantly, successful.

When he returned to London from Cornwall in June, she was at her mother's house in Hampshire and Augustus John was still painting her portrait. A girl with whom Dylan now had a brief affair has written to me about this:

I remember meeting him as an alcoholic cherub, and he was in the Wheatsheaf early one morning — well, elevenish — and we spent the next few days together. (I was running from X who'd decided it would be wonderful if we killed ourselves together. Then I'd borrowed a room from Bob Buhler.) Then we decided to marry — at least we didn't really. Dylan said that, but not to be taken seriously, and he went off to raise money for us to go to Paris. He was to meet a publisher at the Horseshoe and I was to wait for him at the Wheatsheaf, but I waited for hours and hours and hours, and it seems he didn't find his publisher at the Horseshoe and tracked him through pub after pub drinking, of course, all the time. And when they made contact they had a lot more drinks together and in the end he couldn't remember where he'd left me and I went off with someone else. . . .

The next time Dylan and I met we took up from where we'd left off and went to — what was it called, that hotel place down near Villiers Street, with Augustus John. That was when he was talking about Caitlin all the time. "I love you very, very much, but Caitlin's special."

He was a very good lover, I remember. Enthusiastic and softly hairy like a teddy bear . . . You were whomever he wanted you to be. "You have a little girl's body," he said to me, when I certainly hadn't. And a small piece of a snob, too. "You wouldn't believe it, but it's breeding that matters. That's what Caitlin has, and you have. Though you haven't got a lot of other things that Caitlin has."

I have quoted this most personal letter because there are many myths current about Dylan's sex life which are, to the best of my knowledge, untrue. His interest in women was normal, and he satisfied it in a manner that was quite accepted and acceptable in the Soho of his youth. He was no Don Juan, but no more was he frightened or shy of women. On the other hand he never really grew out of his Soho period in this matter. Just as his oddly regressive character constantly, in his writing, drew him back to the scenes and emotions of childhood, so too his attitude towards women — towards all women other than Caitlin, that is — became set during his early period in London. And whereas such an attitude was quite ordinary and natural in a poet of twenty-one playing with playmates of the opposite sex who were art students or would-be actresses or models, it was bizarre when it became that of a famous writer in his thirties towards women with an established position. In America, particularly, his very direct approach to women, and the jokes that he himself made about this ("Why have you come to America, Mr. Thomas?" "In pursuit of my life-long quest for naked women in wet mackintoshes.") led to a great deal of misunderstanding, especially in the years since his death when many who scarcely knew him, or did not know him at all, have tried to explain his life and poems and death using various abstract disciplines of thought. Thus some thought him a sex-maniac, others Freudianly thought that he was impotent or maybe even homosexual at heart. In fact he just liked the girls, and he told them so.

✿   ✿   ✿

Cornwall was not Ireland, and although he did a certain amount of work there, he was also drinking. Nor was he happy about the way his work was going. In a letter to Vernon Watkins, posted on the way to London on April 20th, he wrote:

Polgigga is a tiny place two miles or less from Land's End and very near Penzance and Mousehole (really the loveliest village in England). We live here in a cottage in a field, with a garden full of ferrets and bees. Every time you go to the garden lavatory you are in danger of being stung or bitten. My hostess has unfortunately read too many books of psychology, and talks about my ego over breakfast. . . . The one thing that's saving me — saving me, I mean, not from any melodramatic issues but just from sheer unhappiness — is lots and lots of work. I'm half way through another story and have more or less finished a poem which I want to send you when I'm better pleased with it. But here again I'm not free; perhaps, as you once said, I should stop writing altogether for some time; now, I'm almost afraid of all the once-necessary artifices and obscurities, and can't, for the life or the death of me, get any real liberation, any diffusion or dilution or anything, into the churning bulk of the words; I seem, more than ever, to be tightly packing everything I have and know into a mad-doctor's bag, and then locking it up: all you can see is the bag, all you can know is that it's full to the clasp, all you have to trust is that the invisible and intangible things packed away are — if they *could* only be seen and touched — worth quite a lot.

Earlier in this same letter he had expressed his dissatisfaction with country life. As so often in the country, he longed for the town or the city, and he wrote:

I'm not a country man; I stand for, if anything, the aspidistra, the provincial drive, the morning café, the evening pub; I'd like to believe in the wide open spaces as the wrapping around walls, the windy boredom between house and house, hotel and cinema, bookshop and tube-station; man made his house to keep the wind and the weather out, making his own weathery world inside; that's the trouble with the country: there's too much public world between private ones.

And in Cornwall, with so many friends about — William Scott was now nearby, as was Alfred Janes — his behaviour approximated more to that of the town Dylan than the country Dylan. Mr. J. H. Martin, then a journalist on a local paper who was seeing quite a lot of him at this time, wrote in a letter to the *Times Literary Supplement* of March 19, 1964:

> On his own he was a quiet, reasonable person, but as soon as two or three others arrived he began to put on an act — especially if they were strangers. He had to live up to being Dylan Thomas, the *avant-garde* poet. One evening he poured a glass of beer into my right-hand pocket. Later, as we were walking up Raginnis Hill (we christened it Raginnis-is-good-for-you) he apologized for making me wet and explained that he had not wanted to finish the glass, having already had more than enough.

And Wyn Henderson has told me that one morning he walked over the fields to a remote country pub where the landlord was a friend of his. They did not open the doors at all that midday and by evening, when a worried Wyn came to fetch him home, Dylan was boasting that he had drunk forty pints of beer. Was this, he wished drunkenly to know, a record? Thus did the echo precede, by years, the anguished cry of the dying man in New York. Wyn arranged that a burly farm labourer carry him home, where she washed him like a baby, a performance he thoroughly enjoyed.

His drinking in Cornwall was, however, limited by an almost total absence of money. Wyn has told me an anecdote from this period, characteristic of his attitude towards money. His mother had sent him a pound note, and he immediately invited her to the pub. His first action on entering the bar was to ask the barmaid for two ten-shilling notes in exchange for his pound.

"There you are, Wyn," he said, "one for you and one for me."

Always, if he had money, he shared it with friends, for he was the most generous of men. On the other hand if, as was more usually the case, he had none, then he took it for granted that his friends would share theirs with him. And so great was his certitude that this was the proper way to behave, and such his personal magnetism, that men far less generous than Dylan, far harder-headed about money, came to accept this axiom so far as he was concerned. All sorts of unexpected people took it for granted that they, and indeed everybody else, ought to "look after Dylan."

He was putting the final touches to *Twenty-five Poems* as well as writing his short stories. During this summer and autumn of 1936 he published five stories, three of them in Roger Roughton's Surrealist magazine, *Contemporary Poetry and Prose*, and only nine poems, all of them from the forthcoming *Twenty-five Poems*. He was also writing the beginning of his never-to-be-finished novel, *Adventures in the Skin Trade*. Thus during most of 1936 he was more interested in writing prose — under the influence of James Joyce and of Djuna Barnes — than verse. Vernon Watkins has written about this early prose of his:

These early stories, though less permanent than the poems, display the same sexual preoccupation, the same adolescent groping, through tactile images, from darkness to light, the same pressing, through a multitude of symbols and observations, both imagined and real, towards a place and a condition as familiar and truthful as a field, on which the work of his maturity would rest. Many combine the theme of awakening love with an acute sense of the proximity of death. There is also an element of distrust in the act of creation. The writing of the story, the very pencil with which it is written, becomes a symbol of exaltation and of destruction. In the story "The Orchards," the pencil is described in the act of making a poem:

The word is too much with us. He raised his pencil so that its shadow fell, a tower of wood and lead, on the clean paper, he fingered the pencil tower, the half-moon of his thumb-nail rising and setting behind the leaden spire. The tower fell, down fell the city of words, the walls of a poem, the symmetrical letters . . .

There was, then, in 1935, when "The Orchards" was written, a close link between story and poem, as though the prose, although it contained surrealist elements which did not appear in the poetry, were the reverse side of the same coin. For these words about the pencil are autobiographical: they are clearly Dylan's own words defining his own imaginative situation at the time, a writer distrusting, not himself, but himself as writer. So, beneath the dominant activity of his poetry and the subordinate activity of his prose, there was a third activity: distrusting both. . . .

In the prose, too, there came recurrent moments of severe self-appraisal, moments when what had seemed a masterpiece at the time of writing appeared in retrospect to be only a tour de force. The highly charged language of the symbolic stories reached its climax in what was to be his most ambitious story, the opening of which he left as a fragment — *In the Direction of the Beginning*. He told me after this that he would never again write a story of that kind. . . .

That was in 1938. Meanwhile in 1936 and despite his letter to Richard Church, it was not only in his stories that he was flirting with Surrealism. (Vernon Watkins is quite correct in stating that the dense obscurity of the "sonnet sequence" and some of the other poems from this period had nothing to do with Surrealist theory, though Dylan had told Pamela that he himself was not always sure what they meant.)

June 1936 was the last month of peace in Europe, for the Spanish

Civil War broke out in July, and in London the great International Surrealist Exhibition provides, in retrospect, a grotesque and unhealthy parody of the ball before Quatre Bras. Perhaps its mixture of nightmare and frivolity was well attuned to the enormous cacophony that was soon to come. For it was at least as much a social as an artistic occasion.

Surrealism was already old hat in Paris where it had been born, out of Dadaism, a dozen years before. But to London society it was new, exciting and even shocking. And Dylan, though he was learning fast, was still sufficiently provincial to share in the excitement. It was also anti-social in that it was a slap in the face for accepted values about the very nature of art, and this too would appeal to Dylan even though he himself continued to accept those values. (And this explains the intellectually incomprehensible riddle of why men like Roger Roughton in London and Louis Aragon in Paris managed to be simultaneously Marxists and Surrealists.)

The *Daily Mail* thundered forth, of course, the full philistine disapproval. Beneath huge headlines, A SHOCKING ART SHOW and GIRL SUBJECTS OF SURREALIST PAINTINGS, Pierre Jeanneret described the scene at the private view in the New Burlington Galleries on June 11, 1936:

> The crowd that surged in an unwieldy mass, packed tight as sardines in a tin, at the private view of the "International Surrealist Exhibition," New Burlington Galleries, yesterday, vied in its weirdness with the fantastic pictures and pieces of sculpture it did its best to see.
>
> One girl, dressed in a long white gown, had a thick crimson mesh covering her whole head, face included. She had bright green eyelids and lashes, and carried one of those facsimile legs which are used for the display of stockings in shop windows. Flowers were stuck in the thigh of the leg.
>
> The extremes of Chelsea and hyper-cultured Society stood elbow to elbow. An almost unbearable smell of pungent perfumes filled the air.

Dylan was there, among the pungent perfumes where a learned lecture was given to the accompaniment of an electric bell that made every word inaudible. Anxious to contribute to the fun, he had boiled some string which he passed around in cups, enquiring politely:

"Weak or strong?"

Salvador Dali arrived in a deep-sea diver's suit, and nearly suffocated before Roland Penrose managed to unbolt him. And William Walton attached a kipper on a hook to *Object 228* by Joan Miró. According to T. W. Earp, the art critic of the *Daily Telegraph* who was to become one of Dylan's closest friends, "the 'Object' benefited by the addition."

The party, for such it must be called, went on for a couple of weeks. George Reavey imported Paul Eluard, the French surrealist poet, from Paris for a poetry reading on June 26th, at the gallery. English poets also read; Dylan read a postcard.

Dylan thus found himself involved in the London branch of that international society which must have seemed as remote as the moon to the Swansea boy who had arrived in the capital less than two years before. In every big city there are people, usually rich people, who are avid for new sensations, and some of these will find their thrills and kicks in the sensationalism of ultra-modern art. They often perform a most useful service in that they provide early patronage for misunderstood artists with something new to express, but more often they have small comprehension of the arts and are interested principally in the sensationalism of the work and, perhaps even more so, of the artist. Indeed for some such people the more incomprehensible a painting, a piece of music or — to a lesser extent, for they are not usually very good at reading — a poem, the greater their enthusiasm. Throughout the last hundred and fifty years a long line of charlatans, conscious or unconscious tricksters, has profited (and why not?) from such people's search for a new experience by giving them nothing at all in a new and fancy package.

Dylan, had he been a painter, would have been their natural exploiter. Even as a poet he was, in a way, what they wanted. He was dirty, he was often drunk, he was frequently outrageous. Above all, he was new. What did they care for the sweat and anguish and utter honesty that went into his attempts to write his truth into his poems? They preferred to think that he was an eccentric genius who wrote drunk. And they took him up in London just as later, when he was new in New York, they took him up there too. And he played the part they wished him to play. As he remarked more than once: "We all have to sing for our supper." But their attentions, though they never interfered with his serious work as a poet, did him no good as a man either in the long run or the short.

In the short run this grand *bal masqué* was a disaster for Dylan. I have, I hope, pictured the comparative innocence of his Soho. There was nothing innocent about the rich sensation-mongers who were having themselves a ball in the name of Surrealism. At the private view one young woman wore, over her head and down to her shoulders, one of those semi-spherical wire contraptions that are used to cover the meat in old-fashioned larders. To it were pinned scores of red roses, completely hiding her face. She was the meat, what would nowadays be described as a call-girl, and had recently been involved in a notorious sex scandal. Her interest in the arts was nil, and she had gonorrhea.

Dylan took his friend Ruthven Todd, a Scottish poet of his own age, to her house in Mayfair late one evening, for a last drink. On the doorstep he whispered to Ruthven:

"Watch out, they've all got the clap in here."

This did not worry Ruthven, who was only interested in that last drink, drank it, and left. A few days later a lugubrious Dylan greeted him in the Wheatsheaf with the news:

"I've got it."

If he told Ruthven, one may be sure he told others too. Dylan's misfortune was soon common knowledge among his friends. His own attitude was as usual ambivalent: on the one hand he was disgusted and ashamed, as any normal man must be, while on the other it was, in an obscure way, a proof of manhood, of the fact that he had grown up, and, since he had caught it from so notorious a woman, almost that he had "arrived."

Friends saw to it that he was treated in a nursing home, but in those days before sulfa drugs and penicillin it would be several weeks or even months before he was completely cured. And during this period total abstinence from alcohol was essential. He made the obvious and usual decision: he would return to Swansea, he would go home. It was in these inauspicious circumstances that he wrote what is probably his first love-letter to Caitlin that has survived.

Caitlin, Caitlin my love I love you, I can't tell you how much, I miss you until it hurts me terribly. Can you come up to London before I go to Wales again, because I think I shall have to be in Wales for a long time, a couple of months almost; I've been ill with bronchitis and layringitis or something, no voice at all, no will, all weakness and croaking and spitting and feeling hot and then feeling cold, and now I'm about but quavery and convalescent and I must see you. I haven't seen or written to you or let you know I'm alive — which, at the moment, and remembering neurasthenically my days of almost-death, I don't think I was — since Wednesday, the 21st of April, when I lost you in the morning, found money, and shouted on the wireless. . . .

The letter continues in most passionate terms, begging her to come and see him, or at least to telephone, and ends with a postscript that he has to be abstemious.

She did not come up, and he made his retreat to Swansea early in July. It was the bitterest of them all, and the last to Cwmdonkin Drive, for early in the following year his father at last sold that house and Mr. and Mrs. D. J. Thomas moved to a much smaller one in Bishopston, a village just outside the town. Dylan felt ill, and of an illness which he must disguise from his mother's sympathy and from most, if not all, of his Swansea friends; perhaps only once again was he to be so tortured by guilt, and later he described these months as the most horrible of his life: he could not even drink; he had no money; and Swansea seemed to him more provincial and constricting than ever. These were ashen days.

Yet soon enough there was a very real ray of sunshine. Dylan had met Richard Hughes, the novelist, during an earlier return visit and they had taken a liking to one another. The National Eisteddfod, that Welsh convention of late eighteenth century origin at which druids preside and bards are honoured, was being held that year at Fishguard. There was also a painting competition, for which Fred Janes had entered a picture and which Augustus John was to judge. Fred, who was also at home in Swansea, suggested to Dylan that they borrow Fred's father's car and drive to Fishguard for the judging. Dylan improved on this, with the proposal that they ask if they might call on Richard and Frances Hughes, at Laugharne Castle, on the way. Hughes replied, inviting them to lunch. Dylan probably knew that Augustus, an old friend of the Hughes's, and with him Caitlin would be staying at Laugharne. It would seem probable that she had told him so, in reply to the letter quoted above. It also seems likely that she had not informed Augustus of this.

The account of this meeting, as given by Augustus John in his autobiography, is quite misleading. He speaks of finding Dylan seated alone by the roadside and of introducing him to Caitlin and to Richard Hughes, both for the first time, and tells how Dylan and Caitlin fell into one another's arms in the back of his motor car. The real story of that day, for most of which Fred Janes was present, is rather different.

After lunch with the Hugheses on the 14th, in their pretty pink Georgian house which is called the Castle because it abuts on the ruins, Augustus and Caitlin set off for Fishguard in Augustus's large and very fast car, a six-cylinder Wolseley. Dylan and Fred followed in Fred's father's car, an older, slower and small machine. The judging took place, a lot was drunk, and in the evening the four of them set off for Carmarthen, where they proposed to dine, travelling as before. Augustus was driving even faster now over the bad Welsh roads, and in St. Clears Fred's car broke down. Dylan was transferred to Augustus's car, while Fred remained in St. Clears to see about having his father's repaired. Later he returned to Laugharne, dined at the Castle with Richard and Frances Hughes, and slept at Brown's Hotel.

Dylan and Augustus and Caitlin had dined, though that may well be a euphemism, in Carmarthen. Then Dylan insisted that Augustus take him, too, back to Laugharne, but this the old painter refused to do. He was by now thoroughly annoyed by Dylan and Caitlin's public love-making. Was he jealous? It is possible. Did he know about Dylan's illness? It is probable, as so many people in Soho did. Thus it seems likely that mingled with normal jealousy there was an element of paternal responsibility towards the young girl as well. In any event tempers rose, and eventually it came to a fight in the car park. Dylan was often pugnacious, but he was quite useless with his fists and always got the worst of it. Augustus, though some forty years his senior, had little trouble in knocking Dylan down. Then he and Caitlin got into his large motor car and drove away. And Dylan made his way back sadly to Swansea. But he had found her once again.

*   *   *

He spent most of that summer and autumn in Swansea, though his usual visits to London began again in September. During July and August he was working on the proofs of *Twenty-five Poems.* The proof copy actually bears the title *Twenty-three Poems,* and it was the additional two, *Then was my neophyte* and *Today, this insect,* which he was now rewriting from the early notebooks. He was seeing a great deal of Vernon Watkins at this time, whose advice he sought. He was also working at his stories, which he now envisaged as a book. He talked of writing a play, too, but so far as I am aware no word of this ever got on to paper. And there was some question of a travel book about Wales, but again this came to nothing.

On September 10, 1936, *Twenty-five Poems* was published and was immediately acclaimed, reviled, applauded and insulted.

Edith Sitwell had written, in the previous February in the *London Mercury:* "Here . . . is a young man who has every likelihood of becoming a great poet: I know of no young poet of our time whose poetic gifts are on such great lines." And now, reviewing his second volume in the *Sunday Times,* she felt her earlier judgement amply confirmed. "I could not name one poet of this, the youngest generation, who shows so great a promise, and even so great an achievement." A correspondence ensued, in which Edith Sitwell forcefully defended her views.

Desmond Hawkins, who had written one of the few reviews of *18 Poems*, and a favourable one too, was rather disappointed with the new book. Writing in the *Spectator* he praised it but feared that: "On the whole he has been less successful than before in subduing his material to a communicable form." The anonymous reviewer in the *Times Literary Supplement* admitted: "That Mr. Thomas is essentially a poet is certainly proved by the symbolical quality of his language," but went on to confess that he could not make head nor tail of what the poems were about, and advised readers not to try. Randall Swingler, then a Marxist, writing in the *New English Weekly*, spoke of his "tremendous and chaotic rhetoric, the product of a boisterous, almost brutal, Fancy, but unshaped by the power of Imagination." He then went on to contrast Imagination with Fancy, and added, as he must: "Fancy dissociates itself from any social reference at all." G. W. Stonier reviewed both books together in the *New Statesman and Nation* and he, too, preferred the first one. He found himself, he complained, in a dilemma, and this is apparent in his review. Reluctant to admit his inability to understand the new poems, he praises them in one paragraph and talks about "blowing and spouting, eerie bombast" in the next. Glyn Jones, too, mixed praise with reserve. He said, on the one hand, that these poems marked a considerable progress from the rather narrow themes and forms of *18 Poems;* on the other he suggested that Dylan had perhaps "begun guying himself."

In fact, as is usually the case before a writer's reputation is firmly established, the critics — with the exception of Edith Sitwell, who wrote as a poet and not as a reviewer — were hedging their bets. But on one point they were agreed: this was an important book. And no one was more surprised than Richard Church to find that the public agreed, and actually bought it. The original impression of seven hundred and fifty copies at two shillings and sixpence went at once. A second impression was immediately followed by a third and a fourth and soon 3000 copies had been sold. This was and is a very large sale for "difficult" modern poetry in England. Francis Hope, writing in the *Review,* July 1964, states that Auden's *Poems*, published in 1930, sold 3500 copies in seven years and *The Orators*, published in 1932, only 2000 in eleven. John Betjeman, who is the only English poet whose ultimate popularity has rivalled Dylan's in recent years, published *Continual Dew* in 1937, and he tells me that only some 1600 copies of this brilliant, witty and modish book were sold in its first year. Both he and Auden appeared to be far more popular poets, in their very different ways, in the 1930s than did Dylan. Certainly they were very much easier ones. And if Dylan's apparent obscurity had perhaps a certain fashionable appeal in that Surrealist era, Auden's dialectical skill and political wit could command at least as much in Left Book Club days, while for the vast bulk of the reading public, interested neither in Surrealism nor Communism, Betjeman's skill and charm were extremely attractive. That Dylan's poems, in those early days, won so large a public can be interpreted in at least two ways. Geoffrey Grigson reached the conclusion, though not at this time, that it was all one great confidence trick played by the poet on the public. I find this quite unacceptable, and prefer to believe that it was the profundity and ultimate human simplicity of Dylan's view of the world, combined with his brilliant and original poet's skill, that won his poems their audience, both then and later. In any event Dylan became a famous poet during that winter of 1936-1937.

He did not become a rich one. Dent's turned down the book of stories he was hoping they might publish: Richard Church feared lest they be obscene. Nor did any American publisher yet dare to publish his poems, though several were interested. He must have made something considerably less than one hundred pounds out of *Twenty-five Poems*, and the occasional guinea or two that he got from the sale of poems or stories to magazines most certainly did not provide an income on which even a single man could live.

He was ceasing to wish to live a single man. He had been seeing Caitlin on his visits to London. In an undated letter, probably written in November or early December of 1936, he was urging her to live with him.

Nice, lovely, faraway Caitlin my darling,

Are you better, and please God aren't too miserable in the horrible hospital? Tell me everything, when you'll be out again, where you'll be at Christmas, and that you think of me and love me. And when you're in the world again, we'll both be useful if you like, trot round, do things, compromise with the They people, find a place with a bath and no bugs in Bloomsbury, and be happy there. It's that — the *thought* of the few, simple things we want and the *knowledge* that we're going to get them in spite of you know Who and His spites and tempers — that keeps us living I think. It keeps *me* living. I don't want you for a day (though I'd sell my toes to see you now my dear, only for a minute, to kiss you once, and make a funny face at you): a day is the length of a gnat's life: I want you for the lifetime of a big, mad animal, like an elephant. I've been indoors all this week, with a wicked cold, coughing and snivelling, too full of phlegm and aspirins to write to a girl in hospital, because my letter would be sad and despairing, and even the ink would carry sadness and influenza. Should I make you sad, darling, when you're in bed with rice pudding in Marlborough Ward? I want so very much to look at you again; I love you; you're weeks older now; is your hair grey? Have you put your hair up, and do you look like a real adult person, not at all anymore beautiful and barmy like the proper daughters of God? You mustn't look too grown up, because you'd look older than me; and you'll never, I'll never let you, grow wise, and I'll never, you shall never let me, grow wise, and we'll always be young and unwise together. There is, I suppose, in the eyes of the They, a sort of sweet madness about you and me, a sort of mad bewilderment and astonishment oblivious to the Nasties and the Meanies; you're the only person, of course, you're the only person from here to Aldebaran and back, with whom I'm free entirely; and I think it's because you're as innocent as me. Oh I know we're not saints or virgins or lunatics; we know all the lust and lavatory jokes, and most of the dirty people; we can catch buses and count our change and cross the roads and talk real sentences. But our innocence goes awfully deep, and our discreditable secret is that we don't know anything at all, and our horrid *inner* secret is that we don't care that we don't. . . .

I love you so much I'll never be able to tell you. I can always feel your heart. Dance tunes are always right: I love you body and soul: — and I suppose body means that I want to touch you and be in bed with you, and I suppose soul means that I can hear you and see you and love you in every single, single thing in the whole world asleep or awake.

This letter is so revealing and, incidentally, shows such perceptive understanding of his own nature and of hers, that comment would be superfluous. It is enough to say that the room in Bloomsbury, bugfree or not, was never found. In February of 1937 he was still writing from Cwmdonkin Drive, this time to David Higham.

David Higham had become his agent in the previous autumn, was to remain so all his life, and looks after the affairs of his estate to this day. For many years it was an onerous, unprofitable and above all thankless task. Indeed authors' agents seldom get thanked by the authors they serve. Human nature being what it is, and being perhaps exaggerated even beyond what it should be in the case of many writers, successful authors will tend to begrudge their agent his 10 per cent while unsuccessful ones will blame him for their failures. David Higham, in his care for Dylan's literary property, has certainly had his full measure of abuse

— though less from Dylan than from others — over the past thirty-odd years. But it should be recorded that had he not done everything in his power to help Dylan overcome the almost insuperable problems of living as a poet, Dylan's family would certainly be poorer, Dylan himself would probably have died even earlier, and the world would have lost some fine poems. As early as February 1937 he was writing quite truthfully to Higham, after apologizing for offering his stories through another agent:

My capacity for even the simplest business undertaking is negligible: it sounds as though I'm trying to plead the notorious vagueness of the Dreamy Poet Type B classified by Punch, but really I'm a complete nitwit when it comes to replying to people, organising anything, making any sort of deal, keeping my tiny affairs in order, and even, in this shame-making case, just sending to *one* agent the very little, and very uncommercial, work I do. None of that vagueness is a respectable excuse, I know: But my new resolutions are for Punctuality and Order and I *will* keep them.

He goes on to ask Higham if he can find some publisher who will advance him five pounds a week to travel through Wales and write his Welsh travel book. None would. And on February 11, 1937, he wrote to David Higham the last letter, known to me, from his childhood home. In it he said:

I'm coming up to London tomorrow, but will be there only a few hours before going on to Cambridge; I'm returning to London on Wednesday; could we meet sometime in the morning? I'll ring you up anyway on that morning, and find out. I wish it would be possible for us to meet somewhere outside; I get more terrified of offices every day.

David Higham has told me that from then on Dylan seldom came to his office, and preferred meetings in the pub. As for the Cambridge visit, he was to address a literary society. And surprisingly enough, he decided in Swansea that for this outing he ought to have a dinner jacket. He borrowed Tom Warner's. Dylan's parents were on the point of moving to Bishopston, so this is the last we shall hear of Cwmdonkin Drive. It was also the last that Tom Warner was ever to see of his dinner jacket.

When collecting material for this biography I found that one story, which recurred with the regularity of a metronome, concerned Dylan's thefts of other men's clothes. From Swansea to Seattle they vanished with him — hats, socks, trousers, ties and above all shirts. Ten years after his death, when carrying out the melancholy task of looking through the musty suitcase that had brought his few possessions back from New York, I thought of pocketing a tie as a memento — a return for how many? — but I soon realized that none of them looked as though it were his. What did he do with all these clothes? I doubt if in my life I have bought as many shirts as he stole. And he did on occasion buy clothes, too: a strange raincoat bedizened with a profusion of belts, buckles and flaps which, in his Swansea newspaper days, he thought becoming to his profession; a suit which, in pre-London poet days, he had dyed bottle-green, and which prompted a Swansea barmaid to say to Charles Fisher, who was looking for him, "He's just left. Oh, Mr. Fisher, *he was like a green man from the sea*"; and later, in his film days, more than one very loud check suit, fit for a successful script-writer.

Clothes were always important to him, for he liked to dress the part. Caitlin has described him, setting off for a poetry reading, "Dressed up, like a puppy's supper, dapper and spruce or as near as he could get to it," asking her if he should wear a hat, wondering whether a bow tie or a long one would look best and always choosing the spotted bow. Bill McAlpine recalls the careful scrutiny in the morning mirror, and the inevitable request for assurance from his wife, Helen, that he looked all right before setting out for the day. And I remember him, staying with me, anxious because Caitlin was coming up from Wales and his shirt was dirty, and he *must* look neat and tidy when Cat arrived, and the rummaging through my meagre drawers for shirt, tie, socks, once even trousers that had to be rolled like Prufrock's.

The importance of clothes was one of self-expression. What might be called his basic style of dress was always indicative of the persona he was presenting to the world in that particular period of his life, modified perhaps by the mood of the day and always subject to accident. (He had an extraordinary capacity for losing clothes which he should have been wearing, and not just overcoats or hats. He once lost a pair of shoes, and he and a friend had to retrace his steps through the pubs and clubs of the previous day's drinking to find them. Shirts became mysteriously separated from his torso.)

Grigson has commented on the "'nineties-style" poet who first appeared in London in 1933, to be rapidly replaced by the turtle-necked tough. Now, early in 1937, which was when I first met him, this had become yet further accentuated towards a romanticized, proletarian dirtiness. And the reasons for this were twofold.

He remained above all and beyond all the poet, but during the winter of 1936-1937 his vision of "the poet" was deeply influenced by the Spanish Civil War. Quite a number of his friends and contemporaries had gone to Spain to fight. Some, such as John Cornford, who according to Ralph Abercrombie had left with a copy of *18 Poems* in his pocket, had already died there. Dylan had no intention of following their example, but he was passionately on the side of the Republic. His rejection of bourgeois values was thus reinforced, and one of those values was cleanliness. He rejected that with the others. Nor was he alone in so doing. I remember meeting Giles Romilly, then a Communist, at the Café Royal at about this time. I sat next to him, and he stank. Thus did dirt, for a little while, become a symbol of freedom.

And this merged with Dylan's old-fashioned, nineteenth century view of the poet as *âme damnée*, as Baudelaire's albatross, of the need to plumb Gorky's lower depths and to explore the gutter into which Rimbaud had fallen. Caitlin, in her published letter to her daughter, has written:

I could not bear to see you floundering in the same mudbath of experience that nearly submerged me altogether; and has left me the delinquent wreck I am today. I literally believed all that romantic claptrap about the imperativeness of sinking to the bottom for the sake of spiritual enrichment. You may not believe I could be so fantastically daft, but there was no limit to my daftness: nor Dylan's either, for that matter, in those days. But fortunately, in your sober generation, such bohemian licence: of imagining that every orgy of excess is permitted to the Artist; not to mention the Genius; is absurdly out of date.

Later, after their marriage, Caitlin managed to persuade him that dirt was not an intrinsic part of the poet's uniform. But that poets were special, and therefore should dress specially for the part, Dylan continued to believe for some years. In July of 1938 he was writing about this to Henry Treece, referring to a mutual acquaintance.

He (—— ——) is a professional prig, and dry as dust in the places where he isn't damp. I heard him once sneering at the "childish" idea of poets wearing long hair and corduroy trousers; and if that's not childish, what is? He said Eliot, who was a good poet, dressed and looked like a business man; of course Eliot does, because Eliot is a business man, and a properous one. Empson, Bottrall, MacNeice, and others have professional jobs, and dress to fit them; other poets (or not) are advertising writers (Quennell, Cameron, Tessimond), reporters like Madge, booksellers, clerks; they all wear the uniform of the work that pays them. I like very much the idea of poets dressing professionally, if they are poets alone. I dislike "he's a poet but he dresses like an ordinary chap": I like "he's an ordinary chap but he dresses like a poet."

I have written at such length about this matter of dress because I believe it to be indicative of one aspect of Dylan's complex character. In America it was later said of him, what had been said years before of Heywood Broun, that he looked like an unmade bed. Dylan enjoyed this remark, and quoted it about himself. But the precise way in which the bed was unmade was not solely a matter of chance. The sleeper had made sure that it bore his very personal imprint, for Dylan was as sensitive about clothes as he was about everything else that directly concerned him.

His habit of purloining his friends' clothes was one that they resented as seldom as they regretted the small loans he often needed. (Philip Toynbee has told me that once, after staying with him overnight, Dylan went off in the only really expensive shirt Philip had ever owned. He grumbled about this later that day to Ivan Moffatt, who was horrified and said: "You mustn't mention it to Dylan. He'd be so hurt!") But this habit, too, is relevant. It derived in part from his almost total inefficiency in dealing with the trivial details of day-to-day life, and this can be easily traced back to his childhood and his mother's loving care. It is difficult to imagine Dylan, in London without Caitlin, taking his own dirty shirts to a laundry; had he ever done so, it is impossible to envisage his retrieving them or even remembering where the laundry was. With a supreme disregard of a bachelor's requirements, all that sort of thing was left to women. Sometimes there might be a girl or a Wyn Henderson to do these chores; if not, they were simply left undone. Sleeping usually where he had finished the evening, if in the morning he decided that he needed a clean shirt he would take yours: your wife or girl could then send his dirty one to the wash. It makes sense in a way.

And then there is, once again as with the question of money, the whole problem of possessions. Dylan quite simply did not believe in property, just as some men do not believe in God. Like all his attitudes Dylan's attitude towards possessions was ambivalent, for he would grumble when somebody stole his own "lovely bed," but in general he despised them. Nor was he unique in this. Such contempt is, after all, one of the great themes of the Christian religion; and in so far as he was ever a Communist in the 'thirties, his Communism, like that of so many others and of most of his friends, was a rejection of the property concept which valued pots above paintings and stocks above sonnets. So why not take his friends' shirts? If this lost him their friendship, then this only proved that they had never really been his friends at all. Later, as I shall show, marriage and the responsibility of being a father were to modify a little, but only a very little, this attitude, at least superficially. But always what he valued was what lay within himself and within others; always it was in the head. The outer display was only a manifestation, like clothing, of the inner reality. And he was beginning to realize, even as early as 1936 if not before, that this was true of poetry too. *Adventures in the Skin Trade* was envisaged as the story of a man who peels off layer after layer of what lies without until at last only the naked man is left, the truth established, the absolute achieved.

The direct antithesis to such a vision is the usual European and American view of the world which judges human beings according to their possessions, which are obscurely regarded as rewards. And when Dylan found himself in the company of people who felt that way he often reacted violently, both against them and their possessions. Particularly if they were patronizing and cruel, this most gentle and sensitive of men could become a small and solitary Attila or Tamburlaine, looting and raping his way through English and American homes.

Just as at school he had to be thirty-third in trigonometry, just as in America he had to be the drunkest man in the world, so in London in 1937 he could not simply be a poor poet; he had to be the most penniless of them all, ever. Therefore such money as he might make or be given had to be spent, given away, even lost immediately. Money had become only another skin to be removed as quickly as possible in his revelation of the absolute Dylan. Like so many, perhaps like all, his attitudes, this one never really changed. It was one of the causes of his ruin. In origin, though, it was no more suicidal than was that of St. Francis.

❁   ❁   ❁

After addressing the Cambridge literary society, where he had a passage with a don who said angrily that he had been reading Blake before Dylan was born and to whom Dylan replied: "And I shall be reading him after you are dead," he spent a couple of months in London. In the late spring he and Caitlin went down to Cornwall, where Wyn Henderson had opened a guest house at Mousehole. And there they were married, on the 11th of July, 1937. Caitlin only informed her mother of this, and Dylan his parents, after the marriage ceremony in the Penzance Registrar's Office had taken place.

9

⊁ ⊀

W HY did Dylan and Caitlin get married? The obvious answer is that they were in love with one another, and this they certainly were. But in that society and at that time they might just as well have gone on living together, as they had been doing for the past month or more. Caitlin was not expecting a baby, and was the last person to insist on matrimony in the interests of respectability. From all Dylan's talk and behaviour, one would have guessed that the bourgeois ceremony in the registrar's office would have repelled him.

Furthermore his financial position was desperate. Only five days before his marriage he was writing to David Higham from Cornwall:

> If I can't obtain some money by early next week, I'll have to move from here to nowhere: and in nowhere I can obviously do nothing. Do please try to raise me a little money, even five pounds, from Dent. I'd be more than grateful, it would, cheaply here in the country, keep me going for some time, and I could again, I'm sure, work hard and well.

And on the 9th of July, 1937, that is to say just two days before his marriage, he added a postscript and had to send this letter without a stamp, for he lacked the one and one-half pence to buy one.

> I hope you've received my pathetic, and now even more disastrously important, letter. As you see from the address above, I've had to move . . . and I shan't be able to stay here long without some almost immediate money. It's hard to work at all under these circumstances.

Caitlin, it is true, was the least mercenary of women. And though repeated grinding poverty and worry were to embitter her in the end, were almost to ruin her life, and were to teach her that money is far from despicable, she herself has admitted, in *Leftover Life to Kill,* that she never really understood it.

Dylan and I fell between the two extremes; and though we both had a great loathing for poverty and squalor and did all we could, which was mostly talk, to get out of it, and achieve that ideal state of bourgeois respectability and armchair comfort we both craved; or to be exact, Dylan did; to me there was nothing between the barn and the Salon; we never quite, though we got pretty near it, achieved it. It was the same with money: we spent hours planning all the sensible, civilized things we would do with it; eking it out on *moderate* enjoyment, like proper people; vowing and swearing before our Holy Maker, never again to indulge in those racketing wastes that wrought such havoc in us; and in which a good half of our lives was spent. But the valuable quality of moderation was totally lacking in both of us; in one was bad enough, but in both it was fatal. So when the eventual lump came: as far back as I can remember, we were living in hopes of a usually mythical lump coming to solve all our problems, past and future; the feel of a couple of crinklers was so foreign, and so intoxicating to us, that an immediate celebration, and a riot of spending on all the things we had wanted so long, and a lot more we had not, but just could not resist; was one of those things that the best people simply *had* to do, and it never seriously occurred to us not to, in spite of the messes we got ourselves into. So the back debts went on pressing, only harder, getting steadily more voracious; and the future was laden with threats and wangling tortures: all the belittling intricacies of money worries. Poor nervous Dylan, who had inherited, besides his Father's hypochondria, his acid pessimism for always anticipating the worst, suffered sleepless nights more than me. I had developed, through never having any, and my mother's lofty teaching, that it is vulgar to speak of money, a happy detachment from it, and, though nobody enjoyed the spending of it more, it was a solemn duty with me, yet I never could make myself feel it really mattered, or appreciate the value of it. And of course it was Dylan had the job of making it.

Certainly when she married him in 1937 she gave no thought to the question of whether or not Dylan could support a wife. They were both poor. They loved each other. They might as well be poor together. What she left out of the calculations she never made was that whereas a single man with tastes and needs as simple as Dylan's — a few beers, a table and chair in a quiet corner, a friend's shirt and a floor to sleep on — can get by on almost nothing, any married couple, even without children, requires considerably more. And when the children began to arrive this perpetual poverty, accentuated by his fecklessness and hers, assumed the snowballing avalanche proportions of a perpetual nightmare which contributed as much as, if not more than, anything else to Dylan's disintegration and death.

All that lay in the future, though not the distant future, at the time of their marriage. But if poverty were, for two people so contemptuous of property, no obstacle to marriage, it was still scarcely an inducement. And I conclude that the motive towards marriage was supplied by Dylan and that it was complex.

He wanted Caitlin above everything, but he also wanted Wales. Though he might live with her easily and openly in London or Cornwall, he could hardly take her to Swansea, to his parents' house, as his mistress. He suffered from a naive delusion that when he went away he became somehow invisible, and that no news of what he was up to trickled back home. This was to some extent true of his parents and of his London life before his marriage. Even then, though, rumours had been reaching D.J., who had indeed once asked his brother-in-law, the Reverend Dai Rees, for advice. (And that clergyman had replied, tersely and by telegram: "Put the boy in a madhouse.") Later, in America, this fallacy that once he was out of sight he was also out of mind increased the further west he travelled, until he believed that he could get away with absolutely anything in Los Angeles or Vancouver because no one in distant New York, far off London or utterly remote Laugharne would ever know. But in Wales, and above all in his father's house, he must appear as respectable as ever he could, and so must Caitlin.

And this leads to a more fundamental motive. He loved her, and he wanted her all for himself, and he was simple enough to assume that marriage would ensure this. She has written at length about the almost stern attitude he adopted towards her in such matters as her clothes, conversation, the frequenting of pubs, control of the children. It is said that in our marriages we usually, instinctively, attempt to reproduce the pattern we observed in our parents', since deep down we assume that that is the "proper" way for a husband and wife to behave. Incredible as it may sound, with some part of his being Dylan believed that Caitlin should behave like Flo Thomas, and should treat him with the respectful awe and obedience that his mother had shown towards D.J. And, what is even more incredible, for some years and in some ways Caitlin did her best to oblige, for she loved him very much and was proud of him too.

David Higham managed to get a further eight pounds from Dent's against "the Welsh travel book," and on July 14th Dylan was thanking him for "getting hold of all that money for me so promptly." It was enough for them to move, and on the next day he wrote to Vernon Watkins:

My own news is very big and simple. I was married three days ago; to Caitlin Macnamara; in Penzance registry office; with no money, no prospect of money, no attendant friends or relatives, and in complete happiness. We've been meaning to from the first day we met, and now we are free and glad. We're moving next week — for how long depends on several things, but mostly on one — to a studio some miles away, in Newlyn, a studio above a fish-market and where gulls fly in to breakfast. But I shall be trying to come home soon for at least a few days, along with Caitlin: I think you'll like her very much, she looks like the princess on the top of the Christmas tree, or like a stage Wendy; but for God's sake don't tell her that.

They remained in Cornwall throughout the summer, and then visited his parents in Swansea, staying first at a pub that had long been one of his favourites, the Mermaid in The Mumbles, and then, when money ran out completely, moving into the cramped little house at Bishopston that had taken the place of 5 Cwmdonkin Drive.

The visit was not an unqualified success. Old Mrs. Thomas was taken aback by her daughter-in-law's style, not only in dress, and gave her some money to buy new clothes. Dylan and Caitlin spent these hard-saved pounds, which Mrs. Thomas had been putting aside through the years against her own funeral expenses, on a riotous evening in Swansea, returning, the story has it, with a solitary brassière to show for their day's shopping. In view of their utter difference of background and point of view it is perhaps surprising that Caitlin got on as well as she did with Dylan's parents, with whom she had to spend a quite inordinate amount of time in years to come. It is, indeed, a credit to all three of them. But it would be an exaggeration to say that they really liked each other, and she certainly hated being dependent on them, or on her own mother, or on friends. She has written, in her published letter to her daughter:

The profound difference: between depending on friends' unpaid hospitality; or depending on the paid hospitality of your own choosing. There is no comparable question of which is the more pleasant.

I have progressively found, what is more, that by paying people: for company, or looking after you, or even loving you; they do it a lot more willingly, more conscientiously: than those who are morally bound to do it. Than those who do it through bonds of family obligation, or sentimental attachment.

For their resentment, and consequent hostility: for being morally held down, and morally made to do it for nothing; is blatantly visible to an objective observer.

The family, most particularly, is the brittlest, most easily breakable staff to lean on: enough to gently lean on it, and it snaps promptly in two. It can only remain intact, so long as you are careful never to lean on it.

But lean on it they did, for they had no choice. From his parents' house they went to her mother's, near Ringwood in Hampshire, where they stayed for nearly six months, that is to say until the spring of 1938. This was an improvement on Bishopston, for at least he could and did work more easily here. Nor did Mrs. Macnamara question the high seriousness of poetry even if she could not always understand his poems. These early months of marriage were, from the point of view of his work, very important ones. As I have pointed out in the last chapter, he now gave up writing those "poetical" stories with Surrealist overtones. He had already begun to write prose of a very different sort: "A Visit to Grandpa's," one of the most successful short stories in the future *Portrait of the Artist as a Young Dog,* was published in the *New English Weekly* in March of 1938. His unfinished novel, *Adventures in the Skin Trade,* which is a not very happy compromise between the two styles, a transitional work, was presumably what the "Welsh book for Dent's" had become. The opening chapter of this had been published in the first issue of Keidrych Rhys's magazine *Wales* in the summer of 1937. And the reason why Dylan could never finish it, though he went on fiddling with it for years can, I think, be ascribed in some measure to just this: it was the product of a transitory style that he could never recapture. I recall, as late as 1944, Dylan beginning to read this manuscript in my house and, after a few pages, tossing it across the room in disgusted irritation.

If his prose was now becoming simpler, wittier and more humanistic, more external, so too, but to a lesser extent, were his poems. His letters to Vernon Watkins and Professor Maud's admirable scholarship show that most of the poems on which he was now working were the old, primarily introspective ones quarried from his Swansea notebooks; but he was also writing about Caitlin, or at least about his feelings for her, and this marked the beginning of a considerably wider view of the world and, perhaps paradoxically, a simpler one. He was now learning about the realities of love; soon he was to learn, as much as a man can, about the realities of birth; and in the war and the bombings the knowledge of death was not only within him but all about him. His greater experience made for longer poems, but also obviated, in some measure, the need for the density and the occasionally obscure subjectivity of *18 Poems* and *Twenty-five Poems*. *Altarwise by Owl-light* had marked a climax. Now he was tentatively beginning to move in another direction.

(It is possible that that sequence of poems was more than a mere personal climax coinciding, not fortuitously, with his marriage, but was the high watermark of "experimental" writing in verse, just as its contemporary, *Finnegans Wake*, was the ultimate in "experimental" prose. Both works marked the end of a battle, in which many of the century's best writers had taken part, against outmoded stylistic conventions. The battle had been won, and from now on the best writers, often the same writers, were to consolidate their victory. Only in the theatre, which is intellectually always a generation behind, has experimentation continued to seem necessary and, at times, exciting.)

Of course this new departure was not undertaken consciously and, to begin with, was largely tentative. There is little trace of it, for instance, in the old poems that he was rewriting. But the *Poem to Caitlin — I make this in a warring absence* — is indicative. He had been working on this poem for a year, and he published it in a first and then in a final version in the spring and summer of 1938. In a much earlier poem he had written that he, in his intricate image, strode on two levels. In this poem he strides on his love's level and also on that of the seashore and seawrack of the Cornish and Welsh coasts. As in the more ambitious but similar poem which he wrote a couple of years later, *The Ballad of the Long-legged Bait*, it seems to me, as it has seemed to others, that the levels are too disparate to provide an architecturally successful edifice such as he was to achieve with his later poems. On the other hand, *I make this in a warring absence* with the fine synthesis of its last line, *Yet this I make in a forgiving presence*, does foreshadow the grandly simple dramatic pathos of the poems that were to come.

It will be recalled that Richard Church had, on behalf of Dent's, turned down Dylan's proposed volume of the early stories on grounds of obscenity (though they have all been published now and seem harmless enough.) Church's expressed horror of Surrealism probably played its part in this decision. Furthermore Dent's, through Higham, were pressing him for delivery of his promised "Welsh book," and Dylan was generally very angry with Church at this time.

Late in 1937 Henry Treece, then a very young poet who was later to be associated with the group called "the Apocalypse," wrote to Dylan, for he was planning to write a book about Dylan's poetry. He had been to see Richard Church who had suggested mildly that perhaps such a book was premature. As an example of Dylan's invective when angered, I quote from his reply to Treece, dated January 3, 1938:

Reavey told me, when I was in town last month, that you were writing a book about my poetry. . . . I think the information actually surprised me more than it must have surprised Richard Church who has said to me, when I told him I was starving, that a genuine artist scorns monetary gain, and who later confessed, with a self-deprecatory shrug and a half-wistful smile that has brought tears to many a literary society, to a slight jealousy — "we're not so young as we were, you know" — of the vitality of modern youth. He thinks like a Sunday paper. I can see him telling you, with that pale, gentle, professional charmer's smile, placing together the tips of his thumb and index finger, as if to express some precise subtlety, "It is perhaps just a *little* too early, don't you think?"

Meanwhile George Reavey had agreed to publish the stories that Dent's had turned down, from the Europa Press (Paris and London). There were to be, in the French manner, two editions, a de luxe one at a guinea a copy for which subscriptions were to be sought and an ordinary, commercial one. Augustus John was then painting one of his two celebrated portraits of Dylan, and this was to be the frontispiece of the de luxe edition. The book was to be called *The Burning Baby: 16 Stories*.

In mid-February Dylan was writing to Charles Fisher that it would appear "next month." In mid-March Reavey sent out circulars to possible subscribers. James Laughlin, a Harvard student who had recently founded the New Directions Press, was interested in buying five hundred sets of sheets to make a small American edition.

However, the English printers shared Richard Church's fears, for they too would have been liable had the Crown instituted a prosecution for obscenity. Reavey tried to reason with them, and with some success, but all this meant a postponement of publication, initially until May first. Then Reavey departed for Paris, and Dylan was soon describing him as "tasteful, noncommittal and useless." On June 16th Dylan wrote to Reavey:

Will you tell me which are the stories, or sections of stories, to which most objection is taken? The only story I can think of which might cause a few people a small and really unnecessary alarm is *The Prologue to an Adventure*, this I could cut out from the book, and substitute a story about my grandfather who was a very clean old man. If, however, objection is taken to the book as a whole, then your suggestion of publication first in Paris seems very sensible. I was approached by Lawrence Durrell, for the Obelisk Press, some time ago, and I am pretty confident that, through Durrell and Miller, it would publish the book. That is, unless you have other Paris plans.

In July Wyn Henderson was attempting to get, for Dylan, a lawyer's opinion on the "words, phrases and sentences to which objection is taken." But by now George Reavey was apparently losing interest in the whole complex problem, and was not even answering Dylan's letters, thus arousing Dylan's anger, who referred to him in the most uncomplimentary terms.

Later that month, though, Reavey came up with a new proposition: that the de luxe edition be printed, as written, in Paris and a bowdlerized edition be published in England. In late August of 1938 Dylan was writing to John Davenport:

. . . I can get nothing clear from Reavey who is certainly not my dream, either, of a literary businessman. I write pathetically to George, but he just won't answer. Publication, he has condescended to tell me on a postcard, of the stories as they stand would lead to imprisonment. What he will not tell me is the particular words, phrases, passages to which objection is taken; these my scruples will allow me to alter without hesitation; but how do I know, without being told, what words etc. the dunder printers and lawyers think objectionable: piss, breast, bottom, Love? I understand, from someone else (Wyn Henderson), that George is going to get the stories done by a Paris smutpress first, then allow the lawyers he has apparently consulted to castrate them for English publication. I just sit and hate. Nobody tells me anything. (There will be, Laughlin tells me, no difficulty about American censorship.)

After which the whole project petered out. David Higham arranged that Dent's publish in the following year a book of poems to include such of Dylan's early stories as would not give offense. This became *The Map of Love* and appeared in August 1939.

The other important publishing event during this first year of Dylan's married life was the beginning of his relationship with James Laughlin of New Directions. This did not get off to a good start. Dylan had written to Laughlin that he was penniless and offered American rights on his future books. Laughlin, however, who had now left Harvard against his father's wishes and was trying to live in Italy and publish books on an allowance of a hundred dollars a month, could only send Dylan sixty dollars as advance against royalties on the first book. On the advice of John Davenport, who was visiting him at the time, Dylan did not sign the agreement. But the following year Laughlin returned to Harvard, his father resumed the financing of New Directions, and Higham's New York correspondent, Ann Watkins, worked out a satisfactory contract for five books. The first of them, *The World I Breathe*, poems and prose from the three English volumes, and three new stories, appeared in December 1939.

All this is running far ahead of Dylan's own story.

He liked Ringwood at first, and in late October of 1937, that is to say a week or two after he and Caitlin had first arrived at her mother's house, he wrote to Vernon Watkins:

This is a very lovely place. Caitlin and I ride into the New Forest every day, into Bluebell Wood or onto Cuckoo Hill. There's no one else about; Caitlin's mother is away; we are quiet and small and cigarette-stained and very young. I've read two dozen thrillers, the whole of Jane Austen, a new Wodehouse, some old Powys, a book of Turgenev, 3 lines by Gertrude Stein, and an anthology of Pure Poetry by George Moore. There are only about 2,000 books left in the house.

But soon enough, and as usual, he began to be homesick for Wales. In February he was writing to Charles Fisher:

I miss our old meetings. Here, apart from Caitlin and a very few immediate people, there's no one to talk to except Augustus John, who can't hear. Swansea is still the best place: tell Fred he's right. When somebody else's ship comes home I'll set up Swansea in a neat villa full of drinks and pianos and lawn-mowers and dumbbells and canvases for all of us, and the villa shall be called Percyvilla.

And in March he wrote to Richard Hughes saying that he and Caitlin were hoping to rent a cottage in Carmarthenshire for the summer and wondering if Hughes knew of "any likely places cheap enough for us."

For there was almost no money at all, and though he could manage to pick up a bit in London, where he went quite often for that specific purpose, he seldom managed to bring much of it back with him. Mrs.

Macnamara was home by now, and even a woman as understanding of a poet's problems as was she could hardly be expected to house and feed Dylan and Caitlin forever. He felt humiliated by a situation from which he could see no escape and which degraded him as a man and impeded him as a writer. On March 21, 1938, he wrote to Vernon Watkins:

I have been in London, in penury, and in doubt: In London because money lives and breeds there; in penury because it doesn't; and in doubt as to whether I should continue as an outlaw or take my fate for a walk in the straight and bowler-treed paths. The conceit of outlaws is a wonderful thing; they think they can join the ranks of regularly-conducted society whenever they like. You hear young artists talk glibly about, "God, I've a good mind to chuck this perilous, unsatisfactory, moniless business of art and go into the City and make money." But who wants them in the City? If you are a money-and-success-maker, you make it whatever you do. And young artists are always annoyed and indignant if they hear a City-man say, "God, I've a good mind to chuck this safe, monotonous business of moneymaking and go into the wilderness and make poems."

And two days later, even more bitterly in a letter to Henry Treece for which, once again, he could not afford a stamp:

Do you, I wonder and hope not, know what it is to live outlegally on the extreme fringe of society, to bear all the responsibilities of possessionlessness — which are more and heavier than is thought, for great demands are made of the parasite, and charity, though soon enough you learn to slip it on with a pathetic feeling of comfort, is a mountain to take — and to live from your neighbour's hand to your mouth? I have achieved poverty with distinction, but never poverty with dignity; the best I can manage is dignity with poverty, and I would sooner smarm like a fart-licking spaniel than starve in a world of fat bones. A poem, obviously, cannot be begun with the strength and singlemindedness it demands and deserves unless there is enough money behind it to assure its completion; by the second verse the writer, old-fashioned fool, may need food and drink. I know I will be paid — and how well, how well — for a poem when it is finished; but I do not know how I am going to live until it *is* finished. If I am going to live on writing any longer, I shall have to give up living, or write in a vacuum. Now I go without cigarettes, the tubular, white ants, in a smoking, swarming country. I feel in the position of the professor who was seen far out in the sea, spluttering, struggling, waving his arms and crying, "I'm thinking, I'm thinking." People on the beach, who knew he was always thinking, did nothing; and he sank.

But the series of long letters he was now writing to Henry Treece are usually more about his work than his life. As with his earlier letters to

Pamela Hansford Johnson they were, at least to begin with, letters to someone he had not met and who admired his poems immensely. Moreover Treece was paying him the very considerable compliment of writing a book about him when Dylan was still only twenty-three and had published only half a hundred poems and half a dozen short stories. And Dylan responded by writing him at great length, in letters that have been much quoted and are of the greatest possible concern to anyone interested in Dylan's development as a poet.

However it must be said that they lack the frankness and freshness of his letters to Pamela and the solid technical revelations of those that he was writing at this same time to Vernon. Although he starts his side of the correspondence with considerable enthusiasm, one soon senses a caution, almost a wild creature's alarm, at Treece's attempts to pin him down, to corner him as he must have felt, even perhaps to "expose" him. And Dylan takes refuge, as he had done in answer to the *New Verse* questionnaire three years before, behind a smoke-screen of semi-abstract verbiage. Perhaps the most quoted passage from this correspondence is in this same unstamped letter of March 23, 1938.

You mention Cameron and Madge. Cameron's verse has no greater admirer than myself, and I respect Madge's verse, though with complete lack of affection. But when you say that I have not Cameron's or Madge's "concentric movement round a central image" you are not accounting for the fact that it consciously is not my method to move concentrically round a central image. A poem by Cameron *needs* no more than one image; it moves around one idea, from one logical point to another, making a full circle. A poem by myself *needs* a host of images, because its centre is a host of images. I make one image — though "make" is not the word, I let, perhaps, an image be "made" emotionally in me and then apply to it what intellectual and critical forces I possess — let it breed another, let that image contradict the first, make, out of the third image bred out of the other two together, a fourth contradictory image, and let them all, within my imposed formal limits, conflict. Each image holds within it the seed of its own destruction, and my dialectical method, as I understand it, is a constant building up and breaking down of the images that come out of the central seed, which is itself destructive and constructive at the same time.

Although Dylan was certainly trying to tell the truth, or a truth, about his method of writing poems, phrases such as "my dialectical method" when coming from Dylan have, in my ears at least, the unmistakable ring of a tin shilling on a bar counter. And when, later in this long letter, he says: "I have read [Hopkins] only in the most lackadaisical way; I certainly haven't studied him, or, I regret, any other poet," he is simply telling a lie, unless he construed the word "study" as part of a university education.

When he met Treece, that summer, he did not take to him particularly, and when the book appeared the following year he did not care for that either. He used to say, in one of his less felicitous puns: "Poems are made by fools like me, but only God can make a Treece." But then he never liked dissection of his verse, and his comments on much that has been published about it since his death would certainly be pungent and certainly unprintable. As Caitlin has written:

He had the same dislike, amounting to superstitious horror, of philosophy, psychology, analysis, criticism; all those vaguely termed ponderous tomes; but most of all, of the gentle art of discussing poetry; not that I was likely to do that. We had a mutual agreement to keep off that touchy subject; and, if wellmeaning friends started an abstruse, intense interpretation of some of Dylan's most obscure lines, which he had long ago forgotten the meaning of himself, it was not long before Dylan was on the floor wrapped up in the carpet, scratching himself, like a flea-bitten hyena, in paroxysms of acute boredom, ending, happily for him, in snoring amnesia.

Early in April of 1938 they returned to his parents' small house in Bishopston, but in May, at last, they had a home of their own. Richard Hughes had found them a fisherman's cottage, furnished. It was one of a row, without any modern conveniences of any sort, not even running water. It was near his own house, and was in Gosport Street, Laugharne.

Laugharne is a strange little place, which fitted Dylan like a single, eccentric, tattered glove. Built beneath the shadow of its ruined Norman sea-castle, it has a portreeve for a mayor, and is a small, decayed, English-speaking "church" town set in a countryside that is "chapel" and Welsh-speaking. The town really has no function at all, being neither a market nor a port, with almost no industry and not even a railway station. Its inhabitants, who have much Dutch and Spanish blood, are quite distinct from their rural neighbours and are themselves divided into those who live Up Street and those whose homes are Down Street: these two factions live a Capulet and Montague existence, with little contact and considerable enmity, and they fight with knives. Built largely of purplish sandstone, it has a plethora of pubs and an atmosphere of tumble-down disintegration that recalls certain decayed seaside places in southern and western Ireland. Apart from Richard

Hughes and the clergyman, almost no people of the professional classes then lived in Laugharne. There was not even a doctor; one came from St. Clears, some miles away. The rector of St. Martin's told Richard Hughes at about this time that the dole was Laugharne's greatest blessing, for it brought two thousand pounds a year into a place with almost no other visible means of support. The most important family were the Williamses, of whom one brother owned the town's principal pub, Brown's Hotel, while another ran the buses and a third owned the electricity generating plant. But they did not run Laugharne.

Nobody did. Even the annual sports were a democratic chaos after Dylan's own heart. "What are the sports?" one disgusted inhabitant rhetorically asked Richard Hughes, and answered his own question: "They are the committee, drunk in a tent." And when Richard Hughes organized a regatta everyone believed that the winning sailboat had carried a hidden outboard motor. The ferryman who in those days would row across the estuary to Ferryside in response to the ringing of a handbell was also the Laugharne barber and was deaf and dumb too.

The place abounded in eccentrics of all sorts. One young member of the Williams clan chose to dress as a Wild West cowboy. The village idiot committed a murder, but got away with it, and while he was awaiting trial the village constable could not arrest anyone else, for the jail had only a single cell. The insanity rate was so high that when visiting day at the asylum came round, Williams ran a bus for the relatives. Dylan maintained, though, that the inhabitants of Laugharne were sane compared to the people of Ferryside across the bay "where they believe everything that anyone has ever said about them."

One of the last pieces that Dylan wrote for the BBC was about Laugharne:

Off and on, up and down, high and dry, man and boy, I've been living now for fifteen years, or centuries, in this timeless, beautiful, barmy (both spellings) town, in this far, forgetful, important place of herons, cormorants (known here as billy duckers), castle, churchyard, gulls, ghosts, geese, feuds, scares, scandals, cherry trees, mysteries, jackdaws in the chimneys, bats in the belfry, skeletons in the cupboards, pubs, mud, cockles, flatfish, curlews, rain, and human, often all too human, beings; and, though still very much a foreigner, I am hardly ever stoned in the streets any more, and can claim to be able to call several of the inhabitants, and a few of the herons, by their Christian names.

Now, some people live in Laugharne because they were born in Laugharne and saw no good reason to move; others migrated here, for a number of curious reasons, from places as distant and improbable as Tonypandy or even England, and have now been absorbed by the natives; some entered the town in the dark and immediately disappeared, and can sometimes be heard, on hushed black nights, making noises in ruined houses, or perhaps it is the white owls breathing close together, like ghosts in bed; others have certainly come here to escape the international police, or their wives; and there are those, too, who still do not know, and never will know, why they are here at all: you can see them, any day of the week, slowly, dopily, wandering up and down the streets like Welsh opium-eaters, half-asleep in a heavy bewildered daze. And some, like myself, just came, one day, for the day, and never left, got off the bus, and forgot to get on again. Whatever the reason, if any, for our being here, in this timeless, mild, beguiling island of a town with its seven public houses, one chapel in action, one church, one factory, two billiard tables, one St. Bernard (without brandy), one policeman, three rivers, a visiting sea, one Rolls-Royce selling fish and chips, one cannon (cast-iron), one chancellor (flesh and blood), one portreeve, one Danny Raye, and a multitude of mixed birds, here we just are, and there is nowhere like it anywhere at all.

When you say, in a nearby village or town, that you come from this unique, this waylaying, old, lost Laugharne where some people start to retire before they start to work and where longish journeys, of a few hundred yards, are often undertaken only on bicycles, then, oh! the wary edging away, the whispers and whimpers, and nudges, the swift removal of portable objects:

"Let's get away while the going is good," you hear.
"Laugharne's where they quarrel with boat hooks."
"All the women there's got webfeet."
"Mind out for the Evil Eye!"
"Never go there at the full moon!"

They are only envious. They envy Laugharne its minding of its own, strange, business; its sane disregard for haste; its generous acceptance of the follies of others, having so many, ripe and piping, of its own; its insular, featherbed air; its philosophy of "It will all be the same in a hundred years' time." They deplore its right to be, in their eyes, so wrong, and to enjoy it so much as well. And, through envy and indignation, they label and libel it a legendary lazy little black-magical bedlam by the sea. And is it? Of *course not*, I hope.

That was the place for Dylan, and he was never happier there than in that first summer of 1938, with Caitlin. She was in the early months of pregnancy and was placidly content to live in a house which Dylan described, in a letter to Henry Treece dated May 16th, as "a small, damp fisherman's furnished cottage — green rot sprouts through the florid scarlet forests of the wallpaper, sneeze and the chairs crack, the double-bed is a swing-band with coffin, oompah, slush-pump, gob-stick, and almost wakes the deaf, syphilitic neighbours. . . ." And a month later, again to Treece, he wrote, when inviting him to stay:

I warn you that our cottage is pokey and ugly, four rooms like stained boxes in a workman's and fisherman's row, with a garden leading down to mud and sea, that our living and cooking is rough, that you bathe or go dirty. You will find my wife extremely nice; me small, argumentative, good tempered, lazy, fumbling, boozy as possible, "lower middle class" in attitude and reaction, a dirty tongue, a silly young man. I hope you like drinking, because I do very much and when I have money I don't stop. There are three good pubs here, the best bottled mild in England, and no prohibitive drinking hours. There are walks, and boats, and nets to pull, and colossal liars to listen to.

He was being, as usual, self-deprecatory, for he was certainly not lazy that summer. He was writing new poems and working up the old ones. (Curiously, he never told Vernon that most of the poems he was sending him were quarried from the old Swansea notebooks and rewritten. He had no hesitation in admitting this to Treece, to whom he wrote: "I have a great deal of material still, in MSS books, to shape into proper poems; and these I will include, quite vaguely (that is, without considering an easily marked, planned, critical 'progress') in future published books. But we can talk about this." He was also writing and publishing the stories that make up the *Portrait of the Artist as a Young Dog*, a title suggested by Richard Hughes, which is surely his happiest and most successful prose work. And he began a collaboration with Charles Fisher, first envisaged as a radio play, then as a novel, entitled *The Murder of the King's Canary*.

He had been playing with this idea for some years — Pamela Hansford Johnson had suggested this title — and in March of 1938 he had written to Fisher from Ringwood:

Murder of the King's Canary: I'd very much like to do it with you because I've got lots of new ideas which I'm too lazy to tell you at the moment. Will it go as a radio play? I'd like to make it, with you, into a novel, make it the detective story to end detective stories, introducing blatantly every character and situation — inevitable Chinaman, secret passages etc. — that no respectable writer would dare use now, drag hundreds of red herrings, false clues, withheld evidences into the story, falsify every issue, make many chapters deliberate parodies, full of clichés, of other detective-writers. It could be the best fun, and would make us drinking-money for a year. Write some time and tell me how you feel about it. I hope to be somewhere about Swansea in the early summer, and we can discuss it properly then.

And from Gosport Street, probably in June, he wrote to him again on this subject:

Also we must get started on the Canary. Dorothy Parker called *her* canary Onan. See you perhaps tomorrow? . . . Have you heard anything about the wireless set? We've found a large room for Caitlin to dance in, and all she needs is music.

The radio was provided, and work begun on the *King's Canary*, though this book was eventually written, in a very different form and in collaboration with John Davenport, two years later.

Other friends came out from Swansea or down from London, Mervyn Levy, Vernon, Norman Cameron, Fred Janes, John Davenport. In early August they moved from their fisherman's cottage to what Dylan described as "a tall and dignified house at the posh end of this small town." Sea View was unfurnished, but with the help of friends and by buying on hire purchase they managed to make it habitable, both for themselves and their guests. And Caitlin did her best as a housewife who had to keep house on almost no money at all. Dylan's favourite food was stew, and she usually managed to provide it. Her stews, which used to simmer away for days or weeks on end, were extremely good; perhaps it was her French blood that taught her how to make that delicious and cheapest of all peasant foods, the *pot au feu*. She kept Sea View clean, too. This domestic side of Caitlin's character is one that hardly appears in her autobiographical writings. When her children were born she was a good and conscientious mother, and in circumstances that were often difficult to the point of impossibility she managed somehow to see to it that they got their meals at regular hours, and were clean and suitably dressed for the time of year. Dylan was, in this respect, quite useless. She has written, in *Leftover Life to Kill*:

The most he ever attempted was a super fry-up of all the leftovers: spattering, in the process, the walls, the floor, and even the ceiling with flying scalding fat; producing in the end, as he invariably forgot it to go on with his book, a black, charred pulp which he smothered in "Daddie's" sauce, and swilled down with fizzy cider for breakfast. As for minding babies while I went out, that was unthinkable and against his strongest codes: to which he never once made an exception! And small repair or adjustment that needed a handy man, was equally out of the question; he was as useless as a penguin with his hands, except for one purpose.

Yet somehow, always, she managed to make a home for Dylan. She was a good wife to him. In that same book, writing of their early married life, she says:

Dylan used to read to me in bed, in our first, know-nothing, lamb-sappy days; to be more exact, Dylan may have been a skinny, springy lambkin, but I was more like its buxom mother then, and distinctly recollect carrying him across streams under one arm; till our roles were reversed, and he blew out, and I caved in, through the pressure of family life, and the advent of holy-fire destroying babies. He read interminable Dickens novels, to which he was loyally devoted, and when Dylan was loyally devoted, no sentimental verbosities would change him, though he did bog down somewhere in *Little Dorrit*. He categorically refused to look at Proust, Jane Austen, Tolstoy, Dostoevski, and a lot of the obvious classics, though I furiously asked him, how could he know he wouldn't like them, without bothering to look; but there is no doubt he knew all right. He probably knew, more than anybody, what he liked, and what he didn't like, and what he wanted, and what he didn't want; without, like most people, having to find out. Once again that fiendish element of his days being numbered, comes into it; and all that sickly stinking stuff about: It had to be, there was no other way; the illogical, poets must die young, ruthless reasoning that made him follow, nobly and foolishly, that exorable pattern.

Frances Hughes remembers calling on them at Sea View that summer and finding them wearing heavy fishermen's pullovers in bed, where he was reading Shakespeare aloud to her. Whatever else they may have lacked, there was at least no shortage of books so long as Richard Hughes lived in Laugharne.

Dylan once told Bill McAlpine that he had never written a line while the pubs were open. This is a typical exaggeration, but like most of his statements about himself, it contains its measure of poetic truth. The pub, for Dylan, was a second and essential home. And so it became for Caitlin, too. In her published letter to her daughter, she writes:

Gradually I got used to pubbing: as easily as to most pernicious habits. Gradually the noisy, tapped and lamped cosiness; the smoked soup enveloping, gravy thick fug of the pub: enveloped me too, with its seducing spell. Its shining rows of villainous bottles; its wicked clinking glasses of manufactured friendships; its muzzy bumbling customers under an unaccustomed escaping aspect: began to gradually seduce me. But more still: the burning upward rush to the head; then the lullabying coma of the alcohol: held me a fast prisoner. . . .

Till, in the end, the pub became for me: and more so even for Dylan; a home: more homely than our own; from home. I can't remember one isolated evening that we spent at home: for the simple reason that I don't think there ever was one.

To contemplate living without a pub to go back to; was homelessness indeed. A long, homeless blank to fill up; like a sheet of blank paper with no inspiration. With no boozing pals in it, to fill it with homely life.

The pattern, like all his patterns, was quickly and almost immutably set. In the morning, work, followed by the pub which in Laugharne would usually mean the kitchen of Brown's Hotel; lunch, perhaps to bed with Caitlin, then work again in the afternoon; in the evening, Brown's Hotel again or the Cross Hands. In *Leftover Life to Kill* she has described their Laugharne when they returned there in 1949. By then she was much occupied with the children, and could not always accompany him as she had done in the early days. But with that exception this was basically how they had lived, always:

He was much better than me at contenting himself with the very simple, I might justly say moronic, life. Because, there is no other possible explanation, he lived in a world of his own: "out of this world," as they so succinctly put it in America. Thus: the best part of the morning in the kitchen of this same high class establishment, putting bets on horses, listening, yes, actually listening for once, open mouthed, to local gossip and scandal, while drinking slow consecutive pints of disgustingly flat, cold tea, bitter beer. Muzzily back to late lunch, of one of our rich fatty brews, always eaten alone, apart from the children; and I can't blame him for that, as there is nothing worse than brawling children's meals. He went so far, like a respectable Victorian father, as not travelling in the same carriage with them, though it was not often that we went anywhere *en masse*, and I cannot blame him for that either. Then, blown up with muck and somnolence, up to his humble shed, nesting high above the estuary: and bang into intensive scribbling, muttering, whispering, intoning, bellowing and juggling of words; till seven o'clock prompt.

Then straight back to one of the alternative dumps: we had long discussions as to which was the deadliest; to spend the rest of the evening in "brilliant repartee." That was a sample day with all the innards and lights taken out.

It was against this background, which inevitably became for her one of utter boredom, that he wrote his best work. And it was her determination that he should write his best work, that he should not compromise commercially, which made just tolerable to her a way of life that most women far more placid than Caitlin would surely find unbearable. There was, of course, a certain amount of social relief, when friends came to stay, but this also meant more work for her in the house. There were evenings with the Hugheses, but here Dylan — fond as he was of Frances and Diccon — was not always happy with their friends.

Augustus John now made them both nervous, and he was a fairly frequent visitor to Laugharne Castle. He had not yet got over his jealousy, and in his tough, materialistic fashion he mocked the young lovers for trying to live on air and even for reading Shakespeare aloud in bed. Charles Morgan was another visitor whom Dylan met there, and for whom he took so strong a dislike that he never ceased to invent the most wildly improbable, and hilariously funny, stories about his whimsy and pomposity; years later, in America, he described something utterly tedious as being "as long as a half an hour with a novel by Charles Morgan." And at least one of these grand people who, Dylan suspected, looked down on him has described meeting him at Laugharne Castle at this time.

This was Captain Lancelot de Giberne Sieveking, better known as Lance Sieveking, who wrote a whole column about himself for *Who's Who* in which modesty is not the predominant note. He had, in 1938, produced a few books and had a job with the BBC. In 1957 he published a volume of reminiscences called *The Eye of the Beholder,* which is about all the famous people he had met; the end-papers are in the form of a genealogical tree, showing through whose introduction he had rubbed shoulders with all these celebrities. Although not myself celebrated enough to feature in his end-papers, I had met this personage at just about this time or perhaps a little earlier, and Dylan's immediate reaction surprises me not at all. Here, then, is a description of Dylan at this time by an initially hostile witness:

He and his wife had a tiny cottage overlooking the estuary, just beyond the castle . . . One day I came out on to the stone-flagged terrace that Williams-Ellis had laid under the new windows of the dining-room. There were several people sitting about, among whom were Frances Hughes, my wife and a rather mysterious lady who was said to be a witch. Conversation was general. Frances introduced me to the young man: "Oh, Dylan, this is Lance." He grunted and frowned at the ground. I made one or two remarks to him, but he only replied with angry growls. Occasionally he cast a baleful glare at the clean white flannel trousers I happened to be wearing, and then looked round as if in the hope of finding a pail of garbage or a pot of tar he could throw over them. He was a stoutish young man, with round, slightly protruding eyes, and a mass of tangled brown curls. His nails were black, and his bare feet dirty. He wore very old corduroy trousers, the flies of which gaped open. His dirty grey shirt was torn. He didn't look as if he had washed for a long time. I wondered why he was so grumpy.

He turned to me at last and said: "No."

A tremendous smell of beer reached me with the word. He got up and walked a few steps on to the grass. . . .

When he returned, his face suddenly lit up in a smile so enchanting that his whole appearance was transformed. He sat down and began to talk to everyone in general, including me. It was obvious that they were all very fond of him, and I could understand why. His personality, once he had thrown off his grumpiness, shone with a sort of endearing bravado. He talked well, and his laugh was infectious. His voice had an astonishingly compelling quality and range. . . .

Richard Hughes wrote a comment on this passage, and Mr. Sieveking very decently printed it as a footnote:

Frankly I don't remember Dylan ever looking or behaving quite so badly: at any rate at such an early date. . . . It wasn't just occasional "charm" made us fond of him . . . it was his genius ("charm's" two-a-penny). He may have sponged on us economically but spiritually it was more the other way about. . . . It was the kind of companionship I badly needed.

Richard Hughes has told me that he never lent Dylan and Caitlin money. Occasionally he would give them what he described to me as small sums. His goodness to them, both now and later, was very great, and Dylan was grateful; from now on there is not an unkind word in any of his letters about Richard Hughes. This is not true about all his friends, nor of everyone who lent Dylan money.

Money was the awful, the almost insuperable, problem, and it remained so, in varying degrees of intensity, until the day he died. Already, with Caitlin expecting a baby, it was acute in the summer of 1938, and for the next two years Dylan had to expend a very great deal of his energy on frantic searches for small sums which were never quite enough even to pay the bills. The desperate appeals to agents and publishers, the sad but ever more skilful begging letters to rich friends and acquaintances — and to poor ones, too — the hopes of some state grant constantly deferred, it makes for depressing and monotonous reading. Nor do I propose to go into it in detail here.

At times Dent's were sending him a small weekly sum; at times, too, so was James Laughlin of New Directions. But for 1938 he had to rely mostly on his friends, and particularly on John Davenport who had come back to England from Hollywood with a lot of film money in his pocket. In the autumn of that year Dylan applied to the Royal Literary

Fund for "an immediate grant of money to help me live and to help me pay for the care of Caitlin and child." For this he had to collect signatures, and some of those literary figures to whom he applied were patronizing, while some refused to sign. His appeal was turned down, on the grounds that he was not an "established writer"; but as he pointed out to Davenport, had he been established he would scarcely have needed to apply. John Davenport arranged that his appeal be reconsidered. There was anxious waiting until it was again turned down, and in October of 1938 his debts drove him out of Laugharne and back to Mrs. Macnamara's charity in Ringwood, there to await the baby due in the new year.

The new year brought no surcease. They managed to return to Wales with the baby in April, but at once it was the same problem all over again, aggravated now of course. Norman Cameron thought up a scheme which might produce a small, steady income. Instead of Dylan touching now this friend, now that, for a pound or two, why not organize those friends who believed it important that he continue to live and write? He suggested a "Dylan Thomas Flotation Fund," with contributions of five shillings a week, and John Davenport was prepared to contribute and help. Throughout that summer before the war Dylan was anxiously enquiring about this. But what, he wanted to know, did Cameron mean when he said that Davenport should act as a "funnel" through which his benefactors should send a series of post-dated cheques? It was all most bewildering. In August only three sure contributors had been found, Cameron, Davenport and Roger Roughton. But, Dylan wished to know, what about Peggy Guggenheim, Brian Guinness, Michael Redgrave? What about Roland Penrose, at whose request Dylan had attended the London unveiling of Picasso's *Guernica* and read some words of his own. They all had large fortunes, and most of them had helped individually in the past.

For a little while this idea of collective patronage appeared a possibility. Despite the Royal Literary Fund, he was an "established" poet among those interested in that art, with two books published and a third about to appear. It should not have been too difficult to find twenty or thirty people prepared to give this poet five shillings a week each, and he, Caitlin and the baby could have managed on five or six pounds. However neither John Davenport nor Norman Cameron was the man to organize such an undertaking. They were both busy with their own work, and though they were both generous with time and money neither was even remotely an organization man.

Furthermore Dylan's habits were by then too well known in London. Some of those approached, knowing that beer then cost about eight pence a pint, interpreted, quite correctly, that their five shillings a week meant in fact one pint, out of how many? a day. And although all of them would probably have been prepared to buy Dylan many pints in London, this is not at all the same as paying for the drink without the conversation. And then it was the war, and the scheme collapsed.

An appeal to the late Edward Marsh, that great patron and benefactor of the arts, produced a sum, probably about twenty pounds. Early in 1940 another appeal was launched, this time through the magazine *Horizon,* by Stephen Spender and Henry Moore. T. S. Eliot was among those who signed it, and those who gave were as varied as Hugh Walpole and Kenneth Clark. But again this was only a temporary shoring up of the dyke.

There was one, minute source of income I should like to mention. In 1939 Emma Swan, then a young American poet, inherited some money and thought she was rich. She asked James Laughlin if there were any poet she should help. He told her that Dylan Thomas was penniless, and for two or three years she sent him twenty dollars a month. They never met. He wrote to her, each month, letters which — alas! — are lost. She has told me that once, years later, she found herself in the same room with him in New York, but did not introduce herself for fear lest it embarrass him.

From the time of his marriage insecurity became, even more than before, a basic condition of his life. Money, which he had never loved nor respected, assumed a positive malevolent role. It became the horrible substance which involved him in begging and lying and cheating. It thus became real. And when that symbol assumes, by its cruel inaccessibility, a negative reality in a man's mind, he will often react by becoming either a miser or a spendthrift. Dylan, in his poverty, was a spendthrift, and so was Caitlin. Who can blame them for such defiance; was that not after all their nature? But the cost they had to pay for it was, as usual, enormous.

Many, perhaps most, women would now have pushed Dylan into taking some sort of job. Another wife might have remarked to Dylan that almost all poets without a private income "worked" as well. She understood, through heart and perhaps through head, exactly what the extent of his energy was, and she was always angry and sad when this was dissipated, away from the real purpose of his being. He had convinced her, more I think than ever he had convinced himself, that he was the pure poet, the *poeta assoluto*. But with the outbreak of the war a problem which had been simmering, for him personally, ever since the loss of Swansea innocence, became acute to Dylan as a poet, as a father and as a man. But that belongs in the next chapter.

In October of 1938 he was writing to Higham that his new book, which was then to be called *In the Direction of the Beginning,* was ready. It contained both prose and verse. John Lehmann turned it down for the Hogarth Press, and it went back to Church, who agreed to publish it. As Dylan wrote next spring, about the obscenity trouble: "Richard Church did the simplest thing by cutting all the best stories out." One that went was the fragment which was to have given the book its title, and so the title became *The Map of Love.* In December of 1938 he wrote to Vernon that he had agreed with Church on fifteen poems and five stories. Only one of the poems, and none of the stories, was unfinished when Dylan and Caitlin left Laugharne for Ringwood in late 1938, there to await the baby's birth: this was Llewelyn's long nativity poem, *If my Head Hurt a Hair's Foot.*

Before leaving Laugharne he had gone to Manchester, on October 18th, to take part in his second BBC broadcast. This was national, not regional, and was called *The Modern Muse:* W. H. Auden, Stephen Spender, Cecil Day Lewis and Louis MacNeice, as well as Dylan, read their own poems. It is sad that this was before the age of tapes, and that so astonishing an assembly of poets' voices should have vanished into the air, for no gramophone record was made. And it is all the more sad since "cultural" broadcasts of this sort were rare before the war, though a few programmes of modern music and verse were sent out from Manchester where John Pudney was then working as a writer-producer. Indeed he, as much as any individual, may be said to have created, in the North, the embryo that was later to grow into the Third Programme. Dylan, who scarcely appreciated being corralled into a studio with a lot of other poets who were not then his friends, wrote tartly to John Davenport:

All the boys were in it, and what a mincing lot we were. Did you hear it? All the poets were born in the same house, and had the same mother too.

They were at Mrs. Macnamara's house for five months this time, and Dylan did not enjoy it. In January, while awaiting his son's birth, he wrote to Charles Fisher: "This flat English country levels the intelligence, planes down the imagination, narrows the a's, my ears belch up old wax and misremembered passages of misunderstood music. I sit and hate my mother-in-law, glowering at her from corners and grumbling about her in the sad, sticky quiet of the lavatory. I take little walks over the bad Earth."

And in March, to Frances Hughes: "We're coming back next Wednesday, the fifth, I think, of April and we're looking forward to it a lot. No more muggy south, narrow vowels, flat voices, flat chests, English Riviera, and housefuls of women. We want to see again the dilapidated Roman emperors, the Mrs. Peounds and Peounds, the petrol-drinkers and bee-swallowers. It's very damp here."

A little bit of money had come in, from an American award, the Blumenthal Poetry Prize, which brought him a welcome one hundred dollars, and Higham had obtained him an advance of fifty pounds from Dent's for *The Map of Love;* but against this there were the expenses of the baby's birth, which took place on January 30th. In December when Lawrence Durrell asked him to come to London to meet Henry Miller — a writer for whom Dylan had an immense admiration — he had not the price of the fare, and Durrell sent him one pound.

Durrell's description of that first meeting, inaccurate in other respects though it is in remembered detail, is a good example of Dylan's timidity and shyness with those whom he regarded as great artists. Durrell wrote, in *Encounter:*

On the evening in question he kept us waiting hours and we were on the point of giving him up for lost when the telephone rang. He said in hollow, muffled tones: "I can't find the flat so I'm not coming." He wasn't tipsy. He just sounded terribly nervous and ill at ease. "Where are you now?" I said, "because I'll get a taxi and fetch you." That startled him. "As a matter of fact," he said, "I'm just too afraid to come. You'll have to excuse me." He then told me that he was telephoning from the pub immediately opposite the house. "Stay there," I said, and ran out across the road to meet him and lay hands on him. I hadn't seen him for some time and he had altered a good deal. He was the golliwog poet of the later portraits . . . He was ruffled and tousled and looked as if he had been sleeping in a haystack. He had a huge muffler round his throat. He was also extremely jumpy and touchy and said he was too frightened to move from the pub and that I should stay there and have a drink with him. This I did, and after a bit his nervous aggressiveness died down and I was able to suggest dinner. I painted a ludicrous picture of poor Henry Miller walking round and round the dinner-table cursing him until I prevailed upon him to come with me. Once we left the pub he completely changed, became absolutely himself, and took the whole thing with complete assurance and sang-froid. Within ten minutes the nervous man was teasing Miller and enjoying [the] good wine — and indeed offering to read us his latest poems, which he did there and then. Miller was delighted, too, and Thomas thereupon launched into a fragment of poetic prose with his curious pulpiteer's thrasonical voice; I didn't awfully like the way he read — and only when I heard him on the radio did I realise the full power and beauty of his voice.

We talked and drank late into the night and altogether it was a splendid evening; and from then on we met fairly frequently, though he would never come direct to the house. He always rang up from the pub and forced me to have a drink with him there before he would come into the house. I don't know why.

Just before leaving Hampshire to return to Wales he wrote a letter to his old friend Bert Trick, filled with pride in his baby son, "a fat, round, bald, loud child, with a spread nose and blue saucer eyes," and with nostalgia for the old days in Swansea:

Oh, I'm set in life now — two stone heavier, but not a feather steadier. Though never again will I fit into Swansea quite so happily and comfortably as I did, for I'll be a hundred jokes and personal progressions behind all my friends. I'll be almost a dead face. Or, worse still, a new face, in which nothing will interest them but the old shades and expressions. I'm strong and sentimental for the town and people, for long filled-in Sundays with you and scrapbooks and strawberry jelly at the end. For readings and roarings with all the grand boys. I'm not meaning to talk like an ancient village outcast — no more than two years separate me. I'll have all the summer, and every summer, I hope, in Carmarthenshire. But one small close society is closed to me. And a social grief is natural. We're all moving away. And every single decisive action happens in a blaze of disappointment.

Dylan's nostalgia for the past, for that lost paradise of innocence which we all carry with us throughout lives that are seldom innocent and never paradisiac, became henceforth an ever stronger theme in his writing. In his life it manifested itself in his unswerving loyalty to his Swansea friends: in a devotion, which seems to increase, towards his parents and particularly his father: and in an urgent homesickness for Wales when in England or, later, America. In his prose, excluding his hack-work, he seldom wrote — except in a very few poems such as *After the Funeral* or *Vision and Prayer* — about any other subject than himself as a boy or as a very young man. It was as though he looked not only inwards but into one particular phase of his life, the phase when he was preparing or writing the poems in his notebooks. And in his later poems, which he once defined to a journalist as "statements on the way to the grave," this emotion is of far greater complexity, and nostalgia itself becomes an inadequate word with which to define it.

He had never lost his conviction that his would be a short life. Nor was this a pose, as his "TB" had perhaps once been, for he was far too sensitive and sensible to play-act in front of Caitlin and to her, too, he said repeatedly that he would not live till forty. Though two stone heavier, thanks largely to the beer he had drunk, and no longer a thin and sickly boy, he was convinced that time was ticking away against him. All the more reason, then, to come to terms, poetical terms, with his own past. As he had put it some years before:

> The ball I threw while playing in the park
> Has not yet reached the ground.

When it does reach the ground, he must no longer be there, and thus all he can hope truly to comprehend is its upward flight, the first stage of its parabola. And from such comprehension much can be understood about the only vital problem, that of the relationship between birth and death. For even when he was young and easy under the apple boughs

> Time held me green and dying
> Though I sang in my chains like the sea.

And now the imminence and soon the reality of war made the eternal and infinite omnipresence of death even more real to Dylan than before. It is by no means coincidental that the two victims of that war whom he should have mourned in poems were a girl child and an old man aged one hundred. And again, in one of his last poems, *Lament*, he completes the circle from his infancy to his own coming death and his own children's infancy, with the obvious implication that the circle must again be completed in their brief lives.

The contemplation of their childhood must also and inevitably have reawakened his absorbed interest, never really dormant, in his own. There is no need here to insist on the mystery of watching a child of one's own pass through all those phases and ages that one has passed through oneself in a personal time that is to each of us so distant as to be magical. It is, since Shakespeare and before, one of the great themes of lyric poetry. And perhaps no poet was ever more conscious of *lacri-mae rerum*, of the *neiges d'antan*, of time's wingèd chariot, than Dylan, who was writing poems of regret even before he had left Swansea Grammar School.

There are also other speculations that are relevant to this subject. There is the question of what I have called Dylan's own regressive character, his frequently infantile behaviour. This is perhaps in some ways a matter more for a psychologist than a biographer. But certainly Dylan found it extremely difficult to deal with an adult's problems, with laundry, money and civil servants. Certainly, too, he preserved infantile habits into early middle age, asking his friends to sing him to sleep, sucking at his bottle or his cigarette, eating sweets and reading trash or watching science fiction films goggle-eyed. Much of this must be accountable to the early, perhaps the earliest, days at No. 5 Cwmdonkin Drive, but it can also be explained in part by the fact that his very powerful brain was devoted, not quite exclusively but almost so, to his work. The trivia of life bored him, his failures to deal with them distressed him, his own dishonesty and partial compromise with the outside world disgusted him, and therefore he looked back to the golden age before women and publishers and tax gatherers, when birth and a child's vision of fresh beauty and death were the realities. Certainly it was there that he found his purest and deepest inspiration.

✳   ✳   ✳

They returned to Sea View in May. Llewelyn was christened in the Anglican church there, his godfathers being Augustus John, Richard Hughes and, by proxy, Vernon Watkins. Dylan had all his three children baptized. Their christenings were, I am sure, the only occasions apart from friends' weddings, in his adult life, when he entered a church to take part in a religious service. And this leads to the much-vexed question of Dylan's religion.

Vernon Watkins has stated, more than once, that Dylan was a religious poet, and I hesitate to disagree with a man who knew Dylan so intimately, and his poems even more so. Personal knowledge, though, is not in Dylan's case of first importance in attempting to establish what were, and what were not, his beliefs and convictions. The actor in him led him to play many parts, while the man of sensibility was always most anxious not to distress his friends. Since Vernon Watkins is himself a religious poet, Dylan when with him would, quite naturally and for that time quite truthfully, give the impression that he fully sympathized with his friend's vision of the world. It was this quality of sympathy, which was by no means feigned, that won him his host of friends, of all conditions and almost all views. A Communist friend might be equally convinced that he and Dylan saw more or less eye to eye. A man as uninterested in politics or religion as was I in the days when I was seeing him would be led to believe that he too had no interest in these matters. He did not, in fact, argue, partly from tact and a desire to please, partly because all abstract argument bored and even worried him. This explains why all sorts of views on all sorts of subjects have been ascribed to him by friends and the friends of friends. He had simply agreed. It may also explain why, on the whole, he liked to keep his friends, or at least his different categories of friends, apart; he had no wish to be caught in the middle of an intellectual cross-fire.

The Reverend Leon Atkin, a Nonconformist minister in Swansea with strongly socialist views and whom Dylan liked immensely (he used to refer to him as "my padre") has told me that in his opinion Dylan was a religious man but not a Christian. The poet and philosopher William Empson, who also knew him well, has described Dylan's religion as a "pessimistic pantheism." And on one point, at least, all can agree: Dylan was not an atheist, though in some of his early poems there are echoes of his father's post-Nietzschean, almost Manichean, concept of an essentially malevolent divinity. Not only was atheism, like any other sort of ism, distasteful to a man who was above all interested in his own sensations: as an artist he could not accept the view that it is all fortuitous chaos on the one hand (or how could he write poems?) nor that it is all a mechanical, behaviourist and therefore ultimately predictable construction on the other (or why should he write poems?).

It would be an exaggeration to say that he had thought this problem through. It would be nearer the truth to suggest that he felt, as a poet, the beauty and glory of the divine concept as revealed to, and by, the great English religious poets, Donne, Vaughan, Crashaw, George Herbert, Hopkins. But it does not follow from this that he was himself such a poet, nor even that he might have become one had he lived. (Though this obviously cannot be ruled out.) His direct knowledge of the Christian religion came from the chapels of his youth, and for them and for the ranting oratory of the preachers he preserved a steady dislike and contempt. His use of biblical and Christian ritual imagery would seem to me no more to prove his Christianity than his use of astronomical imagery indicated that he was an astronomer or that his repeated references to birds make him an ornithologist. Those lovely words and echoes were all there, to his hand, and with his pen he put them in his poems.

And of course it is only by an examination of those poems and of his prose that one can form any real opinion on this question of his religious beliefs. But in the poems, again, he is elusive, so elusive that clever and honest men have read quite contradictory meanings into them. And in this may lie much of his appeal to an age that discovered Kierkegaard. If he was a religious poet, his was a religion that excludes morality, dogma, even sureness of belief. This does not leave much behind, but perhaps it is enough, as for that other Thomas, who also doubted.

There are two brief prose passages that seem to me most revealing. One occurs at the very end of "Conversation about Christmas," which he wrote in the autumn of 1947. After describing the child's day, his own Christmas day as a boy, he writes: "I turned the gas down, I got into bed. I said some words to the close and holy darkness, and then I slept."

Five years later he wrote the well-known introductory *Note* to his *Collected Poems*. This ends:

I read somewhere of a shepherd who, when asked why he made, from within fairy rings, ritual observances to the moon to protect his flock, replied: "I'd be a damn' fool if I didn't!" These poems, with all their crudities, doubts, and confusions, are written for the love of Man and in praise of God, and I'd be a damn' fool if they weren't.

These two simple remarks seem to me to tell his spiritual story. As a boy he spoke those few words. The year before he went into that good night he uttered again what is as close to a prayer as perhaps an agnostic can pray. Yet even in these words one senses the gargoyle's wink above the dangling cigarette.

Aneirin Talfan Davies in his study of Dylan's religious imagery, *Dylan: Druid of the Broken Body*, admits that Dylan was brought up by a father who was a Bible-reading agnostic, but believes to see in his poems a spiritual progress towards Roman Catholicism. It is not my intention to engage in religious polemics; I can only say that neither in his writing, nor in his life, nor in his letters, nor in what his friends have told me can I see any sign of any such progress whatsoever. As his knowledge of the world increased, he was able to employ more subtle religious imagery than that which he had first learned in his Uncle Dai's chapel, Paraclete, but I am sure that it requires much wrenching of language, both his and ours, to speak of him as a believer, in any meaningful sense. He remained an agnostic all his life though at times, perhaps, a reluctant one.*

* Vernon Watkins, who has read these pages, has given me this comment: "If he was, as I believe, religious and Christian, he doesn't need my advocacy, and if he wasn't, he doesn't want it. There is a truth in what Empson writes about "a pessimistic pantheism," as Dylan recognized a great error in the Past and he saw ruin ahead; but every colour and glory and holiness of every creature was real to Dylan, not a one-toned gloomy world, but the most rich and variegated one belonged to his vision of God; and so the pantheism; but I still think and feel that George Herbert meant more to him than even this, and Kierkegaard, whom I used to read to him aloud, pierced him more deeply. I would call Dylan a Blakean Christian but even that would be only an approximation."

10

❧ ❧

O<small>NE</small> of the malicious anecdotes which Dylan used to tell about Charles Morgan was that in a sudden silence, at a party, that distinguished novelist was heard to remark: "I spent twenty years perfecting the use of the colon; and then the war came." Whether the story is true about Charles Morgan, I cannot say. It does, however, express a point of view not at all remote from Dylan's own.

He regarded the war as a personal affront. It interfered with his writing; it dried up such slender sources of income as he possessed; and it was likely to destroy him physically or, at best, to condemn him to an indefinite sentence of military service. On September 3, 1939, he sent Pamela a copy of the newly published *Map of Love,* and beneath the date he wrote: "Dylan-shooting begins." And to Frances Hughes he said that he must bring out another book of poems just as quickly as possible, before "they" got him. "They" were undoubtedly the government and its servants, not the Nazi enemy. A broadcast of poems by Welsh poets, which he and Keidrych Rhys had collected and which was to have gone out on September 6th, was cancelled, for the BBC too was being mobilized. And as a young man of twenty-four he must have expected to be called up very soon, even though married and a father.

The whole prospect filled him with the gloomiest foreboding. His reaction to the war was certainly not unique. We did not go gently, or even willingly, into the Second World War. We knew too much about the First. As Bernard Gutteridge has written:

> The last war was my favourite picture story.
> *Illustrated London News* bound in the study;
> The German bayonet we believed still bloody.

It had hung over all our childhoods and youth, that hideous massacre in the mud, and as we grew up we came to see it not through the eyes of the *Illustrated London News,* nor those of Julian Grenfell or Rupert Brooke, but of Wilfred Owen, Robert Graves and Siegfried Sassoon. We might loathe the Nazis and their cruel and stupid ways, but emotionally and by intellectual inheritance it was not the German people we hated so much as our own politicians and brass hats and merchants of death. The very first poster that "they" put up seemed to crystallize and justify this feeling: YOUR RESOLUTION, YOUR FORTITUDE, YOUR COURAGE WILL BRING US VICTORY.

In varying stages of glumness, apprehension or resignation, with vague memories of "life expectancy six weeks" and dawn strafings and shell shock and trench feet, most of the young men whom Dylan had known in the Wheatsheaf, most of his Swansea playmates and a high proportion of the poets he had met either volunteered for the armed forces or rather drearily awaited the summons to serve their King and Country. There were, however, certain alternatives.

It was possible to go away to neutral America, as did W. H. Auden and Christopher Isherwood, or to neutral Ireland, as did Roger Roughton. Such a course, however, was not open to a man with a wife and child and no money. Some, who hated the idea of soldiering but did not wish to emigrate, compromised and joined the Fire Service. This is what Stephen Spender did, and several other writers and painters too; but they were hardly recruiting firemen in Laugharne. There were said to be "reserved occupations" in the BBC, the Ministry of Information and elsewhere. But how to get one, and what qualifications for such a job had the author of three volumes of poems to offer? Finally, and again remembering the First World War, there were those who declared themselves to be conscientious objectors. These men then had to appear before a tribunal which decided whether or not their objections were genuinely those of conscience. Political or personal objection was inacceptable; religious objection — particularly if the man belonged to a pacifist sect such as the Quakers or the Plymouth Brethren — often brought complete exemption. This was the course that Dylan originally chose.

His attitude towards the war was concrete, personal and firm. He hated it, in all its manifestations. He wished neither to kill nor to be killed. The experience of soldiering held no appeal for him whatsoever. Indeed, the very sight of soldiers annoyed him, even before the war began. In July he had written to Treece, from his father's house at Bishopston:

My father's house is stuck on a crowded piece of beautiful landscape — This Way to the Cliff scenery — and surrounded by 4000 Territorial soldiers. Girls hot and stupid for soldiers flock knickerless on the cliff. We're returning to Laugharne tomorrow. There are only 50 soldiers there. What are you doing for your country? I'm letting mine rot.

And three days before the Germans invaded Poland he wrote to his father from Sea View:

These are awful days, and we are very worried. It is terrible to have built, out of nothing, a complete happiness — from no possessions, no material hopes — and a way of living, and then to see the immediate possibility of its being exploded and ruined through no fault of one's own. I expect you both are very anxious too. If I could pray, I'd pray for peace. I'm not a man of action; and the brutal activities of war appal me — as they do every decent-thinking person. Even here the war atmosphere is thick and smelling: the kids dance in the streets, the mobilised soldiers sing Tipperary in the pubs, and wives and mothers weep around the stunted memorial in the Grist. Our own position is, *so far,* quite comfortable.

On September 11, 1939, he wrote to Glyn Jones: "I want to get something out of the war, and put very little in (certainly not my one and only body)." And three days later, to John Davenport:

I am trying to get a job before conscription, because my one-and-only body I will not give. I know that all the shysters in London are grovelling about the Ministry of Information, all the half-poets, the boiled newspaper-men, submen from the islands of crabs, dismissed advertisers, old mercuries, mass-snoopers, and all I have managed to do is to have my name on the crook list and a vague word of hope from Humbert Wolfe. So I must explore every avenue now, I can't afford to leave an Edward Marsh unturned. Because along will come conscription, and the military tribunal, and stretcher-bearing or jail or potato-peeling or the Boys' Fire League. And all I want is time to write poems, I'm only just getting going now, and enough money to keep two and a bit alive. . . . My little money-sources — (apart from anything else) — are diminishing or dying. Soon there will not be a single paper paying inadequately for serious stories and poems.

I can speak and act too. Do you know of anything for me? Does the film-world want an intelligent, young man of literary ability, self-conscious, punch-drunk, who must (for his own sake) keep out of the bloody war, who's willing to do any work — provided, of course, that it pays enough for living?

But nothing turned up, and he resigned himself reluctantly to registering as a conscientious objector and facing the tribunal. To Bert Trick he wrote, in late September:

I'm trying to complete by December a book of short stories, mostly potboilers, called temporarily *Portrait of the Artist as a Young Dog*, stories towards a provincial autobiography. They may be amusing eventually, but the writing of them means the writing of a number of poems less. They are all about Swansea life: the pubs, clubs, billiard rooms, promenades, adolescence and the suburban nights, friendships, tempers and the humiliations. The book is on contract. I get too little regularly for the job. I am commissioned to write another prose book by the middle of next year. . . .

What are you doing in the War? I'm very puzzled. When it's necessary I'm going to register as an objector, but also because I want to get something out of the mess if possible. My little body (though it's little no longer, I'm like a walrus) I don't intend to waste for the mysterious ends of others. If there's any profiteering to be done, I in my fashion wish to be in on it. But my natural and, to me, sensible greed and opportunism will come unfortunately to nothing; I'm sure of that. I know a few wires but they only tinkle when I pull them. So I'm afraid that I shall *have* to take the tribunal. Is there any possibility of getting a job in Swansea? I don't know how you feel about all this, but I can't raise up any feeling about this war at all. And the demon Hitlerism can go up its own bottom. I refuse to help it with a bayonet. To talk about keeping Hitlerism out of this sink of democracy by censorship and conscription, mystery-mongering and umbrella-worship, atrocity circulation and the (thank God mostly unsuccessful *so far*) fostering of hate against bewildered and buggered people. How long? Only to encourage the rebellious pacifism of anti-social softies like myself.

In October he was trying to give these very inchoate and frankly selfish views some sort of theoretical justification. He was Against the War and he now canvassed the support of other writers who he thought might feel as he did. It is possible, too, that he was trying to establish his own position as a pacifist before facing the tribunal. He wrote almost identical letters to a number of writers in his attempt to compile a sort of symposium which he hoped that Robert Herring might publish in his magazine. To Rayner Heppenstall he wrote, on October 27th:

I'm trying to get together, for publication in any unsqueamish paper (preferably *Life and Letters Today*), a collection of objections to war from writers mostly of our age. Not just general objections, but the statements of fellows who aren't going to support the war at all. I don't know how you stand now, but, if you do thoroughly object and intend to stay by your objections, will you write your reasons in a fairly brief statement? — in any way you like, of course. I think the publication, especially in a widely circulated popular-literary magazine, such as *Life and Letters,* will, or might, do, at this time, a lot of good. This is not meant to be a Peace Pledge front, it's no party or union thing at all, just the statements of individual . . .

And he goes on to list three writers from whom he has already received such statements, two of whom were, as it happens, Welsh Nationalists, the third a member of the Communist Party, and he gives the names of three more to whom he is writing.

Here, as in his much earlier "political" letter to the Swansea *Guardian* quoted on pages 78–80, there is once again that curious incoherence that came over Dylan whenever he tried to write about politics or any other semi-abstract subject. This master of the English language then flounders like a foreigner. And this is surely because he did not really "believe in" politics. He might go round saying he was a Communist or a socialist or a pacifist, but what he really believed was summed up in a sentence that he had written to Bert Trick in 1935: "Historically, poetry is the social and economic creed that survives." And he summed it up again, in Communist Prague in 1949, when he was heard to shout: "I am a Communist, but am I also a bloody fool?" If such pronouncements as these have any meaning at all, which is doubtful, it is surely that Dylan had no comprehension whatsoever for politics as that word is normally understood.

In writing to Rayner Heppenstall he had chosen quite the wrong man, for that patriotic Yorkshireman was a determined anti-Nazi who was about to volunteer for the army. He sent Dylan a sharp reply, and soon enough the idea of the manifesto or symposium petered out.

On December 9, 1939, he sent the typescript of the *Portrait of the Artist as a Young Dog* off to David Higham's partner, Laurence Pollinger — Higham had himself re-joined the army — with an urgent request that the balance of the advance, forty-five pounds, be sent him at once. He needed it to pay a pressing debt. And this was the last substantial payment he was to receive from Dent's for several years, for he had no other book published in England until after the war.

On December 18th of that year both he and Caitlin took part in the Laugharne Entertainment which Frances Hughes had organized in aid of the Red Cross. Item Number Two of the Entertainment was: "Tap Dance by Mrs. D. Thomas," and this was followed by a one act farce called *The Devil Among the Skins* by Ernest Goodwin. Dylan played the part of the tanner, which I understand is the lead, though I have not read the play. He acted it very well, and the little Laugharne audience enjoyed the whole Entertainment. This was a winter of endings, for all that was beginning was a war. And so far as I know this was the last time that Dylan appeared upon a stage until the readings of *Under Milk Wood*, at the Young Men's Hebrew Association, in New York in the year of his death.

After the Entertainment Dylan and Caitlin went back to the Hugheses' house and drank and were happy in the kitchen. It was then, Richard Hughes has told me, that Dylan said to him: "What the people of Laugharne need is a play about themselves, a play in which they can act themselves." This may well have been the genesis of *Under Milk Wood* which fits, far more, the mood of the writer who had just finished the *Young Dog* than that of the poet who was about to write *There Was a Saviour*. But with all Dylan's writings the roots lie deep, and almost always deep in his Swansea youth. As early as 1932 or 1933, when staying with Bert Trick in his bungalow at Caswell Bay, Dylan had spoken of his wish to write a sort of Welsh *Ulysses*, a story encompassed within twenty-four hours.

Milk Wood passed, in his mind, through many phases. Certainly Laugharne, Dylan's Laugharne, is the place, though in some ways the village resembles New Quay more closely, and many of the characters derive from that seaside village in Cardiganshire where he lived at the end of the war. In 1943 or thereabouts he outlined the plot to Richard Hughes. A village is declared to be, collectively, mad; an inspector is sent down from London to certify the village insane; the inhabitants give their evidence, and while they and we are convinced of their sanity in a world that has gone crazy, the inspector, who comes from that world of war and greed, regards them as condemned out of their own mouths.

A year or so later, after the revelations of the German concentration camps, Dylan outlined the idea to me one afternoon in an underground drinking club in Chelsea called the Gateways. The village was declared insane, anti-social, dangerous. Barbed wire was strung about it and patrolled by sentries, lest its dotty inhabitants infect the rest of the world with their feckless and futile view of life. They do not mind at all, though they grumble about the disappearance of the buses. The village is the only place that is left free in the whole world, for the authorities have got it wrong. This is not the concentration camp; the rest of the globe is the camp, is mad, and only this little place is sane and happy.

He rightly discarded all this superstructure when he wrote the play, for he was far too skilled a writer to underline his points. But the meaning remains and has been accepted, and this surely accounts for the enormous popularity of a play that was, for its generation, as meaningful in its own way as were George Orwell's last novels in theirs. In it he said something that we wished to hear. He did not say it perfectly, for the play was never really finished, and had he lived he would certainly have revised the ending. Even so it is a small masterpiece, perhaps the best play for sound radio ever written, and it began in Richard Hughes's kitchen, in Laugharne, on December 18, 1939.

They spent the first Christmas of the war, as they had spent the last two of the peace, with Caitlin's mother at Ringwood. Once again it was a long visit, for it was not until the middle of March that they returned to Laugharne. And now time was running out for Dylan: he expected to be called up, with the rest of his age group, that summer. Augustus John, whom he had seen in Hampshire, had suggested to him that he write to Sir Kenneth Clark, then head of the Ministry of Information. Dylan did so, both before and immediately after his return to Wales, asking if there were any possibility of a reserved job, particularly in the Ministry's film division. But there were not.

At the same time he was writing to Stephen Spender urgent and desperate letters asking for financial help. And it was now that Spender, Henry Moore and Herbert Read, acting through Peter Watson's magazine *Horizon*, set about raising money for him. A job was obviously becoming essential.

For in Wales he had attended a conscientious objectors' tribunal, either as a spectator or as witness, and had heard several young men plead exemption, always on religious grounds. What he regarded as the mean faces and bearing of the objectors and the hypocrisy of their claims disgusted him, and he was quite sure that he could never produce such arguments on his own behalf. He did enquire of a Welsh Nationalist leader whether Welsh Nationalism were sufficient reason to be exempted; apparently he seriously considered becoming a Welsh Nationalist in order to avoid conscription. But the man to whom he had written was not at all sympathetic and told him, bluntly, not to be so silly. And Dylan now abandoned the idea of pleading conscientious objection.

On the other hand he still had no luck in finding a job in a reserved occupation. The best that Sir Kenneth or rather Lady Clark could offer was an introduction to Victor Cazalet. Cazalet was a very rich man and a patron of the arts. He commanded an anti-aircraft battery which he had equipped at his own expense, and for the first few months of the war it was almost a private army. Many painters and writers enlisted in it: at least they would have one another's company and their battery commander's understanding of their own particular problems. This must have been the only artillery battery in the history of the British Army to have its own librarian, in the person of James Pope Hennessey. There were quite a number of semi-private armies coming into existence at this time, a swarming, as of bees, of men with similar tastes and mutual friendships. Evelyn Waugh has described this quite natural process in his wartime novel, *Put Out More Flags,* natural that is to Englishmen with their tendency to form clubs and join associations, but anathema to the nameless staff officers and civil servants who were busy transforming the young men of Britain into anonymous personnel. Indeed they already had their eye on Victor Cazalet's battery, nor was it to preserve its semi-private nature much longer. But this Dylan did not know, and he decided to volunteer for that battery — where he had apparently been promised a niche — rather than wait to be called up and sent wherever the army chose to put him. Anti-aircraft artillery, being almost entirely a defensive arm, also appealed to his pacifist emotions.

So early in May he set off from Laugharne to Llandilo to volunteer. And he returned in a state of the utmost depression. The doctors who had carried out the medical examination had pronounced him C-3, because of his weak lungs. Their verdict upset him immensely.

For some years now he had believed himself to be healthy. Now the old nightmare was revived, and though the reason he was declared C-3 was almost certainly asthma combined with a tendency to a bronchial condition, he once again immediately interpreted this as "TB." He was frightened and worried.

Furthermore while his physical rating ruled out a posting to Victor Cazalet's battery, it did not, as he soon discovered, mean that he was exempt from military service. He was still liable to be called up and posted to some non-combatant unit such as the Army Pay Corps. In fact he was in a military limbo, where it was impossible to plan for the future. Thinking he was going to go into the army he was about to give up Sea View and had ceased payment on his hire purchase furniture, which was likely to be taken away at any time. He thus found himself with a wife and child — who would have received a small allowance had he joined the army — but with the prospect of no home, no money and no work. A few days later the Germans began to overrun France, and the war became earnest indeed. But what was he to do? He would have had to be a man with iron nerves to go on writing *Adventures in the Skin Trade* in such circumstances. On May 13, 1940, he wrote to Stephen Spender, from his father's house at Bishopston:

I've had to sneak my family away from our home in Carmarthenshire, because we could no longer obtain any credit and it was too awful to try to live there, among dunning and suspicion, from hand to mouth when I knew the hand would nearly always be empty. I've had to leave all our books and clothes, most of my papers etc., and unless I pay our most important debts, quickly, everything will be sold up: the beds and china and chairs and things that we've managed, with difficulty, to collect over three years. Now, until some money comes, we're staying here in my father's house: he's a very poor man and finds it, himself, hard to live: we're almost an intolerable burden to him, or, rather, we will be very soon. I'm writing only poems now, those extremely slowly, and can expect very little money for them. I do not want to write another straight prosebook yet; it would eventually get me some money, I suppose, but it would mean ten or more poems less, which, I think, would be sad and silly for me. And when I am called up, if only to be a latrine-minder, I shall obviously have less and less time in order to gain me even a few occasional pounds. My wife and myself have not a private penny. I do, a lot, want to return to Laugharne, Carmarthenshire, pay our debts, find ourselves in our own home again, live there working quietly until I am needed; and then to leave my family there, knowing they are, at least, clothed and housed. My debts amount almost exactly to £70. If I could get £100, I could settle everything and make a new start there: ensure food for the two others for a long time to come. If I cannot pay these debts and have a little to live on, there's no hope at all: everything we have collected and built up will go and I do not see where and how my wife and child can merely live. I cannot go away leaving them nothing but debts and their lodging in another's poverty. I'd sooner die with them, and this money worry is making a nervous fool of me when I want to be, and can be, solid and busy.

But his friends saved him. On June 2nd he was writing to Peter Watson, from Laugharne:

Thank you very much for sending on the two cheques. I never thought I'd have so much, and was frightfully pleased: I'll be able to settle everything now. As you see, I've gone back to this place.

It could, at best, be only a reprieve. Even Laugharne was beginning to be affected by the war, as Richard Hughes went off to join the navy, the young men vanished into the army, France collapsed, and the talk was all of invasion. Dent's decided against publishing a book of poems built around *18 Poems*, which was now out of print, and Dylan sold the copyright in those poems, outright, to the Fortune Press for some fifteen pounds without informing his agent of this foolish act. (Ten years later Higham, acting on Dylan's behalf, managed to buy back the copyright for approximately ten times this sum, so that they might be included in *Collected Poems*.) In June Vicky Neuburg died, and Dylan wrote a sad little note, and in Dublin his friend Roger Roughton gassed himself, which upset Dylan greatly. His world, like everyone else's, was dissolving fast. Clearly he could not hope for another publicly collected subsidy, even had the international situation been less overpowering. He was never a man to uproot himself voluntarily, but he and Caitlin could not go on as they were. Yet what was he to do? All his efforts had so far come to nothing. At this moment John Davenport once again came to his help.

John Davenport was a few years older than Dylan. A heavily built, indeed immensely strong man, he had at Cambridge acquired a considerable reputation both as a boxer and a poet. But he abandoned boxing, and poetry, sadly, abandoned him, though in 1940 he was not yet fully aware of this. (In 1931, when he felt poetic inspiration flagging he had asked T. S. Eliot for advice. Eliot had recommended that he not force his muse, and that he return to her in ten years' time. This advice he accepted, but when he sought her again in 1941 she had fled.) He has since become one of the best-known non-academic critics of literature writing in English, a man of immensely wide culture, multilingual, a pianist of distinction, a connoisseur of painting, and a wit. Both physically and intellectually this great bull-of-a-man whose mind is so fastidious that it has prevented him from any commitment other than occasional criticism is almost the exact opposite of bone-snapping, coughing, cocky Dylan who gave himself away in every sense, and in almost every line he ever wrote.

They had met and become friends in the very early, Parton Street bookshop, days. Then John had gone to America, with his first wife, Clement, the daughter of a rich Bostonian. He writes me:

I went to Hollywood to write a film for Robert Donat. RKO bought a thing I'd written for him about Clementine Sobieska and Charles Wogan — Old Pretender stuff. After some months the producer discovered that the Young Pretender wasn't Charles II. He'd got the two Charlies mixed up, and was cross with me for cheating him out of Nell Gwyn. All very vexing. He was a tiny little man who really wanted to do a film about the abdication of Edward VIII. James III and Charles III threw him. He wanted a wedding in Westminster Abbey and all. Rome wasn't good enough. Luckily Donat broke his contract at about that time, and I moved to another studio. I finished up with $750 a week.

In 1937 both he and his wife inherited substantial sums of money, and John decided that this was a good opportunity to come home. He bought a large manor house on the edge of Marshfield, a small and agreeable country town in Gloucestershire. Until the outbreak of the war he was European story editor for MGM, but his contract was automatically cancelled on September 4, 1939. He had spent most of his inheritance on the house, and of course the film income had disappeared, but there was still his wife's money. To Dylan, whom he had helped more than once since his return, John Davenport appeared a millionaire. The Rouaults and Picassos and the great Tanguy that is now in the Museum of Modern Art still hung on the walls; the two concert grands in the music room were still in tune; the thousands of books were in their shelves, and there was wine in the cellar.

In that hot and fantastic summer of 1940 — the last summer, as many of us then thought — John Davenport saw little purpose in economizing or planning against the future. And he gave his hospitality and what remained of his money to his friends. His wife later designed the sets for the Royal Opera House, Covent Garden, and most of their guests were musicians, but he also extended an indefinite invitation to Dylan and Caitlin. In the middle of June they took little Llewelyn down to his grandmother's at Ringwood and themselves went to Marshfield, where they stayed for over three months. Dylan, describing the household to Vernon on August 8th and a little later in another, undated letter, wrote:

I'm staying here in John Davenport's house. He's an amateur writer and musician, extremely able, weighing nineteen stone. It's a big house, full of books and pianos and records. There are lots of other people staying here too: Lennox Berkeley, Arnold Cooke . . . who are both professional composers, Antonia White, and William Glock. Aren't they nice names? Davenport and I are writing a fantastic thriller together, so I haven't done a poem for a long time although there are 2 I want to write badly: both nightmares, I'm afraid. On Europe etcetera please do bettera. . . .

I think this house must be marked, and the letters opened. Really. The house, as I told you, is full of musicians, all are young men, not one is in the army, one has a German name, there *was* a German staying here some time ago, and there have been five lighting offences in about six weeks.

When Dylan refers to John Davenport as an "amateur writer" it is his rather naive way of saying that John did not, like himself, apparently have to depend solely on what he could earn with his pen. Dylan would never have collaborated with an amateur writer in the pejorative sense of that word. Nor was John one of those rich men on whom, increasingly as the years went by, Dylan battened merely because he was rich. Caitlin might complain that life at Marshfield was passed "in a gilded cage" but then her pride led her to resent even normal hospitality and she was growing increasingly suspicious of Dylan's talent for exploiting his friends. For Dylan, John was a friend who liked and understood his poems. Had their situations been reversed, Dylan would have behaved as John was doing.

The routine at Marshfield during that summer of 1940 was soon established. John had furnished one room in the style of a public house bar, complete with beer, and thither he and Dylan would retire after breakfast to work on *The Death of the King's Canary*. Caitlin would then usually go to the gardener's cottage, which was empty, carrying Mozart records to play on the portable gramophone while she danced. At midday they would bicycle out to a real pub for a beer or two. In the afternoons Dylan and Caitlin would go to bed. Then, sometimes, Dylan would work on a poem or on the *Skin Trade*, and in the evenings there was music and talk and drinks and, frequently, the visit of the policeman to complain about the blackout. At night, increasingly, there was the broken drone of German bombers overhead. Dylan wrote to Vernon:

In this house Caitlin and I have our bedroom on the top floor, and so far we haven't got up even when the German machines are over us like starlings. But I think we'll have to, soon. My mother wrote and told me that people are sleeping on the Gower beaches, in barns and hedges. I went to see a smashed aerodrome. Only one person had been killed. He was playing the piano in an entirely empty, entirely dark canteen.

The Death of the King's Canary is a satirical fantasy, somewhat in the style of Wyndham Lewis's *The Apes of God*. It concerns the election of a poet laureate (the King's canary) at a confused and confusing banquet in a country house where a circus, complete with freaks and fat lady and clowns, is installed in the grounds. All the more prominent English poets of the day are present and become increasingly intermingled with the circus people, whom they come to resemble as the proceedings grow more and more orgiastic. The poets are drawn so very much from life, and so easily recognizable both as public and private faces, that the book is considered libellous and cannot be published at present.

Dylan and John wrote alternate chapters, though it is possible that part of Dylan's contribution was in fact what Charles Fisher had written for the original collaboration of 1938, and of which John Davenport knew nothing. Dylan was certainly, by now, capable of such sleight of hand when writing prose. The verse parodies were all written by John Davenport except for the satire of William Empson. This was by Dylan. The July 1942 issue of *Horizon* was devoted to the work of William Empson, and Dylan there printed his satire, with the odd subtitle of "Homage to William Empson." It has not been reprinted since. It is curious that Dylan did not write more of the verses in the *King's Canary*. He was an excellent parodist and enjoyed writing, or at least making up impromptu, parodies all his life. His self-parodies were, in my memory, particularly funny.

It was while staying at Marshfield, and through John Davenport's help, that at last he got a job of sorts. This was writing scripts for the Latin American Service of the BBC. On the 25th of August, 1940, the first of these was broadcast, in Portuguese, to Brazil, and he was commissioned to write another, about Christopher Columbus, with which John Davenport helped him, "an exciting one" as he wrote to Vernon. He told him that he hoped this work would go on, adding: "I'll have to go to London so often, once — and if ever — this job really gets going." But it did not. He only did one more talk for the BBC in the next eighteen months.

Nevertheless in September he did go to London, and Caitlin returned to Bishopston with the baby. John Davenport had obtained fifty pounds from Lord Howard de Walden for Dylan; it was he, it will be recalled, who had written the libretto for *Dylan: Son of the Wave* many years before, though this is purely coincidental. Dylan was most anxious to find work and also to get Caitlin away from Marshfield, where her flirtations with another of the Davenports' guests were making Dylan cross and jealous. It was an angry parting, the first perhaps of many. She did not at all appreciate being shipped back to Swansea while he set off, as she imagined, to have a high old time in London.

This was at the beginning of the blitz, the capital was being bombed every night and often by day as well, and a less propitious moment in history to look for work in London could scarcely be imagined. However, Dylan was lucky.

Through John Davenport again he had met, or perhaps re-met, Ivan Moffatt. In pre-war days Ivan Moffatt, the son of an American painter and decorator and of Iris Tree, the actress, had been living in his father's luxurious flat in Fitzroy Square, and it would seem improbable that he and Dylan should not have met then. However it was only now that they became friends. He was an American and therefore had not been called up. And he was in films.

He was an apprentice director with Donald Taylor, himself a film producer of great distinction who at that time had a company, Strand Films, which was rapidly acquiring a near-monopoly in the making of high quality documentary films for the Ministry of Information. Donald Taylor, moreover, was far from being a simple-minded film tycoon and no man was ever less of a bureaucratic disciplinarian. After many years of film making and of working with the most distinguished producers of documentaries, he had not only absorbed the whole technical bag-of-tricks but had also realized that film technique — of which something like a fetish had been made in the 'thirties — was merely a means to an end, and that a good film, even a documentary about wartime transport, requires a good writer as well as good cameramen, cutters and so on. He was therefore collecting, at Strand, a team of writers whose work he admired.

Ivan Moffatt could not have approached a better man on Dylan's behalf nor a more sympathetic one. He knew and liked Dylan's poems, though it must here be emphasized once again that Dylan, in 1940, though well known in certain circles, was not a famous poet. There cannot then have been many film producers who had ever read a line of his. He also had a personal reputation, which he made no attempt to conceal, and which was calculated to scare off a conventional businessman, but this Donald Taylor was not. Ivan Moffatt appealed, as well, to the generosity and kindliness of Donald Taylor's nature. Not only, he said, was Dylan penniless: he was also too sick to be in the army. It was essential that something be done for him at once.

They met at a pub in St. Martin's Lane one warm September evening. The bar would normally have been crowded at that hour, but London itself was half empty and most of those who remained went home as quickly as ever they could, to be near their families and their shelters before the night, and the bombers, arrived. They met in an almost empty pub.

Donald and Dylan took an immediate liking to one another, which grew stronger with the years. The relationship between employer and employee is not always an easy one, and with so touchy, proud and self-conscious an artist as was Dylan its difficulties might easily have led to disaster. Instead it became one of close friendship and mutual understanding. Donald soon realized that Dylan was not only a fine poet but also a fine film craftsman. Dylan for his part, while not infrequently bored by the scripts on which he was asked to work, never made the cardinal error of many writers new to films; he did not regard his work as a prostitution of his talents, nor did he believe he should assert his artist's integrity by adopting a patronizing attitude towards his employer's needs. On the contrary, Dylan was fascinated by films — had he not been film-struck all his life? — and he was in this, as in all other aspects of his work whether as reader, actor or writer, a pro. Donald Taylor recognized this rapidly, and with delight. Dylan was soon on the payroll of Strand Films, first at eight pounds and later at ten pounds a week, and throughout the war this was his financial anchor. Donald Taylor at that time only paid himself a salary of twenty pounds a week from his most profitable firm, so Dylan's was a very decent salary.

Nor was that the end of it. Donald Taylor did not insist that the writers he employed keep any sort of office hours. Provided that they did their work, and met their date-lines, he was quite uninterested in how they did it or where. When Dylan was in London there was an office for him if he wanted it. If he preferred to be in Wales or anywhere else, Donald had no objection. And for the first six months of their association Dylan, who was extremely frightened of the bombing, was usually working in Wales. Those conferences between writers, directors and producers which occupy so much of film people's time were carried on with the greatest informality, often in the Café Royal at lunchtime, often in the pubs in the evening, or in the Boogie-Woogie or some other night-club later. And at these sessions Strand Films paid the food and drink bills. In fact Dylan not only received the essential security of his salary, but also, when in London, a high proportion of his expenses.

Over and above this, there was nothing in Dylan's contract to prevent him doing any other work he might wish to undertake. And later in the war he did a fair amount of broadcasting — the list, as complete as I have been able to make it, of his broadcasts is given in Appendix 1 — as well as writing poems and talks. Finally, though this was not technically a reserved job, he was under the indirect protection of the Ministry of Information and thus safe from being called up. Donald Taylor had given him, in fact, precisely the job for which he had been looking.

Caitlin did not approve and for mixed reasons. She told Donald Taylor, and frequently, that he was corrupting Dylan. She believed that Dylan was wasting his talents and his brief time, and who can say that she was wrong? She had married a poet, but for three years he wrote almost no poems. The film scripts which, for the next decade, consumed most of his energy and time, have been or are being published, and surely there can be little doubt that though these may be skilled and interesting, they are infinitely less important — I use the disagreeable word deliberately — than the magnificent poems he was still to write, not to mention those that he might have written. She interpreted Donald Taylor as the man who, by money and night-clubs, had seduced Dylan away from his art, who had changed Dylan's innocence to cynicism, and who thus had stolen her Dylan away. And she hated Donald Taylor for having done this.

On the other hand Dylan, as she herself has written, was a man who always knew exactly what he wanted to do. He wanted now to be in films. Furthermore, within a few months he took a step which seems to me to reveal a great deal about his state of mind. For seven years he had been quarrying in his early notebooks, rewriting the poems of his astonishingly fecund adolescence. When he went from Marshfield to London he left the notebooks behind; and in the spring of 1941 he sold them to Bertram Rota, the dealer in manuscripts and rare books, and eventually they found their way to the Lockwood Memorial Library in Buffalo. It would be hard to imagine a more significant gesture on Dylan's part, a greater renunciation of the past, than this. Those notebooks were his youth, those notebooks were his poems, those notebooks were Dylan the young poet. Had he wished to continue, to repeat himself, they contain scores of poems that he could have continued to rewrite. The money, as always, was welcome, but this was one of the less desperate moments. Dylan, who was surely aware of all the implications of his action, was the richer by a hundred pounds or so. Bills were paid and drinks bought. And that quarry which he had created in his own feverish, fertile youth was closed to him forever. The boy-poet, the Rimbaud of Cwmdonkin Drive, had ceased to exist.

Lyric poets change, or stop or die. Keats died in his twenty-sixth year, and Dylan was twenty-six when he sold his notebooks. Nor do I believe that this is purely fortuitous coincidence. As a small child he had told his mother that he intended to be "better than Keats," and all his life that great poet was, as it were, the model against whom he measured himself. Shortly before his death he was to tell John Davenport that he was so tired; that he could not go on; that he had had twice as long at it as Keats. But now, in 1940, he intended to go on living, and writing. Therefore, his own brand of logic would have told him, the past must be shed, the boats burned. As he remarked to me once: "It's lovely when you burn your boats. They burn so beautifully."

       ✻   ✻   ✻

Donald Taylor's writers, who included Graham Greene at first, always Philip Lindsay, the historical novelist who became perhaps Dylan's closest London friend, and towards the end of the war Julian Maclaren Ross, among others, worked sometimes individually, more often as a team, two or more writers being assigned to a single project. Unfortunately the files of Strand and of its successor company, Gryphon, were destroyed. It is therefore impossible to say precisely what scripts Dylan worked on and when. Nor were all the scripts that were begun finished; of those that were finished, not all were made; and on one occasion a film that had been made from a script of Dylan's was never released, for the Ministry of Information was scandalized by its eccentricity.

This was a documentary called *Is Your Ernie Really Necessary?*, a parody of the government's wartime slogan: "Is your journey really necessary?" One actor played all the parts. Donald Taylor has told me that he remembers two scenes from this semi-Surrealist extravaganza: in one the signalman in his box plays "The Bells of St. Mary's" on his levers; in another the solitary actor is dressed like a chorus girl and, by an optical process, is repeated twelve times so that he appears to be a chorus line. This film only got as far as negative cutting before the Ministry got wind of it. It is now lost.

At first Dylan usually worked as a member of a team, and it is hard to say what he was doing. He worked on films with the most varied subjects: the Nazi leaders; M & B, then the new wonder-drug; a film for

ICI about dyes called *This is Colour;* one about the Home Guard; another about a barrage balloon site. It is said that for this last film he needed the advice of a member of the Women's Auxiliary Air Force. The Waafs were paraded for Dylan's inspection, and one very pretty girl stepped smartly forward saying: "Pick me!" He did, and was apparently not disappointed. Perhaps the most ambitious of his documentaries was *Our Country,* which was made towards the end of the war and is almost as sentimental as its title. A returned merchant seaman wanders about Britain and is deeply moved by all he sees. Such films of his as are known to me or remembered by Donald Taylor and others are listed in Appendix 2, but this list is certainly not exhaustive.

Later, as the war neared its end, Donald Taylor wished to get away from documentaries, and a number of plans for feature films were outlined and some scripts written or begun. One, which never progressed beyond the idea stage, was a film that Dylan and Phil Lindsay were to write together about the life of Dickens; they planned to use, almost exclusively, Dickens's own words taken from the autobiographical parts of his novels. Another was to be a film about Crippen. Another was based on Maurice O'Sullivan's book about the Blasket Islands, off Kerry, called *Twenty Years A-Growing;* Dylan wrote one hundred and thirty pages, or half, of this and the synopsis of the second half before the idea was abandoned. His most complete and successful script was written with Donald Taylor, Taylor supplying the story-line, Dylan the descriptions and the dialogue. It is about the Edinburgh body-snatchers, Burke and Hare, and has been published as *The Doctor and the Devils.* It ran into censorship trouble — the subject is exceedingly gruesome — and has not yet been made, though there is once again talk that it will be.

In September of 1945 Donald Taylor wound up his film company, Gryphon. Thereafter Dylan worked as a script-writer for a number of other producers, particularly for Sydney Box, the managing director and executive producer for Gainsborough, a Rank subsidiary. Here again Dylan worked on several feature films, few of which were finished and none of which was made. He also wrote part of a fantasy about a boy's love for bicycles, starting with a penny-farthing and eventually riding up to heaven, to be greeted by a heavenly choir of bicycle bells, on a sunbeam and a Sunbeam: *Me and My Bike* has been published in a limited edition. Indeed though half a dozen of his scripts exist, or will soon exist, as books, scarcely one, apart from the early documentaries, has yet become a film.

This was not Dylan's fault. Many, perhaps most, writers in England and America who have ever been involved in the film world have had, in varying degree, the same experience. All the producers for whom Dylan worked between 1940 and 1949 — when Gainsborough in its turn was wound up and Dylan's connection with films virtually ceased — have told me that he was not only a very skilled craftsman at words (though less good at constructing a dramatic plot) but also conscientious. There is a story that he was once locked up in a hotel room in Sloane Square with a crate of beer and a script to complete over the weekend, and that he got through them both in two days. Such behaviour is, or was, not at all unusual in the film industry, where chaos, rush and cancellation are the normal order, and where wild enthusiasm is replaced, overnight, by total apathy and loss of interest when some man in a front office in which the script-writer has never set foot changes his mind and does not sign a cheque.

And for most writers this is a frustrating state of affairs, against which cynicism provides the easiest defence. Dylan was, in his poems, the very opposite of a cynic, but his film work — during the war he called it, rather touchingly or perhaps cynically, "my war-work" — became increasingly a mere job, and this became markedly more his attitude after the war when he was no longer working with Donald Taylor and their friends. It was done, more and more, simply for the money. After all, a writer is a writer because he wishes to communicate his ideas or emotions, perhaps to the millions, perhaps to his mistress, perhaps, as Dylan wrote, to:

> . . . the lovers, their arms
> Round the griefs of the ages,
> Who pay no praise or wages
> Nor heed my craft or art.

It is depressing to write film after film that is never made. And by the time Dylan was working for Gainsborough, though he did his work well, he had few illusions left. One of the scripts he then wrote was *The Beach at Falesa*, which is based on the story of that name by Robert Louis Stevenson. Although it contains a few good phrases, it is obviously hack-work. Mr. Jan Read, who was then scenario editor at Gainsborough, has written in his introduction to that also unmade script which is now published in book form:

It was my task to keep an eye on progress, and this was anything but easy. His habit was to spend every penny of any advance before beginning work and there would be desperate messages, begging for further advances to pay the tradesmen or buy Christmas presents for the children, so that scripting could continue. Writers ourselves in the scenario department, we did our best for him; but he remained the wonder and despair of the studio accountants. When he did get down to the script he wrote at great speed. . . .

As a person I found him charming and without sides or pretensions. He was unpunctual, it is true, to the extent of turning up for a script meeting a day or two late — generally with some such disarming excuse as that he had only a few minutes ago 'phoned his agent to enquire the date. When he did arrive at Lime Grove it was always in a rumpled blue serge suit, looking like a merchant seaman on shore leave. There was never much work done on those occasions; instead, we inevitably adjourned to the Shepherd's Bush Hotel to down pints of beer and listen to his Welsh stories, which he told beautifully. . . .

Thomas was not the man to bother overmuch with technical requirements. Most of the points agreed in discussion he used to forget long before returning to Oxford and work. . . .

This was late in his life and chronologically this description belongs in the next chapter of this biography. Six years earlier, Julian Maclaren Ross had come to work for Donald Taylor in Golden Square. In an article published after his own death, in the *London Magazine* for December 1964, Julian described his first meeting with Dylan, and their subsequent collaboration at Strand Films:

We travelled up together in the lift at No. 1 Golden Square without speaking, neither knowing who the other was. Dylan wore a green porkpie hat pulled down level with his slightly bulging eyes: like the agates we used as Alley Taws when I was a boy in France, but a darker brown. His full lips were set low in a round full face, a fag-end stuck to the lower one. His nose was bulbous and shiny. He told me afterwards that he used to rub it up with his fist before the mirror every morning until it shone satisfactorily, as a housewife might polish her doorknob. . . .

They found that they were to share an office, and collaborate on a script about the Home Guard, a subject concerning which they were both totally ignorant. They began to invent:

His cigarette waggled up and down as he spoke and his face was screwed up in a frown against the smoke, but he removed the fag-end only when it was burnt right down. But even when he mumbled you could understand every word, though his voice was low-toned and he spoke fast. I've heard people who should know better do imitations of him with a sing-song Welsh accent, but a slight intonation on certain words — "Daughter," for instance, — was all he really had.

They spent the evening drinking, and the next morning Dylan had one of his atrocious hangovers.

He started suddenly to sneeze. Sneeze after sneeze convulsed him and he tried to smother them in a large red bandanna snatched from out of his sleeve.

"That's a nasty cold you've got."

"Not a cold. It's the drink coming out."

The drink was also coming out in sweat, and I said: "Look here Dylan, I don't feel too good myself. Why don't we have a bottle up here, to guard against these hangovers in future?"

"A bottle?"

"Whisky. We could go halves. I know a fellow can get it on the black market. I'll ring him now if you like."

"Whisky? *In the office?*" He seemed absolutely appalled.

"Don't be silly, why not?"

But Dylan firmly shook his head. "Not for me. You please yourself of course, but I won't if you don't mind."

Indeed he never drank when he was working, except sometimes a little fizzy, almost non-alcoholic cyder. Of Dylan's attitude towards his film work, Maclaren Ross writes:

Contrary to what is often said, he was extremely interested in the film-medium, while I at that time was obsessed by it, though it's doubtful whether we either of us had the true Documentary Mind. What we really wanted to script were Features, and together we planned among other subjects a mystery-film to be written in collaboration, entitled *The Whispering Gallery* or *The Distorting Mirror*. We both had a penchant for pictures of this sort and spent much time in tracking down vintage examples all over London. . . .

Our own film was to be a deliberate throwback to *Caligari* and *The Cat and the Canary* in its original Paul Leni version, and Dylan provided the basic idea. A party of assorted people are being shown by a guide round the whispering gallery of a stately home open to the public, when suddenly a voice says out loud: "I'll have this place." Owing to the acoustics no one can tell who spoke, camera pans to various faces, and the film begins, with the heir many times removed ironing out methodically and by remote control all those in his way. He was to recruit his murderous accomplices in a deserted amusement park, and to be seen unrecognizably reflected in the Hall of Mirrors, hence the alternative title. We could never decide whether this super-villain was to be male or female, and Dylan was in favour of both: i.e. a character whose sex is changed by an operation half way through.

We also shared another ambition, which was to write a film script, *not* a treatment as the story-form is called, but a complete scenario ready for shooting which would give the ordinary reader an absolute visual impression of the film in words and could be published as a new form of literature. Carl Meyer, the co-author of *Caligari* and creator of many of the great early German silents, who invented the mobile camera or rather caused it to be moved about, is said to have written such scripts; but neither Dylan nor I could get hold of a script by Meyer, and the only ones we knew which almost succeeded in doing what we had in mind were those printed in *The Film Sense* by Sergei Eisenstein.

The rules we laid down for ourselves were that the script had to be an original specially written in this form and not any kind of adaptation, and that actual film production must be possible. Our main obstacle consisted in the camera-directions, which if given were apt to look too technical, and if omitted would lose the dramatic impact of, for instance, a sudden large close-up, which Dylan however hoped could be conveyed by one's actual choice of words. In fact we were attempting the wellnigh impossible, as anyone who has read the printed versions of *Marienbad* or *L'Immortelle* by Robbe-Grillet will realize, and perhaps Dylan himself in *The Doctor and the Devils* came as close to it as any writer ever will.

Was Dylan wrong to do this film work, as Caitlin then thought? It is impossible to give an objective judgment. Certainly it was a great drain on his energies, and it would surely have been better for us, and perhaps for him, if he had been devoting that energy to poems. Between 1941 and 1944 he wrote, or at least finished, almost no poem, though he was working on some of those that later appeared in *Deaths and Entrances*. However, without Donald Taylor's persistent interventions with the Ministry of Labour Dylan would certainly have been "directed" into some other form of work far less congenial, or perhaps even into the army. Though his comparative silence as a poet can be ascribed, in part, to his script-writing, his actual physical environment was also responsible. During a large part of this period he had nowhere to live, and above all nowhere to write. The idea that a poet can write difficult and truthful poems on his knee between Hammersmith and Trafalgar Square is a romantic fallacy. He may think of poems in the tube, as Dylan did, but he cannot write them there. And it is now necessary to go back in time to explain his homelessness.

In the autumn of 1940 Caitlin had gone to Bishopston, with the baby. She stayed there until the new year, when the centre of Swansea was bombed and burned out in three terrible air-raids. Dylan had been up and down from London, and now Caitlin, Llewelyn aged two, and another woman also with a small child rented a very small cottage at Talsarn, near Lampeter in Cardiganshire, safe from the bombers. Dylan sometimes stayed there when down from London, sometimes at a pub called The Castle in Lampeter, for the cottage was very crowded. The landlord of The Castle remembers Dylan shutting himself up in a back room and getting on with his film work. Then, in the late spring, Frances Hughes invited them to Laugharne Castle, which was filled with children and where she was a grass widow. There they spent the summer, Dylan again travelling up and down from London, a journey that in wartime took six, seven or twelve hours of cold, darkness and discomfort. In London he had no sort of home or even room and dossed down with friends. It was, from every point of view, an immensely unsatisfactory way of life, and in the autumn Caitlin brought Llewelyn up to London.

They had nowhere to go and one evening, like figures from some Victorian melodrama, the three of them arrived on Sir Alan Herbert's doorstep in Hammersmith. Through John Pudney, who was then the Herberts' son-in-law, they had met A. P. Herbert and his wife. Now they had heard that Sir Alan's studio next door was not in use, for he was away at the war, and Lady Herbert let them have it. It was not a place that was meant to be lived in and when Sir Alan had worked there he had been writing without the omnipresence of a wife and very small child. Dylan went off to Golden Square in the mornings and came back late at night. And in May of 1942 he was writing:

Llewelyn is going away tomorrow, for a few weeks, to his grandmother, quite near Salisbury. Just outside Fordingbridge. I have to move from Hammersmith Terrace, and am trying to get a house in St. Peter's Square to share with some people who have furniture. You don't know, I suppose, anyone who has any furniture stored in London and who would want to give it a good home? The only things I have are a deckchair with a hole in it, half a dozen books, a few toys and an old iron. These would not fill even a mouse's home. It is very good sometimes to have nothing; I want society, not me, to have places to sit in and beds to lie in; and who wants a hatstand of his very own? But sometimes, on raining nostalgic Sunday afternoons, after eating the week's meat, it would, however cowardly, whatever a blanketing of responsibility and conscience, be good to sprawl back in one's own bourgeois chair, bought slippers on one's trotters.

But the house in St. Peter's Square came to nothing. Caitlin returned to Talsarn, Dylan to his London nomad's life with occasional visits to Wales. On August 30, 1942, he was writing to Tommy Earp from Talsarn:

> At war myself with the Celtic gnats under a spitfire sun,
> Reading that twenty poems make fifteen cartridge cases,
> Commandos are trained to be cannibals and bombs weigh a hundred ton,
> Poison is dropped from the sky in the shape of hipflasks and chequebooks,
> Pigs can be taught to firewatch and hens to lay handgrenades:
> O the summer grew suddenly lovely as the woodland rose in a phalanx
> And the painted privates I thought were bushes moved in their Nash parades.

I have been here for over a week with Caitlin, with milk and mild and cheese and eggs, and I feel fit as a fiddle only bigger; I watch the sun from a cool room and know that there are trees being trees outside and that I do not have to admire them; the country's the one place you haven't got to go out in, thank Pan.

That summer Caitlin was pregnant again, with the baby that was to be Aeron, named after the Welsh river on whose bank she had been conceived. And in the autumn of 1942 Llewelyn was once again despatched to his grandmother's at Ringwood and she returned to London. For Dylan had at last found a place for them to live.

This was a sparsely furnished studio off Manresa Road, Chelsea, No. 3 Wentworth Studios. It has gone now, this row of single-storey dwellings, and it is remarkable that it had not fallen down then, war or no war, but somehow it survived the bombings, glass roof and all, though when rain fell the water came in under the door and dripped steadily through the roof. Their new home consisted of one big room, with an archaic bathroom, and a kitchen behind a curtain. There were a lot of books, most of them Dan Jones's. There was a huge double bed and later a bassinet for the baby. Bill Brandt's excellent photograph shows Dylan and Caitlin standing behind the big, round table, the only one. There was a gramophone, and records everywhere. To the walls were pinned Dylan's own pictures, his "literary pictures" as he called them, as well as paintings by Janckl Adler, a friend whose violent colours appealed to Dylan, and reproductions of Henry Moore's "shelter drawings." There was a rich smell of stew, and the rich sound of Dylan's voice talking or reading poems, and beer in bottles, and music. It was rickety and ramshackle, and for Caitlin it must have been an awful place in which to keep house and for Dylan a difficult room in which to work since there was no solitude. But to a visitor like myself it seemed immensely snug and warm, at night, in front of the fire, after the pubs had closed.

Aeron was born in a nearby hospital in March of 1943, and the three of them went on living in the studio until early the following year when the renewed German raids — there had been none on London since 1941 — made the glass-roofed studio too dangerous a place for a baby.

It was while they were in Wentworth Studios that I was seeing most of Dylan and rather less of Caitlin. I was in the United States Army, an intelligence officer working in Grosvenor Square on the invasion plans, and my future wife and I had rented a very small furnished house in Godfrey Street, Chelsea, a few hundred yards from their studio. It had a minute guest room, with a desk, and here Dylan used to come and work when he did not have to go to the film company. I was away all day at my office, and Dylan used that little room as his, keeping very regular hours. Sometimes he would still be there when I came home in the evening. I recall, on one occasion, apologizing because I had disturbed him, and I remember his genial reply: he wished he had a sign to hang outside his door, the opposite of those that one finds in hotel bedrooms, a sign that said PLEASE DISTURB. It was about now that he began intensively to write poems once again, and I believe that he wrote nothing else in my house, so the loan of that little room may have contributed to his second flowering.

In the evenings I would change out of uniform, though this was strictly against regulations, and after we had eaten our wartime meal (I remember a particularly curious starling pie) Theo and I would usually, indeed almost always, go to one or more of the Chelsea pubs, the Australian, the Crossed Keys, the Red House, the Markham, not the Six Bells for it had been bombed, the Pier Hotel, the Anglesea, the Princess, but above all the King's Head and Eight Bells, which despite its name is only one pub, down on Cheyne Walk, beside the river. In most of them, and particularly in the Eight Bells, we were likely to run into Chelsea friends, Peter Rose Pulham, John Davenport, Norman Douglas, Philip Lindsay, Maurice Richardson, Brian Howard, Ferdinand Helm, Francis Rose, Francis Butterfield, Michael and Diana Gough and many more, as well as friends of theirs or ours who had come from other parts of London or who were transient soldiers, sailors, airmen passing through. It was thus that I first met Aircraftsman (or was he a Sergeant?) Vernon Watkins and also Dan Jones, dressed, to Dylan's annoyance, as an army captain.

And Dylan, when not drinking up West with his film people, was frequently there, Caitlin less so. We would play shove ha'penny — Dylan was very good at shove ha'penny — sometimes darts, occasionally in the Queen's Elm bar billiards, another game at which Dylan was skilled, and drink beer, and talk. Spirits were then almost unobtainable, and even the beer often ran out, which was why we had to have so many pubs to choose from. We knew which day the brewers delivered to which pubs. But the Eight Bells, which had not yet been modernized and then had a very pretty, very cosy saloon bar, was our favourite.

Superficially, perhaps, these Chelsea pubs in wartime resembled the Soho ones of the 'thirties. Here, as there, a high proportion of the customers were connected with, or at least interested in, the arts. Here, as there, bourgeois values were at a discount, though most if not all of us were sprung from the middle class. Nevertheless the atmosphere was not at all the same.

The average age was much older, for one thing. Many people who would have preferred to entertain at home were driven out by the near-impossibility of buying bottles. (I remember once, passing Robert Herring's house, with Dylan. Herring usually did have drink, and Dylan suggested we take one off him. Herring answered the door himself and said at once that he could not ask us in as he was entertaining. Dylan replied: "Not very," and we walked across the street to the Eight Bells.) The painters and writers among us, myself excepted, had by then established reputations, no matter how small and eclectic these might be. Most of us had wives, or divorces behind us, or a girl with whom we lived a married life, and many, like Dylan, had children too. The age of innocence was past.

And then this was wartime, and a curious bond linked most of the "regulars" who came to drink together at the Eight Bells. Not only was it wartime, but the peak of Britain's war effort was approaching fast. The mobilization of Britain's manpower had been completed, yet here were these young men in their twenties and thirties who were almost all of them, and usually by their own choice, civilians. It is true that they were all, by law, engaged upon some sort of war work, whether as firemen, employees of the BBC or of the Ministry of Information, but they had, as it were, opted out of the one massive experience that was even then being shared by most of their contemporaries and friends. To translate a German phrase of the period, just as Auden and some others hoped to spend the war in neutral America (in many cases soon to return from it in American uniform), so our friends constituted a very small "inner emigration." They turned their backs on the war, which they regarded at best as a bore, at worst as a trick played on them by society. And none felt this more strongly than Dylan. Indeed he would go up to soldiers who were total strangers and tell them that they were damned fools to be in the army. This did not endear him to men who were seldom in the army by choice, and on at least one occasion such a soldier knocked Dylan down.

In part this attitude was political, a relic of the left-wing views that had been prevalent in the 'thirties. In part it was arrogance, though Dylan himself would never have said, as Cyril Connolly did, that he was the culture we were fighting to defend. It was not that this "inner emigration" was pro-German; quite the contrary. But it was scarcely pro-British either, and certainly not pro-American. Only Russian victories seemed to arouse a limited measure of enthusiasm. And thus a curious paradox had arisen. These men, whose political views so far as they had any had led them to identify themselves with the masses emotionally and to alienate them from their own class, now found that those same views had also alienated them from the overwhelming majority of their compatriots. It is probably true that in most cases their pre-war identification had been largely subjective and illusory, but their wartime alienation was real. And in many cases this was the root cause of much unhappiness and failure.

Dylan, like most of us, had never wished to be a soldier and certainly not to kill other people. But, again like most of us, he had screwed himself up to join the army in the summer of 1940. For a variety of reasons he was upset, disoriented, when he was turned down. The boy-poet died. He then found himself in a world that is perhaps the most enclosed, the most artificial, and the most introspective of all, the film world. By day he had little choice but to accept their values. And he spent his evenings with men who did their best to ignore the war, to be cynical about it all (were not the German concentration camps mere atrocity stories churned out by the British yellow press?), who often boasted of their skill in side-stepping the fate of their contemporaries. I have read that when Wellington's soldiers at last returned from the Peninsula and France in 1814 they were received with the same patronizing boredom by the dandies of Almack's. Because Dylan was the man he was, he adopted these colours, *to some extent*. But real cynics do not walk up to strange soldiers and insult them. And a real cynic could never have written *Ceremony after a Fire Raid* or *Among Those Killed*. Dylan was playing a part, not for the first time nor the last. Caitlin did not approve.

Jack Lindsay, Phil's brother, in an unpublished volume of his autobiography, recalls an incident in Wentworth Studios at this time, 1943:

During my Chelsea leave I came up against the deep inner conflict in Dylan, that found its outer expression in his relations with Caitlin. One morning I drifted into their rambling apartment. Dylan lay sore-headed abed, making a few gruff remarks as he smoked. Caitlin said that late at night, after we others had gone, he had torn up his poems in disgust and thrown them into the rubbish-tin.

"You rescued them," I said. "That's the job of the poet's wife. To rescue his poems from the rubbish-tin when life gets too much for him."

She shrugged, and her handsome face with its faint golden glow sharpened in a shrewish way. "No you're quite wrong. It's the last thing I'd do. Dylan's corrupt. Corrupt right through and through. It's not for me to save him from himself. If he can't do it himself, let him rot."

I was startled, shocked. My too-simple picture of Dylan as the pure lyric poet crumpled up, and I realized that I knew nothing of him or of his poetry. My only course was to start from the beginning all over again and look at the real poet, not my fantasy of him. I was also hurt on Dylan's behalf, wanted to say something that would ease the situation for him, without annoying Caitlin, who had spoken with a quiet but deadly intensity. I couldn't think of anything to say, and stole a sidelong glance at Dylan. He went on smoking grumpily as if he hadn't heard his wife's words or as if they were not worth comment. Finally, he spat, coughed, and asked about Phil.

I gathered he had had to undergo the shame of rescuing the torn manuscript himself, under Caitlin's scornful eyes. She had known he wouldn't sacrifice the poem, and he had to admit that she was right and that the tearing had been only a romantic gesture, an act of self-demolition that he couldn't sustain. . . .

Caitlin, in her anger, flailed like a whip-ray not only at Dylan but also at those whom she considered responsible for his decay. It became to her incomprehensible that his friends should admire him, and when she saw such admiration she struck. David Tennant, who owned the Gargoyle and was a drinking companion with plenty of drinks to offer became, he has told me, the Devil in Caitlin's eyes. But above all she blamed his corruption, as she called it, on the film industry and particularly upon Donald Taylor. But was she right to do so? What else could Dylan have done after that medical examination at Llandilo in 1940? Her fierce Irish answer was that he should have gone on writing his poems, being himself, the man she had loved and who had fathered her child. But how could he? The dismal trek between dreary Bishopston and gloomy Ringwood, the subsidies from friends, the whole, miserable business of pennilessness was bad enough and hard enough in peacetime. In time of war it was not even feasible. He knew that it could not go on.

And, more important perhaps, he must have known that the poetry could no more go on as it had been doing. The first rapture was exhausted; Keats was dead; he had aged beyond his notebooks. He might yet salvage an exquisite, youthful poem like *The Hunchback in the Park* and print half of it as he had written it in his teens, but the quarry was closed, for he had worked its marble to the end of his abilities. He needed a rest, a change, a rest from writing youthful Dylan Thomas, a change from being the young Mr. Thomas who had left Swansea long ago. It may be — who can say? — that Victor Cazalet's anti-aircraft battery would have been the best solution. It may be — who can deny it? — that Donald Taylor's film unit was the second best. Certainly, by 1943, he was ready and anxious to start writing poems again. But henceforth they were to be very different poems. And perhaps the strangest aspect of the dozen or so poems he was still to write is their blinding honesty and their sadness. They have no trace whatsoever of the cynicism, of what Caitlin called the corruption, that henceforth and increasingly, though not immediately, infected his life and his conversation. There was a split here that promised ill for the future.

*   *   *

Let me say at once that I did not sense this at the time. Although I thought I knew him well — well enough to ask him to be best man at my marriage in 1944 — I realize now that my knowledge of him was as superficial as was most other people's. He certainly never talked to me about his poetry. I recall once asking him a question about "poetry" and getting a characteristic reply:

"I am not interested in poetry. I am only interested in poems."

We drank and laughed and talked about everything, as it then seemed to me, except that and politics and religion and the war, and we play-acted. When the pubs closed we would go back, with a couple of quarts of bitter and a friend or two, to our little house or, later, to our flat in Paultons Square and play "Russian plays." This was a very simple game, for we made up the Chekovian script as we went along. Dylan always insisted on being Natasha, with a cushion stuffed inside his pull-over and a great deal of Theo's make-up on his cheeks.

On one occasion we had been with him and Tommy Earp, the art critic. Tommy was an almost incredibly etiolated figure with the most exaggerated Oxford accent I have ever heard. When an undergraduate before the First World War he had once been arrested for being drunk and disorderly in an enormous basket of strawberries at Covent Garden. Next morning the magistrate asked him why he had climbed into the basket, and Tommy, in flutey tones, had replied:

"For valetudinarian reasons, purely valetudinarian reasons!"

"Don't address me as if you were the President of the Oxford Union," the magistrate had snapped.

"But I am," wailed Tommy, "I am!" And he was.

Thirty years later, in the Eight Bells, Dylan was telling Tommy and myself how greatly he disliked Goethe. "I hate Goethe," he said, and he had made this odd pronouncement before, both to me and to Vernon. I was quite sure that he had never read Goethe and knew almost nothing about him. I suspect that this hatred was a "received idea" taken from D. H. Lawrence's rude little poem about the Olympian. Furthermore I had no doubt that Dylan and the young Goethe, the poet of *Sturm und Drang* and of the *Ur-Faust*, would have got on extremely well. I said as much, and Tommy backed me up. We were talking about facts now, and poems, and Dylan became very interested. Later, in my flat, we played a Goethe-play, Dylan being the young Goethe who meets himself, the old Goethe, played by Tommy Earp, while I was totally miscast as Schiller. A few days after this I heard him telling someone what a great poet Goethe was, and why. This was how he acquired his general knowledge, for he now read almost no prose except trash.

He would also act in public, as it were. Donald Taylor has written:

The great thing to remember about Dylan was that he was a complete chameleon and could adapt himself to any company and play any role. He was, in fact, a natural born actor. Frequently during our association we would decide in the morning what role we were going to play when we went out for a drink, and this is perhaps why so many people have so many different recollections of him. His favourite role was that of a Welsh country gentleman for which in later days he dressed in hairy tweeds and carried a knobbed walkingstick. Alternatively he could be a BBC actor and verse reader, for which he wore a light grey smooth tweed suit. The role of the drunken Welsh poet with "fag in the corner of the mouth, and dirty raincoat, and polo sweater" sometimes lasted for a week or more, but no longer. He had an extremely flexible voice and could suit it to any of these roles.

I do not recall anything as deliberate as this, but I have a vivid memory of an incident in the famous pub, the Cheshire Cheese, forever associated with American tourists in search of Dr. Johnson's ghost. Dylan and I had gone up to Fleet Street one morning. He had some business to do in a newspaper office, I had my hair cut, and we were to meet in the Cheshire Cheese. I arrived there, in my American uniform, a few minutes before he did, and was immediately seized upon by one of the professional bores who expect drinks in exchange for Johnsonian anecdotes. Dylan arrived and recognized at once what was happening. Without a word being exchanged between us we rounded on the Johnson bore and gave it to him. I became, for half an hour, a lecturer from Harvard, a Johnson specialist, Dylan a professor of English literature from the University of Wales, the author of several scholarly works about the Doctor. Indeed, we had met at the Cheshire Cheese especially to discuss the great lexicographer in so congenial and suitable an atmosphere and were only too delighted that our new friend was also apparently interested in his evergreen personality. Our erudition was enormous, our anecdotes almost incredible. I hope that some of them passed into his own repertoire, for by the time we had finished with the poor man he had so far forgotten himself that he was buying us drinks.

On another occasion when we were with a somewhat ponderous American academic I had met in the army, who in real life was a real professor of English literature, I invented an Elizabethan poet called Tom Blackamore, and we persuaded the professor, though I fear only for the evening, that Blackamore was perhaps the greatest master of the sonnet form England has ever produced and a man whose influence on Shakespeare has been, amazingly, ignored. Dylan quoted many passages from Blackamore's powerful, indeed astonishing, sonnets. And the professor (who was, if I remember correctly, an expert on Sir Walter Scott and the North British novel) was forced to agree that Blacka-more was a very exceptional poet indeed.

Sometimes Dylan and Theo and I, and occasionally Caitlin, would be alone together after the pubs closed. We then usually read poems. I remember Dylan reading a lot of Hardy and particularly *To Lizbie Browne,* a poem of which he was very fond (John Betjeman tells me that he also remembers hearing Dylan read this entrancing poem most beautifully, some years later, in Margaret Taylor's house in Oxford). Lawrence he read, too, and Ezra Pound's *In Kensington Gardens,* and Blake's *London* as well as much else, and Yeats's later poems, and Keats. We were limited by the comparatively few books I had in London at that time. *The Golden Treasury* was one that we passed back and forth, but it was a Victorian edition and did not contain enough of the Metaphysical Poets for his taste. Apart from Cowper, Burns, Smart and above all Blake, I do not recall him reading any eighteenth century poet. I do recall one evening when I was reading Gray's *Elegy.* Dylan became increasingly restive, and at about verse twenty he gave a great yawn and said:

"Oh, for God's sake shut up!"

I do not remember hearing him read any of his contemporaries except Norman Cameron and, much more, Vernon Watkins. He thought very highly of the *Ballad of the Mari Lwyd,* which I heard him read more than once. Another of Vernon's poems that he read was the fine *Portrait of a Friend.* And it is a ghost story that I am now about to tell.

Early in 1938 Dylan had sent Vernon a photograph of himself which arrived cracked down the middle. Vernon then wrote his very well-known poem which begins:

> He has sent me this
> Late and early page
> Caught in the emphasis
> Of last night's cartonnage,
> Crumpled in the post,
> Bringing to lamplight
> Breath's abatement,
> Over- and under-statement,
> Mute as a mummy's pamphlet
> Long cherished by a ghost.

In a poet's terms and a style that has distant echoes of Dylan's own, Vernon writes of his poet friend, and the poem ends:

The superhuman, crowned
Saints must enter this drowned
Tide-race of the mind
To guess or understand
The face of this cracked prophet,
Which from its patient pall
I slowly take,
Drop the envelope,
Compel his disturbing shape,
And write these words on a wall
Maybe for a third man's sake.

After reading it to Theo and myself, one night in the spring of 1944, Dylan closed the book and remarked, in an entirely matter-of-fact tone of voice:

"And of course the third man, Constantine, is you."

Certainly nothing could have seemed to me more absurd, in that spring of apprehension before the invasion of Europe, than any suggestion that twenty years later I should be writing this book. Nor was that what Dylan meant. What he did mean, I think, was that Vernon was explaining Dylan to me, his listener. Yet it is ghostly, is it not?

There is one more small personal anecdote that I should like to tell before I send the young man I then was offstage. I had been writing before the war, both in English and in French, both in prose and in verse, but had published very little. (I had translated a poem of Dylan's into French which had appeared in *La Nouvelle Saison,* Paris, in 1938, the first of his poems to appear in translation.) In 1942 I had written a never-to-be-published short story, and three years later I was reading this semi-Surrealist work to Dylan, seated before the fire in Paultons Square. He told me, tactfully and truthfully, that it was no good. Theo had of course heard this story before, indeed more than once, and had taken a violent dislike to it. She thereupon picked up the typescript and tossed it on the flames. It was the only time I ever saw Dylan shocked.

"She burned your work!" he said. "How wicked, how wicked!"

But I knew, and she knew, that there were several carbon copies of this masterpiece in my drawer. And when this was explained Dylan forgave her, though perhaps less quickly than I. It was not the sort of dramatic gesture he appreciated. Perhaps it reminded him too much of the incident Jack Lindsay has described earlier in this chapter.

And, finally, there is the question of Dylan's sponging and stealing. I have no recollection of Dylan asking me for money, though at this time, as an American officer, I was quite rich by his and my standards. I do recall hearing him elaborate a scheme for extracting yet more money from a very rich man to whom he was already heavily indebted: the scheme did not involve telling the truth. He may have asked me for a taxi-fare from time to time, but then I may equally well have asked him for a half-a-crown. Certainly he never tried to exploit me beyond wearing my shirts and eating my Hershey bars.

He had a reputation as a thief, and I believe that it was, in some measure, justified. As early as the spring of 1941, when a guest at Laugharne Castle, he was writing to Bertram Rota, the bookseller, offering him first editions of modern novels. They may, of course, have been his father's. Later, after the war, many people were to complain that objects were missing when Dylan had been to stay. In 1943 Theo did once catch him walking out of our little Godfrey Street house with her electric sewing machine. This was a rather valuable instrument of which she was almost inordinately proud and which he would have regarded as quite useless and fit only for the pawn shop. She told him to put it down, which he did, and with the expression of the Swansea schoolboy caught cheating at maths and in a ham actor's tones of outraged innocence, he asked:

"Are you accusing me of *stealing?*"

"Yes," she said.

"Well!" he replied, and bore no ill feeling.

Some weeks later, at a party of ours, Caitlin decided to dance. Theo saw Dylan roll up a small rug, which he was carrying out into the hall. Suspiciously she asked him what he was doing with her rug. With immense dignity he replied that he was afraid Caitlin's dancing might damage it.

To myself, in a period of lonely unhappiness just after the war, Dylan and Caitlin were kind and generous in every way, and by this I mean food, drink, friendship, time and sympathy.

*   *   *

When the Germans began bombing London again, early in 1944, Dylan found a cottage near Bosham, in Sussex, where Caitlin went with the baby and the poodle puppy Theo and I had given them. Dylan himself was back and forth between there and London. They were there for some three months, and Dylan hated Bosham. The whole countryside was alive with soldiers being assembled for the invasion. Later he wrote to Vernon:

The Sussex months were beastly. When it wasn't soaking wet, I was. Aeroplanes grazed the roofs, bombs came by night, police by day, there were furies at the bottom of my garden, with bayonets, and a floating dock like a kidney outside the window, and Canadians in the bushes, and Americans in the hair; it was a damned banned area altogether. They worshipped dogs there, too, and when a pom was born in one house the woman put out the Union Jack.

I believe it was this cottage that had a particularly revolting earth closet at the end of the garden, with a well-like shaft. Dylan told me, during one of his frequent visits to London, that it wasn't the rats at the bottom he minded, it was the magpies halfway up.

All this year, 1944, they kept on the Manresa Road studio, but were seldom there together. From Bosham they went to stay for two months with Donald Taylor in his house near Beaconsfield. Donald and Dylan were then collaborating on *The Doctor and the Devils*. In July he, Caitlin and Aeronwy went down to Wales, to escape the flying bombs. For some weeks they stayed with his parents, who had now moved from Swansea out to Llangain, for Dylan's Aunt Dosie had died and his mother had inherited one of the pair of cottages, a mile or so from Fern Hill, just across the estuary from Laugharne. It was even more cramped than Bishopston had been. Dylan hoped to find a house in Laugharne again, but there was none to be had. At last he discovered a bungalow a few miles up the coast, at New Quay in Cardiganshire, which he rented for a year. The studio was supposed to be his home during his visits to London, but he felt lonely and unhappy there, and preferred to stay with friends. Bill McAlpine, an engineer and young poet whom he had recently met, and his wife Helen frequently put him up. They were to become very close friends, both with Dylan and with Caitlin, and remained so.

As usual he was working much better in Wales. In 1944 and 1945 he finished, and published, ten poems which are surely among the finest that he wrote, including as they do *Poem in October*, *Refusal to Mourn*, *This Side of Truth*, *The Conversation of Prayer*, *A Winter's Tale*, *Fern Hill*, and *In my Craft or Sullen Art*. These are the poems of his maturity, as are the eight other poems he was to write in the remaining eight years of his life. This period at the very end of the war was indeed a second flowering, a period of fertility that recalls the earliest days, all the more as these poems were usually much longer, much more complex, and polished to a far greater appearance of simplicity than the early poems had been. They provided nearly half the poems for *Deaths and Entrances,* his fourth book of verse, which appeared in February of 1946 and which really established his reputation as a major poet of his time.

All these poems were first published in periodicals, most of them in the monthly magazine *Horizon* which Cyril Connolly, helped by Stephen Spender, edited and which, almost single-handed, kept culture alive during those long, bleak years of war. In a BBC broadcast Connolly has said of Dylan:

Dylan, I thought then, was not an ideal contributor. A very long poem like *The Long Legged Bait* upset our meagre paper ration. It had to go into very small print, which he resented, and he refused to come and correct the proofs, so that there were some appalling misprints — I remember Jew for dew was one of them for which I got all the blame. Later on he gave us such marvellous poems as *Fern Hill, A Winter's Tale, Deaths and Entrances, A Refusal to Mourn the Death of a Child* and *In Country Sleep.*

Dylan was now harassed by money worries. This was the beginning of those difficulties which were to lead him into lecturing in America and eventually being mobbed to death, like Orpheus and the Thracian women.

Nor could the Muse defend her son. In the war years he could still look very fresh and attractive, although his cynical persona had descended on him. He really preferred to enclose all literary conversation in a kind of capsule of ridicule and parody. I used to buy his poems spot cash from his wallet as if they were packets of cocaine. . . .

This great outpouring of poems was not all that he was doing at New Quay during that year. He was still working on films, and he had begun to write *Milk Wood.* At the prompting of Aneirin Talfan Davies, of the BBC's Welsh service, he had started to broadcast those talks which were later collected and published as *Quite Early One Morning;* the first of these went out in February 1943. Many consider them to be his finest prose. The talk which was to give that book its title went out in December of 1944.

His life at New Quay, in the bungalow called Majoda which he said was made principally of asbestos, was much as it had been at Laugharne before the war and would be again when he returned there later. The evenings were always spent in the pub, usually the Black Lion, with the baby tucked away till closing time in the landlady's bed upstairs. (Llewelyn was still with his grandmother at Ringwood.)

But New Quay was, at that time, a considerably more sophisticated seaside town than Laugharne. It had always been something of a place to which middle-class people retired, and in 1944-1945 it also harboured a group of transients who had gone there — as in a way had Dylan — to "escape" from the war. Dylan drank with these people, as he drank with the butcher, the baker and the candlestick maker, and so did Caitlin. But he drank beer, while she drank spirits, and in increasing quantities. And the rows got worse.

Jack Lindsay, in the unpublished volume of his autobiography from which he has kindly allowed me to quote, has analyzed with great dialectical subtlety Dylan's and Caitlin's relationship. Although I do not agree with all his premises, nor with all his conclusions, I do agree that the public Dylan, what Ruthven Todd has called "instant Dylan," the life-and-soul of the saloon bar, the man who had to establish an apparently intimate relationship at once with every man (and, more dangerously and hatefully for Caitlin, with every woman) became for her a contemptible and corrupt public figure. This was not what she had loved and married, this amateur actor who was prepared to play the buffoon if that were the only way to attract attention, surrounded by yearning, admiring women and men, their faces creased by guffaws, whom she knew he despised but whose admiration and laughter he wanted and, increasingly, needed. Nor was this even the man she knew at home, the honest poet who took such pains that he would write and rewrite a line fifty or a hundred times until he was quite sure that he had achieved poetic truth.

And so, in public, she sometimes scowled and gulped her whiskies, and demanded that attention be directed to her, not solely to Dylan, made scenes, and at home, at night, there were the terrible rows. It was not so bad in New Quay as in London. Yet he always had to be going off to London, and she had a pretty good idea of what went on up there. She had seen it often enough, and her imagination was powerful enough to make a gaudy canvas from the sketches of her knowledge. I have seen him, in 1945, in London, neat and clean and happy that she was coming up; and I have seen her arrive, angry and suspicious. Nor were her suspicions always unjustified. And then the row.

It was to get steadily worse as he grew more famous, until at last it almost killed her love for him. With what pitiful weapons she could muster, and those encumbered by nappies and stewpots and dishcloths, she was fighting Dylan the entertainer, the character she hated and who became increasingly Dylan the drunken buffoon, for the sake of Dylan the poet, whom she loved. It was worst of all, she thought, in America. And when she arrived in New York, where he was dying, and asked: "Is the bloody man dead yet?" it was to the buffoon she referred, for the death of the poet broke her heart.

❅   ❅   ❅

There is one New Quay incident that must be mentioned here, for it attracted wide publicity in the summer of 1945. This was an attempt to murder Dylan.

A woman whom Dylan had known when they were both children in Swansea was married to a man who was then a commando officer. He had been fighting in conditions of great strain and danger behind the German lines in Greece. With the departure of the Germans and the outbreak of the Greek civil war, he found himself having to fight his former Communist allies, who had, he felt, betrayed himself and his comrades. He had seen horrible scenes. In the spring of 1945 he came home in a state of comprehensible nervous exhaustion. He brought with him — and this was not unusual in those days — a large arsenal of very dangerous weapons. He found his wife and child installed in a bungalow next to Dylan's and Caitlin's. Indeed to this overstrung man the two families appeared to live almost as one, and he soon darkly suspected that he had stumbled upon a *ménage à trois*. He also found that he was in a village where patriotism was at a discount, where the war was ignored, and where pacifism and Communism were accepted as the norm, while what he and his comrades had been doing so dangerously was shrugged off as a stupid bore.

Dylan was late with a film script. Donald Taylor sent down some of his people to help and urge Dylan to finish it. One was a Russian secretary of whom Dylan was extremely fond, for she mothered him at Gryphon, doing his typing and generally looking after him. She was a member of the Communist Party. They worked at the script, and when the day's work was done they went as usual to the Black Lion where a great deal was drunk. The Russian secretary made several remarks which caused the battle-weary commando officer to lose his temper. He insulted her, and was stupid enough to bring up the fact that she was Jewish at a moment in time when every paper was filled with the horrors of the German concentration camps. It seems that she clawed at his face, and that he struck back. Dylan and the other men present threw him out. His wife remained behind. The commando officer went to another pub and brooded.

Later that night he came to Dylan's bungalow, where his own wife also was, and fired a sten gun into it. The bullets went straight through its thin walls, and the women put the babies inside the brick chimney, the only solid part of the building. He then kicked in the door.

Somehow Dylan managed to get his gun away from him. The officer now produced a hand-grenade from his pocket and announced that he would blow them all to smithereens unless his gun were returned to him immediately. At the trial, Dylan was asked what he did then.

"Naturally," he said, "I handed it back to him."

Eventually the man departed with his wife and child. He was prosecuted for attempted murder, but was found innocent on the grounds that provocation had been such as to deprive him temporarily of his reason.

This incident upset Dylan greatly, and New Quay was never the same for him again. But though it was upsetting it was regarded, neither by him nor by his friends, as a very weird incident, for the atmosphere in Britain at the very end of, and just after, the war was not so different from that which prevailed throughout the rest of Europe. No enemy army had marched through these islands, but the armies of liberation, those of the British and those of their allies, had done so, leaving the usual wreckage behind them.

That atmosphere might be described as one of exhaustion shot through with violence and hatred. We read about the concentration camps, and we wondered which pub would have beer tonight. We were horrified by Hiroshima, which seemed to make it all meaningless, and we wanted out. I went to America and came back, still a soldier. But I knew that I could get away from it all, and could take my wife with me. Dylan envied me this escape, for we often discussed it during that first winter after the war. He, too, wished to go to America, but his problems were far more complex than mine. With such means as he had, pulling such strings as he could pull, like millions before him, he planned to escape. As Goethe had written: *"Amerika hat es besser."*

11

⊱ ⊰

DYLAN's life in the eight years that were left to him after the war can, for biographical convenience, be divided in two. From 1945 to 1949 he was living in England with trips to Ireland, Italy and Czechoslovakia. In the summer of 1949 he returned to Laugharne, which once again became his home until his death. During this period he went four times to America and once to Persia.

Throughout the summer of 1945 he was trying, with mounting desperation, to find a home for himself and his family in or near London. This was intended to be merely temporary, for he was planning to emigrate to America as soon as possible. He had a dedicated admirer in New York, whom he had not then met, in the person of Oscar Williams, the anthologist. Williams had included poems of Dylan's in his anthologies and had also placed·others with various American magazines, in particular *Poetry* (Chicago). In a very long letter to Oscar Williams, dated July 30, 1945, Dylan asked for his help and expressed his dissatisfaction with life in Britain.

I have been trying to find out what legal etc. complications I will have to go through before leaving this country for America. First of all, because I have no financial independence, I have to be assured — or, rather, the American Embassy over here will have to be assured — that on arriving in America, there is a job, or there are jobs, waiting for me; that I will not become a liability to the United States. There must be a sponsor, or sponsors, who will sign a declaration saying that I and my dependents will *not* be allowed to become liabilities. So what is the first step? The American Embassy has given me several printed forms to be sent to whoever I imagine will employ me in the States and guarantee me a living. If I send these official forms to you, could you do anything about them? That is, could you approach *Time* — whom you suggested as possible employers, if only for part of my time — and get some definite promise, however small, from them? If that could be arranged, then, after the returning to the American Embassy here of the signed "We-won't-let-the-bugger-starve" declaration, and after the final examinations, interviews, and okayings, physical and political, I could sail within three months.

There was also some question of Theodore Spencer, who was a poet, a professor of English at Harvard, and a friend of Augustus John's, finding him work as a lecturer at Harvard or perhaps in the library there. And then maybe Oscar Williams could find him a patron?

A patron would do just as well, to say that he will look after me and mine in luxury, New York, or even in a kennel, Texas. I should most like to read, library, or lecture at Harvard. Time and Harvard. . . .

I should bring my wife, my son aged now 6½, my daughter aged now 2½. Their names are Llewelyn and Aeronwy. They are quite nice hell. My wife's name is Caitlin, she is Irish. We would all come together because I do not want to return to this country for a long time.

The rain has stopped, thank Jesus. Have the Socialists-in-power-now stopped it? An income tax form flops through the window, the letterbox is choked with dockleaves. Let's get out, let's get out.

Later. I have been out. I went to the Edwinsford Arms, a sabbath-dark bar with a stag's head over the Gents and a stuffed salmon caught by Shem and a mildewed advertisement for pre-1914 tobacco and a stain on the wall, just above my head, that I hoped was beer. I had some beer with a man who said he was shot in the groin in the last war, and who, unable to have a woman ever since, blames it on the dirty Jews. He said, "Look what they did, the moochin," and showed me a scar on his calf. I said that I thought he said he had been shot through the groin. "And the calf, and the calf," he said in a terrible temper; "And the calf, the bloody yids." He is an official in some Department — a Department set-built for the early German films — that investigates the authenticity of discharged soldiers' pension-claims. "Every time I see "psycho-neurosis" on a discharge paper, I say 'lead-swinger.'" He told me the best way to boil lobsters, which was detailed and painful. I told him Norman Douglas's recipe for raping a dog. . . . He told me how he had once made a child of six drunk. It began to rain again, great wrathful drops. We parted enemies. I rode back on a bicycle through the justice-must-be-done-let's-rain-on-sinners rain, and the bicycle wheels through the pools and slush on the roads asked the same monotonous and inane questions as the boiler-pipes once asked Gorki: Have you got any rubber? Do you want some fish? Cows under crying roadside trees, looking over the estuary, weed and webfoot mud, waited for Royal Academicians. Snails were coming out; a P.E.N. Club of slugs crossed the road; Manchester, Manchester, fetch a pocket handkerchief, said the engine over the hill; you could hear little boys in desolate back-gardens facing the depressed water, slapping each other on the stomach.

In December of 1945 he was again writing to Oscar Williams for help and also to J. L. Sweeney, who had written the introduction of Dylan's *Selected Writings* which New Directions were preparing for publication the next year. In Chicago he had been awarded the Levinson Poetry Prize, by *Poetry* (Chicago) and he was beginning to be appreciated in America. He sensed that that was the place for him.

Nor was this a momentary whim of the immediate postwar months. In November 1946 he was still determined to get across, and was writing to his American publisher, James Laughlin IV:

I think I can, from this side, with the active help of Edith Sitwell, manage to get jobs — lecturing, reading, etc. — to be awaiting me in America. But from *your* side, and from you personally, I want to know that there is *immediate temporary accommodation* for the four of us (Dylan, Caitlin, Llewelyn, Aeronwy) when we arrive in New York, and a house in the country for us pretty soon afterwards. I hope I'm not being dictatorial. What I want to say, again, is that I want to work a lot and very much, but that those things have got to be seen to (as you promised) before I leave here.

And the other importance: even if, from this side, Edith contrives to get for me a few American lectures etc. I still won't have the money to take the four of us on ship, plane, raft, or even by carrier pigeon.

Caitlin is insisting that I write to you in this way: if she did not insist, I would still be writing this way. I hope that we, together, have a successful author-and-publisher existence: but it *must* be in America and it *must* be through you. Can you write, or cable, me as soon as possible? These, to be dull, are the facts once more:

(1) I want to come early in the New Year to the States.

(2) I will not come unless I bring my family with me.

(3) I need the money to take us over.

(4) I want somewhere temporary for us to stay when we reach New York.

(5) I want somewhere, after that, preferably in the hills, and certainly in the country, where we can live.

(6) Where we live must be somewhere near whatever place you think that I can best earn my living (mostly by broadcasting) in.

(7) I want to write a lot.

(8) What I write is, by our agreement, yours without any condition to print, publish, in America.

(9) And this, most importantly, must be soon.

This letter suggests that Caitlin was at this time as eager as Dylan to move across the Atlantic, but nothing came of it. Then there arose the possibility of his being offered a job at the University of Virginia, and again he was hopeful until this scheme, too, collapsed. Finally in 1949, when John Malcolm Brinnin offered him the chance of an American lecture tour for the following year he accepted with alacrity and enthusiasm.

I have gone into this matter of his American plans in such detail for two reasons. The first is that it knocks another Dylan Thomas legend on the head. It is widely believed in certain circles in England and Wales that Dylan was somehow lured or bribed to go to America, largely against his will and entirely against Caitlin's, there to be mobbed to death "like Orpheus and the Thracian women." On the contrary, he had been doing his best to get to America for some five years before at last he made it, and thereafter he went back whenever he could. What happened when he got there is another story, but certainly there was never any need to inveigle Dylan into going to the United States.

The second reason is that for the first four years after the war, at least, Dylan was hoping to emigrate shortly with his family. His English arrangements therefore continued to be of an essentially temporary nature. Nor would it be true to say that all Dylan's arrangements had always been of this sort. Before the war Sea View had been his, and his family's, home. And after 1949 the Boat House was to be such a home once again. But in the years between the unsettled and unsettling way of life, inevitable perhaps in wartime, was protracted unduly into the peace. All the plans that he and Caitlin made were of a makeshift quality, to cover the next few months before their departure for America.

It would thus be wrong to blame the unsettled and unhappy way of life that he now evolved for himself and his family solely on his feckless ways and his increasing, drunken irresponsibility where money was concerned. It was just as much the other way about. Domestic and financial insecurity, and the hideous worries that those entail for a man of Dylan's temperament, made it increasingly difficult for him to do any serious and sustained work. Though he never ceased to do such work, hack jobs offered the quickest apparent solution to his money problems, while drinks, and the laughter of friends or even of strangers, were the easy means to escape from anxiety.

When he left New Quay and came to London with Caitlin and Aeronwy in September of 1945, they had nowhere to go, for he had long given up 3 Wentworth Studios. It was not easy, then, to find anywhere to live in London. And Dylan's way of life during his frequent visits to the capital that summer had certainly not been conducive to finding a home. I quote a letter of his to David Tennant, the owner of the Gargoyle, dated August 28, 1945.

Across the counties, from mean, green, horse-thieving Wales, I raise one Playercoloured aspen hand to salute and supplicate. The last time I saw you, you had just gone from the Prince of Wales, and who am I to blame. The rest of the day was dark, shot with fire, a hummingtop of taxis and glasses, a spinning sight of scowls and leers seen through the wrong end of a telescope made of indiarubber, a rush of close-ups, strange mouths and noses flattening themselves on one's own in places that seemed to be now a Turkish bath, now a lavatory, now a gymnasium for midgets, bar, hothouse, hospital, knockshop, abbattoir, crematorium, revolving cathedral and, at last, a bed only an inch from the ceiling. I'm coming to town again on Thursday, calm but gabbling, a patient on a monument: beer only for me, for weeks, for health, forgive me, for Christ's sake, for sanity, four freedoms.

Do you know of any flat, small house, in London or fairly near that I could rent? I am getting desperate here. We *have* to move. There has never been, for me, anything more urgent than this. I have to find somewhere to live in, if only for a few months. Do you know of anybody? Would you ask some of the people you see? God, I'd be grateful. I'm going out of my mind here, and can do no work. There *must* be somewhere. Do do, do do do ask and see for me, David. I can't go on like this, travelling eight hours to spend a weekend with Caitlin. . . . Do your best for me, about finding some hole in the wind to lay down my two heads.

He asked Tommy Earp to find them a cottage in Hampshire, my wife searched Chelsea for him, he begged Donald Taylor to discover anything, anywhere. When they arrived they stayed, in fact, for several weeks in my very small Chelsea flat. I was in America at the time, and after a while Theo could no longer stand the noise and the confusion and moved in with her mother. A little later the woman who owned the house, and who lived upstairs, informed my wife that unless the Thomas family departed forthwith she would cancel our lease. So they stayed with the McAlpines for a while, then with John Davenport and his new wife, and finally came to rest, in late November, in a basement in Markham Square, Chelsea.

This little flat belonged to Noel Blakiston who was persuaded to let it to them by Caitlin's sister, Nicolette. She occupied the rest of the house with her children and her husband, Anthony Devas, the well-known portrait painter. So they had once again been forced back upon their relations, though the two families saw little of one another. Dylan and Devas had long been on very bad terms; nobody wanted them in the house, nor did they wish to be there. It was not a state of affairs that was ever intended to be anything but an emergency stop-gap. Furthermore Caitlin wished, at last, to have Llewelyn with her. He had spent almost the entire war with her mother and her other sister, Brigid, in Hampshire. And as he was now nearly seven it was time to start thinking about his formal education. Oxford is as good a place as any to think about that sort of thing.

They spent Christmas with A. J. P. Taylor and his wife, Margaret. It will be recalled that as early as 1935 Dylan had spent some weeks with them in Derbyshire, when Alan Taylor was teaching modern history at Manchester University. He had subsequently become a fellow of Magdalen College, Oxford, where he and his family spent the war in a house on the river, just outside the college walls, called Holywell Ford. A few yards away there was what might be described as a very large summerhouse or studio, on the water's edge, which the Taylors let furnished. It is a curious building, very rustic, a one-room *cottage orné* resembling a circular log cabin, with cooking facilities but no plumbing other than an outdoors earth closet. An ideal retreat for a single person or a young married couple during the summer months, it was hardly designed to house a family of four. But Dylan and Caitlin were delighted to have it, pending their departure for America. They moved in towards the middle of March, 1946, immediately after Dylan's discharge from St. Stephen's Hospital, London. They were to remain there for a whole year.

He had collapsed with alcoholic gastritis and was also in a state of nervous hypertension. The thorough medical examination which he underwent during the four days he was in hospital showed, however, that there was nothing organically wrong with him — the medical report still exists — and that the "cirrhosis of the liver" to which he had been alluding darkly in recent years was as imaginary as his "TB." He suffering, above all, from nervous exhaustion, and he explained to the doctors that unless he drank he could not sleep.

One contributory cause to his nervous condition was undoubtedly the publication, on February 7th, of his fourth volume of poems, *Deaths and Entrances*. Like most established writers he pretended to be quite impervious to criticism and, again like most writers, this was a defensive pose. He minded desperately what the reviewers said. It would take him years to forgive and forget an unkind or unfair notice, and even an appreciative one could arouse his scorn and ire if he felt that the writer had praised him for the wrong reasons. Furthermore *Deaths and Entrances* was, as he well knew, the book that must decide, one way or the other, his standing as a poet. Had he been a mere boy-wonder, a shooting star that had burned itself out and fizzled into films, or had he developed into a major poet? He himself could not be sure. Such questions are answered, in the short run, by the critics, though it is needless to say that they do not always get the answer right, but if they damn, then the chances of a later reappraisal are indeed slender.

The answer was overwhelmingly in his favour. The reception of *Deaths and Entrances* might be summed up in the closing sentence of Norman Cameron's review, published by the *Tribune*: "Mr. Thomas, even in his earliest work, could do 'magnificent things with words.' Now he can do magnificent things with poems."

And the book sold well, too. Within a month or two the first edition of 3000 was exhausted and Dent's were printing a second, to be followed by a third and a fourth. Henceforth he was to be a famous poet. But the strain had been great.

To this must be added the normal strain — normal to him, that is — of life in London, "the capital punishment." He had never been able to take it for long, and seldom if ever had he taken it for as long as this.

And there was the mounting financial worry. Donald Taylor had wound up Gryphon Films in the previous September and Dylan's steady ten pounds a week had come to an end. Now and for the next two years his only regular source of income was the BBC, for whom he wrote, read and acted. But even this was not truly regular, for he never drew a salary, being paid per script or per broadcast. Between September 1945 and March 1946 he had done eleven broadcasts, mostly reading poems on the Eastern Service, beamed to Asia. During the next year, while he was living at Holywell Ford, he did fifty-three more, now principally for English audiences. The BBC's Third Programme had come into existence after the war. Dedicated to the propagation of culture, all sorts of culture, it provided an outlet for poems and for poets such as had never before been offered by any broadcasting system anywhere. Those who listened to the Third Programme in England included virtually everybody interested in the arts who could receive it, and to them Dylan's voice soon became extremely well known. And this certainly helped to spread his fame as a poet, for many of those who heard his magnificent voice now also wished to read him. Thus did the actor once again come to the assistance of the poet. However, in other ways the poet's dramatic *Doppelgaenger* was not altogether the poet's friend. For Dylan continued to act after he had left Broadcasting House; the poet became overshadowed by the brassy orator.

This was in part due to the nature of his employment with the BBC. Many of his friends were now on the staff of that curious institution which, in his day, had a total monopoly. It suffered from its own institutional schizophrenia, for its huge but penny-pinching hierarchical bureaucracy showed many of the qualities of a minor government department — say the Post Office, which in fact controlled and controls it — while at a lower, but more public, level it was and is staffed by men of a very different type, dedicated to entertainment or information or culture. The producers who employed Dylan were numerous, but the principal ones were Roy Campbell, Louis MacNeice, John Arlott, Aneirin Talfan Davies (for the Welsh Service) and, later, Francis Dillon and Douglas Cleverdon. Roy and Louis were themselves poets of great distinction, but there the resemblance ceased. Roy Campbell has been described as the South African equivalent of a Texan, a big, outdoors man, given to violence. He was, I think, the only distinguished English poet of his generation publicly to support Franco during the Spanish Civil War. His long poem on this theme, *Flowering Rifle*, contains some blistering invective against the fashionable left wing poets of the 'thirties who "engaged" in that war from afar. Later he developed a habit of knocking one such poet down on sight. Dylan, never a man to let politics interfere with friendship, liked drinking with him, heavily.

Louis MacNeice, elegant as his own verses, courteous, rather remote, the son of an Irish bishop, with an aristocratic profile that might have been carved from some rare and very hard wood, had a gentle wit and when he wished it, which was seldom, a biting tongue. He too spent a great deal of time with Dylan in the George or the Stag or the Dover Castle, which were the BBC's pubs. So too did John Arlott, who is perhaps better known as a commentator on cricket matches than as a producer of poetry broadcasts. And so did a mass of other people, actors, writers and musicians who, like Dylan, were casual labourers in the BBC's factory-cum-ministry. It was Sir Thomas Beecham who first called the George "the Gluepot," for his musicians were so frequently stuck in there.

It was in these pubs, or in the M. L. Club which was open in the afternoons when they were closed, or in the Tavern at Lord's cricket ground which was also able to provide drinks on summer afternoons, that many programmes were planned and casts engaged. Dylan would meet his friends and drink beer and get work. There was no harm in that, though some who have been casually employed by the BBC have found this procedure uncomfortable and tedious. For with one Mac-Neice or Campbell or W. R. Rodgers one also gets, inevitably, half a dozen bores and hangers-on. With Dylan, the life-and-soul, one got a dozen. And they got him. And they did not let him go.

He had come up from Chelsea or Oxford, had done his work, his broadcast or his recording, he wanted a drink, and there they were, waiting to hear the famous poet hamming himself, to see him progress, glass by glass, from nervous exhaustion to wit, buffoonery and final drunkenness. By then he, and they, would have gone the half-mile from the BBC pubs to the Soho ones of his youth. His old Swansea friend, Charles Fisher, was back from the war, had a job in the House of Commons, and has described how many such an evening ended.

Looking for Dylan and not finding him. In the days of his early celebrity, not long after the war ended, innocent friends of mine at a loss for an occupation were anxious to meet the man who had become a legend in his own lifetime. Often and often someone would say to me just as the pubs were about to close in shabby Soho, "Let's look for Dylan." Ugh. But we would move briskly about, scanning the faces of the later drinkers (it would be all of ten o'clock in the Intrepid Fox, the Wheatsheaf, the Prince of Wales, the Bell, the French Pub, the Marquis of Granby) at each and every one of which the proprietor would say: "E woz ere but he gorn." Undismayed, we would continue to look in the bars of the Gargoyle, the Colonade, Club Eleven, the Caves de France and other such places as had leave to sell drinks until midnight. Ah. Here is the green man at the height of his acclaim. He sits in a corner propped up by two walls, a smouldering, soggy firework sending up stars of singular lucidity. His admirers surround him. What will he do next? they wonder. Will he burst or explode? A long silence. Dylan moves his head. A dozen necks crane forward alert to gather crumbs of irreverence or, perhaps, to learn how to write a poem. "A pint if I may," he rumbles in that deep belly-voice that makes audiences shiver. The pint is quickly fetched. "Oh, Mr. Thomas," says its provider. "What do you think of the new Italian poets?" In a voice fatally like the enquirer's but mincing, effeminate, Dylan repeats the question as an expression of disgust with the whole business. "Oh, Mr. Thomas, what do you think of the new Italian poets?" The subject is dropped.

More silence, followed by more questions. It is obvious from twenty feet away that Dylan is feeling sick. But as long as he can speak, he never gives up. "Tell that doorkeeper dressed like a huntsman to keep those goldfish quiet." He talks in a variety of accents, changing voices like a stage spy changing beards, by turns to Kensington, or BBC, or purest establishment as affected by Nina Hamnett who probably was. He has a target, and the target is pretentiousness wherever he finds it — but especially in the Mandrake after twelve o'clock. His favourite weapon is a Welsh accent, or rather a Swansea accent thin as a worn kitchen knife. "Who are 'iw, I presiwm?" It would be wrong to say that his presence makes anyone uncomfortable, but it encourages them to be cautious. He is so much drunker and more sure of himself than the others, besides being more articulate, if only sporadically. In addition he is ruder, or potentially ruder, at a time when in leading circles in London it is the fashion to be rude in public. All in all it is a formidable presence, as expected. Dylan is wearing nondescript clothes of homespun appearance; flannel or corduroy trousers bagged at the knees, a stained tweed jacket and a dark shirt with a loosely knotted tie. He looks like an unmade bed (I forget who thought up the phrase, but it is a good one).

He smokes continually, and once he has put a cigarette in his mouth he does not touch it until it is finished. He wears his cigarette. His curly hair is uncombed, his stomach bloated, his face flushed, his eyes luminous, but only when he speaks.

At this period I was working in the Commons and was rarely free before eleven at night, by which time Dylan's plans were far advanced, and so was he. Friends though we were, he was usually drunk and I was usually sober when the evening ended, and there are limits to the advantages which sobriety gives one.

Then the taxi back to Chelsea or later, if he did not spend the night in London, the hired car to Oxford. In London he would share the bed of any woman who would have him, more or less regardless of age or beauty, for what he sought in her bed was companionship, snuggling up, rather than passion. Or he would stay with friends, usually now the McAlpines, or he would doss down on the floor of David and Virginia Tennant's little flat beneath the Gargoyle. The next day, since he had no work to do, was likely to be an all-day pub crawl, perhaps with Roy Campbell, if he too were free, perhaps with David Tennant or some other crony. These, according to what David Tennant has told me, always began on the dot of 11:00 A.M. at the Cock Tavern in Fleet Street, "progressing slowly from one pub to another, usually ending up at the Coal Hole in the Strand, and finally at Finch's in the Tottenham Court Road." In the afternoons they would sometimes go to one of the few music halls that still existed. These, and science fiction or horror films, were the only sort of theatrical entertainment Dylan now enjoyed. Then would come the evening round of pubs and clubs and at last the hired car. He would frequently arrive back in Oxford having spent all his money and with nothing to show for this broadcast but a stupendous hangover. On occasion he had not the price of the car, and the Taylors would have to be awakened and the money borrowed to pay the driver. It was not a satisfactory way to earn an unsatisfactory living. Caitlin was becoming increasingly bitter. The rows got worse.

He not only had to go to London for the BBC but also to Cardiff and other outlying stations. And then there were the script conferences as well. Dylan was almost always punctual and sober when he arrived, and he did his work with the conscientiousness of the professional he was. It was afterwards that the drinking and the near-pathological extravagance began. But he also accepted other, unpaid engagements, to read to students, poetry societies and the like. He did this partly because he was too generous a man to refuse such an invitation, but partly, too, because he derived an increasing pleasure in being made much of. (In a letter to Charles Fisher dated March 1947 he said that he had written no poem for a whole year.) At such poetry readings he was often less conscientious. If he were receiving no fee he would expect to be paid in drinks. Sometimes he was drunk before the meeting began. There were even occasions when he did not turn up at all. Then he would write elaborate letters of apology.

He devoted an enormous amount of time to these letters, and some of them are indeed minor masterpieces, as are also some of his begging letters. In 1949 he was invited by the Swansea branch of the British Medical Association to be their guest of honour at their annual banquet. He did not turn up. Perhaps this was deliberate, for such a function would have frightened him, particularly in his own home town, but it was more probably out of alcoholic lethargy. On his way down from London he had stopped off in Bristol to have a few drinks with his old friend Mervyn Levy. This had taken several days, on one of which the Dylanless dinner took place. Weeks passed, and reports of the Swansea doctors' anger at his rudeness reached him. At last he wrote to the secretary of their association as follows:

I owe you so many apologies I don't know where to begin, but as I must begin somewhere let me please say, shaggy forehead to ground and tail wagging in desperate effort at propitiation, how very sorry I was not to have been able to answer at once your kind and charming, censorious and forgiving, letter — which I did not deserve a bit but which I was deeply delighted to have. (Looking back, for a second, at what I've written, I see that an unfriendly eye — a Swansea doctor's eye, for instance — could interpret me as meaning that I think I did not deserve your censoriousness. That is far from the case. Indeed, I thought that your remark about having wished, on October 20th, to murder me in cold blood to be little short, or shorn, of lamb-like. I should have wished upon myself the Death of a Thousand Cuts; and especially if I were a surgeon.) But I'm apologising now, in the first place, for what must have seemed to you the final rudeness, the last straw. . . . I mean the fact that I did not acknowledge straight away your incredibly lenient letter of nearly a month ago. I plead that the collected will of the Members of the Swansea Branch of the British Medical Association, working by a clinically white magic known only to their profession, drove me, soon after my inexcusable non-appearance at their Annual Dinner, into a bag of sickness and a cropper of accidents from which I have not yet fully recovered. The first effect of this malevolent mass medical bedevilment I experienced a week after the Dinner when stopping, heavily disguised, at Swansea in order to try to learn how really execrated I was in the surgeries and theatres, the bolus-rooms and Celtic lazarets, of a town I can approach now only in the deepest dark and where certain areas, particularly around the hospital, are forever taboo to me. I felt sudden and excruciating pains, and when I whimpered about them to a friend he said "Whatever you do, don't get ill in Swansea, it's more than your life is worth. Go in with a cough and they'll circumcise you." So I knew what the position was, and I took my pains home. But even at home, word of my unworthiness had reached the doctors' ears, and I was treated like a leper (fortunately, a wrong diagnosis). Ever since then I have felt unwell. A little later I had an attack of gout — undoubtedly the result of some Swansea specialist sticking a pin into a wax toe — and a little later still was set upon by invisible opponents in the bogled Laugharne dark and fell down and cracked my ribs. So that when your very nice letter was forwarded to me — needing medical attention, naturally I could not spend Christmas in Wales where every doctor loathed my every rib — I was in bed, in London, feeling like hell, unable to write a word, unable even to answer you, to thank you for your forgiveness and for all you said about my part in "Swansea and the Arts." I want to thank you now, belatedly but most gratefully, for that letter. And I do hope you understand why I did not answer it long, long before.

This leads me to try to make an apology for a far more serious breach of courtesy and good faith, and one of which I am profoundly ashamed. I felt, and knew, it to be a great honour when I was invited to be your chief guest and to propose the toast to the British Medical Association at your Annual Dinner. I looked forward a very great deal to that evening, though not without much knocking at the knees, and wrote a long, but not, I hope, too ponderous address, and demothed my monkey-suit, and borrowed some proper shoes, which hurt, and went up to London a few days before, on a radio job, with all the good intentions in the world. The evening of the 19th, when about to set out for Paddington, an acquaintance of mine said: "I have a new, very fast, sportscar, a present from my Mother" — who should know better — "and I will drive you down to Wales like winking. We will spend the night at Bristol." The car *was* very fast, he *did* drive like winking, and we *did* spend the night at Bristol. Just outside Bristol, he drove his car into a telegraph post and buckled it, which I hope drove his mother mad. And we spent the night, sick and shaken, in a hotel that frowned at our bruises and blood; and when I crawled out of bed on the afternoon of the 20th I could not find my acquaintance — the police, I was told, had called to see him — nor his buckled car in which I had left my bag, in which I had left my strenuously worked-upon address, my suit, my borrowed, hurting shoes. I looked round several garages; it wasn't there. And I was far too timid to dare to enquire at the police-station the whereabouts of car, acquaintance, bag, suit, address, or shoes. And anyway, by now it was too late to catch a train which would get me to Swansea in time to deliver, in the suit I hadn't got, the address I couldn't find.

I should, I know, have informed you of this sad, sordid story the very next day. But I put such a confession off and off and off until it seemed too late to matter: by this time, I realised, I was among the doomed.

Written down cold, months after, it does, I agree, sound a thin tall story. The unfortunate fact is that I am one of those people to whom these stories really do happen.

I hope you will be able, somehow, to accept this preposterous excuse, although it is so very lately given. And I hope you will be able to convey my most heartfelt apologies to your colleagues for all the inconvenience, and worse, caused by my failure to attend their Dinner.

And I hope, last of all, that because one Welsh writer has proved himself unworthy of the honour they were so generous to bestow upon him by their invitation, they will not, in future, think that no Welsh writer can be trusted. No Welsh writer can.

It was difficult, indeed almost impossible, to be angry with Dylan for long. Nor must it be imagined that he was, at this time, always as Charles Fisher has described him in Soho.

Mervyn Levy, writing in *John O' London's* on November 29, 1962, described an earlier visit of Dylan's to Bristol, in 1947:

The last time I sang to him was in the small hours, one night in 1947 when he arrived in Bristol without warning, in the battered car of a mutual friend, en route from London to Oxford where he and Caitlin were then living in the grounds of Magdalen College. Not the best route perhaps, but delightfully typical. At this time I was lecturing for the Department of Adult Education in the University of Bristol, and teaching at the West of England College of Art. A furious battering around 2.30 a.m. was irritably attended by Mrs. Musgrave, my landlady, and soon my own door was under fire. "Mr. Levy! Mr. Levy! quickly, please! Some terrible men are asking for you!" I tore into my trousers, pulled on a jacket, and stumbled downstairs. In the hall stood Dylan, his hair matted in damp coils. Against the open door a light drizzle was falling. Tony Hubbard, his companion, grinned a greeting at me from the driving seat of an ancient sports car. A crate of beer, many of the bottles already empty, occupied the whole of the back seat.

"Mervy!" said Dylan. "Mervy! We've come to see you!" They wanted me to help them find an hotel for the night, and within a few minutes, greatly to Mrs. Musgrave's relief, we were trundling down the long hill of Park Street, the old car clanking and groaning, and the bottles jigging in a jingle of joy. At the bottom of this hill is the Royal Hotel on College Green. Three damp men and a crate of beer at two o'clock in the morning had to be given a little thought. But at last a battery of tips established the only point of contact with us that he really understood, and two single rooms were made available. The crate was quarantined at reception, except for two bottles which Dylan stuffed into his pockets. Tony went to his room and I accompanied Dylan. Inside the narrow little room, he pulled off his sodden jacket, threw it on a chair, sat on the bed and shelled off his shoes, the laces still securely knotted. Loosening his tie, a crumpled, porky little man tottered to the wash-basin for the tooth-glass. . . . Grabbing at a bottle, Dylan slipped into the warm cocoon of the bed, still wearing his trousers, shirt, socks and tie.

"You first, Mervy," he said. In this way we finished the two bottles, chatting away about little personal things. Dylan knew many members of my own family. It was a little after 3.30 a.m. "I'm tired, Merv," he said — "Bloody tired. Sing me the song. You know." I sang:

> "I am the bandalero,
> The gallant bandalero,
> I rule the mountains and I claim
> As contraband what comes my way. . . ."

I turned off the light and slipped out of the womb.

Dylan had intended to return to Oxford with Tony the following morning. But he was exhausted. He knew that if he stayed in Bristol for two or three days he would be able to recuperate some of his lost energies. I drink very little and, without the crushing stimulus of other imbibers, Dylan was quite able to resist the more devilish temptations of the bottle. Tony departed alone and for three peaceful days, as happy as the lamb white days of our childhood, we ate well, drank with extreme modesty, and spent long hours in the news cinemas, where Dylan felt snug and safe.

At this same period another old friend, Ruthven Todd, ran into Dylan in London and was shocked by the condition in which he found him. Ruthven was then living a bachelor's life in a cottage at Tilty, Essex. He persuaded Dylan to go back there with him for a few days. In his unpublished memoirs Ruthven has described how extraordinary was the change as soon as they were out of London. The two poets drank beer in the village pub, Dylan enchanted the farm labourers with his relaxed and easy manners, they played darts and ate largely. His powers of recuperation were still quick and great.

From Dylan's point of view Oxford was, psychologically, halfway between the city and the country. When at home he did work, on his broadcasts and his film scripts, in a quiet room that A. J. P. Taylor had obtained for him in college. But there were plenty of pubs in Oxford and plenty of people for Dylan to drink with. During this first post-war year a high proportion of the undergraduates were men in their late twenties, back from the wars. They were thus only four or five years younger than Dylan, and were not to be treated as schoolboys. A number of them were only too pleased to spend their evenings drinking with the famous and amusing poet, so here once again he had a ready-made audience.

With the university staff he had less to do. He was, inevitably, suspicious and mistrustful of the members of the English faculty, though I am told that he was always perfectly civil and courteous to the English dons. Yet the academic attitude towards literature made him, as usual, uncomfortable. On the other hand with Ernest Stahl, now professor of German in the University, and his wife Kathleen, both he and Caitlin struck up a close and enduring friendship. And there were one or two other dons whom Dylan liked, among them Dr. A. L. Rowse, the historian. But it would be quite incorrect to think that Dylan was in any way involved in the life of the university.

Dylan's and Caitlin's relations with their host and hostess were complex. Thus he was aware of Margaret Taylor's great kindness to himself and his family, and he expressed his gratitude in such ways as were open to him: for example, when she showed him a dozen or so of her poems, he wrote her a detailed criticism running to over two thousand words, and if he did not much like her poems at least he paid them the compliment of his full attention. On the other hand he had no hesitation in exploiting that kindness, particularly when he began to feel that she was intent on reforming him. There is a story, which Margaret Taylor assures me is untrue but which is characteristic of how others saw their relationship, that on one occasion, when he was drinking with friends in the bar of the George in Oxford, she came in. He was not pleased to see her, and made some disagreeable remark. She replied: "But, Dylan, I have given you everything you ever asked for." He answered at once. "No you haven't. You haven't given me a caravan." She gave him one at once, which he used as a workroom. The truth is that she owned two caravans and let him have one.

Caitlin came increasingly to resent her status as the recipient of charity and, perhaps even more, Margaret Taylor's somewhat possessive manner towards the whole Thomas family and to Dylan in particular. Alan Taylor wearied quite quickly of this brawling, noisy family on his doorstep and often in his house. He wearied, too, of their incessant demands for money. The Taylors had children of their own to think of. True enough, it was Margaret's money, not his, that she was giving them, but when she sold a picture off his walls in order once again to get them out of debt, he blew up. Relations between Alan and Margaret deteriorated and within a few years they were divorced. It would seem probable that her patronage of the Thomas family contributed to the break-up of their marriage.

And this in turn aroused Caitlin's jealousy. She had reason enough to be bad-tempered. Dylan would frequently disappear for days on end, to make money as he said, leaving her and the children in the summer-house, and he would come back sick and, quite often, penniless as well. She had to borrow, and scrape credit, and accept Margaret Taylor's condolences, and be reminded that after all she was married to a genius. Caitlin came to dislike Margaret Taylor intensely, and when she thought wrongly that Margaret was copying her highly personal style of dress she, in her turn, blew up.

Dylan was always basically loyal to Caitlin despite his infidelities and his increasing neglect of her. If ever he had to take sides, he took hers. And he did so now. Their relationship with the Taylors became an ever unhappier one, and yet it went on for years. It was a great relief to Dylan and Caitlin when they managed to get away for a couple of weeks, in August of 1946, to Cahirciveen in Ireland. They went with Bill and Helen McAlpine to attend the famous Puck Fair in County Kerry. Dylan wrote to John Arlott: "Ireland was grand: I ate myself daft, but have now recovered." And then they returned to Holywell Ford, via Blaen-Cwn, where Dylan's mother was ill.

It must be remembered that throughout this summer and winter — and the winter of the 1946-1947 was not only one of the coldest England has known in modern times, but was also marked by repeated breakdowns of the coal, fuel and electricity systems — Dylan was still hoping to get his family to America. These hopes, however, were beginning to fade. Meanwhile Dylan's friends were becoming alarmed by his obvious and rapid deterioration, and since they valued the poet far above the entertainer they were distressed by his predicament which, as they thought, prevented him from doing his real work. Edith Sitwell in particular was most anxious that the spiral should somehow be broken. For her generation and her class foreign travel had always provided the easiest, quickest and most pleasant escape when an English situation, whether emotional or financial, appeared insoluble.

The Authors' Society had at its disposal a Travelling Scholarship Fund, and the committee then consisted of Dame Edith, chairman, Dilys Powell, Raymond Mortimer and John Lehmann. In the spring of 1947 a sum of one hundred fifty pounds was bestowed on Dylan, with the strong recommendation that his travels should be in Italy. Further financial assistance was provided by private individuals, and Dylan was assured of three months away from it all, without the need to earn his bread and butter. His friends hoped that during this holiday he would write poems once again and, even more important, get himself back on the rails so that when he returned home he could write more.

It was also agreed that when they did return he and his family could no longer continue to live in A. J. P. Taylor's summerhouse. With her now customary generosity Margaret Taylor searched the countryside. At last she found a semi-derelict farmhouse, somewhat euphemistically called the Manor House, just outside the village of South Leigh which is near Witney in Oxfordshire. She bought it, and had water laid on against their return from Italy. They set off on April 8, 1947, taking with them not only their own children but also Caitlin's sister Brigid and her son Tobias. Thus Caitlin need not be perpetually tied to the hearth. The journey took three days, for they had chosen the wrong route; they lost their luggage at the Italo-Swiss frontier, but recovered it; and finally they arrived at Rapallo. This was the first time that Dylan had ever been out of the British Isles.

In one sense the Italian visit was a success. Dylan began to write again, to write poems, that is, and *In Country Sleep* was mostly composed in the villa outside Florence to which they moved after a few weeks on the Italian Riviera. This long and beautiful poem was intended to be one of at least four parts that together would have constituted his longest and greatest work. Two other of the poems, *Over Sir John's Hill* and *In the White Giant's Thigh*, were finished, but the fourth, which was to give the whole not only its title but also a cosmological significance, was never written: *In Country Heaven* thus remains three magnificent poems, but they are uncompleted fragments. In me, at least, these poems evoke much the same aesthetic reaction as do Michelangelo's slaves, still half imprisoned in the shapeless stone from which they are carved.

The theme of this, Dylan's last, major work is one of great complexity, though in these poems his diction has an apparent simplicity by comparison with his earlier style. Like almost all his poems, and those of most other poets, they cannot be "translated" into prose. In July of 1951 he described them to John Malcolm Brinnin as "poems in praise of God's world by a man who doesn't believe in God." They are, in a way, his personal valediction or *nunc dimittis* to the physical world, the world of nature that he loved, of country beauty and fleshly joys. Yet for him the reality of death had always formed an intrinsic part of that world. *In Country Sleep* is a poem for his little daughter but for her, too, death "the Thief as meek as the dew" is waiting. *In the White Giant's Thigh* the dead women

> Who once in gooseskin winter loved all ice leaved
> In the courters' lanes, or twined in the ox roasting sun
> In the wains tonned so high that the wisps of the hay
> Clung to the pitching clouds, or gay with any one
> Young as they in the after milking moonlight lay
>
> Under the lighted shapes of faith and their moonshade
> Petticoats galed high, or shy with the rough riding boys,
> Now clasp me to their grains in the gigantic glade,
>
> Who once, green countries since, were a hedgerow of joys.

And above the estuary, *Over Sir John's Hill*, the hawk on fire, the killer, hangs still above the little birds, who

> Young
> Green chickens of the bay and bushes cluck, "Dilly dilly,
> Come let us die."

But *In Country Heaven* transcends, or at least was intended to transcend, Dylan's personal awareness of mortality. He was acutely conscious of the menace that has hung, like his hawk, over our world since Hiroshima. And to his knowledge of his own impending death he now compounded his fear, a fear that was almost a commonplace of the period, lest this whole lovely planet burn. The unwritten poem was to have expressed this. He wrote of it, in a talk that is reprinted in *Quite Early One Morning:*

The poem is to be called "In Country Heaven." The godhead, the author, the milky-way farmer, the first cause, architect, lamp-lighter, quintessence, the beginning Word, the anthropomorphic bowler-out and blackballer, the stuff of all men, scapegoat, martyr, maker, woe-bearer — He, on top of a hill in heaven, weeps whenever, outside that state of being called his country, one of his worlds drops dead, vanishes screaming, shrivels, explodes, murders itself. And, when he weeps, Light and His tears glide down together, hand in hand. So, at the beginning of the poem, he weeps and Country Heaven is suddenly dark. Bushes and owls blow out like candles. And the countrymen of heaven crouch all together under the hedges and, among themselves in the tear-salt darkness, surmise which world, which star, which of their late, turning homes in the skies has gone for ever. And this time, spreads the heavenly hedgerow rumour, it is the Earth. The Earth has killed itself. It is black, petrified, wizened, poisoned, burst; insanity has blown it rotten; and no creatures at all, joyful, despairing, cruel, kind, dumb, afire, loving, dull, shortly and brutishly hunt their days down like enemies on that corrupted face. And, one by one, those heavenly hedgerowmen who once were of the Earth call to one another, through the long night, Light and His tears falling, what they remember, what they sense in the submerged wilderness and on the exposed hair's breadth of the mind, what they feel trembling on the nerves of a nerve, what they knew in their Edenie hearts, of that self-called place. They remember places, fears, loves, exultation, misery, animal joy, ignorance, and mysteries, all *we* know and do not know.
The poem is made of these tellings. And the poem becomes, at last, an affirmation of the beautiful and terrible worth of the Earth. It grows into a praise of what is and what could be on this lump in the skies. It is a poem about happiness.

The concept was thus almost Miltonic in its scope. Nor can it be pure coincidence that he read extracts from the ten books of *Paradise Lost* over the BBC in 1947 and learned whole passages by heart so that when Hugh Mackintosh quoted a line one evening, in the Saville Club, Dylan quoted the next fifty. And it is possible that it was because of its essentially abstract nature that he never succeeded in transforming the concept into a poem; for he was not granted the time that he would have needed to perform the poetic metamorphosis that would have enabled him to transmute these ideas into his own terms.

As early as 1933 he had written to Pamela Hansford Johnson:

The body, its appearance, death, and disease, is a fact, sure as the fact of a tree. It has its roots in the same earth as the tree. The greatest description I know of our own "earthiness" is to be found in John Donne's Devotions, where he describes man as earth of the earth, his body earth, his hair a wild shrub growing out of the land. All thoughts and actions emanate from the body. Therefore the description of a thought or action — however abstruse it may be — can be beaten home by bringing it onto a physical level. Every idea, intuitive or intellectual, can be imaged and translated in terms of the body, its flesh, skin, blood, sinews, veins, glands, organs, cells, or senses.

Through my small, bonebound island I have learnt all I know, experienced all, and sensed all. All I write is inseparable from the island. As much as possible, therefore, I employ the scenery of the island to describe the scenery of my thoughts, the earthquake of the body to describe the earthquake of the heart.

It is clear from the earlier passage that Dylan's views on his function as a poet had not changed in the fifteen-odd years that had passed, though he was now no longer limited to his own "small, bonebound" island. To have made the inverted sublimation of the ideas behind the unwritten *In Country Heaven* would indeed have been an enormous task, and had it been successful it might well have been one of the greatest poems in the English language.

Yet even if he had lived, it is permissible to doubt whether *In Country Heaven* would ever have been completed as a work of unity, just as it is permissible to doubt whether Michelangelo's slaves would ever have become a unified group. When Bill McAlpine asked him where *In the White Giant's Thigh* fitted into the whole, Dylan replied airily: "I don't know yet, but it'll fit in somewhere." He was no Milton, he was no builder of cathedrals. And of course he was aware of this. To John Davenport he once described his position in the history of English poetry as "captain of the second eleven." This was not at all a modest self-appraisal, for he well knew the qualifications that are required for selection to the first. To continue his homely metaphor, *In Country Heaven* might well have won him his cap, and once again there is no reason to doubt that he was aware of this. And the three poems of *In Country Heaven* that he did write are considered by many, including myself, to be among his finest work.

Edith Sitwell's hope that Italy might enable Dylan to start writing poems again was thus fulfilled. But in another sense his visit was less successful.

He did not like Italy. In April of 1934, when he thought he was in love with Pamela, he had written her:

Shall we live on an island, somewhere in the Mediterranean, writing and reading, loving and sleeping, singing our sweet rude rhymes to the seals? I love you darling.

But four years later, when Lawrence Durrell had suggested that he come to Corfu for the summer of 1939, Dylan had replied:

I think England is the very place for a fluent and fiery writer. The highest hymns of the sun are written in the dark. I like the grey country. A bucket of Greek sun would drown in one colour the crowds of colour I like trying to mix for myself out of a grey flat insular mud. If I went to the sun I'd just sit in the sun; and that would be very pleasant but I'm not doing it. . . .

By 1947 when Dylan arrived in the villa they had been lent near Florence — the Villa Beccaro, at Scandicci — his early prejudices had become hardened by habit. The villa was beautiful, indeed luxurious, and in mid-May he described it, on a postcard to his parents:

This is our house. Really, it's a hundred times nicer than this picture, which gives little idea. It's on the hills, above Florence, some five miles or more from the centre, from the great Cathedral dome which we can see from the sunbathing terrace above the swimming pool. And I hope that sounds grand enough. It's a very big villa, with huge rooms and lovely grounds, arbours, terraces, pools: we have a pinewood and a vineyard of our own. There are cypresses and palms all around us, in the wide green valley below with poppies among the vines and olives, and in the higher hills. Our garden is full of roses. Nightingales sing all night long. Lizards scuttle out of the walls in the sun. It is lovely.

The life, though, did not really appeal to him. Ten days later he was writing to John Davenport:

This pig in Italy bitterly knows — O the tears on his snub snout and the squelch in the trough as he buries his flat, Welsh head in shame, and guzzles and blows — that he should have written, three wine vats gone, a porky letter to Moby D. or two-ton John; but with a grunt in the pines, time trotted on! The spirit was willing: the ham was weak. The spirit was brandy: the ham was swilling. And oh the rasher-frying sun! . . .
To get to the city, we go by horse-and-trap to Scandicci and then suffer in the tram for twenty-five minutes. One can order a car from Florence, but it costs about 3000 lire — thirty shillings. . . .
We have got to know lots of the young intellectuals of Florence, and a damp lot they are. They visit us on Sunday. To overcome the language, I have to stand on my head, fall in the pool, crack nuts with my teeth, and Tarzan in the cypresses. I am very witty in Italian, though a little violent;

and I need space. Do you know anybody in Florence to have a drink with? I met Stephen Spender a few weeks ago. It was very sad. He is on a lecture tour. He is bringing the European intellectuals together. . . .

The omnipresent black market depressed and shocked him almost as much as the poverty of smashed, post-war Italy. And he found the increasing heat almost intolerable. On June 5, 1947, he wrote to his parents:

It is terrifically hot today: ever since June began. It is useless to try to do anything between mid-day and 4 in the afternoon. And it will get hotter day by day. Florence lies below us, through the vines and olives, in a rippling haze.

Today there is a fiesta in Mosciano, and Brigid and Caitlin and the children are going. I am going to work. I cannot work usually in this house, even though it is large. Aeronwy and Tobias make a terrible din together, though Aeronwy is good enough by herself. So I work in a room in the peasant's cottage which is part of this estate: a good room, small and plain, looking into a wild wood. I am working on a long poem, but so slowly. And after it is finished, I want to write a radio play.

The heat was strange, and then there was also the question of what to drink. To Donald Taylor he wrote: "The heat is sizzling, the wine overpowering, the villa enormous." Dylan was a beer-drinker, but the Italians had then not yet begun once again to import German beer, and the national product was thin, gassy, tasting faintly of straw. When I arrived in Italy the following year I found myself forced to drink the cheap, acidulous wine, which was neither thirst-quenching nor good for the nerves. Accustomed as Dylan was to absorbing large quantities of liquid, he drank a great deal of this cheap wine and in Florence was frequently drunk. Professor Tedlock, in his symposium *Dylan Thomas: The Legend and the Poet,* has published a description of Dylan as seen through the rather bewildered eyes of Mario Luzi:

Entering the Giubbe Rosse [a well-known Florentine café] late of an evening, he was to be found entrenched behind a small forest of bottles, a full glass in his hand, and one wondered whether those large pale blue eyes were gazing upon something ineffable or merely into vacancy. He would begin to speak, then lapse into silence, perhaps because the listener did not understand English, perhaps because what he had to say was inexpressible in any language. He talked little, preferring gestures of comprehension or dissent, remaining isolated within his own solitude, his friendliness apparent in the offering of drink.

His wife's problem was to push him into a taxi and get him home. One evening, expected to supper with the poet Montale, he was reluctantly dragged from his bed and remained drunk all the evening. Invited on other occasions to their houses by his translator Bigongiari and Rosai, the painter, he seemed at first to enter the conversation, a glow of fiery youth in his eyes, but almost at once fell back in his chair and slept heavily.

If this is a good example of the writing of the Florentine intellectuals, and if many of them were so unobservant as to think that Dylan had blue eyes, his somnolence becomes more than excusable. To Ronald Bottrall, whom he had known slightly in England and whom he had met again during a visit to Rome that he thoroughly enjoyed, he wrote on June 20th:

I like the people I don't know in the streets, but not the writers etc., who are nearly all editors, I meet in the cafés. So many live with their mothers, on private incomes, and translate Apollinaire. They talk of "letters." Montale seems to be an exception. . . .

One Sunday, when he saw a group of them toiling up the hill towards the villa, he hid in a closet until they had gone.

Llewelyn was unhappy outside Florence, for there were no boys with whom he could play. And Dylan, too, was lonely, indeed almost homesick. He spent a lot of time listening to John Arlott broadcasting his commentary on the England-Australia cricket matches, and he wrote a great many letters to friends, urging them to come and stay, but none did. He had hoped particularly that Bill and Helen McAlpine would manage a visit. Unfortunately they could not, and on July 14th he wrote to them:

What a really big pity, and everybody waiting, from the torpedo lizards in the hairy pool — remind the gardener to change the water! — to the pick-axed and pneumatic-drilled mosquitoes in the guests' bedroom — remind the parlourmaid to take the bottles and the gorgonzola off the bed! We had planned such a lot of things to do, and all with wine: picnics, prickstrips, titlicks, nipsicks, gripwicks, slipthicks, tipsticks, liptricks, etcetera etcetera, parties, expeditions. Perhaps we can all come to Italy next year, and do things on a pig scale.

By mid-July he was writing to Tommy Earp:

I am awfully sick of it here, on the beautiful hills above Florence, drinking chianti in our marble shanty, sick of vini and contadini and bambini, and sicker still when I go, bumpy with mosquito bites, to Florence itself, which is a gruelling museum. I loved it in Rome, felt like Oppenheim on the Riviera, but we have been here, in this villa, two months and I can write only early in the morning, when I don't get up, and in the evening, when I go out. . . . We *really* do have an enormous swimming pool, (into which I have been only once, by mistake), and our own vineyard, olives, mosquitoes, and small Italian mice with blue chins. I have written a longish poem. . . .

A few days later they packed up and moved to Elba, to Rio Marina. Dylan loved this place, while Caitlin, Brigid and the children had the sea. To the McAlpines he wrote on July 26th and again on August 1st:

Lucky Napoleon! This is a most beautiful island; and Rio Marina the strangest town on it: only fishermen and miners live here: few tourists: no foreigners. Extremely tough. Something like a Latin Cahirciveen. Notices "Fighting Prohibited" in all bars. . . .
And the green and blue transparent yachted winkled and pickling sea. We are rarely out of it, except to drink, eat, sleep, sing, ——, walk, dance, ride, write, quarrel, climb, cave and cafe crawl, read, smoke, brood, bask in the lavatory, over the parroty fruit-market. There is no winter in Elba; cognac is threepence a large glass; the children have web feet; the women taste of salt. . . .

They stayed there for two weeks, and returned to England on August 11th. It was not an auspicious arrival. The McAlpines had invited them to stay, but were out when they arrived. Dylan attempted to climb in through a window, fell, and broke his arm. And thus ended the only foreign holiday Dylan ever took.

❊   ❊   ❊

Back in England, Dylan and Caitlin had, at last and for the first time in seven years, a house in which to live. The Manor House, South Leigh, which Margaret Taylor had bought specifically to house them, was a large cottage or small farmhouse in a field on the far edge of that straggling village. It had a small and run-to-seed garden, was white-washed without, and apart from the electricity that Margaret had installed was without modern conveniences of any sort. There was never a bath, for instance, during the eighteen months that they were there. Llewelyn went to Magdalen College School, and Aeronwy was at home. The caravan was towed out and installed in the field in front of the house. Later, after Caitlin in a moment of pique had tried to tip it on its side with Dylan in it, he prudently moved it to the orchard of Mr. Green, the postmaster and grocer who also acted as village taxi-driver, at the other end of the village, next to the pub.

Writing from South Leigh to John Davenport, in late September of 1947, he said:

> The above is my permanent address until they find out. . . . Our Manor is a cottage, but only five minutes from Witney and exactly twenty-five from Oxford. Do come down. Only one small, single spare bed so far.

South Leigh had obvious and considerable advantages over Holywell Ford, but it had its drawbacks too. It was, for one thing, much more isolated. Dylan immediately resumed his BBC and film life, and his return journeys were now longer and his arrivals even less predictable than before. Although friends did come to stay and Harry Locke, the comedian, and his wife had a cottage in the village — as, next year, did the McAlpines — Caitlin had to spend an unconscionable amount of time alone with the children in this isolated little house. And from the spring of 1948 she had to look after his parents as well.

D. J. Thomas had been ailing for some time. In fact he had never really recovered since his tongue cancer of 1932, and had gradually become a semi-invalid. He was now losing his eyesight as well. The pride and fire had almost all gone out of him and he was becoming a husk of himself. He had lost his pot-belly, did the crossword puzzles of which both he and Dylan were so fond, and awaited the end. People who only knew him in his last years find it hard to recognize in him the English master at the Swansea Grammar School whom his pupils there had known. The spectacle of his decline distressed Dylan greatly and inspired one of his last poems, *Do not go gentle into that good night*.

And now, in the winter of 1947-1948, his mother fell and broke her knee. She was taken to Carmarthen Infirmary. Dylan's sister Nancy went from Brixham to Blaen-Cwm to look after D.J. and be near her mother. Nancy had served in the Field Army Nursing Yeomanry during the war, and had married her second husband, Gordon Summersby, in India. He was trying his hand as a commercial fisherman at Brixham, but this was not proving a very successful venture, and he was seriously considering a return to India. Dylan went down to Blaen-Cwm and described what he found there in an undated letter to Caitlin:

> Here it's snowbound, dead, dull, damned; there's hockey-voiced Nancy being jolly over pans and primuses in the kitchen, and my father trembling and moaning all over the place, crying out sharply when the dog barks — Nancy's dog, — weeping, despairing. My mother, in the Infirmary, with her leg steel-splintered up towards the ceiling and a 300 lb. weight hanging from

it, is good and cheerful and talks without stop about the removed ovaries, dropped wombs, amputated breasts, tubercular spines and puerperal fevers of her new friends in the women's surgical ward. She will have to lie, trussed, on her back with her leg weighted for at least two months, and then will be a long time learning, like a child, to walk again. The doctors have stuck a great steel pin right through her knee, so that, by some method, the broken leg will grow to the same length as the other one. My father, more nervous and harrowed than I have ever seen him, cannot stay on here alone, and Nancy cannot stay with him, so she is taking him back with her to Brixham until my mother can leave the infirmary. My mother will therefore be alone in the infirmary for months. No one here will look after the dog Mably, and Nancy cannot take him back to her tiny cottage as she has, already, a Labrador retriever: they didn't know what to do but to have Mably destroyed, which is wrong, because he is young and well and very nice. So I have said that I will take him.

In late April of 1948, Mrs. Thomas came out of the infirmary. Dylan went down to Brixham and decided there and then to bring his parents back to South Leigh by ambulance. The old couple obviously could not live alone, Nancy's cottage was too small, and in any case she and her husband were going abroad. So Dylan brought them back with him, first to the Lockes' cottage which he rented, then to the Manor House itself. This was intended as a temporary measure, but for the rest of Dylan's life they were to remain dependent upon him, or rather upon Caitlin, though Summersby helped financially. Here was a further, and extremely gloomy, burden for her to bear.

Relations with the Taylors deteriorated, as Dylan failed to pay the small rent agreed upon. Margaret, however, did not allow this to affect her warm, protective feelings, which she expressed somewhat too freely for Caitlin's liking. Margaret Taylor's frequent visits to South Leigh could be relied upon to spark off a row between Dylan and Caitlin. Dylan spent less and less time at home. Their Oxford friends have told me that Dylan could still, in company and in drink, shake off his ever-mounting worries and fears, and at least for a while, until he sank into a glazed stupor, be his old, witty, charming self. Caitlin, on the other hand, became increasingly bitter and violent in public, especially when Dylan was present and the centre of attention.

There is a tragi-comic anecdote told me by Bill McAlpine that perhaps symbolizes this. Shortly before Christmas of 1948 he and Dylan bicycled from South Leigh to Witney. Their wives wanted them to do some Christmas shopping, which, after the requisite number of beers, they did and Dylan's basket was full of nuts. He was in collision with a lorry, fell off, and an old lady who happened to be passing remarked to the little figure lying in the road: "You've split your nuts, sonny." Bill found that Dylan had broken a tooth, and an arm as usual. He took him straight to the Radcliffe Infirmary in Oxford where Dylan's arm was set in plaster. Although he must have been in considerable pain, his flow of humour kept the nurses and interns in fits of laughter. Then an ambulance was provided to take him home. Dylan somehow persuaded the ambulance men to stop at all the pubs on the way. At last this odd little party arrived at the Manor House and Dylan asked the ambulance men in for a drink. Caitlin took one look at his arm in plaster and exclaimed, bitterly:

"Play-acting!"

In early 1948 one of the worst blows of all had fallen. Dylan had never filed an income tax return, and now the Inspector of Taxes caught up with him. A vast sum in back income tax was demanded in most menacing tones, vast that is by Dylan's standards, though even had it been small it would have been difficult enough for him to find it. He was liable to criminal prosecution and to the confiscation, at source, of his entire, erratic income. Margaret Taylor hurried up to London to see David Higham on his behalf, and Higham proceeded, as best he could, to sort out this problem too. He put the business into the hands of an accountant named Leslie H. Andrews. It cannot have been an easy job, since these tax claims went back many years. Dylan had, of course, kept no accounts of any sort, and had a habit of not turning up for meetings with his agent and his accountant. Somehow, however, Higham and Andrews between them managed to pacify H. M. Inspector of Taxes, but at a cost to Dylan in money, and therefore in worry, that was a major contributory factor in his decline and death. For henceforth a substantial percentage of his earnings — which varied according to Andrews's success with the tax people, but which was never less than a third and was at times almost twice that — was deducted at source to pay off the accumulated debt. He had reached an age and enjoyed a reputation which should at least have made some financial security obtainable. Yet from now until his death he was never, for a single day, free of financial terror. The vultures roosted on the roof-tree of the Manor House, South Leigh.

In the summer of 1948 he went to work for Sydney Box at Gainsborough Films. His contract assured him of one thousand pounds a year

[303]

as advance against three feature scripts which he was to write within the year, and for which he was to receive one thousand pounds each on delivery. Ralph Keene, who had once worked for Donald Taylor, had suggested this to Box, and it should have solved Dylan's basic financial problem, as his salary from Strand Films had done throughout the war. But now so much of the money was snatched by the Inland Revenue before he ever saw it that it solved little. Furthermore only one script, *The Beach at Falesa*, adapted from R. L. Stevenson's story of that title, was finished before Gainsborough was wound up, almost overnight, in the spring of 1949 by its parent company, the Rank Organization. The other two scripts on which Dylan had done a considerable amount of work therefore remained unfinished and unpaid for.

So far as publishers were concerned, Dylan, in these last years, was signing almost any contract that would produce a little immediate money. He was not the first, or the last, writer to do this. Graham Greene persuaded Eyre and Spottiswoode to give Dylan an advance against *Adventures in the Skin Trade*, which he promised once again to finish. He never did. Dylan persuaded the Princess Caetani, the American lady who edited and owned the international avant-garde magazine *Botteghe Oscure* in Rome, to buy the unfinished *Under Milk Wood*. He promised to finish it rapidly, but did not, and also sold it elsewhere without informing Higham. Dent's wished to issue a new edition of *18 Poems*, and paid one hundred and fifty pounds to buy back the copyright that Dylan had sold for some fifteen pounds to the Fortune Press during the war. They were not prepared to offer any further advance. Higham, however, persuaded them to bring out *Collected Poems* instead. For this Dylan did get an advance, but he wished to write a long poem as preface. This took him one whole year, and even when that was done Dent's had the greatest difficulty in getting him to correct his proofs. E. F. Bozman, the editor at Dent's, has said that Dylan was almost incredibly dilatory where his own financial interests were concerned.

The BBC, who had been pleased with Louis MacNeice's English version of *Faust*, commissioned Dylan to do a similar version for broadcasting of *Peer Gynt*. When he failed again and again to meet the dateline in his contract, they threatened to apply the ultimate sanction and have him totally black-listed from all BBC programmes. Once again Higham came to the rescue and this threat, which if applied would have cut off one of Dylan's principal sources of income, was withdrawn.

Still, it would be curious to know what was the mental process of the BBC bureaucrat who was prepared to silence one of the most powerful and popular voices the BBC ever had at its disposal because the owner of that voice was also a writer who had failed to keep a contract.

Weighed down by worry, sick with alcohol, swamped by work he must have known he could never complete, burdened with his parents' endless complaints, snapped at by Caitlin, mourned over by Margaret, disappointed by America, wearied of the incessant travel between Oxford and the BBC, and above all homesick for Wales and a happier past, Dylan wished to return to Laugharne.

In the autumn of 1948 he wrote to Frances Hughes to find out if the house called the Castle, that Richard Hughes had once rented and now left, was available. It was not. But again Margaret Taylor came to his help. She sold South Leigh and with the proceeds bought for him the Boat House, Laugharne, and a cottage called the Pelican House, opposite Brown's Hotel in Laugharne's main street, was rented, though not by her, for his parents. They all moved there in May of 1949, and Dylan commemorated his departure from England in the following broadcast, which went out on June 23, 1949:

Before I came back to live in Wales, a very little time ago, I was travelling on a morning train from Oxford to London when, suddenly, the desire to live neither in Oxford nor in London, or to travel between them, came very near to knocking me down, which would not be difficult.

I was, at that moment, chillily perched on a stool, old from sleep, at the tumbler-circled counter in the bellying buffet-car, watching, over my black, lace-collared, but Liffeyless glass, the corpse-grey liver-sausage and dredged tea, the putty rolls and washing-day lager, being wolfed and lapped by furtive, small, damp physicists and large, ball-playing, booming boys with bulldog pipes and scarves as thick and many as a cabman's waistcoats.

There, all about me, chastely dropping, with gloved and mincing, just-so fingers, saccharine tablets into their cups of stewed Thameswater, or poising their cigarette-holders like blowpipes, or daintily raising, the little finger crooked, a current bun to the snapping flash of their long, strong teeth, tall and terrible women neighed: women inaccessible as goat crags, nowhere, on all this smacked and blossoming earth, at home except on lofty, cold bicycles with baskets at the front full of lettuce, library books, and starchless bread, aloofly scything along the High, the wind never raising their sensible skirts, and their knitted pastel stockings full of old hockeymuscles.

There, all about me, long thin accents with yellow waistcoats and carefully windswept hair, one lock over the eye, bleated and fluted. In a drawl of corduroy at the tea-urn, vowels were plucked and trussed.

Tiny, dry, egghead dons, smelling of water-biscuit, with finickety lips and dolls' bowties like butterflies poisoned and pinned, solved the crossword puzzles behind their octagonal glasses and smirked their coffee up.

Slade-fringed, cowlike girls in, may be, hessian, put down the books they could not read and turned big, mooing eyes towards the passing landscape they could not paint.

One ox-broad, beardless boy, tattooed with his school colours, manfully drank up his gin and lemon, wishing it were all lemon.

And there I watched that dottle-tasting liquid history of scorched and shaken tea passing the lips and going the gastric rounds of gaunt and hairy horn-rimmed lecturers in French who tapped their Gaulloise on their Sartre and saw, with disdain, the pretty gasworks ripple by, ebullient Didcot come and go, red Reading fly by like a biscuit: they were bent on an existentialist spree.

And then and there, as I watched them all, desire raised its little fist.

I did not want to be in England, now that they were there.

I did not want to be in England, whether they were there or not.

I wanted to be in Wales.

Let me be fair, however much I dislike it. The men and women, and the others, in that carriage were not England. I do not point to one group of people, however repellent, and say, "That, to me, is England. Help, let me out!" I distrust the man who says, "Now *that* is England," and shows me a tailwag of rich tweedy women babytalking to their poodles. That is no more England than a village cricket match is.

No, my desire not to be in England rose and crowned me at that very moment; and that is all.

For a long time, indeed, I have been fated of living among strangers in a dark and savage country whose customs and tribal rites I shall never understand, breathing an alien air, hearing, everywhere, the snobcalls, the prigchants, the mating cries, the tom-toms of a curious, and maybe cannibal, race. The reverence paid to the cultural witch-doctors sickened me, as did their ritual pomp, their odorous courts, and the periodic sacrifices of the young. I wanted to sit no longer, as I had sat for years in that narrow-vowelled jungle, alone as it seemed, by my log fire — (a bright light keeps the beasts at bay) — rolling the word Wales round my tongue like a gobstopper of magical properties, ringing the word like a bell, making it rise and fall, whisper and thunder like the Welsh sea whose fish are great Liberals, fond of laverbread and broth, and who always, on Sundays, attend their green and watery chapels.

Alone there, the wolves of Middlesex mewling outside my llanwigwam fire, I used to think, to keep me company, of the bits and pieces of sounds and pictures, tunes and colours, places and persons, that meant my home tome. The outpost Englishman, monkey-suited for dinner in the exotic bush, toasts Piccadilly in whiskey, or so I have read. I could not put on steeplehat and red flannel petticoat and drink to the bright lights of Llanstephan in light ale. All I could do was remember, and I am good at that.

I could remember, to keep me going through the long Saxon nights, the smell of the streets on Sunday, palpable as bombazine. The scooped hollow sound that Sunday made as I woke: religion in a black seashell. The melancholy endless mothballed avenues of Sunday in the sunken suburbs, where not a lawnmower stirs. The tinroofed chapels where I trebled Aberystwyth and made calf eyes at the minto-sucking girls. The primitive, dark promenade of hidden loves after chapel, the long, low Sunday whistle to make the girls turn round, and, always, mine had glasses. The rattle of the milkcart Monday morning, and the first tram hissing like a gander to the steelworks. The hunchback streets on Sunday morning, men with white mufflers and lean dogs waiting for a miracle outside the pub shut like a tomb, and the beetles passing them by with their noses and brollies in the air. The sound of the colliers' voices at night left on the air above the crippled street. *"Nosda, Will." "Nosda, Shoni." "Nosda, Evan." "Nosda!"* No star. And the stars coming out sweet as the smell of fish and chips. Anything, anything would do to remember to ward off the pinstriped wolves. Remember the shop at the corner, Mrs. Evans the Pop, full of liquorice, bootlaces, lamp oil, pear drops, and a smell that was comfier than roses. The front parlour, which nobody ever entered save the preacher on special occasions or sometimes the committee members of the Mothers' Union or the rare relatives from England or another foreign country, and, of course, the family mourners every now and then to sit on the edges of the unused chairs and hear the voice of the clock ticking their own lives away between the two china dogs.

But all this was easy stuff, like settles in the corners, hams on the hooks, hymns after stop-tap, tenors with leeks, the hwyl at Ebenezer, the cockles on the stalls, dressers, eisteddfodau, Welshcakes, slagheaps, funerals, and bethelbells. What was harder to remember was what birds sounded like and said in Gower; what sort of a sound and a shape was Carmarthen Bay; how did the morning come in through the windows of Solva; what silence when night fell in the Aeron Valley.

I could not remember, try as I might, if I was a different man, if a man at all, when cockily bulking in Wales than when flinching in London from traffic and other writers or guiltily buttonholing the Soho night to unbosom my buckets of woes.

I knew, as I walked the City, the snarl of the grimestones of the bread-and-butter streets. Did the pavements of my home town bounce with a different cry?

I knew, oh I knew, what my face looked like in the cracked, advertisement-bitten looking-glass of the skies over Fleet and Wardour. Had I, awaking, the same face, then, in the shaving-glass of the sky propped above the Welsh sea's sink?

I could not remember, try as I might, if the old, booted body that bore its grumbles and juices so scowlingly up Portland Place to do its morning rant was the same as that which, hoofed with seaweed, did a jig on the Llanina sands and barked at the far mackerel.

Lost and blown about in London town, a barrel-shaped leaf, am I still the same, I said to myself, as that safe and sound loller at the corners of Wales who, to my memory, was happy as a sandman.

How could I answer my silly questions unless I went back to Wales?

And now that I am back in Wales, am I the same person, sadly staring over the flat, sad, estuary sands, watching the herons walk like women poets, hearing the gab of gulls, alone and lost in a soft kangaroo pocket of the sad, salt West, who once, so very little time ago, trundled under the blaring lights, to the tune of cabhorns, his beautiful barrow of raspberries.

The properties of my memory remain.

Still the rebuking chapel has a cold eye and a sweet voice. Sunday, still, wears spiderweb gloves, blows its nose in an umbrella, and smells of wet fur.

Market Day still clucks on the cobbles among the cockles and clogs, ducks, drakes, and gaiters, babyshawls, fishfrails, parchs and baskets.

Saturday night wears its cap on the side of its brilliantine and is full of pints.

I know that I am home again because I feel just as I felt when I was not at home, only more so.

And still there are harps and whippets on the castled and pitheaded hills.

12

WHILE still living in South Leigh Dylan had made his second journey abroad, this time to Prague as a guest of the Czechoslovakian
government, where he attended the inauguration of the Czechoslovak
Writers' Union. He flew to Prague on March 4, 1949, and was there for
a little less than a week. The congress, which was to "create a programme of artistic activity" for Czech and Slovak writers, lasted only
for two days, but there were the customary banquets and visits to the
theatre. Delegates came from all over the world, particularly of course
the Communist parts of it, and Dylan afterwards told Aneirin Talfan
Davies that he had been the only non-Communist present.

It was the Czechoslovak cultural attaché in London, Aloys Skoumal,
who had invited him. Skoumal is himself a translator — he has translated Swift and Lewis Carroll, among others, into his own language —
with a wide knowledge of English literature. He has, I am told, an
especial fondness for "Celtic" writers, and the two writers whom he
invited to attend the Prague Conference — which I believe was the first
international literary get-together to be held in that city since the Communist *coup d'état* of just over a year before — were Louis MacNeice
and Dylan Thomas, both of whom he knew personally.

Louis MacNeice did not even bother to reply. In the 'thirties he had
been far more active politically, and far more to the left, than had Dylan, but he had remained politically alert in a way that Dylan had never
been. Dylan now signed, more or less automatically, any document,
whether Communist-inspired or not, which talked of peace and freedom. Thus he signed the Stockholm Peace Petition and the Rosenberg
Petition. Louis was much more aware of what was going on in the world,

and refused to lend his name to Stalinist propaganda. For this was the chilliest period of Stalinism, when it was impossible for any real poet to publish in Russia or Russian-occupied Europe. Socialist realism, that is to say hymns to Stalin and poems about tractors and so on, was all that was permitted. So Dylan went to Prague alone.

This visit to a Communist country was something of an eye-opener to him. He rapidly discovered that in any totalitarian state there are two sorts of writers, the official ones, in this case the socialist realists, whose congress he was attending, and the unofficial ones, the "modern" poets and novelists, with whom his sympathies lay and whose company he infinitely preferred to that of those others. The answer to Lenin's famous question "Who whom?" was not hard to find in Czechoslovak literary circles at that time.

Jirina Haukova met Dylan almost as soon as he arrived. She was later to translate some of his poems. In a letter to me she has described his visit to Prague:

I was employed in this time at the Ministry of Information but I met Dylan unofficially. He came to Prague the day I saw him and he took part in the session of Writers' Union. I went to see him in the hall of the Hotel Flora. I knew his photo but nobody such was sitting there. The photo was very old, a photo of a young lyrical man. I recognised him only by his hair. He had got fat. I told him: "You are bigger now." He laughed and said: "I'm fat." I suggested him to go and see the Old Town of Prague. He agreed and was looking forward to Pilsner beer. I asked him why did he come to take part in the session of Writers' Union. He answered: "Why not? I'm left." We went out, in the old town he was enthusiastic by the gothic churches and modern style houses. Moreover he recognized every pub and we went always in for one Pilsner beer. Dylan showed by hand: "A big one," and every waiter understood him. We talked about the literature and about the translating of his poetry. In this time it was quite impossible to publish modern poetry in our country. I asked him what he would do if he would be in our country and could not publish. He said he would never write social realistic literature; he would rather take a job and write what he wished. "A real poet must stand everything," says he, "and it doesn't matter if he publishes or not."

Prague was under snow in these days and Dylan liked it very much. He had on a new coat with a cap — "a flying coat" as he said — he bought it for the trip to Prague. He looked as Jack Frost in this coat with cap in the snow. Everybody looked on him. It was snowing and snowing and Dylan said, he had imagined Prague just so. He had the shoes with the nails and he was again and again falling on the slippery snow. As he saw the next pub we always stopped in; at last we went on the castle and we sat again in an old pub where he got a new big one and the Czech slivovice. There came some friends and we spoke again and again about poetry and about the situation when the poet could not publish. He told me his friend in England was the poet MacNeice. He appreciated Eliot's early poems and poems of Edith Sitwell. We descended from the castle, it was still snowing. We held each other by the hands and Dylan stretched his arms out and cried: "Your snow, your snow, I could catch all your snow into my bag and take it with me."

I took him home, where came some friends and we spoke again about poetry. He said Blake was the greatest poet and he read us his poems. He didn't want to meet more official people and to take part in the official entertainments and receptions. . . .

The next day we invited one of the best Czech poets, Vladimir Holan, and some literary friends to meet Dylan. It was unforgettable evening. Dylan didn't know Czech and Holan didn't know English but they spoke about poetry and they understood one another. They showed together by the hand who was great poet and who was greater. Thomas then told us the first version of his *Milk Wood*. At the farewell Holan told him to salute all living and dead English poets. Dylan said he was terribly glad he had met Holan and the others. He felt his duty should be to stay with us.

I should like to say: we didn't know Dylan as an irresponsible drunkard, but the man who was very friendly, sincere, open, sensitive and fully aware of his literary and human responsibility.

He himself, writing to Caitlin on the fifth, paints a slightly different picture. But then he had two censorships to consider, that of his hosts and that of his wife:

I arrived in Prague about 24 hours ago, was met at the airport by an elderly woman and a young man who took me at once to a reception in the House of Parliament where hundreds of Czechs, Slovaks, Russians, Rumanians, Bulgarians and Hungarians were drinking wine. After, dinner: really incredibly bad food but nice people. After that a party to say goodbye to two Greek film-men who were returning to the Greek war. Today, hours of Congress and translators. Lunch with an old Czech friend of Norman Cameron's. After, more Congress and each guest made a speech. Including me. Tonight, a Smetana opera. Tomorrow, more speeches, and a broadcast. . . . All this has nothing to do with writing — I mean, all this multilingual congressing. But Prague is so beautiful. And bitingly, savagely cold; you, my love, would die of it. . . . Nobody here, so far, allows me to go into a cafe, pub, or dive. They prefer parties in the home. We don't agree. But they are a wonderfully friendly people. I do hope we can come here together. . . .

And finally here is the text of the address he is purported to have given to this congress. The English original does not exist, but only the

Czech translation, which I have had re-translated back into English. These are therefore not Dylan's own words, though the opening paragraphs sound like his thought. The last, however, does not ring true to me. Here I may well be wrong. Dylan's skill at ingratiation was, as I hope I have shown, very considerable, and it is possible but most unlikely that he may have produced this mimicry of the Stalinist claptrap that he had been hearing from the official writers at the congress.

As the only Englishman present at this meeting I must say, by way of introduction, that I am Welsh. As a Welshman, I repeat, I am by choice a poet. A Welsh poet who has no other wish than to write poems, but unfortunately I must work to live.

I feel very honoured and proud to be among writers from so many countries, professional writers. When a poet will be able to earn his living in England by writing poems, then at last the immoral and impertinent idea will be dead that poetry is merely a sort of youthful hobby.

This is my first visit to Czechoslovakia, but God willing and with the friendly consent of the "Union of Czechoslovak Writers" it will not be the last. For the first time I have seen a writers' organization. In theory and at second hand I knew that this was a great idea, and now I have seen in practice and directly that it can be a good one. When I get home I shall tell every writer I meet that the great dignity and value of literature can only be fully realized with the help of a writers' organization, an organization owning both a daily paper and a magazine. I should like to say to every writer here — which as a private individual I am not entitled to do, though I do not hesitate to say it — that I convey to you the sincere and genuine friendship of all serious English and Welsh writers.

Yesterday at the Ministry of Information I saw a film about Czechoslovakia's "Great February." This film should be shown all over the world so that people all over the world might see how you danced and sang on February 6th, 1948. The faces in the crowd reveal the delight and pride that your people took in the birth of the new People's Republic, the beauty of simple people, proud and joyful, with the rhythm of history visible in their every gesture.

This visit to Prague was to cause him some trouble with the American authorities when he applied for his second entry visa, three years later, at the height of the McCarthy period. In 1950, however, when he applied for his first, it was not held against him.

*　　*　　*

The move from Oxfordshire to Laugharne, in the first week of May 1949, was not an easy one, for Caitlin was in the seventh month of pregnancy. (Colm, their third and last child, was born on the 24th of

July.) Not only did Dylan have to move his own family — less Llewelyn, who stayed at school in Oxford — but also his parents to their new home. And the Boat House is difficult to reach. But before I describe Dylan's best-known home, I would point out one fact that seems to me relevant to his biography. From the summer of 1938 until his death in 1953 there was almost no period when Caitlin, besides looking after him as best she could, was not pregnant or looking after a child less than six years of age, or both, and this with no help at all, except occasionally that of her sister Brigid or some woman with whom she had struck up an acquaintance. To Dylan, with his peasant roots and his old-fashioned, almost Puritanical views, this may well have seemed the normal life for a wife and mother. To Caitlin, the dancer from a different background where nannies are not regarded as the ultimate, aristocratic evil, it did not. She loved her children, and she looked after them, but her life was slipping away in damp Oxfordshire and damper Laugharne.

Much has been written about the romantic Boat House, perched on stilts at the end of its "breakneck of rock" like one of Dylan's herons above the great estuary, at the end of the long walk — it is inaccessible by car — which is now called Dylan's Walk. It is an up-and-down place, its roof almost level with the path, from which another steep path leads down to the front door, its stilts reaching to the mud, with a narrow, veranda-like catwalk about it on the two seaward sides. Across the double bay lies, to the right, Sir John's Hill, to the left Llanstephan, faraway. When the tide is miles out thousands of seabirds dig for seaworms or little stranded fishes and screech or mew their apparent distress. The cockle-women work the closer shore. When the tide returns it almost laps at the house's foundations. Except for the mud, all is steep, inside and out, a dangerous house in which to bring up small children.

Above the cottage and a few yards along the Walk is the wooden shack where he worked in the afternoons. It had a coal-burning stove to keep him warm in winter, a large table, a chair and an old chest of drawers. The floor was usually deep in work-sheets as he struggled with his play, *Under Milk Wood,* or worked slowly, oh so slowly, at his last poems, often writing and re-writing a single line fifty times or more, until at last he was satisfied that he had achieved poetic truth. Here there was never any compromise. When the Princess Caetani asked Vernon Watkins to implore Dylan that he send her the rest of *Milk Wood,* his answer was that he would rather let her down than himself:

though the play might be in a fit state for reading or broadcasting, he was not yet satisfied with it for publication. And so he worked on. To the walls were pinned photographs of Walt Whitman, Thomas Hardy, D. H. Lawrence, W. H. Auden, a reproduction of a portrait of Blake, a Modigliani print, a few nudes. The view from the windows is vast; it was a fine place to work.

And these first months back in Laugharne were a happy period, apart from the incessant money worries. Between his arrival at the Boat House in May of 1949 and his first trip to America in February of the following year, he only did six broadcasts, and two of those were from Wales. Thus he had few of the gruelling trips to London. Both he and Caitlin loved the new baby, and she was never happier than when she had a child at her breast. It was almost an Indian summer. It was also the last period of happiness he was to know.

In May, a fortnight after his return to Laugharne, he received a letter from John Malcolm Brinnin. Brinnin was and is an American poet, a couple of years younger than Dylan, whom Brinnin had admired enormously for many years. He had heard of Dylan's wish to come to the United States. In his famous book, *Dylan Thomas in America,* Brinnin has written:

When, in 1949, I was offered the directorship of the Poetry Center of the YM–YWHA (Young Men's and Young Women's Hebrew Association) in New York, I accepted this position with one thought foremost in my mind: at last I could myself invite Dylan Thomas to come to America. My first act in my new position was to write to him.

Dylan replied at once, accepting the offer, and suggesting January or February as a suitable date. He also asked Brinnin to try and arrange other readings for him. After consultation with Dylan's literary agent in New York — who had no knowledge of how to arrange a lecture tour — Brinnin, at that time equally ignorant, agreed to take on this job, for which he was to get an agent's percentage of 15 per cent. Such was the basis of a relationship which soon assumed, for Brinnin at least, a far greater significance. He was, in his own phrase, Dylan's "reluctant guardian angel, brother's keeper, nursemaid, amanuensis, bar companion." And, as his book clearly shows, his emotions became deeply involved as well.

Brinnin arranged an intensive and extensive series of readings for Dylan, back and forth across the United States and up into Canada, the whole trip to last the better part of three months. A more experienced arranger of such tours might have hesitated to ask any man to carry out such a schedule, and one who knew Dylan's physical and mental state would surely not have driven him so hard. But Brinnin was only doing what Dylan wished. He wanted to give as many readings, and thus make as much money, as possible, and to Higham he wrote, in December of 1949: "These alone . . . make, for me, the prospect of my visit *extremely* worth while." Even before he set off he was writing to Selden Rodman, the poet and editor who had invited him to Haiti, about the possibility of a second trip to America, this time with Caitlin, in 1951.

The Laugharne months had been a period of physical and mental recuperation. He doubtless felt up to the demands that were about to be made on him, for on January 12, 1950, he answered a letter from Princess Caetani in which she must have said that his drinking in London had frightened her. He wrote:

Yes, I think I am frightened of drink, too. But it is not so bad as, perhaps, you think: the fear, I mean. It is only frightening when I am whirlingly perplexed, when my ordinary troubles are magnified into monsters and I fall weak down before them, when I do not know what to do or where to turn. When I am here, or anywhere I like, and am busy, then drink's no fear at all and I'm well, terribly well, and gay, and unafraid and full of other, nicer nonsenses, and altogether a dull, happy fellow only wanting to put into words, never into useless, haphazard, unhappy action, the ordered turbulence, the ubiquitous and rinsing grief, the unreasonable glory, of the world I know and don't know.

He went up to London with Caitlin in mid-February, got extremely drunk at a farewell party, and flew to New York on February 20, 1950. Caitlin went back to Laugharne, to Aeronwy and Colm.

It is not my intention to write at length about Dylan's life in America. This has been done, most competently, by John Malcolm Brinnin, who is reliable as to the facts when he was present, and almost always when he was not. The points on which I disagree with him, which are few and usually disagreements of interpretation, will emerge later in this chapter.

Dylan in New York was not essentially different from Dylan in London. He toddled about the bars and bookshops, asked women to take him to their beds, talked to other poets, and behaved outrageously at literary parties. Brinnin has described in detail one such party on the second night after Dylan's arrival.

We went up into a room buzzing with writers and editors, some of whom were old friends of mine. Wystan Auden was there, James Agee, Louis Kronenberger and the Trillings, Lionel and Diana, and James and Tania Stern and Charles Rolo, Katherine Anne Porter and many others. As Dylan, by a loud and awkward entrance, seemed to demand considerably more attention than the party was disposed to grant him, becoming again the very figure of the wine-soaked poet, I looked at Auden and winced inwardly. I could not help feeling that his eyes showed more than a hint of accusation, that before the evening was out he would somehow say, "I told you so."

At the end of the party Dylan lifted Katherine Anne Porter up to the ceiling and held her suspended in mid-air. Though Miss Porter, being a Southern lady as well as a distinguished author, showed no signs of being unduly distressed at such behavior, Brinnin and a little group of witnesses were "half amused, half appalled" by it. Auden had already gone, but presumably he had seen enough to be reinforced in the doubt which he had previously expressed to Brinnin, during an encounter in the subway, whether it was *wise* to invite Dylan to the United States at all, "in view of his London reputation for roaring behavior."

From Dylan's point of view, he went there to make quick and easy money. The wisdom of so doing did not enter into his calculations. For here he was the actor, not the poet, and few actors have ever been sufficiently wise to realize that Hollywood stardom, for them, may be a foolish alternative to Shaftebury Avenue or even to Swansea repertory. He went to America to play Dylan Thomas, and he picked up Katherine Anne Porter: the stories of his drunkenness, his lechery, his outrageous remarks spread, and this was one form of his self-expression: he gave them more and more of it, from coast to coast, and they loved it: they wanted more yet, they wanted drama, and at last he gave them that as well.

New York is not London, though Dylan tried to pretend that in a way it was. In London there was always Paddington Station and the train to Wales: in New York there was, ahead, a continent to be barnstormed, mesmerized, astonished, shocked, delighted, and, with luck, raped and looted. In London there were close friends who understood, like John Davenport or Roy Campbell; in New York there were new friends, who knew only Dylan-in-America and therefore scarcely understood, or friends and acquaintances from a more or less distant past, such as Ruthven Todd, Len Lye, George Reavey or W. H. Auden, and these were rapidly swamped and lost to Dylan's sight in the great continental tide of those who wished to see the drunken, irreverent legend turned to flesh. Scale changes quality. What Charles Fisher had seen in Soho, three or four years before, became an almost monstrous exhibitionism as thousands wished to enjoy the voyeur's pleasure of seeing the famous poet drunk. Brinnin writes:

He roared across the continent creating the legend that still grows and changes and threatens altogether to becloud the personality of the man who wrote the poems of Dylan Thomas. At first it was a legend at least tenuously related to plausible actions and conversations in plausible places. But soon, like all legends, it snowballed through fact and fancy alike, and became too big and complicated to allow for the separation of truth from malice, fantasy from the easier forms of hyperbole. If Dylan had done and said all that was reported as truth, he would not have been tolerated in even the most liberal of surroundings; if his rumoured carousals and lecheries had been as outrageous and consistent as they were said to be he would have been hauled off to jail or committed to an asylum. It was as if Dylan were the vehicle by which imagination might ride out of academic doldrums. Since he was expected always to say and do shocking things, and since he very often failed to do either, certain elements of his public, determined to keep Dylan as their poet-clown, made up stories of what he *should* have done and said. In the long run, of course, this became more a comment on his public than on him.

Several years later Wynford Vaughan Thomas collected memories of Dylan Thomas for a programme that the BBC put out on the tenth anniversary of his death. Earle Birney remembered a scene after a reading in Vancouver:

And then a vulturous descent of reporters fell on our party. No reporter could believe that Thomas wanted to do anything but get drunk as rapidly as possible. A photographer arrived. The waiters were apparently tipped to set up a table in another room with dozens of tumblers full of beer on it. Dylan was lured away to it on the pretext of a phone call, photographed without warning for local posterity, like a pig in a swill pen, and exhorted to pour our thin ale down his gullet while more cameras clicked. In the end he complied, of course, as much out of amiability as out of alcoholism. And he had another appearance to make that evening. Somehow he managed it, but afterwards he was the victim of the hospitality of well-meaning literati, and well-healed squares, party sycophants and culture-vultures all trying to get into the act, to live within the Thomas legend, above all to see what the Great Poet and Tippler was like when absolutely stoned.

One American lion-hunter was ever prepared to abduct the famous poet. With no apparent shame, he recorded for Wynford Vaughan Thomas:

I have two children and I thought that I would want my son and daughter to be able to say that they had seen and heard the great man, and I was prepared to drag them down from their cots to see and hear Dylan Thomas. So I said he had to come along and I was very firm and decisive about it. Of course I had several cohorts to back me very staunchly. They started to shout: "Yes, you've got to go along with us." So he let himself be led like a lamb to the slaughter and I got him into my car. But I did a rather Machiavellian thing. I placed one very attractive girl on each knee of Dylan Thomas to hold him down should he want to get out, and he did want to get out. All along the way he kept on shouting: "I want to go to a pub, take me to a pub!" My heart sank for him and I felt rather sad because obviously he didn't want to come to my place but, as I said, I felt I owed a duty to my children and I wasn't going to let him escape me.

He did not, of course, encounter maniacs wherever he went, but the atmosphere that preceded him was increasingly tinged with something like hysteria. Yet he struggled on across the continent. He liked San Francisco, that beautiful city: there he was among people, the principal being his hostess, Ruth Witt-Diamant, who did not regard him as a perambulating freak. He liked Chicago, and he told me that its Skid Row fascinated him more than anything else in America. There, too, he found friends, including Mrs. Ellen Borden Stevenson. In Los Angeles, or rather in nearby Hollywood, there was his old friend, Ivan Moffatt, who told Dylan that he could get him a job writing film scripts there any time. There were other English writers, and Christopher Isherwood took him to Charles Chaplin's house, which Dylan regarded as an immense honour, for Chaplin was, in every way, his hero. To judge by the sour little note in Chaplin's autobiography, he does not seem to have shared Dylan's delight at this meeting, though he graciously agreed to send a telegram to Laugharne saying that Dylan was with him. In Washington he stayed with Mr. and Mrs. Francis Biddle, and saw how the really rich live and acquired, in his usual fashion, some really good shirts.

But New York was where most of his friends were, and New York acquired, for him, some of the qualities of home. Shortly after his first arrival George Reavey had taken him to the White Horse Tavern in Greenwich Village, and there Dylan found a bar that resembled, superficially at least, a London pub. It became, in English parlance, his local.

One of the many new friends he made in America, and perhaps the one he liked most, was Theodore Roethke. Before ever Dylan came to America, he had expressed a desire to meet Roethke, for he admired his poems more than those of any other American poet of his generation with the possible exception only of Robert Lowell. Nor was he disappointed. Roethke was a huge German-American from the Middle West — his grandfather had been Bismarck's chief game-keeper before he emigrated — who loved drink and women and poetry and laughter and talk. He was a companion after Dylan's own heart and with him, at least, the mask could be dropped. Roethke wrote in *Encounter*, shortly after Dylan's death:

It is difficult for me to write anything, stunned as I am, like many another, by the news of his death. I knew him for only three brief periods, yet I had come to think of him as a younger brother: unsentimentally, perhaps, and not protective as so many felt inclined to be — for he could fend for himself against male and female; but rather someone to be proud of, to rejoice in, to be irritated with, or even jealous of. . . .

The demands on his body and spirit were many; his recklessness, lovely. But even his superb energies felt the strain, I should say, on lecture tours when he was set upon by fools. Any kind of social pretentiousness disturbed him, and particularly in academia. The bourgeois he did not love. He could, and did, act outrageously, on occasion, snarling from one side of his mouth to a gabbling faculty wife that nobody ever came to America except to get fees and drink free liquor; only to wish, wistfully, the next five minutes, to someone he respected, that he could stay in this country for a time, and maybe even teach. But even in black moods, his instinctive sweetness and graciousness would flash through. More than any other writer or artist I know, he really cared for and cherished his fellow-men.

I first met him in 1950, in New York. John Brinnin had written twice that Dylan Thomas wanted to meet me. I found this hard to believe, but when I came down from Yaddo in May, still groggy from my own private wars with the world, it seemed to be so.

Someone had lent me an apartment up-town; he was staying down-town on Washington Square. We sometimes alternated: one would rout out the other, different days. He had been built up to me as a great swill-down drinker, a prodigious roaring boy out of the Welsh caves. But I never knew such a one. Some bubbly or Guinness or just plain beer, maybe; and not much else. We would sit around talking about poetry; about Welsh picnics; life on the Detroit river, and in Chicago (he greatly admired *The Man with the Golden Arm*); the early Hammett; and so on. Or maybe bumble across town to an old Marx Brothers movie, or mope along, poking into book shops or looking into shop windows. . . .

He had a wide, detailed and active knowledge of the whole range of English literature; and a long memory. I noticed one day a big pile of poems — Edward Thomas, Hardy, Ransom, Housman, W. R. Rodgers, Davies, and others — all copied out in his careful hand. He said he never felt he knew a poem, what was in it, until he had done this. His taste was exact and specific; he was loyal to the poem, not the poet; and the list of contemporaries he valued was a good deal shorter than might generally be supposed.

He was one of the great ones, there can be no doubt of that. And he drank his own blood, ate his own marrow, to get at some of that material. His poems need no words, least of all mine, to defend or explain them.

It is not my intention here to give a detailed itinerary of Dylan's first, or indeed of any of his American trips. This will be found in Appendix 3, compiled in 1962 as a dissertation by Thelma L. B. Murdy, then of the University of Florida. Melodramatic accounts of Dylan Thomas in America abound, and have grown since his death, while the sober statements of friends such as Roethke have faded from the public memory. But the best voice of all is surely Dylan's own. He wrote frequently to his parents and to Caitlin, particularly during this first tour. His reactions, during later ones, were not very different.

New York frightened him at first, and on February 25, 1950, that is to say four days after his arrival and thus subsequent to the late-night levitation of Katherine Anne Porter, he wrote to Caitlin:

My darling far-away love, my precious Caitlin, my wife dear, I love you as I have never loved you, oh please remember me all day and every day as I remember you here in this terrible, beautiful, dream and nightmare city which would only be any good at all if we were together in it, if every night we clung together in it. . . .

He describes John Malcolm Brinnin as "a terribly nice man," and after more endearments, he goes on:

I love you, and I love our children, and I love our house. Here, each night, I have to take things to sleep: I am staying right in the middle of Manhattan, surrounded by skyscrapers infinitely taller and stranger than one has ever known from the pictures: I am staying in a room, an hotel room for the promised flat did not come off, on the 30th floor: and the *noise* all day and night: without some drug I couldn't sleep at all. The highest, heaviest lorries, police-cars, firebrigades, ambulances, all with their banshee sirens wailing and screaming, seem never to stop; Manhattan is built on rock, a lot of demolition work is going on to take up yet another super skyscraper, and so there is almost continuous dynamite blasting. Aeroplanes just skim the tips of the great glimmering skyscrapers, some beautiful, some hellish. And I have no idea what I am doing here in the very loud, mad middle of the last mad Empire on earth: — except to think of you, and love you, and to work for us. I have done two readings this week, to the Poetry Center of New York: each time there was an audience of about a thousand. I felt a very lonely, foreign midget orating up there, in a huge hall, before all those faces; but the readings went well. After this country weekend, where I arrange with Brinnin some of the rest of my appallingly extensive programme, I go to Harvard University, Cambridge, Boston, for about two days, then to Washington, then back to New York, then, God knows, I daren't think, but I know it includes Yale, Princeton, Vassar — three big universities, as you know, old know-all — and Salt Lake City, where the Mormons live, and Notre Dame, the Jesuit College, and the Middle West, Iowa, Ohio, Chicago — and Florida, the kind of exotic resort, and after that the mere thought makes my head roar like New York. To the places near to New York, Brinnin is driving me by car; to others I go by myself by train; to the more distant places, I fly. But *whatever* happens, by God I don't fly back. Including landing at Dublin, Canada and Boston, for very short times, I was in the air, cooped up in the stratosphere, for 17 hours with twenty of the nastiest people in the sky. I had an awful hangover from our London do as well; the terrible height makes one's ears hurt like hell, one's lips chap, one's belly turn; and it went on forever. I'm coming back by boat.

I've been to a few parties, met lots of American poets, writers, critics, hangers-on, some very pleasant; all furiously polite and hospitable. But, apart from on one occasion, I've stuck nearly all the time to American beer, which, though thin, I like a lot and is ice-cold. (I arrived, by the way, on the coldest day New York has had for years and years: it was about 4 above zero. You'd have loved it. I never thought anything could be so cold, my ears nearly fell off: the wind just whipped through that monstrous duffle.) But, as soon as I got into a room, the steamed heat was worse: I think I can stand zero better than that, and, to the astonishment of the natives, I keep all windows open at the top. I've been, too, to lots of famous places: up the top of the Empire State Building, the tallest there is, which terrified me so much I had to come down at once; to Greenwich Village, a feebler Soho but with stronger drinks; and this morning John Brinnin is driving us to Harlem. . . .

And now it must look to you, my Cat, as though I am enjoying myself here. I'm not. It's nightmare, day and night; there never was such a place; I would never get used to the speed, the noise, the utter indifference of the crowds, the frightening politeness of the intellectuals, and, most of all, these huge phallic towers, up and up and up, hundreds of floors, into the impossible sky. I feel so terrified of this place, I hardly dare to leave my hotel room — luxurious — until Brinnin or someone calls for me. Everybody uses the telephone all the time: it is like breathing: it is now nine o'clock in the morning, and I've had six calls: all from people whose names I did not catch to invite me to a little poity at an address I had no idea of. And most of all most of all most of all, though, God, there's no need to say this to you who understand everything, I want to be with you. If we could be here together, everything would be all right. *Never* again would I come here, or to any far place, without you; but especially never to here. The rest of America may be all right, and perhaps I can understand it, but that is the last monument there is to the insane desire for power that shoots its buildings up to the stars and roars its engines louder and faster than they have ever been roared before and makes everything cost the earth and where the imminence of death is reflected in every last power-stroke and grab of the great moron bosses, the big-shots, the multis one never sees. This morning we go down to see the other side beyond the skyscrapers: black Harlem, starving Jewish East Side. A family of four in New York is poor on £ 14 a week. I'll buy some nylons all the same next week, and some tinned stuff. Anything else?

To his father, now a very sick man, and his mother he wrote the next day in much the same terms about his journey and the strange city in which he found himself:

Brinnin took me touring over half of this mad city: Broadway, Harlem, the Wall Street area, the East Side (where the Dead End Kids come from). I drank huge icy milkshakes in the drugstores, and iced lager beer in the Third Avenue saloons almost every one of which is kept by an Irishman. I ate fried shrimps, fried chicken, a T-bone steak the size of a month's ration for an English family. I went to the top of the Empire State building, the tallest skyscraper in the world, had one look at the nightmare city, and came down quickly.

And then he set off on his travels. From Kenyon, on March 13th, he was writing to Caitlin:

I wrote you last from be-Biddled Washington. Then I sweated back to New York. Then I read in Columbia University, New York. Then I flew to Cornell University, read, caught a night-sleeper-train to Ohio, arriving this morning. This evening, in an hour's time, I do my little act at Kenyon University, then another night train, this time to Chicago, I never seem to sleep in a bed any more, only on planes and trains. I'm hardly living; I'm just a voice on wheels. And the damnedest thing is that quite likely I may arrive home with hardly any money at all, both the United States *and* Great Britain taxing my earnings — my earnings for us, Colum, Aeron, Llewelyn, for our house that makes me cry to think of, for the water, the heron, old, sad, empty Brown's. I am writing this in a room in Kenyon University, and can find no paper or sharp pencil and am too scared to go out and find somebody to ask.

Her replies, which had to go through John Malcolm Brinnin and then catch him on the wing as he hurtled across the continent, were not reaching him. On March 16th, using the paper of the Quadrangle Club, Chicago, he wrote to her:

This is not, as it seems from the address above, a dive, joint, saloon, etc. but the honourable and dignified headquarters of the dons of the University of Chicago. I love you. That is all I know. But all I know, too, is that I am writing into space; the kind of dreadful, unknown space I am just going to enter. I am going to Iowa, Illinois, Idaho, Indindiana, but these, though mis-spelt, *are* on the map. You are not. Have you forgotten me? I am the man you used to say you loved. . . .

On April 5th, in a train that was taking him from San Francisco to Vancouver, he wrote to her:

Please forgive, Cat dear, the nasty little note I sent about your not writing: it was only because I was so worried and so deeply in love with you. This is going to be the shortest letter because I am writing it on a rocking train that is taking me from San Francisco — the best city on earth — to Vancouver in Canada. . . .

The train is going so fast through wonderful country along the Pacific coast that I can write no more. As soon as I get on stationary land I will write longly. I said San Francisco was the best city on earth. It is incredibly beautiful, all hills and bridges and blinding blue sky and boats and Pacific ocean. I am trying — and there's every reason to believe it will succeed — to arrange that you and me and Colum (my Colum, your Colum) come to San Francisco next spring when I will become, for six months, a professor in the English department of the University. You will love it here. . . .

I spent last evening with Varda, the Greek painter, who remembers you when you were fifteen. I wish I did. . . .

Next day, as he had promised, he wrote her a long letter from Van-couver, which he described as "a quite handsome hellhole" and "more British than Cheltenham." Malcolm Lowry, the author of *Under the Volcano*, had come down from the mountains to see him. In San Fran-cisco, he told her, he had been out to see Henry Miller at Big Sur, and described him as "gentle and mellow and gay." He had a lot more to say about the beauties of that city and the excellence of its sea-food, and went on to talk, like any other paterfamilias, of the shops and the presents he hoped to bring home to her and the children. (This is not the visit to Vancouver described earlier in this chapter; that took place in 1952.)

On May 7th he was back in New York, with only one more reading to do at Princeton and two in New York City, the last on May 18th. He wrote to her, from the Hotel Earle on Washington Square:

It will not be so long now, in terms of days and weeks, before I come back to the true world; but, in terms of lonely, sleepless nights, of heartbreak and horror it is an eternity. I do not yet know when I can get a boat to sail back on; I know I cannot travel any more by plane. . . . But boats are hard to get, because of American tourists travelling to Europe, especially to Italy and Holy Year. I have a good chance of getting a boat a few days after May 15th, but dare not bank on it. So I reserved a passage, anyway, for June 1st. . . .

Sometimes I think I shall go mad, and this time properly, thinking of you all day and night as I fly over the continent from university to university, hotel to hotel, stuffed-shirt to stuffed-shirt, heat to heat. It is getting abominably hot. Since I last wrote I have been in Florida, Wisconsin, Indiana, hell getting hotter all the time; I have been in Detroit, the worst city, the home of motorcars; and in and out of New York. I have been so exhausted I was quite incapable of writing a word. After readings, I fell into bed, into sweaty half-awoken hope you got the £17 cheque from San Francisco and the one last week from Boston. And I hope they helped a little. . . .

And on June 1st he sailed for home on the *Queen Elizabeth*. These quotations from his letters show, I think, how sad, lonely and exhausting were these American journeys. This is evident, too, in Brinnin's much more detailed account of these tours. However, it must be borne in mind that Dylan was anxious to stress these aspects when writing to Caitlin. He knew that she, in damp and dreary Laugharne, was darkly suspicious that he, in distant America, was behaving in the manner she disliked most; furthermore, from her as from all the few women he had loved since infancy, he wanted compassion. This is not a derogatory remark; the three Marys are considerably more essential to our vision of the world than is the Freudian's Jocasta, or perhaps even the poets' Athene.

He brought back little money with him, little more than the eight hundred dollars Brinnin had secreted in a handbag that he was sending as a present to Caitlin. By all accounts his extravagance in America, though petty, was almost insane. He never mastered the currency, and when he paid for a round of drinks he would not bother to pick up the change, while a one dollar bill and a twenty were all the same to him. He would give money to anyone who asked for it, and quite a few did. Poets, real or self-styled, were never refused. Among the crowds of hangers-on in the bars he frequented there were some who were far more interested in the free drinks and the hand-outs than in poems or poets. New York's Bohemia was closer to Skid Row than London's. And Brinnin has described his own mounting despair as he tried, and failed, to control Dylan's finances.

While Dylan had already earned thousands of dollars in the United States, his bank account was dwindling at an alarming rate. In spite of my determination to keep free of such concern, his relentless need for money had led me to becoming miserly about his funds and painfully reluctant to meet his requests for new amounts. I could not understand why he carelessly spent fifty and sixty dollars every day, or why, with Caitlin continually requesting money for household accounts, he paid no heed to my warnings that unless he cut down on his spending he would return to Wales empty-handed. He did send modest amounts to his wife now and then, but when I suggested that we deposit in his local bank in Carmarthen for safe keeping all the money except what he would need for basic expenses, he balked. At the onset of his travels it had seemed reasonable to estimate that he might go home with about three thousand dollars in cash. Soon this figure was revised to two thousand dollars. When, day by day, it became apparent that even this amount was too much to hope for, I despaired of his returning with anything at all. In our talk at the San Remo, I showed him his accounts, but he looked at these only, it seemed, by way of politely thanking me for my trouble, and turned away to order another drink. Dylan could not have known it, but his indifference to the accounts over which I had worked many hours left me dispirited and hopeless.

I must here echo Blake's proverb of hell: *Enough, or too much.* Enough has been written about Dylan's sex life in America to spare me the need to burden the reader with these tedious and repetitive tales. In his loneliness he asked women of all sorts and conditions to go to bed with him. Some did; others were scandalized. And the scandals spread, were multiplied and enlarged, both before and after his death, until in legend this exhausted, often drunk and frequently sick man has become a veritable Priapus, who could surpass the Hercules of the Thirteenth Labour and deflower all the virgins of Bennington or Vassar in a single night, after which he would chase all the female faculty members around the campus before breakfast. In fact, with Dylan, it was mostly talk: he liked "talking bawdy" which is far less acceptable in America than in England, drunk he propositioned women directly and publicly, and when he flew on to the next university he left an astonished, scandalized, angry or amused audience behind him.

The stories, inflated and often incredible, floated back to England, and a contrary legend was there created: that Dylan was set upon by great crowds of American nymphomaniacs. He was quite willing to play this part, too, when he came home. When I questioned him about it, he told me that it was "all those deans' wives" who would not give him a moment's peace. I must have looked incredulous, or perhaps he suddenly remembered that I am American and know my country fairly well, for he gave his embarrassed snigger of a laugh and changed the subject.

But far more important than these legends is the fact that in New York, and for the first time since he had met Caitlin, he had what might be called a love affair. Brinnin has given her the name of Sarah, and that will do for this book, too. Brinnin describes her as follows:

She held an important job in publishing to which she brought extraordinary intelligence, an executive sense of responsibility, and that air of professional sophistication governed by the Madison Avenue fashion journals. She had been highly educated, had taught for several years at one of the leading women's colleges, and was knowledgeably devoted to Dylan's work from the time of its earliest publication. These qualities, combined with her dark handsomeness and social poise, made her precisely the sort of woman from whom one would expect Dylan only to flee.

Their liaison was not a secret — in such matters Dylan kept few secrets — and when she came to London, in September of 1950, and Dylan introduced her to his friends and took her to Brighton, nobody had any doubts as to what their relationship must be. To Brinnin, who was also in London at that time, he said:

"John, what am I going to do?" His face, suddenly sober, showed bewilderment and his eyes were set upon something far away.

"About what?"

"I'm in love with Sarah, and I'm in love with my wife. I don't know what to do."

Of course Caitlin heard about it, down in Laugharne, through the usual woman friend. And of course she was extremely angry. She had heard other stories about his American tour; she knew he had come back with almost no money; and now he was apparently importing his American mistresses into England. Her fury was comprehensible and colossal.

Dylan back-pedalled frantically. He wrote to friends imploring them to tell Caitlin that Sarah meant nothing to him, that he loved only his wife. He begged Caitlin not to leave him. He promised never to see Sarah or to correspond with her again. Sarah, meanwhile, had left England. She knew nothing of Dylan's promises to Caitlin. And when she returned to London that winter she wrote to him, as had been arranged, at the Savage Club which he had recently joined. What happened next was recounted by her, in a letter to Brinnin, of January 1951 after she had left London again:

Thank you, so much more than I can begin to say here, and just now, for writing as you did. And the pictures, which in my happily timeless suspension here seem to have been taken centuries ago, are wonderful to have, and help eradicate the woes of my second London quite entirely. For you are quite right, and neither of us needs, thank God, to contemplate any disillusion. I wrote you a whining little note last week, which crossed your fine envelope packed with the best, and I spoke in that of a letter from Dylan. And the explanation did lie, as he discovered only when he got my letters from here, and as I suspected all the time, in the fine Italian hand of the grey lady, ——. I won't attempt to tell it all here, and there's no need, but Dylan was ill with pleurisy and then pneumonia all the weeks I was in London, and she collected his mail for him at his club every morning. What she did with them neither of us will probably ever know, but he saw none of my letters and messages, nothing. She came to see me off at the air station when I finally did give up and go back to France, laden with her flowers and dulcet doom, and even now she sends me poisonously cheerful letters about how lucky I am to be out of England. But that's the end of it now, with all its soap-opera bubbles broken, finally.

What the "grey lady" did with all the letters was to give them to Caitlin, for it was she who had informed her about this liaison in the first place. It is not hard to imagine what the Christmas spirit was like in Laugharne in 1950. Dylan's and Caitlin's marriage was very near the breaking point when, early in January of 1951, he left for Persia with Ralph Keene — known to all his friends as Bunny — to make a documentary film commissioned by the Anglo-Iranian Oil Company. His letters to Caitlin show how grievous was now the rift between them. The first two of these letters are undated:

All these strange, lost days I love you, and I am lost indeed without you, my dear wife. This is so much further than America, and letters will take so much longer to travel to you and yours to me if you will ever write to me again oh *darling* Cat. And if you do not write to me, and if you do not love me any more, I cannot go on, I cannot go on sleeplessly thinking, "Caitlin, my Cattleanchor, my dear, does not love me, o God let me die." I can't live without you; I can't go travelling with this long, wan Bunny through this fearful strange world unless I am sure that at the end we will be together again as we are meant to be together, close and alone except for our cuckoo whom I miss very very very much, more than I could dream of. But you: I miss you more than I would miss my life although you *are* my life. I can see now, in this grand over-hot Oil-Company Guest House where we are staying, your smiling and your anger, your golden hair and blue eyes and our wedding ring from a cracker.

He had not heard from her when next he wrote, from Tehran:

There's no meaning to anything without us being together. I love you all the day and night, and I am five thousand miles away. Until I hear from you, Cat, every minute of the day and night's insane. I have to dope myself into nightmare sleep with tablets from Bunny's enormous medicine-chest. I wake up before it is dawn, in this great undersea bedroom under snow-mountains, and turn the echoes of your voice over and over in the dark, and look into your blue beautiful undersea eyes five thousand miles away: they're all that is real . . .

The long Bunny is still in bed, groaning: he has a "little chill" he says, has a huge fire in his room, two hotwaterbottles, an array all over his bedside table of syrups, pills, syringes, laxatives, chlorodyne, linaments and compresses: he uses a thermometer every hour. And I? I go with horrible oil-men to interview horrible government-men; I sit in the lounge of this posh Guest House for horrible oil-men and listen to Scotch engineers running down the Persian wogs; I go with a pleasant Persian guide through endless museums, palaces, libraries, courts of law, houses of parliament, till my feet and my boredom bleed. What for, what for? Only the bazaar was wonderful, Tehran bazaar, the largest in Persia . . . miles of covered bazaar, smelling of incense and carpets and food and poverty. And women with only their eyes showing through tattered, dirty, cobble-trailing thin black sack-wraps; or lifting their wraps high to miss the mud and showing men's ragged trousers or baggy black bloomers; and lots of them with splayed and rotting high-heel shoes. Only the very poor — that is, the vast majority — of women wear these wrappings, not only of black but of grey, earth-brown, filthy white — and they wear them only to cover up their rags. They huddle their horrible poverty inside these chadurs as they slip-slop through the foul main streets or the shouting, barging aisles of the bazaar. Often there are babies huddled in with the poverty. And beautiful dirty children in little chadurs slip-slop behind them. The poor in the streets and the bazaar wear every kind of clothing, so long as it's dirty and wretched. Men wear little rimless bowlers, or caps like scavenging tram-conductors, and old army overcoats, British, German, American. Poor children all have cropped heads. Well-to-do children have their eyes darkened with Kohl or mascara.

The only water for the poor in Tehran — the capital city of Persia — runs down the public gutters. I saw an old man pissing in the gutter, walking away a few yards, then cupping his hands and drinking from it. This running cesspool is the only drinking and washing water for the poor. . . .

There is no nightlife at all in Tehran. Moslems are not supposed to drink, though some do. Only in one or two expensive hotels for Europeans can one buy a drink. There seems to be no fixed price for any drinks. I was charged

[328]

six shillings for a bottle of beer, Bunny twelve shillings for a small whiskey. Only in well-to-do houses — and in this Guest House for oil men — can one drink at all. In four days I have had eight pints of beer: all lager. . . .

By January 16th he was in Ahwaz, on his way to Abadan. Still no letter had come from her, and he wrote, almost in desperation, begging for a word that she wanted him back:

Perhaps you have said "He is dead to me." And if you say that indeed I will be dead . . . Oh, it would be wonderful to be with you, to be in your lovely arms, my love. It's seven o'clock in the morning; I'm lying in bed; already it's awfully hot; together we could be happy, we could go out into the garden in the sun, into the striped street, on to the river banks. Yesterday evening, just before dusk, I saw four men, in long Arabian dress, squatting in a circle on a tiny mudbank in the middle of the river. The mudbank was just large enough to hold them. The sun was going down quickly, the river was rising. The four men were playing cards. . . .

When at last he did hear from her it was a hard, unloving letter that he received. From Isfahan he wrote:

Your letter, as it was meant to, made me want to die. I did not think that, after reading it so many times till I knew every pain by heart, I could go on with these days and nights . . . knowing that, a long way and a lifetime away, you no longer loved or wanted me. . . . But the bloody animal always does go on . . . I cannot live without you — you, always — and I have no intention of doing so. I fly back, from Tehran to London, on . . . the 14th February. I shall cable you from Tehran the time of my arrival. You said, before we parted, that you would come up to London to meet me on my return. You will not, I suppose, be doing that now. If you are not, will you please — it is not a great deal to ask — leave me a message at the McAlpines. I will not come back to Laugharne until I know that I am wanted: not as an inefficient mispayer of bills, but as myself and for you. . . .

However, when he returned to England she agreed that they go on living together. The Persian film was cancelled for political reasons — Mossadegh had confiscated the assets of the Anglo-Iranian Oil Company only a few days after Dylan and Bunny Keene had left — and Dylan and Caitlin spent the spring and summer of 1951 in Laugharne. But she never truly forgave him, nor did she ever really trust him again. She continued to threaten, intermittently, that she would leave him. Yet how could she, without money, with a baby boy and a girl of eight attending the village school? She was trapped, and as she drank more heavily her outbursts of temper became increasingly violent and uncontrollable. There were still times, particularly when they were alone to-gether and Dylan was working, that were happy, but even this was a happiness built on sand. Caitlin had given Dylan the only sort of secu-rity, emotional security, that he had known since childhood and now, by his own folly, this too was undermined.

Robert Pocock's ex-wife, Sheila, has told me of an incident at the Boat House that must date from about this time or perhaps a little later. Dylan was at the bottom of the steep stairs, Colm at the top. Dylan told the little boy to jump, which he did, and Dylan caught him. Then he turned to Sheila and said:

"You see, there's one human being still trusts me."

The near break-up of his marriage, which could only mean the end of his life, is reflected in his poem *Lament*, written shortly after his return from Persia. Of this poem he wrote to Princess Caetani, on March 20, 1951:

I have a poem nearly finished, which will be about 50 or 60 lines long and is coarse and violent: I will send it as soon as it is done — when I can, if I can, shake off this nervous hag that rides me, biting and scratching into insomnia, nightmare, and the long anxious daylight . . .

I want to write poems so much — oh, the old pariah cry! — but I worry too much: I'm at my worries all day and night with a hundred crochet hooks. . . .

And during this summer of 1951 he did write poems. This was, in-deed, his last true flowering as a poet. In addition to *Lament,* he com-pleted *Poem on his Birthday* and *Do not go gentle into that good night,* began the long *Prologue* to *Collected Poems* and finished about half of *Under Milk Wood.* All these, except the *Prologue,* were published by Princess Caetani in her *Botteghe Oscure,* the portion of *Milk Wood* there bearing the title of *Llareggub: A Play for Voices.*

Again with the exception of the *Prologue,* these were the last poems he was to complete. In the two years of life that remained to him he only wrote the unfinished *Elegy,* which Vernon Watkins was able to assemble as a finished poem from Dylan's worksheets after his death, although Vernon is the first to assert that there is no telling whether or not Dylan would have published it in this form. Dylan also wrote some of the charming verses for *Under Milk Wood* in 1952 and 1953, but he would never have ranked these with his poems. The only other original work he was to produce were his talks for American audiences and for the BBC, two book reviews, and one short story called, quite simply, "A Story." Thus when, in the summer of 1951, a young man who was writing a thesis about Dylan Thomas asked him a few, rather naive, questions, he was, unbeknown to himself, asking Dylan to sum up his life's work. Richard Jones published Dylan's answers to these questions in the *Texas Quarterly*, Winter 1961, with the rather misleading title of *Dylan Thomas's Poetic Manifesto*, which it is not, for it is merely his reply, courteous as usual, to five questions. This is the reply:

You want to know why and how I first began to write poetry, and which poets or kinds of poetry I was first moved and influenced by.

To answer the first part of this question, I should say I wanted to write poetry in the beginning because I had fallen in love with words. The first poems I knew were nursery rhymes, and before I could read them for myself I had come to love just the words of them, the words alone. What the words stood for, symbolised, or meant, was of very secondary importance; what mattered was the *sound* of them as I heard them for the first time on the lips of the remote and incomprehensible grown-ups who seemed, for some reason, to be living in my world. And these words were, to me, as the notes of bells, the sounds of musical instruments, the noises of wind, sea, and rain, the rattle of milkcarts, the clopping of hooves on cobbles, the fingering of branches on a window pane, might be to someone, deaf from birth, who has miraculously found his hearing. I did not care what the words said, overmuch, nor what happened to Jack & Jill & the Mother Goose rest of them; I cared for the shapes of sound that their names, and the words describing their actions, made in my ears; I cared for the colours the words cast on my eyes. I realise that I may be, as I think back all that way, romanticising my reactions to the simple and beautiful words of those pure poems; but that is all I can honestly remember, however much time might have falsified my memory. I fell in love — that is the only expression I can think of — at once, and am still at the mercy of words, though sometimes now, knowing a little of their behaviour very well, I think I can influence them slightly and have even learned to beat them now and then, which they appear to enjoy. I tumbled for words at once. And, when I began to read the nursery rhymes for myself, and, later, to read other verses and ballads, I knew that I had discovered the most important things, to me, that could be ever. There they were, seemingly lifeless, made only of black and white, but out of them, out of their own being, came love and terror and pity and pain and wonder and all the other vague abstractions that make our ephemeral lives dangerous, great, and bearable. Out of them came the gusts and grunts and hiccups and heehaws of the common fun of the earth; and though what the words meant was, in its own way, often deliciously funny enough, so much funnier seemed to me, at that almost forgotten time, the shape and shade and size and noise of the words as they hummed, strummed, jigged and galloped along. That was the time of innocence; words burst upon me, unencumbered by trivial or portentous association; words were their spring-like selves, fresh with Eden's dew, as they flew out of the air. They made their own original associations as they sprang and shone. The words "Ride a cock-horse to Banbury Cross" were as haunting to me, who did not know then what a cock-horse was nor cared a damn where Banbury Cross might be, as, much later, were such lines as John Donne's "Go and catch a falling star, Get with child a mandrake root," which also I could not understand when I first read them. And as I read more and more, and it was not all verse, by any means, my love for the real life of words increased until I knew that I must live *with* them and *in* them, always. I knew, in fact, that I must be a writer of words, and nothing else. The first thing was to feel and know their sound and substance; what I was going to do with those words, what use I was going to make of them, what I was going to *say* through them, would come later. I knew I had to know them most intimately in all their forms and moods, their ups and downs, their chops and changes, their needs and demands. (Here, I am afraid, I am beginning to talk too vaguely. I do not like writing *about* words, because then I often use bad and wrong and stale and wooly words. What I like to do is to treat words as a craftsman does his wood or stone or what-have-you, to hew, carve, mould, coil, polish and plane them into patterns, sequences, sculptures, fugues of sound expressing some lyrical impulse, some spiritual doubt or conviction, some dimly-realised truth I must try to reach and realise.) It was when I was very young, and just at school, that, in my father's study, before homework that was never done, I began to know one kind of writing from another, one kind of goodness, one kind of badness. My first, and greatest, liberty was that of being able to read everything and anything I cared to. I read indiscriminately, and with my eyes hanging out. I could never have dreamt that there were such goings-on in the world between the covers of books, such sand-storms and ice-blasts of words, such slashing of humbug, and humbug too, such staggering peace, such enormous laughter, such and so many blinding bright lights breaking across the just-awaking wits and splashing all over the pages in a million bits and pieces all of which were words, words, words, and each of which was alive forever in its own delight and glory and oddity and light. (I must try not to make these supposedly helpful notes as confusing as my poems themselves.) I wrote endless imitations, though I never thought them to be imitations but, rather, wonderfully original things, like eggs laid by tigers. They were imitations of anything I happened to be reading at the time: Sir Thomas Browne, de Quincey, Henry Newbolt, the Ballads, Blake, Baroness Orczy, Marlowe, Chums, the Imagists, the Bible, Poe, Keats, Lawrence, Anon., and Shakespeare. A mixed lot, as you see, and randomly remembered. I tried my callow hand at almost every poetical form. How could I learn the tricks of a trade unless I tried to do them myself? I learned that the bad tricks come easily; and the good ones, which help you to say what you think you wish to say in the most meaningful, moving way, I am still learning. (But in earnest company you must call these tricks by other names, such as technical devices, prosodic experiments, etc.)

The writers, then, who influenced my earliest poems and stories were, quite simply and truthfully, all the writers I was reading at the time, and, as you see from a specimen list higher up the page, they ranged from writers of school-boy adventure yarns to incomparable and inimitable masters like Blake. That is, when I began, bad writing had as much influence on my stuff as good. The bad influences I tried to remove and renounce bit by bit, shadow by shadow, echo by echo, through trial and error, through delight and disgust and misgiving, as I came to love words more and to hate the heavy hands that knocked them about, the thick tongues that had no feel for their multitudinous tastes, the dull and botching hacks who flattened them out into a colourless and insipid paste, the pedants who made them moribund and pompous as themselves. Let me say that the things that first made me love language and want to work *in* it and *for* it were nursery rhymes and folk tales, the Scottish Ballads, a few lines of hymns, the most famous Bible stories and the rhythms of the Bible, Blake's Songs of Innocence, and the quite incomprehensible magical majesty and nonsense of Shakespeare heard, read, and near-murdered in the first forms of my school.

You ask me, next, if it is true that three of the dominant influences on my published prose and poetry are Joyce, the Bible, and Freud. (I purposely say my "published" prose and poetry, as in the preceding pages I have been talking about the primary influences upon my very first and forever unpublishable juvenilia.) I cannot say that I have been "influenced" by Joyce, whom I enormously admire and whose Ulysses, and earlier stories, I have read a great deal. I think this Joyce question arose because somebody once, in print, remarked on the closeness of the title of my book of short stories, "Portrait of the Artist as a Young Dog," to Joyce's title, "Portrait of the Artist as a Young Man." As you know, the name given to innumerable portrait paintings by their artists is, "Portrait of the Artist as a Young Man" — a perfectly straightforward title. Joyce used the painting title for the first time as the title of a literary work. I myself made a bit of doggish fun of the painting-title and, of course, intended no possible reference to Joyce. I do not think that Joyce has had any hand at all in my writing; certainly his Ulysses has not. On the other hand, I cannot deny that the shaping of some of my "Portrait" stories might owe something to Joyce's stories in the volume, "Dubliners." But then "Dubliners" was a pioneering work in the world of the short story, and no good storywriter since can have failed, in some way, however little, to have benefited by it.

The Bible, I have referred to in attempting to answer your first question. Its great stories of Noah, Jonah, Lot, Moses, Jacob, David, Solomon and a thousand more, I had, of course, known from very early youth; the great rhythms had rolled over me from the Welsh pulpits; and I read, for myself, from Job and Ecclesiastes; and the story of the New Testament is part of my life. But I have never sat down and studied the Bible, never consciously echoed its language, and am, in reality, as ignorant of it as most brought-up Christians. All of the Bible that I use in my work is remembered from childhood, and is the common property of all who were brought up in English-speaking communities. Nowhere, indeed, in all my writing, do I use any knowledge which is not commonplace to any literate person. I *have* used a few difficult words in early poems, but they are easily looked-up and were, in any case, thrown into the poems in a kind of adolescent showing-off which I hope I have now discarded.

And that leads me to the third "dominant influence": Sigmund Freud. My only acquaintance with the theories and discoveries of Dr. Freud has been through the work of novelists who have been excited by his case-book histories, of popular newspaper scientific-potboilers who have, I imagine, vulgarised his work beyond recognition, and of a few modern poets, including Auden, who have attempted to use psychoanalytical phraseology and theory in some of their poems. I have read only one book of Freud's, "The Interpretation of Dreams," and do not recall having been influenced by it in any way. Again, no honest writer today can possibly avoid being influenced by Freud through his pioneering work into the Unconscious and by the influence of those discoveries on the scientific, philosophic, and artistic work of his contemporaries: but not, by any means, necessarily through Freud's own writing.

To your third question — Do I deliberately utilise devices of rhyme, rhythm, and word-formation in my writing — I must, of course, answer with an immediate, Yes. I am a painstaking, conscientious, involved and devious craftsman in words, however unsuccessful the result so often appears, and to whatever wrong uses I may apply my technical paraphernalia. I use everything and anything to make my poems work and move in the directions I want them to: old tricks, new tricks, puns, portmanteau-words, paradox, allusion, paranomasia, paragram, catachresis, slang, assonantal rhymes, vowel rhymes, sprung rhythm. Every device there is in language is there to be used if you will. Poets have got to enjoy themselves sometimes, and the twistings and convolutions of words, the inventions and contrivances, are all part of the joy that is part of the painful, voluntary work.

Your next question asks whether my use of combinations of words to create something new, "in the Surrealist way," is according to a set formula or is spontaneous.

There is a confusion here, for the Surrealists' set formula was to juxtapose the unpremeditated.

Let me make it clearer if I can. The Surrealists — (that is, super-realists, or those who work *above* realism) — were a coterie of painters and writers in Paris, in the nineteen twenties, who did not believe in the conscious selection of images. To put it in another way: they were artists who were dissatisfied with both the realists — (roughly speaking, those who tried to put down in paint and words an actual representation of what they imagined to be the real world in which they lived and the impressionists who, roughly speaking again, were those who tried to give an impression of what they imagined to be the real world.) The Surrealists wanted to dive into the subconscious mind, the mind below the conscious surface, and dig up their images from there without the aid of logic or reason, and put them down, illogically and unreasonably, in paint and words. The Surrealists affirmed that, as three quarters of the mind was submerged, it was the function of the artist to gather his material from the greatest submerged mass of the mind rather than from that quarter of the mind which, like the tip of an iceberg, protruded from the subconscious sea. One method the Surrealists used in their poetry was to juxtapose words and images that had no rational relationship; and out of this they hoped to achieve a kind of subconscious, or dream, poetry that would be truer to the real, imaginative world of the mind, mostly submerged, than is the poetry of the conscious mind that relies upon the rational and logical relationship of ideas, objects, and images.

This is, very crudely, the credo of the Surrealists, and one with which I profoundly disagree. I do not mind from where the images of a poem are dragged up: drag them up, if you like, from the nethermost sea of the hidden self; but before they reach paper, they must go through all the rational processes of the intellect. The Surrealists, on the other hand, put their words down together on paper exactly as they emerge from chaos; they do not shape these words or put them in order; to them, chaos is the shape and order. This seems to me to be exceedingly presumptuous; the Surrealists imagine that whatever they dredge from their subconscious selves and put down in paint or in words must, essentially, be of some interest or value. I deny this. One of the arts of the poet is to make comprehensible and articulate what might emerge from subconscious sources; one of the great main uses of the intellect is to *select*, from the amorphous mass of subconscious images, those that will best further his imaginative purpose, which is to write the best poem he can.

And question five is, God help us, what is my definition of Poetry?

I, myself, do not read poetry for anything but pleasure. I read only the poems I like. This means, of course, that I have to read a lot of poems I don't like before I find the ones I do, but, when I *do* find the ones I do, then all I can say is, "Here they are," and read them to myself for pleasure.

Read the poems you like reading. Don't bother whether they're "important," or if they'll live. What does it matter what poetry *is*, after all? If you want a definition of poetry, say: "Poetry is what makes me laugh or cry or yawn, what makes my toenails twinkle, what makes me want to do this or that or nothing," and let it go at that. All that matters about poetry is the enjoyment of it, however tragic it may be. All that matters is the eternal movement behind it, the vast undercurrent of human grief, folly, pretension, exaltation, or ignorance, however unlofty the intention of the poem.

You can tear a poem apart to see what makes it technically tick, and say to yourself, when the works are laid out before you, the vowels, the consonants, the rhymes or rhythms, "Yes, this is *it*. This is why the poem moves

[335]

me so. It is because of the craftsmanship." But you're back again where you began.

You're back with the mystery of having been moved by words. The best craftsmanship always leaves holes and gaps in the works of the poem so that something that is *not* in the poem can creep, crawl, flash, or thunder in.

The joy and function of poetry is, and was, the celebration of man, which is also the celebration of God.

It is interesting to compare this document — which was never intended for publication, and which must therefore not be regarded as a poet's testament even though it corresponds in time with the end of his life as a poet, and though he used much of it to introduce a reading of poems at the Massachusetts Institute of Technology on March 7, 1952, which speech was quoted earlier in this book — with both the verse *Prologue*, far more of a testament, and with his earlier replies, in particular to the *New Verse* questionnaire of 1934. It then becomes apparent that while there was no change of purpose, almost no change of view, in the seventeen years that had elapsed, there was a widening and a deepening both of perception and of humility. He was, in fact, the same poet only more so.

During this summer of 1951 he went to London very little. He did only one broadcast from there, about Persian oil, in April, and one about the Festival Exhibition which he had to visit before talking about it over the Welsh Service in June. That is why he was able to work at his poems. But this was the last time. For almost all the rest of his life, the actor took over.

Caitlin had mumps that summer in Laugharne. Margaret Taylor bought a cottage for herself there, as did Bunny Keene's ex-wife. Dylan's father was by now almost blind, but he and Dylan still did the *Times* crossword puzzle together in the mornings. Debts piled up as usual, and the endless correspondence about back income tax went on. Brinnin came to stay, with his friend Bill Read. Brinnin, in Caitlin's eyes, was now the arch-seducer, far worse than Donald Taylor had ever been in happier years long past. But she realized, now, that Dylan was only too anxious to be seduced. Brinnin's account of his stay at the Boat House does not make comfortable reading. Nevertheless it was agreed that Dylan should attempt to retrieve his finances by another American tour in the spring of 1952: it seemed the only way to deal with his creditors. But this time Caitlin was to go with him. Indeed she flatly refused to spend another winter in Laugharne. And since Dylan had to make money broadcasting, they moved to London, with the children, in late September. Once again Margaret Taylor found them a place to live. This was a basement flat in a house she owned in Camden Town, at No. 54 Delancey Street. Even the old caravan was brought down from South Leigh and installed in the yard at the back of the house. They lived there until Dylan and Caitlin sailed for America in January of 1952.

Over six years had now passed since the end of the war, and five since last they had lived in the city. The atmosphere of London, even of Dylan's London, had changed. The Labour government had come and gone. Another war was now being fought, in Korea. Stalinism was at its height, and in America Joe McCarthy was nearing the zenith or nadir of his brief and peculiar career. Dylan's politics, such as they were, had not changed, but they seemed curiously old-fashioned in this London: it now required no courage to be left-wing in a country where the Left had just held stodgy and respectable office for half a decade, while vociferously to belong to the extreme left at this time was less indicative of sensitivity and intelligence than the reverse. Dylan had remained stuck with the political emotions he had quite honourably imbibed in the 'thirties; still, he was fully prepared to deny them, and to sign any document, in order to obtain his visa for the America of McCarthyism. After some difficulties caused by his Prague trip, he got the visa.

In other and more subtle ways time was leaving him behind. Increasingly isolated by alcohol, by anxiety, by the fact that he now read almost nothing save trash or poems he had read before, by his nostalgia and preoccupation with his personal past, this poet who had been the epitome of all that was avant-garde was, quite quickly, becoming almost out of date. The new generation of poets that was arising as the post-war period ended looked at the legend, and then at the poems, with a cool eye. Such is the habit of the young, such is the cycle of fame, and it is as irrelevant to the value of his poems that he be regarded as old-fashioned in 1952 as was the fact that he had been the very newest voice in 1935. In any case this devaluation of his reputation which was beginning before his death was limited to a very small circle of poets and critics. As for the general public and those reviewers who write for them in the Sunday papers and the large circulation magazines, Dylan's greatest triumph was still to come, with the publication of *Collected Poems* and the production of *Under Milk Wood*. This was equally true of England and America.

This loss of contact with the very young — a fate which afflicts all writers, and which is not always an unbearable hardship — was aggravated for Dylan by the fact that he was also losing touch with many of his contemporaries, for reasons that were not literary. His friends remained loyal, often astonishingly loyal, to him. But men and women who had enjoyed being in the Wheatsheaf with him before the war, who had delighted in his company in the wartime pubs and in the immediate post-war misery, now found it tedious to spend many evenings watching him get drunk in the Mother Redcap or Finch's. Oscar Wilde once reproached André Gide, who was avoiding his old friend during Wilde's post-prison, Parisian decline, with the remark: "I was never ashamed to be seen with Verlaine, even when he was drunk." During this last, sad period most of Dylan's friends were certainly not ashamed to be seen with him, but many were exasperated by him.

Those who were prepared, endlessly, to drink beer and move from pub to dingy pub, and become involved in scenes and rows, tended more and more to be young snobs, prepared to put up with anything in order to touch genius, or middle-aged failures who, like Dylan, had never grown out of the habits and attitudes of their youth, or men with money but no self-confidence who were reassured in their own esteem when they could pay for, and watch, a man so much their better engaged upon self-destruction.

All this I have on hearsay, but reliable hearsay. I never spent a whole evening with Dylan after I returned to England in 1950. I met him, or less often him and Caitlin, occasionally at lunchtime when I was in London for the day, always by accident and usually in the back bar of the Café Royal, and we drank and laughed and had a good time together. Nor did I ever go to Delancey Street. But from all accounts those winter evenings in Camden Town, and the shattering rows that ended them in the basement flat crowded with children and laundry and warring people and spectators, must have been sad indeed.

Kingsley Amis was then an almost unknown poet, not yet thirty, who at that time took a very cool view of Dylan, though he has since become more sympathetic. In the *Spectator* in 1957, he described an evening with Dylan. I do not think that this is an unkind portrait of the legendary figure as he was, in his own Swansea, in 1951. In order to double-lock Amis's pseudonym, I must say that the "Welsh painter" was not, in fact, a painter at all. This is what Amis saw:

In the spring of 1951 Dylan Thomas accepted an invitation to give a talk to the English Society of the University College of Swansea. The society's secretary, a pupil of mine, asked me if I would like to come along to the pub and meet Thomas before the official proceedings opened. I said I would like to very much, for although I was not at that time an enthusiast for his verse I had heard a great deal, in Swansea and elsewhere, of his abilities as a talker and entertainer of his friends. And after all, the fellow was an eminent poet and had written at least one book, the *Portrait of the Artist as a Young Dog*, for which my admiration had never wavered. I arranged with my wife and some of my friends that we would try to get Thomas back into the pub (we anticipated little difficulty here), and thereafter to our house for coffee and a few bottles of beer. I got down to the pub about six, feeling expectant.

Thomas was already there, a glass of light ale before him and a half-circle of students round him. Also in attendance was a Welsh painter of small eminence whom I will call Griffiths; in the course of the evening he told us several times that he had that day driven all the way down from his home in Merionethshire on purpose to meet Thomas, whom he had known, he said, for some years. Except for Griffiths, I think we all felt rather over-awed in the presence of the master, and the conversation hung fire a little for some time. Thomas looked tired and a bit puffy, though not in any way ill, and if, as I was told later, he had already been drinking for some time he gave no sign of it. He was in fact very sedate, perhaps because of the tired-ness, or, what would have been perfectly explicable, through boredom. He was putting the light ales down with regularity but without hurry; I congratulated myself on having bought one of them for him. There was some un-inspired talk about his recent visit to America. Then he announced in his clear, slow, slightly haughty, cut-glass Welsh voice: "I've just come back from Persia, where I've been pouring water on troubled oil."

Making what was in those days my stock retort to the prepared epigram, I said: "I say, I must go and write that down."

He looked round the circle, grinning. "I have," he said.

After a few more remarks about Persia had been exchanged, Griffiths, who had been getting restless, shifted his buttocks along the leatherette bench, raised his bearded chin and asked: "What about a few of the old limericks, Dylan?"

Thomas agreed, though without the slightest enthusiasm. I thought it possible that he was not greatly attached to Griffiths, who now began to recite a long string of limericks, bending forward along the seat and address-ing himself exclusively to Thomas, indeed at times fairly hissing them into his ear. The content was scatological rather than obscene, with a few refer-ences to vomiting and dirty socks thrown in.

Thomas went on apparently ignoring Griffiths, sitting there placidly drinking and smoking, gazing over our heads and occasionally wrinkling his parted lips, no doubt a habit of his. When he did this he lost his faintly statuesque appearance and became a dissolute but very amiable frog. All at once he roused himself and told some limericks back to his associate. They were, however, distinctly funnier. The only one I remember cannot be reproduced here, on grounds of possible offence to the Crown. Griffiths said he had heard it before.

After some minutes of this antiphon, the secretary, speaking I think for the first time since introducing me, told us it was time to get along to the meeting. Thomas jumped up and bought a number of bottles of beer, two of which he stuffed into his coat pockets. He gave the others to Griffiths to carry. "No need to worry, man," Griffiths kept saying, "Plenty of time afterwards."

"I've been caught that way before."

The bottles were still in his pockets — he checked up on this several times — when in due course he sat rather balefully facing his audience in a room in the Students' Union. About fifty or sixty people had turned up: students and lecturers from the college mainly, but with a good sprinkling of persons who looked as if they were implicated in some way with the local Bookmen's Society. With a puzzled expression, as if he wondered who its author could be, Thomas took from his breast pocket and sorted through an ample typescript, which had evidently been used many times before.

His first words were: "I can't manage a proper talk. I might just manage an improper one." Some of the female Bookmen glanced at one another apprehensively. The rest of the talk I forget *in toto*, except for a reference to "crew-cut sophomores from the quarter-back division," and something about the fierce, huge matrons who, according to him, infested American literary clubs. His theme, in so far as he had one, was indeed his experiences while lecturing on and reading poetry in the United States, and his tone was one of pretty strong contempt. Aside from this, much of what he said seemed good sense and was phrased as such, but rather more was couched in his vein of sonorous whimsy, well tricked out with the long impressionistic catalogues, strings of compound adjectives, and puns, or rather bits of homophone-play — the vein he used in his broadcasts. Stopping this rather than concluding it, he said he would read some poems.

The one that sticks in my mind most was "Fern Hill," which he recited with a kind of controlled passion that communicated itself to every person in the room. For the most part, though, he read the works of other poets: Auden's "The Unknown Citizen," Plomer's "The Flying Bum" (the Bookmen got a bit glassy-eyed about that one) and Yeats's "Lapis Lazuli." His voice was magnificent, and his belief in what he read was so patent as to be immediately infectious, yet there was something vaguely discomforting about it too, not only to me. Although obviously without all charlatanry, he did here and there sound or behave like a charlatan. This feeling was crystallised for me when he came to the end of "Lapis Lazuli." He went normally enough, if rather slowly, as far as:

"Their eyes mid many wrinkles, their eyes,
Their ancient, glittering eyes . . ."

and then fell silent for a full ten seconds. This, as can readily be checked, is a very long time, and since his still rather baleful glare at his audience did not flicker, nor his frame move a hair's breadth, it certainly bore its full value on this occasion. At the end of this period his mouth dropped slowly and widely open, his lips crinkled like a child's who is going to cry, and he said in a tremulous half-whisper:

". . . are gay."

He held it for another ten seconds or so, still staring and immobile, his mouth still open and crinkled. It was magnificent and the silence in the room was absolute, but . . .

Not very long afterwards we were all back in the pub, Griffiths included. With his performance over, Thomas's constraint had disappeared, and he was clearly beginning to enjoy himself. Griffiths, however, was monopolising him more and more and exchanging a kind of cryptic badinage with him that soon became hard to listen to, especially on one's feet. The pub, too, had filled up and was by now so crowded that the large group round Thomas soon lost all cohesion and started to melt away. I was not sorry to go and sit down at the other end of the room when the chance came. It was at this point that my friends and I finally abandoned our scheme of trying to get Thomas up to my house when the pub shut. After a time the girl student who had been with us earlier, and who had stayed with Thomas longer than most, came over and said: "You know, nobody's talking to him now, except that Griffiths chap."

"Why don't you stay and talk to him?"

"Too boring. And he wasn't talking to any of us. Still, poor dab, he does look out of it. He was in a real state a little while ago."

"How do you mean?"

"All sorry for himself. Complaining that everybody'd gone and left him."

We all felt rather uncomfortable, and rightly. Although I can vividly recall how tedious, and how unsharable, his conversation with Griffiths was, I am ashamed now to think how openly we must have seemed to be dropping Thomas, how plain was our duty not to drop him at all. Our general disappointment goes to explain our behaviour, but does not excuse it. We were unlucky, too, in encountering him when he was off form and accompanied by Griffiths. At the time I thought that if he had wanted to detach himself and talk to the students he would have found some means of doing so: I have since realised that he was far too good-natured ever to contemplate giving anybody the cold shoulder, and I wonder whether a talent for doing that might not have been something that he badly needed. One of us, at any rate, should have found a way of assuring him that he was being regarded that evening, not with a coltish mixture of awe and suspicion, but sympathetically. Then, I think, we should have seen that his attitude was the product of nothing more self-aware or self-regarding than shyness.

It was some ten months after this that he and Caitlin set off for his second American tour. In literary circles over there, which had been generally slower to acclaim his poems, the reaction was likewise delayed. His poems were still ultra-modern, his behaviour still astonishing. And on this trip he proceeded once again to delight his audiences, now bigger than before, with his magnificent readings, and to amaze his hosts and their guests afterwards. If his now celebrated lechery was somewhat bridled by the presence of his wife, the spectators were compensated by a series of shattering public rows between Dylan and Caitlin as they clawed and fought their way back and forth across the Union. Again, almost no money was brought home, for to Dylan's extravagance there was now added Caitlin's. Llewelyn was turned away from his school, for Dylan had omitted to pay the fees; this was a particularly shameful and humiliating episode. Dylan paid dearly for his discovery of America, for in so doing he sacrificed the first object of his writing, which was the discovery of himself.

And by now it is the summer of 1952, they are back at Laugharne, and there is little more of this sad tale to tell. Dylan was working, but sporadically and very slowly, at *Milk Wood*. Another American tour was arranged for the spring, at which the play for voices was to be read as the principal attraction. He was doing his broadcasts, mostly as a reader, and the poems he chose have been published by the producer of the series, Aneirin Talfan Davies, in collaboration with Professor Ralph Maud, with the title *The Colour of Saying*. This choice reflects, in some measure, Dylan's own taste, but rather more his belief in what would appeal to his Welsh and to his American audiences; many of the poems that Dylan loved most are not included. Dylan the entertainer is here also Dylan the impresario, selling, along with his fine voice, his love for other men's poems. He read them, as he had read poems to his audiences across the United States, most carefully and with great skill. It would seem probable that no modern poet, and certainly no actor, but only this actor-poet has read other men's words as beautifully and with such understanding as did Dylan, and fortunately the recordings exist to prove, or disprove, this assertion in the ears of posterity.

During that summer and winter of 1952-1953 he was frequently ill. He arrived back from America in June in a state of exhaustion, went to watch the cricket at Lord's, sat in the sun, and suffered what he called sunstroke, followed by what he called pleurisy. He went home to Laugharne. In October he was writing to Oscar Williams: "I've had pneumonia and worse." In November he was in bed "with bronchitis," and in February with flu. And his gouty toe, which had been hurting him for some years, was getting worse.

His finances were, as usual, in even worse shape than was he. The Inland Revenue decided that he must pay tax, to the tune of £1907, on the earnings of his first, 1950, American tour. Mr. Andrews set about contesting this. Then the National Health Service officials joined in the hunt. Dylan had not been buying his insurance stamps, and they threatened immediate prosecution unless he paid them fifty pounds twelve shillings and sixpence. In October Margaret Taylor, who was not a rich woman and whose limited resources had been almost exhausted by past generosity, began to talk of selling the Boat House unless he paid her some rent. This danger, too, hung over his head for the rest of his life. He spent an increasing amount of the limited time that was left him writing desperate letters to friends and publishers in attempts to raise money.

Dent's agreed to publish a collection of short pieces, mostly those he had written for broadcasting, which at last appeared posthumously as *Quite Early One Morning*. They were still unwilling to publish his early stories that Richard Church had turned down fifteen years before. On the other hand they were prepared to reconsider *Adventures in the Skin Trade* provided Dylan were willing to finish it; he agreed to do so and a very little further work was done on it. Meanwhile they were begging him for the final draft of the *Prologue* and for the corrected proofs of *Collected Poems*. At last, in September, he sent these to Bozman at Dent's. He said that the *Prologue* had taken him a year to write, during which time he had written no other poem. This *Prologue* is of most intricate construction. The first line rhymes with the last, which is the one hundred and second, the second with the penultimate, and so on until, at its centre, lines 51 and 52 are a rhyming couplet. It seems an almost pointless convention to have chosen, and by the time he had finished it Dylan suspected this. He read it to Louis MacNeice, and when that most sensitive ear failed to grasp the poem's construction, Dylan was downcast.

The late Charles Fry, popularly known as the "chocolate publisher," of the now defunct firm of Wingate Ltd., had commissioned a book of American impressions. During his tour with Caitlin she had kept a diary which was meant to provide him with the basic material for this book. To the best of my knowledge no word of this book was ever written, and early in 1953 Fry threatened to sue for the return of his advance. Once again Higham came to the rescue and persuaded Wingate's to accept an option on *Under Milk Wood* instead. But with a quite remarkable absence of judgment, Fry, when he saw the unfinished manuscript, preferred to sell it to Dent's for the advance he had given Dylan. Dylan did not profit from this deal between the two publishers. No more did Wingate's. Had Fry published *Under Milk Wood* it is possible that Wingate's might not now be defunct.

In December of 1952 Dylan agreed to write a children's book of Welsh fairy tales for yet another publisher, but again no work was done on this. Princess Caetani had paid for the whole of *Under Milk Wood,* but had received only half of it. Even that immensely kind woman was showing signs of impatience, and enormously long letters of apology were written to her, too. Indeed, if the amount of time and energy he was now giving to his letters of apology and to <u>his</u> requests for money had been devoted to his work, he could probably have finished *Milk Wood* and perhaps more in 1952. But he found it increasingly hard to do real work. He did his broadcasts; he wrote his letters; he read to poetry societies; and *Under Milk Wood* progressed with almost incredible slowness. He was a sick, unhappy man, and very tired.

Collected Poems was published on November 10, 1952, when there was one year less one day of life left to him. It was received by the critics with fanfares. With scarce a dissenting voice, he was acclaimed a great poet. When the book appeared in America four months later its reception was equally rapturous. And the public went to the bookshops and bought it. In the last year of Dylan's life it sold ten thousand copies in the English edition alone, and in the year after his death a further twenty thousand. In America sales were even higher. He was awarded Foyle's literary prize, two hundred and fifty pounds for the best book of the year. The gramophone records he had made in America were selling well, and were to sell better. In fact the financial nightmare was coming to an end, and Caitlin in her widowhood has been a rich woman. But Dylan, cruelly, never saw the end of the long, his lifelong, tunnel of money worries. He died as he had lived, penniless, and a charitable fund had to be opened for his widow and children. And I think that it was this endless awful anxiety that contributed, more perhaps than anything else, to his decline and death. It tormented him all his life and, with monstrous irony, like some bird of prey that had been gnawing at his liver, it flew away as soon as he became a corpse.

Whatever pleasure or encouragement he might have derived from the reception of *Collected Poems* was cast into the blackest shadow by the fact that his father, blind and in great pain, was dying. On December 15, 1952, D. J. Thomas died. Dylan's distress was very deep. As has perhaps become apparent in the course of this book, Dylan's relationship with his father was one of great importance and considerable complexity. In some ways Dylan's whole life work had been a justification of himself in D.J.'s eyes. And in the last Laugharne years they had become close friends, too. D.J. had mellowed, and had come to admire his son. When Dylan was at home there was never a day that he did not go to see his father, to chat and do the crossword together and, so long as D.J. still could cross the street, to drink a pint in Brown's. And now he was gone. Aneirin Talfan Davies has told me of meeting Dylan in Swansea, during his father's last days. They went to a café and Dylan sat, almost silent, hour after hour, drinking coffee.

D. J. Thomas had asked that he be cremated. Dylan could not bring himself to enter the crematorium, but the man who was with him did, and saw fit to tell Dylan how his father's skull had burst like a bomb in the heat of the furnace. When he added, outside the crematorium, that they were now breathing D.J.'s body, Dylan turned away and vomited.

In April his sister died, in distant Bombay. This was no such blow, for they had never been close. But the past was coming to an end. If Dylan were to go on, he had henceforth to live in the future. And the future was a temporal dimension which he had seldom taken into account. Nevertheless he was prepared, with a heavy heart, to try, for he loved God's world. And the future still meant, for him, America. On April 16, 1953, he set off across the Atlantic once again. It was not a happy departure. To Brinnin he had written, on March 18th:

In the beginning, as Treece said in one of his apocalapses, was the bird; and this came from Caitlin, who said, and repeated it only last night after our Boston-Laugharne babble, "You want to go to the States again only for flattery, idleness, and infidelity." This hurt me terribly. The right words were: appreciation, dramatic work, and friends. Therefore I didn't write until I knew for certain that I could come to the States for a visit and then return to a body and hearth not irremediably split from navel to firedog. Of course I'm far from certain now, but I'm coming. This unfair charge — flattery, idleness, etcetera — kept me seething quiet for quite a bit. Then my father died, and my mother relied on me to look after her and to stay, writing like a fury, pen in paw, a literary mole, at home. Then a woman — you never met her — who promised me a real lot of money for oh so little in return died of an overdose of sleeping drug and left no will, and her son, the heir, could hardly be expected to fulfil *that* kind of unwritten agreement. Then a publisher's firm, which had advanced me money for an American-Impressions book of which I never wrote a word, turned, justly, nasty, and said that I had to do the book by June 1953 or they would set the law on me. Then Caitlin was going to have another baby and didn't want it. Then Margaret bloody Taylor said that she was going to sell the ricketty house we wrestled in over our heads and live bodies. So this was the position I was in, so far as my American visit was concerned: — Caitlin was completely against it, and was going to have a baby; my mother was against it, because I should be near her and working hard to keep the lot of us; and I was reluctantly against it, because I was without money, owing to an unexpected suicide, and I could not, naturally, leave a mother and pregnant wife and three children penniless at home while I leered and tubthumped in Liberty Land; and the publishers were legally against it, because I had to write a book for them quickly; and on top of all that the final reason for my knowing that I could not come out this spring was the prospect of the rapid unhousing of dame, dam, chick-to-be, and the well-loved rest. (I write like a cad. I should whip myself to death on the steps of my Club for all this.) Well, anyway; I won a prize, for the book of the year, of £250, which put paid to baby . . . And a brother-in-law in Bombay said he would look, from a distance, after my Mother's welfare. And Margaret bloodiest Taylor has, temporarily, relented. And I think I can give the demanding publishers the script of "Under Milk Wood" (when finished) instead of, for instance, "A Bard's-Eye View of the U.S.A." and Caitlin's hatred of my projected visit can be calmed only by this: that after no more than six weeks' larricking around I return from New York with enough money to take Colm, her and me for three winter months to Portugal where all, I hear, is cheap and sunny.

Such was the front that Dylan presented to the outside world: such were not the thoughts that filled his sleepless nights.

This, his third, American tour was, to judge by Brinnin's account and by what others have told me, a somewhat more placid business than the first two had been. America was no longer strange to him, and therefore was less frightening. Although he got drunk, there were whole periods during these six weeks when he did not. But as for infidelities, Caitlin was quite right. He spent a night with Sarah — who had passed through a marriage since last he had seen her in 1950 — and he started his relationship with Liz Reitell, the new secretary of the Poetry Center of the YM–YWHA in New York who was thus Brinnin's principal assistant.

He even managed to do some writing during this American trip. *Under Milk Wood* was to be read, solo, at the Fogg Museum, Harvard, on May 3rd and again by a cast of actors which included Dylan at the

Poetry Center on May 14th and May 28th. It was still not finished, and up to the very last moment on all three occasions Dylan was writing more material, some of which he later discarded. The play was an immediate success, which helped Dylan. And since Liz Reitell was a woman, it was in many ways easier for her to look after Dylan than it had been for John Malcolm Brinnin.

More important for a future that was never to be was his meeting with Stravinsky. I quote from *Conversations with Stravinsky* by the composer and Robert Craft: the speaker is Igor Stravinsky.

I first heard of Dylan Thomas from Auden, in New York, in February or March of 1950. Coming late to an appointment one day Auden excused himself saying he had been busy helping extricate an English poet from some sort of trouble. He told me about Dylan Thomas. I read him after that, and in Urbana in the winter of 1950 my wife went to hear him read. Two years later, in January 1952, the English film producer, Michael Powell, came to see me in Hollywood with a project that I found very attractive. Powell proposed to make a short film, a kind of masque, of a scene from the Odyssey; it would require two or three arias as well as pieces of pure instrumental music and recitations of pure poetry. Powell said that Thomas had agreed to write the verse; he asked me to compose the music. Alas, there was no money. Where were the angels, even the Broadway kind, and why are the world's commissions, grants, funds, foundations never available to Dylan Thomases? I regret that this project was not realized. *The Doctor and the Devils* proves, I think, that Dylan's talent could have created a new medium.

Then in May 1953 Boston University proposed to commission me to write an opera with Dylan. I was in Boston at the time and Dylan who was in New York or New Haven came to see me. As soon as I saw him I knew that the only thing to do was to love him. He was nervous, however, chain smoking the whole time, and he complained of severe gout pains . . . "but I prefer the gout to the cure; I'm not going to let a doctor shove a bayonet into me twice a week."

His face and skin had the colour and swelling of too much drinking. He was a shorter man than I expected, not more than five feet five or six, with a large protuberant behind and belly. His nose was a red bulb and his eyes were glazed. He drank a glass of whisky with me which made him more at ease, though he kept worrying about his wife, saying he had to hurry home to Wales "or it would be too late." He talked to me about the *Rake's Progress*. He had heard the first broadcast of it from Venice. He knew the libretto well, and he admired it: "Auden is the most skilful of us all." I don't know how much he knew about music, but he talked about the operas he knew and liked, and about what he wanted to do. "His" opera was to be about the re-discovery of our planet following an atomic misadventure. There would be a re-creation of language, only the new one would have no abstractions; there would only be people, objects, and words. He promised to avoid poetic indulgences: "No conceits, I'll knock them all on the head." He talked to me about Yeats who he said was almost the greatest lyric poet since Shakespeare, and quoted from memory the poem with the refrain "Daybreak and a candle-end." He agreed to come to me in Hollywood as soon as he could. Returning there, I had a room built for him, an extension of our dining-room, as we have no guest room. I received two letters from him. I wrote him October 25th in New York and asked him for word of his arrival plans in Hollywood. I expected a telegram from him announcing the hour of his aeroplane. On November 9th the telegram came. It said he was dead. All I could do was to cry.

Dylan was very excited by the prospect of this collaboration and he wrote at once to Caitlin:

And then can you — this is important — make plans well beforehand to be away with me the whole of July. Alone, without Colm or Aeron. You and me. I know that at the end of July Llewelyn comes out of school, but somehow it must be arranged. You and me must, at the beginning of July, go together to Hollywood. We can get a boat from London, direct but slow, to San Francisco, and then fly to Los Angeles in an hour. Outside Hollywood, in a huge easy house in the hills, we're to stay for the month with Stravinsky. I've seen him, just now, in Boston, and we've thought of an opera and it is — for me — so simple that the libretto can be written in the time we're there. That's not just optimistic: it *can* and will be. In advance, I'll be given 500 pounds and our passage, first class, and then another £500 — and then royalties until we die. We'll go back from Hollywood to Laugharne, and, in the winter, we'll go to Majorca. There'll be plenty of money. This time it's working. . . .

Yes, the end of the tunnel, which he was never to reach, was in sight. And though he broke his arm yet again in New York, he flew back to London, on the day after the coronation of Queen Elizabeth II, high-spirited and sober. To Oscar Williams he wrote, from Laugharne, towards the end of June:

I missed you a lot my last days, and was Lizzed away to the plane alone. I almost liked the plane-ride, though; it was stormy and dangerous, and only my iron will kept the big bird up; lightning looked wonderful through the little eyeholes in its underbelly; the bar was open all the way from Newfoundland; and the woman next to me was stone-deaf so I spoke to her all the way, more wildly and more wildly as the plane lurched on through dark and lion-thunder and the fire-water yelled through my blood like Sioux, and she unheard all my delirium with a smile; and then the Red Indians scalped me; and then it was London, and my iron will brought the bird down, safely, with only one spine-cracking jar. And queasy, purple, mag-goty, scalped, I weak-wormed through festoons, bunting, flags, great roses, sad spangles, paste and tinsel, the million cardboard simpers and ogrish plaster statuettes of the nincompoop queen, I crawled as early as sin in the chilly weeping morning through the city's hushed hangover and all those miles of cock-deep orange-peel, nibbled sandwiches, broken bottles, dis-carded vests, vomit and condoms, lollipops, senile fish, blood, lips, old towels, teeth, turds, soiled blowing newspapers by the unread mountain, all the spatter and bloody gravy and giant mouseness that go to show how a loyal and phlegmatic people — "London can break it!" — enjoyed themselves like hell the day before. And, my God, wouldn't I have enjoyed it too! In the house where I stay in London, a party was still going on, at half past seven in the wet, beige morning, that had started two nights before. Full of my news, of the latest American gossip from the intellectual underworld, of tall goings-on, of tiny victories and disasters, aching to gabble I found my-self in a company of amiable, wrestling, maudlin, beetle-skulled men, semi-men, and many kinds of women, who did not know or care I had been so far and wildly away but seemed to think I had been in the party all the whoop-ing time. Sober, airsick, pancaked flat, I saw these intelligent old friends as a warrenful of blockish stinkers, and sulked all morning over my warm beer as they clamoured and hiccuped, rolled rogering down, fell gayly through windows, sang and splintered. And in the afternoon I stood — I was the only one who could — alone and disillusioned among the snorers and the dead. They grunted all around me, or went soughing and green to their Maker. As the little murdered moles in the Scotch poem, like sma' Assyrians they lay. I was close to crying there, in the chaotic middle of anti-climax. It was all too sordid. Oh how I hated these recumbent Bohemians! Slowly, I went up-stairs to bath. There was a man in the bath. And tears ran down my cheeks. Two creatures stretched dead in my bed. And, now, the rain was boo-hooing too all over London. *P.S.* I am sorry to add to this that by the end of the day I was happy as a pig in shit myself, and conducted the singing of hymns with my broken arm, and chased people and was caught, and wound up as snug as a bugger in Rugby. Oh, my immortal soul, and oh, my tissues!

I returned to Laugharne ten days later; and now, in my left mind again, I shall begin to go on with the Adventures in the Skin Trade.

The end of the tunnel might be in sight, but he was still inside it.

In September he was writing to Bozman imploring him for money and asking that it be sent direct to him, and not through Higham who would have been obligated to retain the greater part against income tax debts. Furthermore, Boston University had decided not to finance the Stravinsky opera after all, and although Stravinsky had no doubt that he could himself raise the necessary money elsewhere, this meant that there was no immediate large advance and no free passage to California for Caitlin and himself. Brinnin, who visited them at Laugharne in September, was prepared to organize more *Milk Wood* performances at his Poetry Center in October, and this would enable him to pay Dylan's passage to New York. He could then go on from there to California, where he would be Stravinsky's guest. But he would once again have to go alone, Caitlin following later when the financial imbroglio had been untangled. Such was the plan. There were to be two performances of the revised *Under Milk Wood*, arranged for October 24th and 25th, a few readings in and about New York, and then in November he was to go to Chicago, to stay with Mrs. Stevenson, and from there to Stravinsky's home in California.

Caitlin was opposed to this trip. And Brinnin, when he saw Dylan in Wales, also doubted whether Dylan was in a fit state to undertake the rigours of yet another visit to America so soon after the last. He was having black-outs now. In August he fell downstairs at the McAlpines' and blacked his eye. He fell down walking home in Laugharne and cut his head badly. He fainted in the cinema at Carmarthen and, again, with Philip Burton, the radio and TV producer, in London. He continued to do his BBC work, but he was becoming increasingly erratic and unreliable. He was a very sick man, and Caitlin told him that another American trip would kill him. Yet immediate money, to pay the children's school fees, to pay the bills, to pay the income tax collectors, was essential. And the money was in America.

On October 9, 1953, he left Laugharne for the last time. In Swansea he cashed a post-dated cheque with his old friend Ralph Wishart, Ralph the Books, in whose Aladdin's Cave of a bookshop he had spent so many, many years. He and Caitlin went on to London, where he was to leave her. She was not in a good mood.

Fred Janes has described to me Dylan's last day in Laugharne. Fred had taken Ceri Richards over to the Boat House. Curiously they had never met before, and of course were never to meet again, the man who is perhaps the greatest modern Welsh poet and the man who may be Wale's greatest painter and who, moreover, has derived a great deal of his inspiration from Dylan's poems. It was, Fred has told me, an entirely successful introduction. The two men liked each other on sight. All was sunny, indoors and out, until, as evening fell, Caitlin began to pick a quarrel with Dylan, and Fred, anxious that the mood not be ruined, took Ceri Richards away.

Dylan was in London for ten days. It was there that I saw him, for the last time. It was, as usual, an accidental encounter. I had been to Broadcasting House on some business of my own. So had he, in connection with the production of *Under Milk Wood*. When I left, in the dusk as I recall, I saw his bulky figure in the street ahead of me, headed like myself for the George. I caught up with him — I had not seen him for months — and he suggested that we avoid the BBC pubs and go somewhere where we could have a quiet drink together. We were both entirely sober. We found a bar in which I had certainly never been before, nor I think had he. I do not know what it was called, nor in which street it lay. It was one of a thousand colourless saloon bars, almost empty at that early hour, and we drank two or three pints together.

I had not seen him for many months, and I noticed how subdued, even sad, he seemed. He told me that he had no wish to go to America so soon again for he was, he said, very tired. On the other hand he was clearly proud that Stravinsky should have chosen him to be his librettist, for Stravinsky was one of the great. He outlined the idea of the opera to me, much as Stravinsky has described it. I only remember one further detail. The tree in the new Garden of Eden (and is it fanciful to think that this concept should have been his *Paradise Regained* to follow the *Paradise Lost* of the unfinished *In Country Heaven*?) was to bear leaves on each of which there would be a single letter of the alphabet. Then, when the fresh winds blew and the Tree of Knowledge shed its leaves, the second Adam would re-create, for the second Eve, all words and languages.

We talked, amiably and calmly about this and that, trivia mostly, while strangers drifted in and out of the dark bar. He certainly did not seem to me to be at all suicidal in his attitude, though others who saw him during these days have told me that he talked, almost willingly, of his impending death — but then he had been doing that, in one way and another, for thirty years. I sensed a certain trepidation, which was characteristic, towards the unwritten opera. His respect for the arts was so profound that he was bound to be timorous: were his own abilities sufficient to match those of so great a composer as Stravinsky? And with *Milk Wood* still unfinished, and *In Country Heaven* incomplete, not to mention *Skin Trade*, he must have been aware — though he did not say this—of the difficulty he found in writing any long work. He spoke, I think, of the speed with which he hoped to write the opera. He invited my wife and myself to spend Christmas at Laugharne. I formed the impression that the libretto not only pleased and flattered but also frightened him.

He had wished to go with me to this nameless pub precisely because of its anonymity and in order to escape from "all those people" in the George. After an hour or less he became restless — perhaps because I bored him, though I say this out of false modesty for I do not really believe it, perhaps because he had been the poet and had talked the poet's talk long enough and now wished to be the entertainer once again, cocooned in laughing faces — and he suggested that we go to the other pub. We did. Immediately he was surrounded by the usual people: immediately he became the life and soul of the party, funny, obscene, instant Dylan, quite unlike the man with whom I had just been talking: and after a little while I had to go and catch my train. I never saw him again.

On October 20th he arrived, by air, in New York. Douglas Cleverdon, the producer of *Under Milk Wood* for the BBC, Margaret Taylor, Harry and Cordelia Locke and Caitlin had seen him off the previous evening from Victoria Air Terminal. They had had drinks in the bar there, and only Harry Locke had gone out with Dylan to the bus that was to take him to London Airport. Harry has told me that Dylan was sober, depressed and quiet. The bus was almost empty. He sat in the back, and as it moved off Dylan, through the window, gave Harry the thumbs-down signal. This was the last glimpse that any friend had of him in England. Harry Locke went back and joined the others in the bar.

Immediately, in New York, Liz Reitell took charge of him, and immediately the rehearsals of the new and, as death willed, final version of *Under Milk Wood* began. The strain on Dylan was too great. Drink no longer helped, and he was in a state of near collapse. Liz Reitell had two responsibilities, one to the Poetry Center, the other to Dylan, with whom she was in love. She took him to a doctor who gave him an injection of ACTH (a cortisone-type drug) which briefly pulled him together and enabled him to go on at the Poetry Center. This was then a comparatively new drug, the effects of which were not fully understood. The doctor did warn Dylan against drinking after this injection, but it should have been obvious that Dylan would go on drinking. The combination of alcohol and ACTH can, I am told, be poisonous. He was also taking sleeping pills. It has been said that certain of his friends were giving him pep pills as well. Nevertheless, as John Malcolm Brinnin's account in *Dylan Thomas in America* shows, he struggled on. He managed to do the *Milk Wood* performances, and one reading, and then, on November 3rd, he collapsed.

At 2 A.M. on November 4th he struggled from his bed and despite Liz Reitell's protests insisted that he must go out and have a drink. She did not go with him. After an hour and a half, according to her account, he returned, and said laconically: "I've had eighteen straight whiskies. I think that's the record." This characteristic remark was certainly untrue. Within a matter of weeks his friend Ruthven Todd and Stuart Thomas, a Swansea lawyer, checked on those ninety minutes. He had had perhaps four or five whiskies; eighteen would have killed him outright. But even this was enough to undo him.

Next morning the doctor was summoned again, and another injection of ACTH administered. (One of the noxious qualities of this drug is that it may make the patient liable to any sort of infection. It does decrease strain, however, which is presumably why it was administered.) That afternoon, when he had awoken from a troubled sleep, he developed delirium tremens. Again the doctor was summoned. Yet another injection was given, which Brinnin describes simply as a sedative, but which I am told — though not by the doctor in question, for he does not reply to questions on this subject — was morphine. Within a matter of hours Dylan was transferred to St. Vincent's Hospital, in a coma: and an urgent message was sent to Caitlin to come to the hospital immediately. He never recovered consciousness, and died on November 9th. (The doctor does not appear to have been summoned at once and the hospital authorities were thus initially in ignorance of the various injections that had been previously administered.) The terminal cause of death was pneumonia, but this he contracted while in coma. According to his autopsy the cause of death was: "Insult to the brain," a phrase equally meaningless in British and in American medical parlance.

He was brought back to Wales, and his body lies buried in Laugharne.

Appendix 1

Date	Service	Programme
21 Apr., 1937	Welsh	Life and the Modern Poet (talk)
18 Nov., 1938	Home	The Modern Muse (feature programme)
6 Sept., 1939	Welsh	Modern Welsh Poets (cancelled)
25/26 Aug., 1940	Latin American	The Duque De Caxias (script)
13 Oct., 1940	Latin American	Cristobal Colon (script)
19 Sept., 1941 20 Sept., 1941 26 Sept., 1941 17 Oct., 1941	Eastern American African Pacific	Civilian's war, No. 19. Sailors' Home (talk)
25 May, 1942	Overseas	Books and Authors (talk)
10 Nov., 1942	Home	In Parenthesis (talk)
29 Nov., 1942	North American	Britain to America (talk)
8 Feb., 1943	Welsh	*Amongst those killed in Dawn Raid* (poem)
15 Feb., 1943	Welsh	Reminiscences of Childhood (talk)
8 Aug., 1943	Eastern	Calling All Students — *The Apocalyptic Poets,* by Desmond Hawkins (reading from "A Saint about to Fall")
14 Dec., 1944	Welsh	Quite Early One Morning (talk)
27 Feb., 1945	Home	Porter to the Bards
31 Aug., 1945	Home	Quite Early One Morning (talk)
2 Sept., 1945	Home	New Poems (script and reading)
9 Sept., 1945	Home	Birds, Beasts and Flowers — Selection from D. H. Lawrence (reading)
29 Sept., 1945 13 Oct., 1945	Eastern	Book of Verse (reading)
2 Nov., 1945	Eastern	Famous Contemporaries — Augustus John (reading of script)
14 Dec., 1945	Home	Poetry Promenade No. 8 (reading from own works)
16 Dec., 1945	Welsh	Children's Hour — Memories of Christmas (talk)
5 Jan., 1946	Eastern	Book of Verse (reading of script)
21 Jan., 1946	Eastern	The English Poet Sees India (reading)
9 Mar., 1946 20 Apr., 1946 27 Apr., 1946	Eastern	Book of Verse (reading)

Date	Service	Programme
2 May, 1946	Light	Rogues and Vagabonds — Captain Kidd
4 May, 1946 11 May, 1946	Eastern	Book of Verse (reading)
16 May, 1946	Light	Rogues and Vagabonds — Peacocks Can Be Poisonous
18 May, 1946	African	This is London, No. 9 — Outer Suburb
19 May, 1946	Home	Time for Verse (reading)
19 May, 1946	Home	The World Goes By (reading of script)
6 June, 1946	Light	Rogues and Vagabonds — The German Princess
18 June, 1946	Light	Books and Writers — Modern Poetry (discussion with James Stephens)
14 July, 1946	Home	Time for Verse (reading of script)
15 July, 1946	African	This is London — The Londoner (reading of script)
16 July, 1946	Midland	Poetry Reading — Lord Byron (reading)
27 July, 1946	Eastern	Book of Verse — Wilfred Owen (reading)
24 Aug., 1946 31 Aug., 1946	Eastern	Book of Verse (reading)
1 Sept., 1946	Home	Time for Verse (reading)
28 Sept., 1946	Eastern	Book of Verse (reading)
30 Sept., 1946	Third	"Comus" (took part)
8 Oct., 1946	Home	In the Margin — Welsh Literature (reading of script)
16 Oct., 1946	North American	Freedom Forum (discussion)
17 Oct., 1946	Third	Poetry Reading — Keats (reading)
22 Oct., 1946 23 Oct., 1946	Third	The Careerist
25 Oct., 1946 13 Nov., 1946 2 Jan., 1947	Third	Memories of August Bank Holiday (reading of script)
26 Oct., 1946	Third	The Poet and his Critic (reading)
26 Oct., 1946	Eastern	Book of verse (reading)
29 Oct., 1946	Light	Focus — On Joining Up
30 Oct., 1946	Light	Mr. Popski's Private Army (reading)
2 Nov., 1946	Eastern	Book of Verse (reading)
16 Nov., 1946	Third	The Poet and His Critic (reading)
19 Nov., 1946 20 Nov., 1946	Third	"In Parenthesis" (took part)
22 Nov., 1946	Light	Books and Writers (reading)
28 Nov., 1946	Third	Poetry Reading — Blake (reading)
30 Nov., 1946	Third	Living Writers — Walter de la Mare (reading of script)
2 Dec., 1946	Third	The Shadow of Cain (Edith Sitwell) (reading)
13 Dec., 1946	Home	The Heartless Giant (took part)
14 Dec., 1946 21 Dec., 1946	Eastern	Book of Verse (reading)
22 Dec., 1946	Home	Time for Verse (reading)
27 Dec., 1946	Home	Tonight's Talk (reading of script)
8 Jan., 1947	Home	Wednesday Story (reading) (?) "A Visit to Grandpa's"
18 Jan., 1947	Eastern	Book of Verse (reading)
24 Jan., 1947	West	Literature in the West, No. 1 — Sir Philip Sidney (reading of script)

Date	Service	Programme
1 Feb., 1947 8 Feb., 1947 }	Third	The Poet and his Critic
8 Feb., 1947	Eastern	Book of Verse (reading)
1 Mar., 1947 8 Mar., 1947 }	Third	The Poet and his Critic (reading of script)
20 Mar., 1947	Third	The Ballad of Mari Llwd (reading)
26 Apr., 1947	Eastern	Book of Verse (reading)
9 May, 1947	Welsh	Return Journey (took part of narrator)
29 Sept., 1947	Third	"Comus" (took part in new production)
30 Sept., 1947	Eastern	*Poetry* magazine (reading)
9 Oct., 1947	Home	The Memoirs of the Dog Berganza (Cervantes) (took part with John Chandos)
14 Oct., 1947	Eastern	*Poetry* magazine (reading)
19 Oct., 1947		*Paradise Lost,* Book I
26 Oct., 1947		*Paradise Lost,* Book II
2 Nov., 1947	Third	*Paradise Lost,* Book III
9 Nov., 1947		*Paradise Lost,* Book IV } (reading)
16 Nov., 1947		*Paradise Lost,* Book V
23 Nov., 1947		*Paradise Lost,* Book VI
25 Nov., 1947	Eastern	Book of Verse *Modern Poetry* magazine (reading)
30 Nov., 1947	Third	*Paradise Lost,* Books VII and VIII (reading)
2 Dec., 1947	Eastern	Book of Verse — *Modern Poetry* magazine (reading)
7 Dec., 1947	Third	*Paradise Lost,* Book IX (reading)
14 Dec., 1947	Third	*Paradise Lost,* Book X (reading)
16 Dec., 1947	Eastern	Book of Verse — *Modern Poetry* magazine (reading)
21 Dec., 1947	North American	Window on Britain — A day in a London Mews (reading of script)
23 Dec., 1947	Eastern	Book of Verse — *Modern Poetry* magazine (reading)
28 Dec., 1947 4 Apr., 1948 }	Home	The Autobiography of a Super-Tramp (reader)
12 Jan., 1948	Eastern	Book of Verse (reading)
8 Feb., 1948	Home	*Country* magazine — The Windrush Valley (narrator)
10 Feb., 1948	Light	Books and Authors
14 Feb., 1948	Light	Books and Authors (reading of script)
16 Feb., 1948 1 Mar., 1948 15 Mar., 1948 }	Eastern	Book of Verse (reading)
4 Apr., 1948	Home	Autobiography of a Super-Tramp (reader)
9 May, 1948	Home	Time for Verse (reading)
13 June, 1948	Home	*Country* magazine — Isle of Thanet (introduced programme)
13 July, 1948	Overseas	Book of Verse (reading)
19 July, 1948	Third	The Two Wicked Sisters (reading)
24 July, 1948	Third	The Bard (T. Gray) (reading)
30 July, 1948	Third	English Festival of Spoken Poetry (reading of script)
(?)	Overseas	Book of Verse (two programmes)
17 Sept., 1948	Light	Focus on Boxing (took part)
22 Sept., 1948	Third	The Life of Sub-Human (took part)
28 Sept., 1948	Third	Shadow of Cain (Edith Sitwell) (reading)

Date	Service	Programme
(?)	Eastern	Book of Verse (recorded 29 Sept., 1948)
11 Nov., 1948	Third	In Parenthesis (live repeat)
(?)	Eastern	Book of Verse (recorded 6 Oct., 1948)
15 Nov., 1948	Third	Extraordinary Little Cough (reading)
10 Dec., 1948	Overseas	Looking at Britain, No. 18 — Radnorshire (reading)
22 Dec., 1948	Third	Trimalchio's Dinner
14 Jan., 1949	Third	The Background of Modern Poetry (reading)
23 June, 1949	Scotland	Scottish Life and Letters — Living in Wales (talk)
29 July, 1949	Welsh	*Arts* magazine — Edward Thomas (reading and comment)
24 Sept., 1949	Third	Selected and read own work (*There was a Saviour, If my Head Hurt, Poem in October, In Memory of Ann Jones, A Refusal to Mourn, Ivory Craft*)
24 Oct., 1949	Wales	Swansea and the Arts (introduced, linked and talked)
30 Jan., 1950	Third	The Dark Tower (took part)
23 July, 1950	Home	New Judgement on Edgar Allan Poe (took part)
15 Aug., 1950	Third	Poetry Programme — John Donne (reading)
25 Sept., 1950	Third	Poems and a Commentary
22 Nov., 1950	Third	Poems for Liberty, 1 (reading)
24 Nov., 1950	Eastern	Book of Verse (reading)
13 Dec., 1950	Home	Poetic Licence (chairman of discussion)
26 Dec., 1950	Home	Book of Verse (reading)
10 Jan., 1951	Third	D. H. Lawrence's Poems (reading)
17 Apr., 1951	Home	Report to the People — Persian Oil
19 June, 1951 14 Aug., 1951	Wales	Festival Exhibition (talk)
16 Nov., 1951	Wales	Say the Word (took part)
18 Nov., 1951	Home	Portrait of Athens (took part)
21 Nov., 1951	Third	Retreat from Moscow (reading)
26 Dec., 1951	Home	Question Time (took part)
31 Dec., 1951	Third	The Golden Ass (took part)
14 Oct., 1951	Third	Three poems by Robert Lowell (reading)
26 Oct., 1951	Third	New Soundings
3 Nov., 1952	Home	A Visit to Grandpa's (reading; school broadcast)
14 Jan., 1953	Wales	Three Ballads by Vernon Watkins (reading)
1 Mar., 1953 8 Mar., 1953 15 Mar., 1953 22 Mar., 1953	Wales	Dylan Thomas Anthology (reading)
9 Apr., 1953	TV	Home Town — Swansea (took part)
5 May, 1953	Third	The Anathemeta (D. Jones) (took part)
6 May, 1953	Wales	*Reminiscences of Childhood*
3 June, 1953	Wales	Worthiness of Wales
17 June, 1953	Wales	Quite Early One Morning
13 July, 1953	Wales	International Eisteddfod (talk)
20 Aug., 1953	TV	Speaking Personally (took part)
20 Oct., 1953	Wales	Barbarous Hexameters (reading)
5 Nov., 1953	Wales	Laugharne (talk in programme)
9 May, 1957	TV	*Under Milk Wood*

Appendix 2

DOCUMENTARIES

The Conquest of a Germ
  Production: Strand Films for Ministry of Information
  Producer: Donald Taylor
  Director: John Eldridge
  Script: Dylan Thomas and John Eldridge
  Starring: David Farrar
  Released: February 1942

These Are the Men
  Production: Strand Films for Ministry of Information
  Producer: Donald Taylor
  Devised and compiled: Oswald Hafenrichter and Dylan Thomas
  Verse commentary: Dylan Thomas
  Released: April 1942

This Is Colour
  Production: Strand Films for ICI
  Producer and Studio Director: Basil Wright
  Location Direction: Jack Ellitt
  Camera: Jack Cardiff
  Music: Richard Addinsell
  Commentary: written by Dylan Thomas; spoken by Valentine Dyall, Joseph
    MacLeod, Marjorie Fielding
  Colour
  Released: May 1942

New Towns for Old
  Production: Strand Films for Ministry of Information
  Direction: John Eldridge
  Camera: Jo Jago
  Script: Dylan Thomas
  Producer: Alexander Shaw
  Released: June 1942

Balloon Site 586
  Production: Strand Films for Ministry of Information
  Producer: Alexander Shaw
  Directors: John Banting, Dylan Thomas, Charles de Latour, Alan Osbiston,
    Peter Scott, Desmond Dickinson

Camera: Charles Marlborough
Released: September 1942

Green Mountain, Black Mountain
Production: Strand Films for Ministry of Information
Producer: Donald Taylor
Devised and Compiled: Alan Osbiston and Dylan Thomas
Words: written by Dylan Thomas; spoken by James McKechnie and Brian Herbert
Released: March 1943

Our Country
Production: Strand Films for Ministry of Information
Producer: Alexander Shaw and Donald Taylor
Director: John Eldridge
Script and Commentary: Dylan Thomas
Music: William Alwyn
Made in 1944; released in 1945

Is Your Ernie Really Necessary?
Production: Strand Films for Ministry of Information, in collaboration with Oswald Mitchell (1943)
Directors: Dylan Thomas and Oswald Mitchell
Script: Dylan Thomas
Starring: Hay Petrie
Suppressed by Ministry of Information after first screening

Where Are They Now?
Production: Strand Films for Ministry of Information
Devised: Oswald Hafenrichter and Dylan Thomas
Verse commentary: Dylan Thomas
Date unknown; not released

FEATURES
The Doctor and the Devils
Production: Strand Films
Story: Donald Taylor
Screenplay: Dylan Thomas
Completed in 1944; not produced due to censorship difficulties

Twenty Years A-Growing
(from the novel by Maurice O'Sullivan)
Production: Strand Films
Script: Dylan Thomas
Written in 1944; script unfinished

Suffer Little Children
(alternative title, *Betty London*)
Production: Strand Films
Script: Dylan Thomas and Donald Taylor
Written in 1945; not made
Bought by Gainsborough Pictures Ltd.; some of the material used in a Diana Dors film, *Good Time Girl*

Crippen
(Gryphon)
 Screenplay: Dylan Thomas and Philip Lindsay
 First treatment completed in 1945, but project abandoned due to censorship
   problems

Robert Burns
(from Catherine Carswell's biography)
 Screenplay: Dylan Thomas and Donald Taylor
 Project abandoned in 1945 due to Paramount's announcing a musical biography
   of the poet with Bing Crosby

Three Weird Sisters
 Production: British National Pictures Ltd.
 Screenplay: Louise Birt and Dylan Thomas
 Director: Dan Birt
 Made in 1948

No Room at the Inn
 Production: British National Pictures Ltd.
 Screenplay: Dan Birt and Dylan Thomas
 Director: Dan Birt
 Producers: L. H. Jackson and Ivan Foxwell
 Screenplay finished 1948

Me and My Bike
(film operetta)
 Producer: Sidney Box
 Written during the autumn of 1948 when Dylan Thomas was under contract to
   Gainsborough Pictures. Eventually a film under this title was made by Ralph
   Keene for Gainsborough

The Beach of Falesa
 Written in 1948 for Gainsborough; has now been published

Rebecca's Daughters
 Written in 1948 for Gainsborough

Appendix 3

LECTURES AND READINGS FROM AMERICA
BY DYLAN THOMAS
(From Sound and Meaning in Dylan Thomas's Poetry
By: Thelma L. B. Murdy
University of Florida dissertation, 1962)

Most of the following entries are culled from John Malcolm Brinnin's *Dylan Thomas in America*. For one third of them, however, I am even more directly indebted to Professor Brinnin, who was so kind as to compile the requested information for me from his personal, scattered records. Although the listing is probably incomplete, it is the first attempt to reconstruct Thomas's reading and recording itinerary in America.

Trip I: February 21, 1950 (Tuesday) — May 31, 1950 (Wednesday)

Place	Date	Sponsor
Kaufmann Auditorium New York, N.Y.	February 23, 1950 (Thursday evening)	The YM-YWHA Poetry Center
Kaufmann Auditorium New York, N.Y.	February 25, 1950 (Saturday evening)	The YM-YWHA Poetry Center
New Haven, Conn.	February 28, 1950 (Tuesday, late afternoon)	Yale University
Cambridge, Mass.*	March 1, 1950 (Wednesday afternoon)	Harvard University
Cambridge, Mass.	March 2, 1950 (Thursday morning)	Recordings of his poems for John L. Sweeney's collection in Lamont Library, Harvard University
South Hadley, Mass.	March 2, 1950 (Thursday evening)	Mount Holyoke College
Amherst, Mass.	March 3, 1950 (Friday)	Amherst College
Bryn Mawr, Pa.	March 7, 1950 (Tuesday evening)	Bryn Mawr College
The Institute of Contemporary Arts Washington, D.C.	March 8, 1950 (Wednesday evening)	Robert Richman
Washington, D.C.	March 9, 1950	Recordings of his poems at the Library of Congress

* For personal reminiscences of this reading, see Richard Eberhart's "Some Memories of Dylan Thomas," *Yale Literary Magazine*, CXXII (November 1954), 5-6. This article is reprinted in Tedlock's collection of essays, pp. 55-56.

Place	Date	Sponsor
New York, N.Y.	March 13, 1950 (Monday)	Columbia University
Ithaca, N.Y.	March 14, 1950 (Tuesday evening)	Cornell University
Gambier, Ohio	March 15, 1950 (Wednesday)	Kenyon College
Chicago, Ill.	March 16, 1950 (Thursday)	The University of Chicago
Notre Dame, Ind.	March 17, 1950 (Friday)	Notre Dame University
Urbana, Ill.	March 20, 1950 (Monday)	The University of Illinois
Iowa City, Iowa	March 21, 1950 (Tuesday)	The State University of Iowa
Berkeley, Cal.	April 4, 1950 (Tuesday)	The University of California
Vancouver, B.C.*	April 6, 1950 (Thursday evening)	The University of British Columbia
Seattle, Wash.	April 7, 1950 (Friday)	The University of Washington
Los Angeles, Cal.	April 10, 1950 (Monday)	The University of California at Los Angeles
Claremont, Cal.	April 11, 1950 (Tuesday)	Pomona College
Santa Barbara, Cal.	April 13, 1950 (Thursday)	Santa Barbara Museum and Santa Barbara College
Oakland, Cal.	April 17, 1950 (Monday)	Mills College
San Francisco, Cal.	April 18, 1950 (Tuesday)	San Francisco State College
New York, N.Y.	April 24, 1950 (Monday morning)	Cooper Union
New York, N.Y.	April 24, 1950 (Monday evening)	Museum of Modern Art
Geneva, N.Y.	April 26, 1950 (Wednesday)	Hobart College
Florida Union Auditorium Gainesville, Fla.†	April 27, 1950 (Thursday evening, 8:00 P.M.)	The Creative Writing Collection of the University of Florida Library

* See Floris McLaren's "Dylan Thomas in Vancouver," *Contemporary Verse,* No. 31. (Spring, 1950), 26-27.

† From a letter by Gene Baro and from talks with staff members at the University of Florida who attended Thomas's Gainesville reading, the following account is derived: Through the initiative of Gene Baro, the Creative Writing Collection of University of Florida Library sponsored a lecture by Dylan Thomas. Although Thomas's engagement was originally projected for April 20, 1950, the poet telegraphed Baro from San Francisco to say he was ill and unable to make the scheduled lecture. Since Baro had no address for Thomas, apart from Western Union, he contacted John Malcolm Brinnin and arranged a new date for Thomas's lecture. At 8:00 P.M. on Thursday, April 27, 1950, at the Florida Union Auditorium, Thomas was introduced by Dr. Thomas Pyles and began his readings. Among the selections were poems by Hardy, Yeats, Auden and Betjeman (including *The Arrest of Oscar Wilde at the Cadogan Hotel*). Of his own works Thomas read only a few, among them, *A Refusal to Mourn the Death, by Fire, of a Child in London.* Although publicity was better for Thomas's projected lecture on April 20 than it was for the actual lecture on April 27, the program was rather well attended. No recording was made, because the contract was only for a reading. Thomas stayed in Gainesville at Gene Baro's apartment three or four days. A day or two after the lecture, Baro and Thomas, alone together, read poetry to one another most of the night; the next morning after breakfast Baro persuaded Thomas

Place	Date	Sponsor
Wellesley, Mass.	May 1, 1950 (Monday, late afternoon)	Wellesley College
Waltham, Mass.	May 2, 1950 (Tuesday evening)	Brandeis University
Ann Arbor, Mich.	May 3, 1950 (Wednesday)	The University of Michigan
Detroit, Mich.	May 4, 1950 (Thursday)	Wayne State University
Bloomington, Ind.	May 5, 1950 (Friday)	Indiana University
Bloomington, Ind.	May 5, 1950 (Friday)	Indiana University Lecture on his work with British documentary films
Poughkeepsie, N.Y.	May 9, 1950 (Tuesday evening)	Vassar College
Princeton, N.J.	May 10, 1950 (Wednesday)	Princeton University
Kaufmann Auditorium New York, N.Y.	May 15, 1950 (Monday evening)	The YM-YWHA Poetry Center First full recital of prose—selections from *A Portrait of the Artist as a Young Dog*
New York, N.Y.	May 18, 1950 (Thursday)	Barnard College

Trip II: January 20, 1952 (Sunday) — May 16, 1952 (Friday)

Place	Date	Sponsor
New York, N.Y.	January 30, 1952 (Wednesday)	Columbia University
Kaufmann Auditorium New York, N.Y.	January 31, 1952 (Thursday)	The YM-YWHA Poetry Center
Kaufmann Auditorium New York, N.Y.	February 2, 1952 (Saturday)	The YM-YWHA Poetry Center
New York, N.Y.	February 5, 1952 (Tuesday)	Museum of Modern Art
Washington, D.C.	February 8, 1952 (Saturday)	Institute of Contemporary Arts
New York, N.Y.	February 13, 1952 (Wednesday)	The New School for Social Research
New York, N.Y.	February 14, 1952 (Thursday)	New York University
Burlington, Vt.	February 15, 1952 (Friday)	The University of Vermont
New York, N.Y.	February 18, 1952 (Monday)	Museum of Modern Art
New York, N.Y.	February 21, 1952 (Thursday)	New York University
New York, N.Y.	February 22, 1952 (Friday afternoon)	Recordings of his poems for Caedmon Publishers (TC 1002, Dylan Thomas volume I)
New York, N.Y.	February 24, 1952 (Monday afternoon)	Cherry Lane Theatre

to make a tape, which is now on deposit in the University Library's audio-visual department. The recording is of seven early poems: *From love's first fever to her plague, Especially when the October wind, It is the sinner's dust-tongued bell, If my head hurt a hair's foot, The hand that signed the paper, Once below a time,* and *When all my five and country senses see.*

Place	Date	Sponsor
Millbrook, N.Y.	February 26, 1952 (Wednesday)	Bennett Junior College
Montreal, P.Q.	February 28, 1952 (Friday)	McGill University
New York, N.Y.	February 29, 1952 (Saturday)	Socialist Party
Washington, D.C.	March 1, 1952 (Tuesday)	Institute of Contemporary Arts
Baltimore, Md.	March 4, 1952 (Friday)	Johns Hopkins University
Princeton, N.J.	March 5, 1952 (Saturday)	Princeton University
Massachusetts Institute of Technology Auditorium, Cambridge, Mass.	March 7, 1952 (Monday)	Massachusetts Institute of Technology Introduction to the reading taped live, poems recorded later in the studio (Caedmon TC 1043 Dylan Thomas volume III)
Lincoln, Mass.	March 7, 1952 (Friday evening)	De Cordova Museum
Brattle Theatre Cambridge, Mass.*	March 10, 1952 (Monday evening)	The Poets' Theatre
Boston, Mass.	March 11, 1952 (Tuesday)	Boston University
New York, N.Y.	March 12, 1952 (Wednesday)	The New School for Social Research
Saratoga Springs, N.Y.	March 13, 1952 (Thursday evening)	Skidmore College
New York, N.Y.	March 16, 1952 (Sunday)	Circle-in-the-Square Theatre
University Park, Pa.	March 17, 1952 (Monday)	Pennsylvania State University
San Francisco, Cal.	April 3, 1952 (Thursday)	San Francisco State College
Vancouver, B.C.	April 8, 1952 (Tuesday)	University of British Columbia
Vancouver, B.C.	April 9, 1952 (Wednesday)	A local sponsor
Seattle, Wash.	April 10, 1952 (Thursday)	University of Washington
Berkeley, Cal.	April 15, 1952 (Tuesday)	University of California
San Francisco, Cal.	April 16, 1952 (Wednesday)	San Francisco Museum of Art
Salt Lake City, Utah	April 18, 1952 (Friday)	University of Utah
Columbia, Mo.	April 21, 1952 (Monday)	University of Missouri
Chicago, Ill.	April 23, 1952 (Wednesday)	*Poetry* magazine
Evanston, Ill.	April 24, 1952 (Thursday)	Northwestern University
Milwaukee, Wis.	April 25, 1952 (Friday)	Marquette University
New Orleans, La.	April 28, 1952 (Monday)	Tulane University

(The only instance of Thomas's failure to fulfil an engagement)

| New York, N.Y. | April 30, 1952 (Wednesday) | Masters Institute |
| (?) Washington, D.C. | (?) May 5, 1952 (Monday) | (?) Institute of Contemporary Arts |

* See Eberhart, pp. 5-6 (in Tedlock, pp. 56-57), for personal reminiscences of this reading.

[364]

Place	Date	Sponsor
Storrs, Conn.	May 7, 1952 (Wednesday evening)	University of Connecticut
Annandale-on-Hudson, N.Y.	May 8, 1952 (Thursday)	Bard College
Bronxville, N.Y.	May 12, 1952 (Monday)	Sarah Lawrence College
Hanover, N.H.	May 13, 1952 (Tuesday)	Dartmouth College
Washington, D.C.	May 14, 1952 (Wednesday)	Duncan Phillips Gallery
Kaufmann Auditorium New York, N.Y.	May 15, 1952	The YM-YWHA Poetry Center. Farewell Performance

Trip III: April 21, 1953 (Tuesday) — June 3, 1953 (Wednesday)

Place	Date	Sponsor
Jordan Hall Boston, Mass.	April 25, 1953 (Saturday evening)	Boston University
Bennington, Vt.	April 27, 1953 (Monday, late afternoon)	Bennington College
Syracuse, N.Y.	April 28, 1953 (Tuesday)	Syracuse University
Williamstown, Mass.	April 29, 1953 (Wednesday)	Williams College
Fogg Museum Harvard University, Cambridge, Mass.	May 1, 1953	The Poets' Theatre
Fogg Museum Harvard University, Cambridge, Mass.	May 3, 1953 (Sunday evening)	The Poets' Theatre. The unfinished *Under Milk Wood* presented in a solo performance
Washington, D.C.	May 4, 1953 (Monday)	Institute of Contemporary Arts
Smith Memorial Auditorium Randolph-Macon Women's College, Lynchburg, Va.*	May 5, 1953 (Tuesday evening, 8:00 P.M.)	Public Lecture Committee and the Department of English of Randolph-Macon Woman's College
Kaufmann Auditorium New York, N.Y.	May 8, 1953 (Friday evening)	The YM-YWHA Poetry Center
Auditorium of the Ethical Culture Society on Rittenhouse Square, Philadelphia, Pa.†	(?) May 9, 1953 (evening)	Philadelphia Art Alliance
Cambridge, Mass.	May 11, 1953 (Monday evening)	Massachusets Institute of Technology
Durham, N.C.	May 12, 1953 (Tuesday)	Duke University

* According to Miss W. T. Weathers, no recording of Thomas's lecture was made. But she and a colleague recall that Thomas "did not read a great many of his own poems, and showed a very modest attitude in this respect." After some comments on poetry in general, Thomas read poems by Yeats and possibly by Auden. Of his own poems he read *Fern Hill, Do not go gentle into that good night, A Refusal to Mourn the Death, by Fire, of a Child in London,* and probably also *The Hunchback in the Park* and *In my Craft or Sullen Art* (From a letter of mid-October, 1961)

† Through the kindness of Daniel G. Hoffman, I am able to summarize from his letter dated November 6, 1961, concerning Thomas's lecture in Philadelphia. He recalls that Thomas prefaced the poems with his prose sketch *A Visit to America* and that among the poems he read were Henry Reed's *Chard Whitlow* and

Place	*Date*	*Sponsor*
Storrs, Conn.	May 13, 1953 (Wednesday evening)	The University of Connecticut
Kaufmann Auditorium New York, N.Y.	May 14, 1953 (Thursday evening)	The YM-YWHA Poetry Center Premiere performance of *Under Milk Wood* (Recorded by Caedmon Publishers on TC 2005)
Amherst, Mass.	May 20, 1953 (Wednesday)	Amherst College
Kaufmann Auditorium New York, N.Y.	May 24, 1953 (Sunday evening)	The YM-YWHA Poetry Center
Kaufmann Auditorium New York, N.Y.	May 28, 1953	The YM-YWHA Poetry Center Second performance of *Under Milk Wood*
New York, N.Y.	June 2, 1953 (Tuesday)	Recordings of his poems for Caedmon Publishers (TC 1018 Dylan Thomas volume II)

Trip IV: October 19, 1953 (Monday) — November 9, 1953 (Monday)

Kaufmann Auditorium New York, N.Y.	October 24, 1953 (Saturday evening)	The YM-YWHA Poetry Center Third performance of *Under Milk Wood*
Kaufmann Auditorium New York, N.Y.	October 25, 1953 (Sunday afternoon)	The YM-YWHA Poetry Center Fourth and greatest performance of *Under Milk Wood* and the last performance of it in which Thomas participated
New York, N.Y.	October 28, 1953 (Wednesday)	City College of New York
New York, N.Y.	October 28, 1953 (Wednesday)	Cinema 16 Symposium on Film Art

his own *Do not go gentle into that good night* and *Lament*. Of Thomas's performance, Professor Hoffman says that "he gave the most electrifying literary program the city has ever known." A recording was made of the lecture and a copy exists in the archive of Swarthmore College.

Index

𝔧 𝔨

Sassoon, Siegfried, D.M.T. on, 53
Scott, William, 143, 161, 191
Secombe, Harry, 20
Selected Writings, 279
Sieveking, Capt. Lancelot de Giberne (Lance), 227
Sitwell, Edith, 180–81, 198, 199, 293, 296
Sitwell family, D.M.T. on, 51–53
Skoumal, Aloys, 309
South Leigh, 293, 300–5
South Wales Daily Post (now *South Wales Evening Post*), 63–68, 75, 96
Spectator, 199, 338
Spencer, Theodore, 278
Spender, Stephen, 116, 138, 229, 230, 239, 244, 246, 273
Stahl, Ernest and Kathleen, 291
Stevenson, Mrs. Ellen Borden, 318
Stonier, G. W., 199
"Story, A," 331
Strand Films, 252, 254
Strange Orchestra (Ackland), 69
Stravinsky, Igor, 45, 347–52
Strife (Galsworthy), 59
Stulik, proprietor of the Eiffel Tower Hotel, 157–58
Summersby, Gordon, 301, 302
Sunday Referee (Poets' Corner), 95–96, 100, 104, 111, 118, 120, 141–42, 145
Sunday Times, 198–99
Surrealism, 177–79, 192–95, 334–36
Swan, Emma, 229
Swansea, 66, 95, 102, 143–45, 165, 176, 182, 196–97, 198, 287–89; D.M.T.'s birth in, 3, 21; character of, 17–20; effect of, on D.M.T.'s development, 19–20; depression in, 62–63
 Cwmdonkin Drive, 3, 25–26, 61ff., 102, 128, 196, 201, 202; Cwmdonkin Park, 27–28, 32, 37; Glanbrydan Avenue, 77; Grammar School, 11, 22, 38, 39–51, 57–60, 66, 133; Grand Theatre, 66; Kardomah, 135; Little Theatre, 66–71, 115
Swansea and West Wales Guardian, 80–81
Swansea Evening Post, 166
Sweeney, J. L., 279
Swingler, Randall, 45, 82, 134, 139, 199

TAIG, THOMAS, 70, 77
Talsarn, 260

Taylor, A. J. P., 169, 282, 287, 291–93, 302
Taylor, Donald, 57, 251–57, 259, 266, 267, 272, 275, 281, 283, 298, 304, 336
Taylor, Haydn, 67, 93
Taylor, Margaret, 169, 269, 282, 287, 291–93, 302, 303, 305, 336, 343, 352
Tedlock, Professor, 298
Tennant, David, 160, 266, 281, 286
Texas Quarterly, 331
Tharpe, Runia, 96, 100–1, 115, 142
This is Colour, 255
Thomas, Aeronwy (D.M.T.'s daughter), 261, 271, 280, 300
Thomas, Caitlin (D.M.T.'s wife), 21, 88, 131, 133, 134, 136–37, 271–72; birth, 183; family and background, 182–83; childhood, 183–86; character and temperament, 185–86, 187; physical appearance, 186; as a dancer, 187; as a writer, 187; first meeting with D.M.T., 189; marriage, 208–9; attitude to money, 208–10; as a housewife, 223–24, 225; pubs become second home to, 224–25; birth of first child, 231; against D.M.T.'s scriptwriting, 253, 259; birth of second child, 262; anger at D.M.T.'s "corruption," 265, 274–75; growing dislike of Margaret Taylor, 292, 302; increasing bitterness of, 302, 329; birth of third child, 312; feels her life "slipping away," 313; anger over "Sarah," 326–30; antagonism towards Brinnin, 336; on D.M.T.'s second American tour, 341–42; extravagance of, 342; now a rich woman, 344; opposed to last American visit, 350; final parting from D.M.T., 350. *See also Leftover Life to Kill, Not Quite Posthumous Letter to My Daughter*. For relationship with D.M.T. *see under* Thomas, Dylan Marlais
Thomas, Colm (D.M.T.'s son), 312
Thomas, D. J. (D.M.T.'s father), 3, 4, 10, 16, 25, 38, 54–55, 83, 197, 301, 322; character, 10–11, 13–15; birth and early life, 10–12; career, 11–14; drinking habits, 12–13; religious beliefs, 13; relationship with D.M.T., 15, 33–34, 51, 59, 110, 345; chooses D.M.T.'s names, 23–25; contracts cancer, 102, 110; on D.M.T.'s poems,